Shiping Hua
Feb. 2015

East Asian Development Model

Given the impressive growth in East Asia after World War II, initially led by Japan, the region's development models have been scrutinized since the 1980s. The shared Confucian cultural heritage, strong government guidance, and export led economies were often cited as contributors to the impressive growth. However, major changes have taken place in Asia on and around the turn of the century: Japan experienced two decades of economic slow-down, while World Bank figures reveal that China is poised to become the largest economy in the world in 2014, overtaking the United States.

Bearing this in mind, is it even possible to formulate an East Asian development model in the context of a shifting twenty-first century? And if so, what is it? This book addresses this issue by looking at the economic, political and cultural perspectives of China, Japan and South Korea, focusing on dynamism and potential consensus regarding an East Asian development model. The chapters offer a historical background to the East Asian development model, as well as in-depth case studies of each of the countries concerned to show that whilst the East Asian development model does have distinct characteristics as compared with other areas, and other countries may draw some insights from the East Asian experience, it is not a panacea that fits all circumstances and fits all times.

This book will be welcomed by students and scholars of Asian economics, Asian politics, international political economy and development studies.

Shiping Hua is Calvin and Helen Lang Distinguished Chair in Asian Studies and Director of the Asian Studies Program, at the University of Louisville, USA. He is also "100-Plan Scholar" with Xi'an International Studies University, China.

Ruihua Hu is Dean of the School of International Studies, Xi'an International Studies University, China.

Routledge contemporary Asia series

1 **Taiwan and Post-Communist Europe**
Shopping for allies
Czeslaw Tubilewicz

2 **The Asia–Europe Meeting**
The theory and practice of interregionalism
Alfredo C. Robles, Jr.

3 **Islamic Legitimacy in a Plural Asia**
Edited by Anthony Reid and Michael Gilsenan

4 **Asian–European Relations**
Building blocks for global governance?
Edited by Jürgen Rüland, Gunter Schubert, Günter Schucher, and Cornelia Storz

5 **Taiwan's Environmental Struggle**
Toward a green silicon island
Jack F. Williams and Ch'ang-yi David Chang

6 **Taiwan's Relations with Mainland China**
A tail wagging two dogs
Su Chi

7 **The Politics of Civic Space in Asia**
Building urban communities
Edited by Amrita Daniere and Mike Douglass

8 **Trade and Contemporary Society along the Silk Road**
An ethno-history of Ladakh
Jacqueline Fewkes

9 **Lessons from the Asian Financial Crisis**
Edited by Richard Carney

10 **Kim Jong Il's Leadership of North Korea**
Jae-Cheon Lim

11 **Education as a Political Tool in Asia**
Edited by Marie Lall and Edward Vickers

12 **Human Genetic Biobanks in Asia**
Politics of trust and scientific advancement
Edited by Margaret Sleeboom-Faulkner

13 **East Asian Regionalism from a Legal Perspective**
Current features and a vision for the future
Edited by Tamio Nakamura

14 **Dissent and Cultural Resistance in Asia's Cities**
Edited by Melissa Butcher and Selvaraj Velayutham

15 **Preventing Corruption in Asia**
Institutional design and policy capacity
Edited by Ting Gong and Stephen Ma

16 **Expansion of Trade and FDI in Asia**
Strategic and policy challenges
Edited by Julien Chaisse and Philippe Gugler

17 **Business Innovation in Asia**
Knowledge and technology networks from Japan
Dennis McNamara

18 **Regional Minorities and Development in Asia**
Edited by Huhua Cao and Elizabeth Morrell

19 **Regionalism in China–Vietnam Relations**
Institution-building in the Greater Mekong subregion
Oliver Hensengerth

20 **From Orientalism to Postcolonialism**
Asia–Europe and the lineages of difference
Edited by Sucheta Mazumdar, Kaiwar Vasant, and Thierry Labica

21 **Politics and Change in Singapore and Hong Kong**
Containing contention
Stephan Ortmann

22 **Inter-Ethnic Dynamics in Asia**
Considering the other through ethnonyms, territories and rituals
Edited by Christian Culas and François Robinne

23 **Asia and Latin America**
Political, economic and multilateral relations
Edited by Jörn Dosch and Olaf Jacob

24 **Japan and Africa**
Globalization and foreign aid in the 21st century
Edited by Howard P. Lehman

25 **De-Westernizing Communication Research**
Altering questions and changing frameworks
Edited by Georgette Wang

26 **Asian Cities, Migrant Labor and Contested Spaces**
Edited by Tai-Chee Wong and Jonathan Rigg

27 **Diaspora Literature and Visual Culture**
Asia in flight
Sheng-mei Ma

28 **Alterities in Asia**
Reflections on identity and regionalism
Edited by Leong Yew

29 **Soft Power in Japan–China Relations**
State, sub-state and non-state relations
Utpal Vyas

30 Enhancing Asia–Europe Co-operation through Educational Exchange
Georg Wiessala

31 History Textbooks and the Wars in Asia
Divided memories
Edited by Gi-Wook Shin and Daniel C. Sneider

32 The Politics of Religion in South and Southeast Asia
Edited by Ishtiaq Ahmed

33 The Chinese/Vietnamese Diaspora
Revisiting the boatpeople
Edited by Yuk Wah Chan

34 The Dynamics of Social Capital and Civic Engagement in Asia
Vibrant societies
Edited by Amrita Daniere and Hy Van Luong

35 Eurasia's Ascent in Energy and Geopolitics
Rivalry or partnership for China, Russia and Central Asia?
Edited by Robert E. Bedeski and Niklas Swanström

36 Asian Popular Culture in Transition
Edited by John A. Lent and Lorna Fitzsimmons

37 Sexual Diversity in Asia, *c.* 600–1950
Edited by Raquel Reyes and William G. Clarence Smith

38 Asia's Role in Governing Global Health
Edited by Kelley Lee, Tikki Pang, and Yeling Tan

39 Asian Heritage Management
Contexts, concerns, and prospects
Edited by Kapila D. Silva and Neel Kamal Chapagain

40 Genocide and Mass Atrocities in Asia
Legacies and prevention
Edited by Deborah Mayerson and Annie Pohlman

41 Child Security in Asia
The impact of armed conflict in Cambodia and Myanmar
Cecilia Jacob

42 Vietnamese–Chinese Relationships at the Borderlands
Trade, tourism and cultural politics
Yuk Wah Chan

43 Asianism and the Politics of Regional Consciousness in Singapore
Leong Yew

44 Disaster Relief in the Asia Pacific
Agency and resilience
Edited by Minako Sakai, Edwin Jurriëns, Jian Zhang, and Alec Thornton

45 Human Trafficking in Asia
Forcing issues
Edited by Sallie Yea

46 Democracy or Alternative Political Systems in Asia
After the strongmen
Edited by Michael Hsin-Huang Hsiao

47 European Studies in Asia
Contours of a discipline
Georg Wiessala

48 Corporate Social Responsibility and Human Rights in Asia
Robert J. Hanlon

49 Irregular Migration and Human Security in East Asia
Edited by Jiyoung Song and Alistair D.B. Cook

50 Renewable Energy in East Asia
Towards a new developmentalism
Christopher M. Dent

51 East Asian Development Model
Twenty-first century perspectives
Edited by Shiping Hua and Ruihua Hu

East Asian Development Model

Twenty-first century perspectives

Edited by
Shiping Hua and Ruihua Hu

Routledge
Taylor & Francis Group
LONDON AND NEW YORK

First published 2015
by Routledge
2 Park Square, Milton Park, Abingdon, Oxon OX14 4RN

and by Routledge
711 Third Avenue, New York, NY 10017

Routledge is an imprint of the Taylor & Francis Group, an informa business

British Library Cataloguing in Publication Data
A catalogue record for this book is available from the British Library

Library of Congress Cataloging in Publication Data
East Asian development model (Hua and Hu)
East Asian development model: 21st century perspectives / edited by Shiping Hua and Ruihua Hu.
pages cm. – (Routledge contemporary Asia series; 51)
Includes bibliographical references and index.
1. Economic development–East Asia. 2. East Asia–Economic conditions–21st century. I. Hua, Shiping, editor. II. Hu, Ruihua, editor. III. Park, Yoon S., Need for a paradigm change for the East Asian economy. Container of (work): IV. Title.
HC460.5.E27374 2015
338.95–dc23 2014022761

ISBN: 978-0-415-73727-2 (hbk)
ISBN: 978-1-315-81813-9 (ebk)

Typeset in Times New Roman
by Wearset Ltd, Boldon, Tyne and Wear

MIX
Paper from responsible sources
FSC www.fsc.org FSC® C013056

Printed and bound in Great Britain by
TJ International Ltd, Padstow, Cornwall

For Helen Lew Lang

Contents

Figures

Tables

Contributors

Weixing (Mark) Chen is a Professor of Public Policy Leadership and Chair of the Department of Public Policy Leadership at the University of Mississippi. His research focuses on leadership and leadership succession in China and China's transition. He has published numerous articles in professional journals and contributed chapters to many books on Chinese politics and China's transition. He is the author of *The Political Economy of Rural Development in China, 1978–1999* and editor of a number of books.

Ruihua Hu is Professor of Political Science and Dean of the School of International Studies, Xi'an International Studies University. He has published widely in the areas of Chinese international relations and Western political thought.

Shiping Hua is Calvin and Helen Lang Distinguished Chair in Asian Studies, Professor of Political Science and Director of Asian Studies Program. He has published nine books in English and three books in Chinese, mostly in the areas of East Asian politics, especially Chinese political culture. He is the general editor of two book series: "Asia in the New Millennium" with the University Press of Kentucky and "Contemporary World's Classics: Political Science Series" (translations) with Renmin University Press in China. He is also "Shaanxi 100-Plan Scholar" with Xi'an International Studies University.

Hyug Baeg Im is Professor at the Department of Political Science and International Relations, Korea University. He received his MA and PhD in political science from the University of Chicago. His current research focuses on the impact of the IT revolution and globalization on Korean democracy. His publications include "The Rise of Bureaucratic Authoritarianism in South Korea," *World Politics*, 34(2) (1987); "South Korean Democratic Consolidation in Comparative Perspective," in *Consolidating Democracy in South Korea* (Lynne Rienner, 2000); "The US Role in Korean Democracy and Security since Cold War Era," *International Relations of the Asia Pacific*, 6(2) (2006); "Better Democracy, Better Economic Growth? South Korea," *International Political Science Review*, 32(5); "The Origins of Yushin Regime: Machiavelli Unveiled," in *Park Chung Hee Era* (Harvard University Press, 2011).

John Kennedy received his PhD at the University of California, Davis in 2002. He is an Associate Professor in the Department of Political Science at the University of Kansas. He has consistently returned to China to conduct research on rural politics since 1995, and he is also co-founder of the Northwest Socioeconomic Development Research Center (NSDRC) at Shaanxi Normal University, Xian, China. His research is on local governance, and topics include local elections, tax and fee reform, rural education, health care, and the cadre management system. He has published research articles in *The China Quarterly*, the *Journal of Contemporary China*, *Asian Survey*, the *Journal of Chinese Political Science*, the *Journal of Peasant Studies*, *Asian Politics and Policy*, the *Journal of Diplomacy*, and *International Relations and Political Studies*.

Henry Laurence is Associate Professor of Government at Bowdoin College in Maine, USA. His current research is on media and broadcasting policy in Japan, Britain, and the United States. He is the author of *Money Rules: The New Politics of Finance in Britain and Japan* (Cornell University Press, 2001). Dr. Laurence received a PhD in Political Science from Harvard University and a BA from Oxford, and has held research affiliations at the Reuters Institute for the Study of Journalism and the Nissan Institute for Japanese Studies at Oxford, and at the Institute for Social Sciences at the University of Tokyo.

Patricia L. Maclachlan received her PhD in comparative politics from Columbia University in 1996 and was a research associate at Harvard University's Program on U.S.–Japan Relations from 1995 to 1996. After working for one year as a tenure-track Assistant Professor at the University of Calgary's Department of Political Science, she joined the University of Texas in 1997, where she is now Associate Professor of Government and Asian Studies. She also served as director of UT's Center for East Asian Studies from 2007 to 2010. Dr. Maclachlan's research focuses on the politics and political economy of Japan. Her publications include *Consumer Politics in Postwar Japan: The Institutional Boundaries of Citizen Activism* (Columbia University Press, 2002); *The Ambivalent Consumer: Questioning Consumption in East Asia and the West* (Cornell University Press, 2006), which she co-edited with Sheldon Garon; and *The People's Post Office: The History and Politics of the Japanese Postal System, 1871–2010* (Harvard University East Asia Center, 2011).

Peter Moody, PhD Yale, is Emeritus Professor of Political Science at the University of Notre Dame. He specializes in the study of Chinese politics and Chinese political culture.

Yoon-Shik Park is currently Professor of International Finance at the School of Business of George Washington University in Washington, D.C. In addition to George Washington University, he also taught at Georgetown University and Columbia University. Among his many publications are such books as *The Korean Bond Market: Post Asian Crisis and Beyond*, *Project Financing and International Financial Markets*, *International Banking: Theory & Practice*, *Oil Money and the World Economy*, *The Eurobond Market: Function and Structure*, as well as many articles and reports in the fields of international banking, international finance, global financial markets, development financing, and financial market development. Before entering academia, he worked for the World Bank as a Senior Economist and then served as the Financial Advisor to the Chairman of the Samsung Group in Korea. He has also served as a member of the boards of directors of both Samsung Corporation, a large Korean chaebol, during 1998–2009, and currently the Korea Economic Institute of America, Inc. Dr. Park has been a consultant to the World Bank, Asian Development Bank, International Finance Corporation, Inter-American Development Bank, U.S. Agency for International Development, and other private and public institutions around the world. In addition to his MBA in finance and MA in economics, Prof. Park has received two doctorate degrees: Doctor of Business Administration in international finance from Harvard University Graduate School of Business Administration and a PhD in economics from George Washington University.

Terence Roehrig is Professor at the National Security Affairs Department and the Director of the Asia-Pacific Studies Group at the U.S. Naval War College, and was a Research Fellow at the Kennedy School at Harvard University in the International Security Program and the Project on Managing the Atom. He is the author of the forthcoming book: *Japan, South Korea, and the U.S. Nuclear Umbrella: Extended Deterrence and Nuclear Weapons* (Columbia University Press) and co-author with Uk Heo of *South Korea's Rise: Economic Development, Power, and Foreign Relations* (Cambridge University Press, 2014). He has published articles and book chapters on North Korea's nuclear weapons program, Korean and East Asian security issues, the Northern Limit Line, the U.S.–South Korea alliance, the South Korean Navy, human rights, and transitional justice. Dr. Roehrig received his PhD in political science from the University of Wisconsin-Madison and is a past President of the Association of Korean Political Studies.

Shi Yaojiang is Professor of Economics and Management at Shaanxi Normal University in Xian, Shaanxi Province, China. He is also Director of the Northwest Socioeconomic Development Research Center there. His research interests include the emergence and development of economic enterprises in rural China, as well as the process of political nominations in rural areas of China and how political incentives affect government performance.

Changzoo Song graduated from the University of Hawai'i (Political Science) and taught in Latvia and Ukraine before joining the School of Asian Studies at the University of Auckland, New Zealand, in 2002. His research interests include: nationalism, nation-building, and the changes in nationalist ideology in Korea; Korean diaspora and their identity transformations; and South Korea's diasporic engagement policy and its efforts to build a de-territorialized nation. His works have been published in *Acta Koreana*, *International Review of Korean Studies*, *Asian Ethnicities*, and *IZA World of Labor* among others. Currently Dr. Song is working on how the business class in South Korea has been participating in nation-building while competing with other actors such as the state and *minjung* for a nationalist hegemony in postcolonial South Korea.

Brantly Womack is Professor of Foreign Affairs and holds the Miller Center's C.K. Yen Chair at the University of Virginia. He received his BA in politics and philosophy from the University of Dallas and his PhD in political science from University of Chicago. He is the author of *China Among Unequals: Asymmetric International Relationships in Asia* (World Scientific Press, 2010) and *China and Vietnam: The Politics of Asymmetry* (Cambridge, 2006), as well as over 100 articles and book chapters. He edited *China's Rise in Historical Perspective* (Rowman & Littlefield, 2010) and *Contemporary Chinese Politics in Historical Perspective* (Cambridge, 1991). In 2011 Womack received the China Friendship Award for his work with Chinese universities. He holds honorary positions at Jilin University, East China Normal University, and Zhongshan (Sun Yat-Sen) University. He recently completed a Visiting Research Professorship at the East Asia Institute of National University of Singapore.

Brian Woodall is Associate Professor at the Sam Nunn School of International Affairs at the Georgia Institute of Technology. At the time his chapter was completed, he held the appointment of Fulbright Fellow and Visiting Scholar in the Graduate School of Engineering at the Tokyo Institute of Technology.

Kate Zhou received her BA in English from Wuhan University, an MS in sociology from Texas A&M University and an MA and PhD in politics from Princeton University. She is Professor of Comparative Politics and Political Economy of China in the Department of Political Science at the University of Hawai'i, Manoa. Her main research interests include the dynamics of transition from central planning to market economy. She has published articles on political economy and women's studies, along with three books titled *How the Farmers Changed China: Power of the People*, which was translated into Spanish (El poder del Pueblo, Biblioteca de China Contemporánea, Barcelona, 1998) and *China's Long March to Freedom: Grassroots Modernization.* Together with Lynn White and Shelley Riggs, Kate Zhou has published a new edited book, *Democratization in China, Korea and Southeast Asia?* (Routledge, 2013).

Stephen Zierak, CPCU, retired in 2010 as a Vice President of Swiss Re America, after a long, successful career in property/casualty insurance management. Since that time he has been active in research related to

American domestic and foreign public policy. Mr. Zierak holds a bachelors degree in government from Boston University, and is currently pursuing his masters degree in political science at University of Nebraska, Omaha. He lectures and writes on political matters. Mr. Zierak and his wife, Teodora, reside in Honolulu, Hawaii.

Acknowledgments

Asian Studies Program at the University of Louisville has been running the annual Lang Seminars in Asian Studies, in honor of Helen Lew Lang and her late husband Calvin Lang. The Lang family donated funds to the University for the establishment of the Program in 2011. The majority of the chapters in this volume were papers delivered at the seminars between 2011 and 2013. Staff members at the Asian Studies Program, Stacey Ann Wilson Schoen and Ladye Anna Lorraine Webber, helped with the seminars and the preparation of this manuscript. The editors thank the two anonymous referees at Routledge for their very constructive comments. We are totally responsible for the contents of this book.

Part I

Theoretical perspectives

1 Introduction

The East Asian Development Model

Shiping Hua

"East Asia," as designated by the United Nations, includes China, Japan, Korea, Mongolia, and Taiwan. However, when people discuss the "East Asian Development Model," they tend to use the term generically. A "model" here refers to a pattern of economic characteristics that distinguish a group of countries from the rest. Mongolia is usually not included in discussions about the model, because the country is drastically different from other East Asian countries in terms of economic development and cultural traditions.

Ezra Vogel was among the first to promote the idea of the East Asian Development Model in the 1980s–1990s. His model includes Japan, South Korea, and Taiwan, the so-called Big Three, and the two cities of Hong Kong and Singapore (Vogel 1991). Many scholars seem to agree that there is indeed commonality in Japan, South Korea, and Taiwan in terms of economic performance, external conditions, and social and cultural conditions. Singapore and Hong Kong also share some, though not all, of the similarities.

Among these five countries/regions Japan received more attention, because of the size and its earlier economic take-off after World War II. The Japanese economy reached its pre-war level in merely a decade after the war. The favorable international conditions after World War II seemed to be important for Japan's economic development. For instance, many believe that the Korean War played a very important role in the reconstruction of Japan, because the lucrative American military supplies contracts related to the Korean War helped jump-start the Japanese economy.

The international conditions were also good for the economic take-offs of South Korea and Taiwan after the war. The United States, for security reasons during the Cold War, allowed the Big Three to practice protectionism while keeping its own market open to their exports. The United States could afford to do this at that time because of the relative small size of the economies of the Big Three.

In addition to international environment, domestic and social factors were more important in the rise of East Asia, such as a strong emphasis on education and competent bureaucracy (Kang 1995). The Big Three seem to share the common characteristics of a high level of investment, possibly a result of high savings. They also carried out sensible macroeconomic policies. Other similarities include a homogeneous population, a high stock of human capital, and reasonable income equality (Boltho and Weber 2009). Characteristics also include the concern for stability connected with inflation, and capital control, so that capital does not escape to other countries (Chang 2006).

The Confucian cultural tradition is also important. The Big Three as well as Hong Kong and Singapore were influenced to various degrees by the Confucian culture that stresses industriousness, frugality, education, a respect for hierarchical relationships, and the emphasis on the group rather than the individual (Tu 1996). That paves the way for an interventionist state.

Although the Big Three seem to share similarities in comparison with other countries, important differences among them do exist. For instance, Japan probably benefited from the Korean War more than the other two. In addition, South Korea's economy is growth-obsessed, i.e., regarding growth as the only priority. Taiwan, however, stressed not only growth, but also stability and equity.

Although Hong Kong and Singapore are usually included in the group, they both have distinct characteristics such as their laissez-faire economies and the fact that they are both virtually cities.

The group of the East Asian Model latterly also included the second tier of fast-developing economies in Asia: Indonesia, Malaysia, and Thailand. But, among other things, they differ culturally in the sense that Malaysia and Indonesia are Islamic states where religion has a major impact upon economic structures.

China was not included in the initial discussions of the model, because its economic take-off came later. With China's economic development gaining momentum since the late 1980s, more and more scholars include China in discussions about the "East Asian Development Model." China shares some of the above-mentioned characteristics of the Big Three such as a high level of investment that is related to savings, high dependence on the export market, strong state intervention, sensible macroeconomic policies, a relatively homogeneous population, a high stock of human capital, the Confucian culture, the concern for stability, and capital control.

But Chinese development differs from that of the Big Three in some significant ways. China has had a command economy, in spite of efforts to privatize the country's economy. China is noted for its direct support for state-owned enterprises by the government and a dual system of public and non-public ownership (Baek 2005). The Chinese economy is more globalized in the sense that China's market is more open to the outside. In recent years, about 50–70 percent of China's GDP was related to foreign trade. Unlike the Big Three, especially Taiwan, China's income gap between the rich and poor is larger.

The concept of the East Asian Model has enriched development theories. For some, the East Asian Development Model, which stresses the particularity of East Asia in comparison to other areas, contradicts the Modernization Theory that emerged after World War II. According to Modernization Theory, developments were linear and evolutionary, implying that all countries need to become like Western societies. Modernization Theory disfavors government intervention, believing that the individualism-driven private sector is the key to economic development (So 1990).

Others, however, see the theoretical relationship differently. In a departure from some Third World countries that adopted socialist policies, as the majority of African countries did immediately after World War II, the East Asian countries, especially the Big Three, relied on market forces. This is in accordance with Modernization Theory, as some authors in this book also believe. Therefore, there is no East Asian Development Model (Chang 2006: 18).

The East Asian Development Model also contradicts the so-called "Dependency Theory" that originated from the less developed countries of Latin America. In the 1960s, Dependency Theory was popular. According to the theory, poor countries are poor and will always be poor because rich countries take advantage of them. External factors are the key as to whether a country is rich or not (So 1990).

With the changing shape of the model since it was conceived and the theoretical ambiguity, it is not a surprise that the feasibility of the model was questioned from the very beginning. Actually, some do not believe that there is such a thing called East Asian Development Model. They believe that each country is different. For instance, East Asian countries have a trade surplus with the United States. But that is a particularity of the United States, not related to East Asia, because most countries that trade with the United States have surplus.

The unstable economies of these East Asian countries also cast doubt on the feasibility of the model. Starting in the late 1980s, the Japanese economy was in trouble. Thereafter, Japan experienced more than two decades of economic slowdown. People started to question the model even more following the 1997 economic crisis. This time, not only the Japanese economy, but a group of Asian countries were affected. Meanwhile, starting from the early 1990s, more and more people started to talk about the rise of China, whose economy was affected, but not hit as badly as the other East Asian countries such as Malaysia and Thailand, during the 1997 crisis.

The East Asian Development Model experienced another shock with the 2008 crisis. In fact, some called it "dead" after the 2008 crisis. A major reason is that although the Chinese economy was not hit as badly as most of the other countries, the economic policies of the United States made some scholars question the feasibility of the East Asian Development Model that relies heavily on exports. President Obama discouraged consumerism that caused the United States to have a trade deficit with most countries with which it trades.

Against this background, we have selected a group of articles that deal with the East Asian Development Model from a variety of perspectives, focusing on China, Japan, and South Korea. The selection was made because of the relative importance of these three countries. The focus is on the most recent developments, instead of the early stage after World War II. While most authors in this volume seem to believe that East Asian developments have a pattern that is different from other areas, they do not believe that this model fits all circumstances and all times.

In the following, I will briefly summarize each of the chapters, with particular attention to how the study is related to the East Asian Development Model. The first part of the book contains the first two chapters, dealing with some theoretical issues. In Chapter 2, Park first traces the historical background of East Asian economic development. In pre-modern times, the size of the Asian economy was three times that of the West, while in modern times, before the 1960s, it was about a third of that of the West. Park also remarks that although East Asia has experienced impressive growth from the 1960s through the 1990s, the real cause for the growth is unclear. For instance, he cites scholarly studies to show that the real cause of East Asian growth was probably due to savings, increased labor and capital investment, and the exploitation of labor, not to those positive factors such as Total Factor Productivity. In terms of Total Factor Productivity, East Asia and the West were roughly the same. He also points out that the role played by the government may or may not be constructive in promoting economic growth. Factors such as opening domestic markets to foreign investors may be more important ones. Park believes that with the slowdown of the economies of Japan and South Korea, we need a new paradigm to explain East Asian development.

The following three chapters are largely case studies about South Korea. In Chapter 3, Song believes that South Korea's economic developments have most of the characteristics of the East Asian Development Model. But he focuses on another characteristic that promoted economic growth in East Asia, especially South Korea: nationalism. While the chapter focuses on the positive impact of nationalism upon South Korea's economic developments, he argues that such was also the case with China, Taiwan, and Singapore. Also, since the 1990s, the power of nationalism in mobilizing and disciplining people decreased, because, as the countries became more wealthy, individualism was on the rise. To use nationalism as a tool for economic development is effective only in the early stage of development. Song remarks that while East Asian countries can use nationalism for economic development, other countries such as India cannot.

In Chapter 4, Im argues that before the 1980s, South Korea was viewed as an exemplar case that capitalist development promoted authoritarian politics. The South Korean experience, as well as that of Taiwan, thus contradicted Modernization Theory. After the end of the Cold War, however, South Korea seems to be the exemplar case that democracy outperforms authoritarian regimes in promoting economic development. His argument runs parallel with that of Song in the sense that both divide South Korean development into two stages: the elementary stage and the advanced stage. In the elementary stage, nationalist ideology and authoritarian politics seemed to be compatible with economic development. As the country's economic development reaches an advanced level, nationalist ideology and authoritarian politics are no longer related to economic development. South Korea's case also seems to support the thesis that economic development is good in supporting the sustainability of democracy.

In Chapter 5, Roehrig focuses his attention on the political and economic relations between Japan and South Korea in recent years. But he believes that the success of the economic developments of the two countries was partly based on the East Asian Development Model, and strong economic ties helped to restrain some of the effects of ROK–Japan animosity and provide a foundation for the relationship to weather the political storms that have occurred and will likely occur in the future.

The next three chapters are case studies about Japan's economic development. In Chapter 6, Woodall takes a similar approach to Park, Im, and Song in arguing that the East Asian Development Model is time-sensitive in that certain policies worked under certain historical circumstances only. Thus, the title of the chapter is apt: "The Development of the Developmental State." During the early postwar decades, Japan ruthlessly subordinated all other objectives "to the singular pursuit of increased production, increased exports, and national wealth." By the late 1980s, it was clear that new tools would have to be found to steer an economy driven by cutting-edge high-technology industry. But once established, institutions are "sticky" and difficult to change. Understanding the evolution of the developmental state is critically important for the East Asian states that have adapted the model to suit local conditions, especially South Korea and China, which are progressing through stages that broadly resemble those traversed by the Japanese state at comparable levels of economic attainment.

In Chapter 7, Maclachlan uses the case study of Japan's postwar postal service to demonstrate the tension between the proponents of a growth model that values state paternalism, safety, security, and community, i.e., part of the East Asian Development Model, and those who believe that the ticket to future economic recovery and prosperity lie with the prioritization of market forces and a smaller government, risk-taking, competition, profit-making, and free trade. Very much in line with what Woodall argues forcefully in the previous chapter, Maclachlan demonstrates that although neoliberal forces continue to grow, the survival of vested interests like the postmasters and their ongoing importance to political parties will ensure that deep-seated compromise continues to inform Japan's reformist agenda.

In Chapter 8, Laurence compares state policies to accomplish the transition from analog to digital transmission of terrestrial television broadcasts (DTV) in Japan and the United States. The East Asian Development Model makes people expect that the coordination problems associated with the transition will be best solved by Japan, which is skilled at mediation and providing information, acting in an institutional structure in which private corporate actors accept the legitimacy of state intervention. However, the study found that the Japanese state was no more effective than the U.S. government at managing the digital transition. Indeed, the United States outperformed Japan, which started the process of transition later, completed it later, and achieved consistently lower rates of DTV penetration. In addition, there was little *systematic* difference in the strategies both countries adopted. Both American and Japanese policy-makers employed a mix of market-friendly and state-directed carrots and sticks to accomplish the transition. In both countries, relationships between state and market actors were sometimes antagonistic, at other times cooperative—and both the Japanese and the Americans provided handsome subsidies to both broadcasters and viewers.

The last five chapters are about China. In Chapter 9, Moody discusses the so-called "Beijing Consensus" in the global system. He points out that between the period of the collapse of the former Soviet Union and the 2008 economic crisis, the "Washington Consensus" characterized by the free market seemed to capture the day. After the 2008 crisis, the "Beijing Consensus" seemed to gain more popularity. The "Beijing Consensus" is characterized by a drive for innovation directed and protected by the state; self-determination, meaning the ability of the state to set for itself the terms on which it interacts with the outside world; a concern for maintaining social and political stability; state action to ensure a relatively even distribution of the benefits of growth, avoiding gross disparities of wealth and income. He also points out that the "Beijing Consensus" seems much like the East Asian Development Model, a model that supposedly crashed and burned in 1997.

In Chapter 10, Chen, in contrast to Moody who stresses the similarities between the East Asian Development Model and the post-Mao Chinese economic model, believes that China's economic success could be attributed to a lot of factors, many of which are unique to the Chinese political, social, and cultural contexts and thus can hardly be transplanted. China's political ideology, system, and culture are different from those in the United States and the West, and China is also different from other East Asian countries in that China achieved its economic success under the framework of one-Party rule with capitalism.

In Chapter 11, Zhou and Zierak discuss two models of China's development in the last more than three decades: during the first period, it was bottom-up, i.e., the people took the initiative, while the state allowed it, to liberalize the country's economy. During the second period, it was top-down, i.e, the state followed the example of other East Asian countries and actively guided the country's economic development.

In Chapter 12, like Moody, Kennedy and Shi makes the observation that some aspects of an East Asian model of governance are based on the ideas of New Confucianism. The basic idea is that virtuous leaders are the key to good governance and the notion of rule by virtue and Confucianism is popular among some leading Chinese intellectuals. Using a "vertical survey" of villagers, village cadres, and township and county officials, this study assesses cadre–mass relations (as well as cadre–cadre relations) of contemporary Chinese society. The study has found that the relationship is bad due to lack of coordinated efforts to collect and evaluate information regarding villager preferences and opinions.

In Chapter 13, Womack discusses China's economic development within a globalized world. Similar to those scholars who emphasize the external factors related to East Asian development, such as the Cold War, Womack discusses the necessity for China to switch from relying heavily on exports, a key characteristic of the East Asian Development Model, to increasing domestic consumption, because, he argues, after the 2008 economic crisis, the old model was no longer viable. This was because the global market for China's exports dwindled considerably after the crisis. He focuses on China's diplomacy.

In conclusion, while most authors in this volume share the belief that East Asian development does have distinct characteristics compared with other areas, and other countries may draw some insights from the East Asian experience, the East Asian Development Model is not a panacea that fits all circumstances and fits all times.

Bibliography

Baek, S. (2005) "Does China Follow the East Asian Development Model?" *Journal of Contemporary Asia*, 35(4): 485–498.

Berger, P. and Hsiao, H. (1998) *In Search of an East Asian Development Model*, New Brunswick, NJ: Transaction Books.

Boltho, A. and Weber, M. (2009) "Did China Follow the East Asian Development Model?" *The European Journal of Comparative Economics*, 6(2): 267–286.

Cai, K. (2011) *The Political Economy of East Asia: Regional and National Dimensions*, Basingstoke: Palgrave Macmillan.

Chang, H. (2007) *The East Asian Development Experience: The Miracle, the Crisis and the Future*, London: Zed Books.

Chang, Ha-Joon (2006) "Understanding the Relationship between Institutions and Economic Development: Some Key Theoretical Issues," United Nations University Discussion Paper No. 2006/05, July 2006. Online: www.wider.unu.edu/stc/repec/pdfs/rp2006/dp2006-05.pdf.

Cummings, B. (1999) *The Politics of the Asian Economic Crisis*, New York: Cornell University Press.

Feenstra, R. (2006) *Emergent Economies, Divergent Paths: Economic Organization and International Trade in South Korea and Taiwan (Structural Analysis in the Social Sciences)*, Cambridge: Cambridge University Press.

Haggard, S. (1990) *Pathways from the Periphery: The Politics of Growth in the Newly Industrializing Countries*, New York: Cornell University Press.

Henderson, J. (2011) *East Asian Transformation: On the Political Economy of Dynamism, Governance and Crisis*, Abingdon: Taylor & Francis Books.

Kang, D. (1995) "South Korean and Taiwanese Development and the New Institutional Economics," *International Organization*, 49(3): 555–587.

Li, K. (2013) *Capitalist Development and Economism in East Asia: The Rise of Hong Kong, Singapore, Taiwan and South Korea*, London: Routledge.

Page, J. (1994) *NBER Macroeconomics Annual 1994*, Vol. 9, Cambridge, MA: MIT Press.

Perkins, D. (2013) *East Asian Development: Foundations and Strategies*, Cambridge, MA: Harvard University Press.

So, A. (1990) *Social Change and Development Modernization, Dependency and World-System Theories*, Hong Kong: Sage Publications.

So, A. and Chiu, S. (1995) *East Asia and the World Economy*, Hong Kong: Sage Publications.

Tu, W. (1996) *Confucian Traditions in East Asian Modernity: Moral Education and Economic Culture in Japan and the Four Mini-Dragons*, Cambridge, MA: Harvard University Press.

Vogel, E. (1991) *The Four Little Dragons: The Spread of Industrialization in East Asia*, Cambridge, MA: Harvard University Press.

Wan, M. (2007) *The Political Economy of East Asia: Striving for Wealth and Power*, Washington, DC: CQ Press.

2 Need for a paradigm change for the East Asian economy

Yoon-shik Park

Historical overview of the Asian economy

For many centuries until about 200 years ago, Asia's economy was far more advanced than that of the West. In 1700, the Asian economy was almost three times that of the United States and Europe combined, at 62 percent of the world economy for Asia vs. only 23 percent for Europe and the United States together. As late as 1820, the size of the Asian economy at 58 percent of the world economy was twice as big as that of Europe and the United States combined at only 29 percent of the world economy. However, the Asian economy experienced precipitous decline compared to the Western world, hitting its nadir in 1952, when the Asian economy accounted for only 17 percent of the total world economy, compared to 58 percent for the Western economy in that year. During the two-and-a-half centuries from 1700 until 1952, the relative size of the Asian economy fell from three times that of the Western economy combined to only one-third. In 1952, the Korean peninsula was the fierce battleground of the 1950–1953 Korean War, pitting China and North Korea against South Korea and the U.N. forces led by the United States.

The main cause of the relative Asian economic decline during the previous several centuries is its isolationistic policy. Especially, the largest Asian country, China, whose very name means the Middle Kingdom, considered itself the center of the world and the paragon of culture and civilization, while disdaining all other countries as barbarians. Such hubris cost Asia dearly when the economy in the Western world was rapidly developing through the Industrial Revolution and global exploration and colonization. Until the eighteenth century, however, Asia had been a fertile ground for technical innovations such as gunpowder and the printing press.

Historically, Asia also produced its share of world-renowned navigators and explorers, such as China's Admiral Zheng He (1371–1433). During the fourteenth century, the Yuan Dynasty sought to expand Sino-Arab trade, and the Ming Dynasty continued this tradition, with Admiral Zheng commanding huge fleets to mount seven expeditions to South Asia, the Arabian Peninsula, and as far as East Africa during 1405–1433. Some historical records described with wonder Zheng He's great fleet of gigantic ships, far larger than any other wooden ships in history. These massive ships were capable of accommodating more than 500 passengers along with huge amounts of cargo. From the late fifteenth century, however, China practiced isolationist policies, banning further construction of ocean-going vessels, for example. While Europeans were motivated by "greed and passion" in their world exploration and commercial ventures, the Confucian state of China abhorred mercantile success (Landes 1999: 96–97).

While the Western world encouraged global explorers and business entrepreneurs in the ensuing centuries, Asia's elites were mainly satisfied to be landed gentry, putting less emphasis on business ventures and profits and more on arts, poetry, literature, and other scholarly pursuits. The traditional Asian value system of shi, nong, gong, sang (scholar mandarins, gentlemen farmers, artisans, and traders) has had a persistent impact on the career choices of numerous bright young Asians. Such a value system discouraged many well-educated Asians from pursuing business careers, resulting in slower economic growth in Asia whose economy was mainly based on traditional agriculture instead of manufacturing and trade. During Korea's Choson dynasty (1392–1910), for example, those who passed the civil-service exam could gain entry to the privileged *yangban* class, a scholarly aristocracy. This tradition continues in today's education fever in South Korea (*The Economist* 2013). The essence of the traditional Asian value system nurtured strong family cohesion, emphasis on education and social order, and pervasive influence of government officialdom. At the same time, it encouraged nepotism and cronyism, lack of transparency, pervasive corruption, less emphasis on rule of law and more on relationship, encouraging conformism and discouraging individualism.

However, the Asian economy embarked upon its catch-up race with the West from the 1950s onward, in the midst of, or right after, the Korean War of 1950–1953, when Japan first blazed new trails in industrialization and its robust export drive. From the 1960s, the four Asian tiger economies of Hong Kong, Taiwan, Singapore, and South Korea then followed. From the 1970s, the so-called Asian tiger cubs (Thailand, the Philippines, Malaysia, and Indonesia) also imitated the tiger economies. These eight Asian economies achieved the highest growth rate in the world. During 1965–1990, their per capita income grew at an average annual rate of over 5.5 percent, while the comparable figure was less than 2 percent for the Latin American and Caribbean countries as well as Middle Eastern and Mediterranean countries (World Bank 1993). This Asian growth momentum has infected other large Asian countries. China from the 1980s and India from the 1990s embarked upon the serious industrialization and globalization of their own economies. Now, the twenty-first century is viewed as the Pacific Century, when the global economic center seems to be pivoting from the Atlantic region to the Asia-Pacific arena.

However, there has been some debate on the proper role of government in nurturing the rapid economic growth in East Asia. Proponents of laissez-faire economics have pointed at the relative openness of the East Asian economies and their dependence on private markets to argue for less activist government policies. Others have pointed to deliberate government initiatives such as export promotion and industrialization policies to propose more activist government roles in economic development. There is also a debate on the degree of the increased labor productivity as the main engine of economic growth in East Asia. Total factor productivity, which refers to increased productivity that is not explained by increased capital or labor inputs but the result of new technologies and improved organizations, has been compared among East Asian countries and other advanced industrial countries in North America and Western Europe.

During East Asia's high growth period between 1960 and 1994, however, some have argued that the growth in total factor productivity in East Asia was estimated to be no higher than that of slower-growing advanced countries in North America and Western Europe (Collins and Bosworth 1996). This finding may imply that the East Asian economic miracle has not been the result of Asia's success in skillfully combining modern technology and organizational skills, but rather the outcome of increased labor and capital inputs through personal sacrifices and high savings. If this is the true cause of Asia's economic "miracle," the Asian economic growth momentum may slow down gradually to the same pace as that in the Western advanced countries, as the untapped Asian labor pool is gradually exhausted and its high savings and investment rate declines due to increased consumer spending. Already, Japan's economic performance has been lackluster since the early 1990s, referred to by some as the "two lost decades," and the Korean economy has also slowed down markedly from 9.2 percent per year on average in the 1970s to 4.2 percent in 2000s and only 2 to 3 percent since 2011.

South Korea as a case study

During the disastrous Korean War of 1950–1953, the already poor agrarian economy of South Korea was utterly devastated and its infrastructure severely degraded. Occupying only 0.07 percent of the Earth's landmass and without a single drop of crude oil resources, South Korea was desperate for food aid from the United States for its daily survival. Despite such devastation, the Korean economy has achieved a truly miraculous growth since the 1960s, becoming the world's twelfth largest economy today. Korea's per capita income grew from just $89 in 1961 to over $33,200 in 2013 (CIA, *The World Factbook*, 2014). This so-called "Miracle on the Han River" was achieved by the deliberate government policy of an export-promoting open economy accompanied by rapid development of the manufacturing sector aimed at export markets, as there was simply no domestic consumption power to speak of anyway. Now Korea has become the eighth largest trading nation in the world, with its annual trade volume exceeding $1.1 trillion, from only $500 million in 1962.

The early years of Korea's economic development were full of trials and challenges, but the Korean people overcame those difficulties by exploiting the country's geological and historical situations. Korean entrepreneurs initially took advantage of the advanced technical and marketing skills in neighboring Japan through joint ventures and other cooperative arrangements. After having obtained their initial access to the Western markets with the assistance of Japanese joint venture partners, Korean businesses have then chosen to compete directly with their former mentors in Japan in international markets. As the Korean economy has achieved its initial success, its unique brand image has also advanced and broadened from the economic field to cultural arenas as well, such as the so-called *Hallyu* (Korean Wave) in music, film, drama, sports, and other entertainment areas. Korean economic progress and the *Hallyu* have reinforced each other in enhancing the Korean brand image both economically and culturally, achieving a virtuous circle.

In recent years, however, the Korean economy has notably slowed down, with huge youth unemployment and even higher under-employment. Labor force participation of Korean youth (15 through 29 years of age) currently stands at below 40 percent, compared to over 50 percent for the OECD average. Many of the big Korean industrial giants such as Samsung and Hyundai have increasingly moved their new investments abroad to low-cost regions in South Asia and Eastern Europe. Consequently, many experts have recently raised their voice urging a fundamental paradigm shift in the Korean economic development policy toward a greater emphasis on the service sector of the economy where job growth can be far more rapid. Korea's service sector is grossly under-developed compared to other advanced countries. Korea's service sector *value added* as a share of GDP is well below that of advanced countries. The same is true for its share in the total employment. Furthermore, productivity of the Korean service sector is estimated at one-third that of Switzerland and half that of the United States. Such a poor state is due to the fact that the Korean service sector is concentrated in low-value *infrastructure services* such as wholesale and retail sales, lodging, and food services. Korea's service sector is painfully under-developed in the high-value *knowledge service industries* in banking, finance, insurance, medical services, engineering, telecommunications, research and development, and IT and software services. The urgent challenge facing the Korean economy in the coming years is how to nurture world-class knowledge service industries comparable to Korea's manufacturing giants such as Samsung Electronics and Hyundai Motor Company.

Development patterns of the East Asian economy

The Korean economy has been touted as one of the premier success stories in post-World War II economic development. During the past half-century from 1961 through 2012, the Korean economy as measured by GDP has grown from near zero (less than $3 billion) to almost $1.2 trillion. In 1961, Korea's per capita GDP was only $89, 101th among 125 countries surveyed in that year by the World Bank. At that time, Korea belonged among the world's poorest nations, along with such countries as Togo, Uganda, and Bangladesh. As late as 1965, Korea was poorer than India, with per capita GDP of only $106 compared to $121 in India. But Korea's per capita GDP grew 313 times during the past 48 years to $33,200 in 2013, while India's was only $4,000 in 2013, which was just

33 times larger than that of 1965. Such spectacular economic growth was mainly fueled by Korea's export-promoting open economic policy. Korea's annual exports in goods and services rose from $40 million in 1961 to $718 billion in 2013, an increase of 18,000 times!

For nearly a decade after the end of the Korean War in 1953, Korea's postwar socio-political turmoil hampered any earnest attempts to jump-start economic development. However, Korea embarked upon economic development seriously from the early 1960s after the military took over the government in a nearly bloodless coup in 1961 led by General Park Chung-hee. In the initial stages, however, the country faced formidable challenges. Korea was then an extremely poor agrarian economy, with a negligible domestic consumer market and weak entrepreneurial base. The country suffered from lack of both capital and modern technology, and there was almost no modern business management talent. The founder of today's mighty Samsung Group, the late Chairman Byung-chull Lee, started his business career as a tiny rice-mill operator in his rural home village during the Japanese occupation of the Korean peninsula. The founder of Hyundai Group, the late Chairman Ju-yung Chung, first started his business career as a small car-repair shop operator in Seoul.

Faced with formidable barriers to economic development, the Korean government decided to be the primary force behind modernizing the economy by adopting a government-led industrialization policy. The military government tried to overcome the primitive and small domestic market by focusing its industrial policy on nurturing export-promoting industries to access vast foreign markets instead of a tiny and poor domestic market. In order to conserve meager foreign exchange reserves, the government also encouraged development of import-substituting industries. Thus, it is perhaps not surprising that the first modern business ventures that Samsung Group embarked upon successfully were a sugar-refining business through Cheil Sugar Refining Company in order to substitute for imported sugar, and also a wool textile business (via Cheil Wool Textile Company) to replace expensive imported textile products from abroad.[1] The government also encouraged inward direct investments from modern Western corporations to bring in both technology and management know-how as well as investment capital.

The first-generation Korean entrepreneurs mitigated their lack of modern management skills and industrial experience through foreign joint ventures or technology licenses from advanced countries. Especially, Japanese companies served as the role model for, and often joint venture partners with, new Korean business firms. Samsung Electronics Corporation benefited initially from its early joint venture with Japan's NEC. Today's premier Korean hotel, Shilla Hotel, started initially as a joint venture with Hotel Okura of Japan. The world-renowned Korean steel company, POSCO, was initially funded by a large loan from the Export–Import Bank of Japan and it also benefited from technical assistance from major Japanese steel companies in its early years.

The fact that Korea has achieved almost miraculous economic growth during the past half-century was certainly not due to the fact that Korean people are more intelligent or more hard-working than the people of other developing countries such as India. We know for a fact that Indians as a people are as intelligent and as hardworking as Koreans. So many Indian immigrants to the United States have achieved a level of success to be envied by any Asian immigrant communities. The Indian immigrant community in the United States has produced the former CEO of Citigroup and the current CEOs of both Microsoft and Pepsi, as well as two current state governors in Louisiana and South Carolina. So many Indian immigrants and their descendants in the United States have been active at the highest level in various professions such as finance, medicine, academia, the legal profession, and international organizations like the World Bank and the IMF, etc. If anything, they have been generally more successful than the Korean immigrant community in the United States.

If Koreans are no brighter than Indians as people, then what does explain the historical fact that comparative economic growth rates between Korea and India have been so different during the past half-century or so? The answer lies not in the genetic superiority of Koreans compared to other populations. The Korean economic success is a modern example of Arnold Toynbee's theory of "challenge and response" (Toynbee 1963: 60–79). According to Toynbee, great world civilizations such as those of ancient Egypt in the Nile River Delta and early China in the Yellow River Basin were the results of heroic human endeavors to overcome harsh environments such as frequent flooding and cold winters. Similarly, South Korea faced almost an existential threat from Communist North Korea, which had almost succeeded in overwhelming the South during the Korean War. To counter this grave threat, South Koreans used economic development not so much to become rich for the sake of enjoying material well-being but rather as the means for simple national survival. New businesses were needed to provide enough jobs, especially for its youth, in order to prevent social unrest. The external security threat from Communist North Korea was to be overcome by rapid economic development and industrialization.

For example, few can now refute the compelling role of the Seoul–Busan Expressway in the industrialization of the Korean economy. When the Expressway project was first broached by the government in the late 1960s, however, many doubted the project's economic and financial viability when there was hardly any traffic to justify such a massive investment. The World Bank also refused to finance the project, but the government went ahead anyway on the national security ground. The highway would be vital to move troop reinforcements rapidly from the southern area in case of another North Korean invasion. The highway was also built in such a way as to be used as emergency landing sites for Korean warplanes. A similar logic was used when the government pushed for starting POSCO, which eventually became the world's largest steel manufacturing company and played a critical role in Korea's industrialization. Despite initial opposition from many experts, the project was pushed through by the government as it was deemed essential for Korea's war industries in view of constant North Korean military threats.

In this sense, the Korean economic success was similar to that of the other three so-called Asian tiger economies of Taiwan, Hong Kong, and Singapore, each of which faced its own existential security threats. Both Taiwan and Hong Kong, peopled with refugees from Communist China, had to face both real and imagined threats of invasion by the newly unified Communist China. Singapore, the new, tiny non-Muslim city state that became independent from Malaysia in 1965, was surrounded by the largest Muslim country of Indonesia to its south and by the Islamic state of Malaysia to the north.[2] For these countries, economic development and industrialization were the primary means to secure national survival from much larger and potentially hostile neighboring countries.

Korea pursued a government-led free and open market economy, relying upon international trade as the means to access advanced technology and management know-how as well as huge foreign markets for its exports. In the initial decades of Korea's industrialization in the 1960s and 1970s, the United States was also the most important economic partner for Korea. While the U.S. security umbrella was essential for Korea to pursue its rapid industrialization despite constant security threats from North Korea, the U.S. market was also the most important destination for Korean exports during those early decades. Also, Korea shamelessly pursued a mercantilist policy in its trade with the United States, with an aggressive export drive combined with both overt and covert restrictive measures on imports through high tariffs and non-tariff barriers. The United States magnanimously tolerated Korea's obvious mercantilist policies, mainly because the Unites States recognized Korea's frontier role during the Cold War between the Soviet bloc and the Free World.

Need for a new Asian economic paradigm

In recent years, however, the Korean economy has notably slowed down, with huge youth unemployment and even more serious under-employment. Korea's average economic growth rate was 9.2 percent in the 1970s, 9.8 percent in the 1980s, and 6.6 percent in the 1990s. But its average growth rate slowed down markedly to 4.2 percent in the 2000s, and the economy grew only 3.7 percent in 2011, 2.0 percent in 2012 and 2.8 percent in 2013.[3] Many of the big Korean industrial giants such as Samsung and Hyundai have increasingly moved their new investments abroad to low-cost regions such as South Asia and Eastern Europe. Between 1995 and 2010, Korea's largest manufacturing firms shifted 17 percent of their production to overseas plants (Bank of Korea 2012). As a result, total employment in such companies fell by 2 percent annually. Consequently, the share of workers employed at large Korean companies fell by one-third, from 18 percent to 12 percent. The real Korean unemployment rate, especially the youth unemployment rate, has become unsustainably high in recent years.

The same is true for Japan and, to a lesser degree, China. Asian economies should reorient their economic development strategy from the export orientation to nurturing domestic consumption. At the same time, their economy has to be diversified from the narrow manufacturing focus to the service industries as well, with bold deregulation and liberalization. In this way, the Asian economy can have a more balanced modern economy on the twin foundations of manufacturing and service industries in order to create more jobs and to join the rank of truly advanced countries. Since the 1970s, the world's advanced countries have embarked upon the transformation of their economy from the manufacturing sector toward the service industries. The service sector of G-7 advanced countries accounts for 72 percent of the total value added of their economy, while the comparable figure for the manufacturing sector accounts for less than a quarter of that of the service sector at only 16 percent. The service sector of G-7 countries also provides 75 percent of their total employment, while their manufacturing sector employment stands at only 14 percent. On the other hand, the comparable figures for Korea stand at only 60 percent for value added and 67 percent for employment (Park and Choi 2011).

The economic structure has shifted gradually from manufacturing toward service industries in G-7 advanced countries in recent decades. The manufacturing sector in the United States accounted for 22 percent of total employment in 1970 but it declined to 10 percent in 2007. The Korean manufacturing sector accounted for a peak of 29 percent of the total employment in 1989, but its share has steadily declined over the past two decades to 17 percent in 2008. However, the service sector's productivity in Asian countries such as Korea is estimated at only one-third of Switzerland's and half that of the United States. This productivity gap is due to the fact that the service industries in most Asian countries are concentrated in *infrastructure services* such as wholesale and retail sales, transportation and warehousing, food services and lodgings, real estate agencies, and personal services (McKinsey Global Institute 2013). On the other hand, Asia's service sector is relatively under-developed in the high-value *knowledge service industries* such as banking, finance, insurance, telecommunications, medicine, research and development, etc.

In the financial service industries, Asia's competitiveness is well below that of advanced countries, even though the manufacturing sector in Asia has produced many global winners in electronics, steel, shipbuilding, etc. The main reason for the relative backwardness of the Asian finance industries compared to its manufacturing sector can be traced back to deliberate government economic development strategies during the 1960s through the 1990s to focus on export-led growth. Thus, it is critically important for Asia to nurture the high value-added knowledge service sector instead of relatively low-skilled and low value-added infrastructure service industries. Developing international financial centers in major Asian cities such as Shanghai, Seoul, and Mumbai is one way to advance the banking and financial industries in Asia to the level of globally competitive players. Successful international financial centers also nurture the development of other advanced knowledge service industries such as world-class medical services and educational institutions, sophisticated telecommunications, renowned cultural institutions, etc. (Park 2011).

However, the greatest barrier to modernizing the Asian service sector is the suffocating regulations and bureaucratic meddling by government in most Asian countries. The Asian service sector needs drastic deregulation and far less bureaucratic interference in order for the Asian economy to advance to the next level. The paradigm change for the Asian economy has to start with comprehensive economic deregulation and liberalization, combined with a drastic reduction in the power of government bureaucracy.

Notes

1 The Samsung Group founder, the late Chairman B.C. Lee, had a special attachment to both Cheil Sugar and Cheil Wool Textile Company during his lifetime, even though Samsung Group has since ventured into other and even more successful business fields through such companies as Samsung Electronics and Samsung Heavy Industries, etc.
2 Lee Kuan Yew, Singapore's first prime minister, details in his acclaimed autobiography the serious security threats emanating from its neighboring countries such as Malaysia and Indonesia immediately after Singapore gained independence from Malaysia in 1965. See Lee (2000: chs. 3 and 17).
3 International Monetary Fund, *World Economic Outlook*, April 2014.

References

Bank of Korea, "Impact and Implication of Expanding Overseas Production by Korean Companies," *The Bank of Korea Economic Review*, No. 2012–4, July 2012.

Collins, S. and Bosworth, B., "Economic Growth in East Asia: Accumulation Versus Assimilation," *Brookings Papers on Economic Activity*, 2, 1966.

Economist, The, "Special Report: The Koreas," October 26, 2013.

Krugman, P., "The Myth of Asia's Miracle," *Foreign Affairs*, 73, no. 6 (November–December), 1994: 62–78.

Landes, D.S., *The Wealth and Poverty of Nations*, New York: W.W. Norton, 1999.

Lee, K.Y., *From Third World to First: The Singapore Story: 1965–2000*, New York: HarperCollins, 2000.

McKinsey Global Institute, *Beyond Korean Style: Shaping a New Growth Formula*, April 2013.

Park, J. and Choi, Y., *A Comparative Study of the Service Industries between Korea and Advanced Countries*, Institute for International Trade, Korea International Trade Association, May 2011.

Park, Y., *Developing an International Financial Center to Modernize the Korean Service Sector*, Academic Paper Series, Korea Economic Institute, Washington, DC, October 2011.

Petri, P.A., "Common Foundations of East Asian Success," in D.M. Leipziger (ed.), *Lessons from East Asia*, Ann Arbor, MI: University of Michigan Press, 1997.

Stiglitz, J.E., "Lessons from Four Decades of East Asian Experience," in J.E. Sitglitz and S. Yusuf (eds.), *Rethinking the East Asian Miracle*, New York: Oxford University Press, 2001.

Toynbee, A.J., *A Study of History*, New York: Oxford University Press, 1963.

World Bank, *The East Asian Miracle: Economic Growth and Public Policy*, A World Bank Policy Research Report, New York: Oxford University Press, 1993.

Part II

The Republic of Korea

3 The use of nationalist ideology in the economic development of South Korea

Implications for the East Asian Development Model

*Changzoo Song**

Introduction

In the last few decades scholarly discourses on South Korea's economic development and on that of East Asia in general have focused on the peculiar government–business relationship in these countries; favorable international environment such as the Cold War; U.S. aid programs; and the prevalence of the Confucian traditions of the countries. For example, in his classic paper on the East Asian developmental model, Kuznets (1988) included high investment ratios, small public sectors, export orientation, labor-market competition, and government intervention in economic matters as the common characteristics of Japan, Taiwan, and South Korea. Among non-economic factors, he mentioned ethnic and linguistic homogeneity, relatively compact geography, manageable population size, and Confucian tradition (Kuznets 1988: s35).

State theorists emphasize that the states in East Asian countries were more independent from other social forces and, therefore, they were more able to control the economy and make effective plans for economic development (Johnson 1982; Woo-Cumings 1999). Others also stressed the role of the neo-Confucian traditions of the East Asian countries that helped the rapid industrialization and economic development of these countries (Kahn 1979; Hofstede and Bond 1988; Kim and Park 2003). Herman Kahn, for example, at the end of the 1970s predicted that the prevalence of neo-Confucian values in East Asian countries would bring further development in these countries (Kahn 1979). In explaining neo-Confucian values, Vogel includes a meritocratic bureaucracy, the entrance examination system, the importance of group consciousness, and the goal of self-improvement, and he says that these values contributed to the development of East Asian countries (Vogel 1991). Regarding the "economic miracle" of East Asian "dragons," Vogel also stresses "situational factors" such as U.S. aid, the destruction of the old order, a sense of political urgency, an eager and plentiful labor supply, and familiarity with the Japanese model of success.

Indeed, the developmental experiences of South Korea all seem to have the ingredients mentioned above. Though implied in some studies, however, nationalism or nationalist ideologies, which the governments and elite often intentionally promoted and utilized for capitalist development in these countries, have not been properly emphasized in studies of the economic development of East Asian countries. For example, while scholars have stressed the prevalence of group consciousness among the peoples of East Asian countries, they seldom explored how the states and business elites of these countries mobilized and motivated people using nationalist ideologies to achieve economic growth. Nationalism has been a strong factor behind the rapid economic development of South Korea and other East Asian countries. Certainly, scholars such as Hoselitz (1956), W.W. Rostow (1971), Ernest Gellner (1983), and Liah Greenfeld (1992) mentioned the importance of nationalism in modernization. Nevertheless, in an East Asian context, scholarly discourses on development have paid little attention to the role of nationalist ideologies while more attention was paid to the peculiar state–business relations of these countries. Countries where the states and ruling elite were able to utilize the powerful ideology of nationalism in mobilizing their peoples and resources for economic development have achieved relatively rapid and a high level of development. This is common among the "Asian Tigers" and their model, Japan.

To fill this gap in academic discourse in the East Asian development model, this chapter explores the role of nationalist ideologies in East Asian countries, and the abilities of the states and business elites in utilizing nationalism for economic development. In so doing, it will examine the power of nationalism in motivating and mobilizing both entrepreneurial and working classes and the practice of using the ideology for the achievement of rapid industrialization and economic development. In particular, it will pay special attention to the disciplinary functions of nationalism in regard to workers in the early stage of development. It will also explore how the business elites have used the nationalist ideologies to motivate and control workers and to protect their interests from foreign competitors. While attempting to explain the role of nationalism in the economic development of the East Asian countries in general, the main focus of this chapter is the South Korean case.

Use of nationalism by the state

Nationalism is everywhere and regardless of the ever-increasing level of globalization, it is still the dominant ideology. Nationalism has been particularly strong in East Asian countries, partly due to their colonial history. As a matter of fact, Koreans felt the urgency of industrialization as they had been colonized by Japan, the country that Koreans long considered culturally similar but inferior, and it gave Koreans a strong motivation to rectify past mistakes through successful economic development in the world community (Vogel 1991). In addition, countries such as Korea, Taiwan, China, and Japan are more or less ethnically homogeneous, and they have embraced the ideology of nationalism, focused on ethnicity, more intensely than other countries. In particular, these countries have utilized nationalism more effectively than elsewhere in Asia or Africa. They have done so by efficiently mobilizing their peoples and resources to achieve modernization and economic development.

As we will see, the developmental state of South Korea was particularly good at mobilizing people with the cause of the nation and imbuing people with the idea that the nation and individuals are fundamentally interconnected and share the same destiny. In so doing, the state used nationalism as a tool to give people a clear national identity and attach values to nationalist causes. Thus, the state could encourage people to work for the greater good of the nation.

Then, how has nationalism contributed so much to the modernization and economic development in South Korea and other East Asian countries, and why did this not happen—or happen only to a lesser degree—in other countries in Asia and elsewhere? The answer to this question lies in the fact that South Korea, and other East Asian countries, was able to mobilize, motivate, and control people with nationalism. Typically, this was carried out through various mechanisms including the educational system and other state apparatuses such as the military and state-sponsored mass movements. This was also a part of the modern nation-building process in South Korea.

Building the nation

According to Gellner (1983), industrialization brought the modern nation and nationalism. Industrialization requires the general education system to change traditional communities to industrial ones so that they would be suitable for the new factory and urban lifestyles. However, in the case of Asian and African countries often nationalism preceded industrialization, or neither of them were existent until later stages due to their colonial history. For these post-colonial societies industrialization was needed for survival, and nationalism was a necessary tool for industrialization. In this situation, states, as agencies of industrialization, should develop a program of standardized, hierarchical public education for every member of the community. This requires the "nationalization" of the people, in which process the social and cultural peripheries are assimilated into a larger center, the national community. Thus, the nation-state in the industrial era functions basically as an assimilating agency (Richmond 1984: 5). This is what the South Korean state actively carried out through the general educational system: the homogenization of the people. This nation-building was particularly active in South Korea in the 1960s and 1970s under the leadership of President Park Chung Hee. This period was also accompanied by rapid industrialization and the country's economy showed a remarkable annual growth rate of higher than 10 percent. This rapid industrialization was closely related to the intensification of nationalism.

The process of nationalization in South Korea has also been a process of cultural homogenization. Regardless of the popular belief and official discourse on the homogeneity of Korean society, it is undeniable that the traditional Korean society was regionally diverse and different regions were marked with cultural differences. Before the introduction of modern transportation and communication, Koreans were culturally divided along the lines of region and dialect. Among all the cultural and social differences, linguistic variation was the most salient difference among the regions. Therefore, standard Korean was enforced through the educational system. In addition, as the modern Korean society experienced intensive ideological divisions between the rightists and leftists, a conflict that has been a major force in modern Korean politics, the state education system pursued ideological homogeneity as well.

One of the numerous measures to achieve this goal was adding the *National Ethics* subject to the school curriculum as a separate subject at the secondary and tertiary levels of education. This occurred in 1968 and the subject purported to teach students the "ethical" basis of the Korean nation. The Ministry of Education states that the purpose of introducing the subject was to imbue people with ethics so that they can contribute to the prosperity of the national community and national unification (Son 2009). Other subjects such as *National History*, *Social Life*, and *National Language* also promoted the nationalist ideology among pupils. Textbooks on National History and National Ethics amply serviced the particular version of nationalism that the state intended to instill. In this regard, the South Korean state and ruling elite not only created nationalist ideology, but they also utilized it in pursuing industrialization. It can be said that the process of industrialization in countries such as South Korea was also the process of building a nation.

In Korea, there has been a long tradition of state control of education,[1] and this was even further reinforced during the colonial period when all educational activities were under the direct control of the Japanese Governor-General (Cumings 1981; Kim 1987). This tradition of state-controlled education did not change much in the post-colonial period, and the developmental state of South Korea actively utilized the national educational system in building the nation and propagating its own version of nationalism among the people. As Kedourie (1993: 83–84) points out, where modern states are the main disseminators of nationalist ideology, national educational systems are the main tools of it, and the role of education is essential in the development of nationalism.

Disciplining, controlling, and mobilizing people

In pursuing industrialization, the South Korean state disciplined people, especially the working class, so that the latter would provide inexpensive, reliable, and quality labor for the capitalist industry that was being built. Such disciplinary activity began with school education and often it was completed in the compulsory military service. All of the East Asian countries including South Korea, Taiwan, Singapore, and China have state-controlled educational system and they used to have a compulsory military service system, including in Japan, before World War II.

Ever since education became compulsory in the early twentieth century in East Asian countries, school education was a powerful tool of the state in disciplining their populations. As elsewhere in East Asia, school education was the basis of popular mobilization in South Korea.[2] In particular, during the Park era (1961–1979) the South Korean school system was under the tight control of the state, and the latter promulgated new ideological foundations of the national education system. In 1968 the state declared the National Education Charter, which set the educational goals of the nation as national restoration, industrialization, and anti-communism. It also emphasized Korea's long history as a sovereign nation, strong resistance against foreign invasions, and the cultural uniqueness of the Korean people. The basic goal of the Charter was the "restoration of the nation" (*minjok chunghŭng*), and its eventual goal was "to create a new history by building new ideal individuals for the nation" (Pak 1971: 29–34).

Then, what was the intention and function of such education in regard to nation-building? First of all, it was to create a culturally integrated and homogeneous country, and this would require assimilation and homogenization of the society. To this end, people should embrace a "standard" Korean culture imagined by the developmental state. More importantly, education was to mobilize people and discipline them so that they would fit better into modern industrial society. Controlling people along the line of the state and the ruling elite certainly would be another function and goal of such education. Indeed, the nationalistic spirit inculcated from primary school onwards shaped the South Koreans into a diligent people (Ahmad and Eun 2012: 308).

In imbuing people with nationalism and also disciplining them, the South Korean state also emphasized the physical strength of the members of the nation. "Physical power is national power" was a popular motto during the Park era in South Korea, and the government encouraged people to exercise and promoted many sports activities. It rewarded athletes who gained medals at international games, and the awards for male athletes included exemption from military service, which was mandatory for all young males.[3] The state also introduced a compulsory Physical Strength Measurement System in school and every student who took the national examination to enter tertiary educational institutes had to take this test.

One of the most prominent actions of the state in controlling and disciplining people was the introduction of military training in high school by the end of the 1960s. High school and university students were required to have two hours of military drill each week, which were taught by retired army officers. In addition to the weekly military drill classes, university students had to take actual military drills inside military barracks each year for two weeks. Students were also frequently mobilized for various events and rituals organized or sponsored by the state, where they normally performed military-like marches and march-pasts. These military drill classes and rituals were a deliberate mechanism to discipline young students and through this institution the state extended its ideological and physical control of the future generations.

In this regard, the South Korean state revived the old Student Defense Corps (*Hakto Hoguktan*, 學徒護國團) in 1975, replacing the existing Student Associations both in high schools and in universities. South Korea had a very strong tradition in which student associations were politically very powerful, and they often led anti-government movements. The April Revolution in 1960, which toppled the Syngman Rhee government, is a prime example. Under the new Student Defense Corps system, however, all students were organized into quasi-military units headed by principals of their schools. This was an effective way to divert the powerful political energy of the students from possible anti-government resistance. While such measures were highly oppressive and authoritarian, at least from the state's perspective, this was helpful for stable economic growth, when the international economic and political situation was not favorable for South Korea. For example, there were global recessions due to the two "oil shocks," and communist expansion seemed to be well in progress, especially with the unification of Vietnam by the North in 1975.

South Korea and most other East Asian countries have a system of compulsory military service, which has been an efficient tool for mass mobilization as well as educating and disciplining the masses. In addition to regular military service, the South Korean government also established Local Reserve Army Corps (*Hyangto Yebigun*, 鄕土豫備軍) in 1969. Through this program the state mobilized a few million young males who had finished their military service within the past five to ten years. They were mobilized to participate in military drills in military barracks a few times each year. These occasions were well utilized by the government to imbue them with anti-communist ideology, patriotism, and the need for a stable and strong state to cope with the increasing threats from the North. The government also used these events to propagate its achievements to generate political support for the government during election years.

Such measures are commonly used in all East Asian countries including Japan (before World War II), Taiwan, Singapore, and today's China. As illustrated in Figures 3.1 and 3.2, in China students are required to take similar military drills in schools. This is a norm in most East Asian countries but it would not be practiced or would be simply impossible to practice in other Asian countries such as India. This is one of the characteristics of the East Asian development model.

Figure 3.1 Chinese students visiting the Huangpoa Military Academy in Guangzhou as part of their military education in August 2013.

Figure 3.2 Chinese students visiting the Huangpoa Military Academy in Guangzhou as part of their military drill class in August 2013.

Mass mobilization

During the Park era the state became a mechanism not only to homogenize people for industrialization but also to mobilize and discipline them to maintain social integration in the process of rapid change. In addition, the state successfully promoted nationalist zeal, and translated it into mass mobilization to achieve modernization and industrialization. Throughout its reign, the Park regime in South Korea created various mass organizations and launched mass movements that were designed to mobilize, control, and discipline people. These included the above-mentioned Local Reserve Army Corps, the Student Defense Corps, and the New Village Movement (*Saemaŭl Undong*). These mass-mobilization systems played an important role in controlling the society, strengthening defense, promoting patriotism among the population, and also developing the economy.

Launched in 1970, the New Village Movement was one of the most successful mobilization programs initiated by the South Korean state. As the industrialization projects of the 1960s focused on industrial development, rural areas were relatively neglected and there was a need to narrow the ever-widening gap between agricultural and industrial sectors. It started in a very simple manner when villagers were given a small amount of material incentives—cement and other construction materials—and certain autonomy to develop their own villages. Many villages responded to this stimulation and those that showed good progress were given more incentives. Naturally, leaders engaged in these villages and they led many projects to improve the economic situations of the villages. The movement brought changes not only in the economic life of the villagers but also in the mentality of traditional villagers, and they were motivated to improve their lives. In addition to the small material support, the government also provided them with ideological and moral support by training village leaders and rewarding significant progress. While this movement was considered a great success (Park 1998), the system was also used to control the rural population. This was done through selective material and monetary aids from the central government. Villages that supported the regime would receive more material and monetary aids while others that did not show their support for the regime were left out.

As the movement spread throughout the rural area, villagers, and in fact the whole nation, were urged to get up early, work hard, save more, and explore ways to improve their economic life. In this sense, this movement was a disciplinary measure for the rural population, which had been traditionally outside of the state's disciplining measures. Combined with school education and the Local Reserve Army Corps, the state could deeply penetrate into the daily lives of villagers even in the remotest areas.

Daily rituals

In addition to these mobilization systems, various nationalist rituals were enforced in the everyday life of ordinary people: at workplaces, public performances, and even in villages. In almost all cases, these rituals were connected to nationalism. On a weekly basis schools had Morning Convention, for which all the school's students and teachers gathered together, forming neat rows like an army during its inspection. Such events and rituals were always accompanied by saluting the national flag, singing the national anthem, and reciting the National Education Charter. At workplaces, such rituals were performed regularly. Employees would be gathered every morning before the start of work and the company manager would give a speech, which is normally preceded by saluting the national flag and singing the national anthem (Song 2003).[4] Such rituals were forced even at movie theaters where, at the beginning of each film showing, all of the audience had to stand up and salute the national flag when the anthem was played. At the end of TV programs at midnight, TV stations would end the day's broadcast with the national anthem. Even on streets, at 5 p.m. every evening the national anthem was broadcast with the Oath to the National Flag,[5] and people had to stop and salute the national flag until the anthem ended.

Such rituals can be very effective in promoting and reinforcing national identity among people (Billig 1995). Guibernau also shows the importance of "symbols and repetitive rituals" in strengthening national unity and establishing the boundaries that distinguish a nation from others (Guibernau 1996: 81). As Bloom suggests, the state instilled devotion to its symbolic representatives in its citizens through such measures:

> For nation-building by the state, certain symbolic representatives of the states are indispensable. Either formal or informal individuals, institutions, rituals, and ideologies can serve as the symbolic representative of the state to the extent that they are clearly associated with the state.
>
> (Bloom 1990: 61)

All these efforts of the South Korean state were to propagate a particular type of nationalism, and their impact on the national culture was very deep. Through this mass mobilization the state persuaded people to identify themselves with the state as well as the nation (Park 1993: 81–82). In general, the state in South Korea, as in the case of Japan in the early twentieth century, fostered a particular form of nationalism and it was disseminated through state apparatuses such as the educational system and military service, which also became compulsory for all able-bodied males. By so doing, Park's regime was successful in making the people "willing to work long, hard hours for national pride" (Heo and Roehrig 2010: 79).

Foucault (1982) says the capacity to exercise power consists in three types of relationship: relations of power, relationships of communication, and finalized activities. Together, these three types of relationship constitute the "disciplinary" apparatus necessary for the exercise of power. This is exactly what the South Korean state did. First, it endeavored to produce a relationship of communication with the people, based around the idea of the nation—a system of symbols and signs within which states can immerse the exercise of power. The state also aimed to create objective capacities for the realization of power relations with its people by building various institutions through which it would exert its power over people. Here, the nationalist ideology that elite people shared was the foundation of such a system, and the South Korean state successfully utilized these relationships in training, mobilizing, and controlling its people. Through these measures the South Korean State pushed its economic development program with great success.

Use of nationalism by business elites

As seen above, the developmental state in South Korea actively utilized nationalism to motivate, control, and discipline people, especially the working class, through various state apparatuses (both institutional and ideological). Meanwhile, the business elite of the country also used the nationalist ideologies in a similar manner, particularly to promote harmonious labor relations and to protect their business interests from foreign capital. First of all, nationalism functioned in promoting entrepreneurial spirit among businessmen and the general public. Most of all nationalism gave business activities a moral stance, which is particularly important in Korea where entrepreneurialism was not eminent in its tradition. As a matter of fact, throughout the Chosŏn dynasty, the merchant class occupied the lowest echelon in the social order. This is because neo-Confucianism emphasized moral achievement as the most important virtue, while it discouraged commercial activities during the Chosŏn dynasty.

Modern nationalism, however, encouraged industrial activities and supported entrepreneurialism. For example, since the 1960s the South Korean state emphasized the importance of industrial activities in the name of the nation. National slogans such as *sanŏp ipkuk* ("developing the nation with industrialization") and the more conventional ones such as *puguk kangbyŏng* ("enriching the country, and strengthen its military") were prevalent. They all associated national well-being with entrepreneurism. With such mottos and policies, the developmental state of South Korea gave moral legitimacy to the business class in the country. Entrepreneurs who achieved a high level of exports were rewarded and they were praised as national heroes. Though the business class was seen as lacking nationalist legitimacy in South Korea, as we will see below, it soon began to adopt the nationalist ideology in legitimizing their business activities.

Business for the nation

In Western Europe the bourgeois class was the major force of modern nationalism, and in some cases nationalism was a political instrument devised by the ruling elite to preserve their class privilege and status (Greenfeld 1990). Having an indispensable interest in nationalist politics and culture, the bourgeois class in Western European societies favored a strong national government that would both protect their mercantile and industrial interests from the threats of other countries and secure the domestic market from regional barriers (Nairn 1997). Through such active roles in nationalism, the bourgeois class of most Western countries became a dominant class, and has enjoyed a high level of hegemony.[6] Similar dominance of the bourgeois class in a national community also occurred in some Asian and African countries, in which the bourgeois class also supported nationalism. For example, in post-Meiji Japan the bourgeois class has been active in promoting nationalism and many influential figures in Japanese business circles have been associated with nationalism, such as Shibusawa Eiichi (1840–1931). Even today, the business elite play a significant role in Japan in the development and propagation of cultural nationalism through its support of the ideology of *nihonjinron* (Yoshino 1992: 158).

In contrast to the cases of Western Europe and Japan, however, the business class of South Korea has not achieved hegemonic status. There are both cultural and historical reasons why the bourgeois or business class lack this kind of hegemony in South Korea (Eckert 1990: 116). First of all, as stated above, there has been a contempt for the entrepreneurial class in Korea due to its Confucian tradition. Commerce and industry carried negative connotations in the neo-Confucian tradition and merchants and artisans occupied the lowest statuses in the social hierarchy of scholar-bureaucrats, farmers, artisans, and traders. In addition, under Confucian society a quasi-egalitarian ideal also developed together with the ideals of meritocracy and the moral equality of human beings. In such a tradition, private property, though generally recognized in Korea, was not as highly valued as it was in the Protestant worldview. Such traditions still remain alive in

Korea despite the drastic social changes and the development of the capitalist economy in modern times, which have limited the social power of the newly developed bourgeois class (Eckert 1990).

Second, the collective or cooperative relationship of the Korean business class with the political authorities in both the colonial and post-colonial periods also explains why the Korean entrepreneurial class has not been able to enjoy hegemonic status. Historically, Korean businessmen as a group followed a course of "accommodation, subordination, and obedience to the government in return for monopoly rights and other favours" (Juhn 1977: 10). This was especially true during the colonial period when Korean merchants and small factory owners could not survive in the hostile environment unless they willingly cooperated with the authorities. It was during "developmental colonialism" (Cumings 1997: 162), the later period of Japanese colonialism in Korea when the "Korean majority suffered badly at the precise time when a minority was doing well" (Cumings 1997: 183). Therefore, this small number of businessmen would be branded as collaborators after the liberation.

A similar pattern of close government–business relationships was repeated in the post-colonial period. The South Korean government's economic development strategy in the post-colonial period showed similarities with that of the last decade of the colonial period in terms of government-controlled financing and giving the provision of favorable treatment to a small number of companies in return for their support for the regimes (Woo 1991: 42). Such a collaborative relationship developed by the Korean business elite with the authoritarian regime weakened the nationalist credit of the class. Indeed, there would have been more tolerance for personal and corporate profit-seeking in South Korea if the nationalist credentials of the country's bourgeoisie had been less flawed (Eckert 1990: 138).

Nevertheless, this has been changing steadily in the last few decades and the South Korean business class has been gaining more hegemonic status within South Korean society. In addition, the South Korean business elite's lack of legitimacy did not mean that it has not been active in nationalist politics. As a matter of fact, South Korean capitalists have endeavored to give legitimacy to their business activities by stressing that their activities are fundamental for the nation. While popular perceptions in Korea hold that most capitalists collaborated with Japanese colonial authorities, the political and cultural influence of the South Korean business elite has grown rapidly in the last few decades. In addition, through their growing ideological and cultural leadership, the business elite of South Korea has played an important role in constructing, maintaining, and reinforcing the national identity of contemporary Koreans. Today, the Korean business elite in pursuit of hegemony tend to believe that they should "guide," if not control, the direction of society's cultural and ideological development. For example, Chairman Rho of Hanhwa, one of the biggest conglomerates in South Korea, insists that "*chaebŏls* should go beyond the economic realm" in terms of their influence and that they should take "leadership in cultural projects" (Ungson *et al.* 1997: 132).

In fact, such unfavorable social perceptions of the Korean bourgeoisie have spurred the clan to pursue ways to provide itself with nationalist attributes, especially in the post-colonial era. Members of the South Korean business class tend to identify their corporations as "national" projects rather than "private" projects. For example, Kim Yŏn-su, the founder of Samyang, which is one of the oldest companies in Korea, claims that he decided to be a businessman for the sake of the nation during the colonial period:

> During the colonial period when the social stream was marked with despair and inertia, the youth of the time strove to find ways to work for the nation. Some took up arms against the Japanese authorities for Korean independence while others joined in the cultural movement for the enhancement of national consciousness. In my case, I decided to devote myself to business because I realized that our country was too poor and backward. I wanted to strengthen and enrich our country by developing modern industries. I firmly believed that our country could overcome its backwardness by building a self-sufficient economy and by importing advanced technologies, thereby gaining national independence.
>
> (Kim 1981: 48)

Those Korean capitalists who engaged in business during the colonial period, such as Kim Yŏn-su, tend to legitimize their activities by insisting that they were essentially motivated by love and sympathy for people suffering from colonial exploitation. In so doing, the Korean bourgeois nationalist discourse provides a vision for the prosperity of the national community through their business activities. Most of the mission statements of corporations reflect such principles. For example, the official watchwords of Samsung, a well-known South Korean conglomerate, are *saŏp poguk* ("serving the country through entrepreneurial activities"), *injae cheil* (merit system), and *hamni ch'ugu* (search for rationality), among which *saŏp poguk* is the most important. For Samsung, "serving the country through entrepreneurial activities" specifically means "contributing to national development by increasing employment and by expanding Samsung's business" (Hwang 1993: 184). Similarly, the company motto of Ssangyong, another large conglomerate, is "contributing to the modernization of our nation by working in the areas of key industries." In addition, Ssangyong's founder Kim Sŏng-gon used to urge on his employees by saying, "Let's work, work harder, for the fatherland and the nation" (Yi 1993: 456). In so doing, the business class of South Korea, as the developmental state of the country did, has been participating in nation-building in its own way and using nationalist ideology for the economic development of the country.

Harmonious labor relations: nation–corporation–family

As stated above, the tradition of the Confucian order was very much alive in many aspects of culture and politics in post-colonial South Korea. Especially under the rule of Park Chung Hee, the Confucian character of the country's nationalism gained new dimensions. In particular, unlike the leftist ideology that provokes class consciousness among the proletariat, the developmental state's nationalism emphasized the harmonious relationship between capital and labor. In many speeches, Park placed great emphasis on the idea that modernization should be achieved by the united efforts of people, businesses, and the state. The business elite of South Korea fully supported this view, and they actively propagated harmonious labor relations in the name of the nation's well-being. A harmonious relationship among all the units of the national community was essential to achieve industrialization, and this would be possible when a harmonious relationship exists between capital and labor. Labor should obey management and management should be responsible for the welfare of labor.

The views and visions of business elite are well reflected in the autobiographies of business leaders, as well as in many of their advertisements. In the advertisements of big companies and their owners' autobiographies, we can detect how the business elite of South Korea utilized (and shaped) the nationalism of the country. First of all, the nationalism that South Korean business leaders endorse tends to emphasize the inevitable unity between nation and corporations as a family. It also focuses on the hostile nature of the international environment, taking a realist view on the international community, thus distinguishing "us" from "them." It often views Japan as a national enemy to overcome or defeat.[7]

Nationalism is an ideology that views the nation as a community in which people feel connected to each other (Anderson 1983). In the case of Korean nationalism, as are the cases of Japan and China, the nation tends to be imagined as an extended family, which is well reflected in the terms of *guójiā* (國家) or *kukka* (*kokka* in Japanese) for the "state."[8] In this rhetoric of "nation is a family," individuals are expected to act as loyal and filial members of the family in their relationship with the national community.

From the early stage of capitalist development, the post-colonial South Korean entrepreneurs emphasized the importance of national harmony, especially cooperation between entrepreneurs and workers, for the sake of national development. In so doing, they viewed employers and employees as members of the same family. Therefore, they frequently espouse paternalist rhetoric, and the desired harmony between capital and labor is frequently reinforced in daily discourse by reference to the Confucian patriarchal family system. Top managers of South Korean companies, when they talk about the corporations or nation, tend to stress the importance of Confucian values, especially familial harmony. For them, a corporation is like a family, and the relationship between the employer and worker in a company is often considered as an extension of the parent–child relationship within a family. In such a relationship, the employer also takes the responsibility of supporting his employees. For the employees, obedience and sacrifice are the desired virtues (Song 1994: 388).

One such example is Ch'oe Chong-gŏn, the former chairman of Sunkyung, who promoted a doctrine he names *hansot'pap sikkuron* ("the thesis of we-all-live-under-the-same-roof"). According to this thesis, everybody who works for

Sunkyung is a family member whose life is shared with other members regardless of his/her rank in the company. This doctrine is well represented in his biography, which describes his management philosophy as follows:

> In Sunkyung there was no clear distinction between boss and subordinate. It was always the chairman himself who worked most diligently, and who did the most difficult jobs. Though Ch'oe nominally was the Chairman of the company, he actually behaved like a buddy to everyone in the company. He was always a reliable friend and an available drinking pal to anyone. Since he was such a friendly "boss," the workers did not need labour union to represent their rights, and there could not be any conflict between management and labour. There were always direct channels between the chairman and the workers to talk about problems at friendly drinking parties before they became serious.
>
> (Yi 1993: 527)

As this biography reveals, the consequence, if not the explicit purpose, of the thesis of *hansot'pap sikkuron* is the avoidance of the need for a labor union. In the notion of the "corporation as a family," the personal, friendly, and fatherly character of the business owner simply replaces the institutionalized and impersonal labor union. This corporation-as-family discourse is a logical extension of the doctrine of nation-as-family that the developmental state propagates.

Another aspect of "nation-as-family" and "corporation-as-family" ideology is reflected in the practice of nationalist ceremonies at workplaces, as mentioned above. Nationalist ceremonies, including singing the national anthem, saluting the national flag, and reading out the Charter of National Education, were not unusual practices at workplaces in South Korea through the 1960s, 1970s, and 1980s. For the business elite, such nationalist ceremonies are highly desirable because they serve the interests of the business class in multiple ways. First, practicing nationalist rituals at work provides moral legitimacy to their business activities by connecting the latter with the superior values of nationalism and patriotism. Through nationalist rituals, business management and labor become a concrete part of the national community. Thus, even for workers, labor means not merely production or providing a service, but it becomes a much loftier action of serving the nation. Propagation of such belief, needless to say, is intended to weaken the class consciousness of workers by providing a sense of purpose to the workers who have to endure the toils of labor.

In addition, patriarchal values such as filial piety are extended smoothly to the company owner through such rituals, all the more so because these rituals are normally conducted in the context of the hierarchical relations of the workplace. Usually the head of the business (or his/her representatives) leads the rituals, which often imitate military-style ceremonies. Since such ceremonies are widely practiced in schools and the military, participants are familiar with them and seldom question the rationale. Such rituals also discipline employees by making them stand in rows, sing the national anthem, and salute the national flag before and after work. In this case, corporations use nationalism as a means for disciplining the workforce.

However, the business elites' use of nationalism supplements that of the developmental state. They have disciplined Koreans through subtler means than the state has done. One example of Sunkyung's advertising in the mid-1980s shows the business class urging the nation to work hard to achieve technological development for the future of the national economy. According to the ad, South Korea can become an advanced country if it utilizes and awakens the "dormant national wisdom" that the members of the Korean nation have in their "blood":

> Let's wake the national wisdom that is lying dormant. Our ancestors have developed a unique culture with their skills and creativity. It was the spirit of craftsmanship (*chang'in chŏngsin*) that thus developed an excellent culture, and this spirit is in the blood of our nation. With this very craftsmanship, our ancestors developed technologies creatively, and we inherited the spirit from them. The most urgent task for us now is to build a new era of technological development by awakening the dormant wisdom of our nation. Our dream of making Korea an advanced country will definitely be realized if the young people of our country search for knowledge incessantly and work hard with bountiful creativity.

This advertisement was issued in the mid-1980s when student protests against the authoritarian regime were at a peak. From this we can see that South Korean business elite tried hard to de-politicize student demonstrators in the turbulent time of the 1980s by using nationalist themes. With the financial crisis of 1997 the business elite further emphasized the close relationship and "shared fate" of workers and business. In so doing, the business elite again used paternalism by providing a vision in which South Korea would become one of the most developed nations in the world if business and workers worked together.

Protecting national economic interests

The business elite of South Korea brings the notion of a family-like national community to a Darwinist view of the business world. In their nationalist rhetoric, the South Korean business elite tends to present the world as an arena where groups struggle against each other for scarce resources and markets, in which only the best-adapted and most successful groups will survive. The Korean business elite espouse such a "realist" worldview and it tends to view the basic character of the world as unruly, disorderly, and harshly competitive. Especially since the 1980s, as South Korean corporations expanded to the world market, business leaders more openly propagated a "Darwinist" worldview. In their nationalist discourse, South Korean business leaders proposed that the new century will be marked by ferocious competition among nations and that a "war" will prevail and only the fit will survive (Song 2003).

For example, as South Korea's electronic, shipbuilding, and automobile industries have been competing with Japan in global markets, South Korean business emphasized the need for "overcoming" Japanese or taking it over.[9] After the emergence of China as industrial power in the 1980s, South Korean companies expressed their concern that they would lose their market share to Chinese companies. In this regard, business leaders of South Korea warned South Koreans that the country's industries would be "sandwiched" between China and other advanced countries such as Japan. Using such rhetoric, they provoked the nationalist sentiments of people to protect their own business interests and in so doing they also intended to urge Koreans to raise labor productivity.

Here, they show a dual attitude toward Japan. On one hand, they position Japan as a "national enemy" or competitor that should be "defeated" or "overcome." On the other hand, they tend to urge Koreans to emulate Japanese workers, whose labor productivity is much higher than that of Koreans. In fact, the great majority of Korean business leaders revere Japan as a model that Korea should emulate. Japan's harmonious labor relations and Japanese workers' high productivity have been widely praised by South Korean business elites. Therefore, business leaders of South Korea also tend to emphasize the necessity of learning Japanese-style labor relations. South Korean business leaders have always preferred the Japanese style of "industrial paternalism" to the Western European style of "welfare corporatism" (Lee and Song 1994). In this Japanese system of industrial paternalism, capital guarantees paternalistic protection—i.e., lifetime employment—and labor devotes loyalty to capital. A researcher discusses Korean business leaders who emphasize learning the Japanese work ethic and harmonious industrial relations:

> The business class tends to believe that industrial unionism would empower labour. Therefore, throughout the period of rapid economic growth, the business classes have repeatedly touted the merits of a Japanese-style labour relationship and the high work ethic of workers. Therefore, they selectively adopted Japanese style management skills.
>
> (Song 1994: 254)

The use of nationalist ideology by the business elite for promoting harmonious labor relations and protecting the business interests of Korean companies is much more subtle and sophisticated than the way in which the developmental state used the nationalism to discipline the working class. Thanks to the aggressive efforts of the South Korean bourgeoisie to improve its popular image, it has been successful in gaining more nationalist legitimacy. The fact that many South Koreans today identify themselves with the products of South Korea demonstrates the growth of the ideological power of the Korean business community. Today, Korean products such as automobiles and electronic goods seem to form an important part of Korean identity.

Nevertheless, the strategies of the business elite of the country did not seem to work well after the 1990s when South Korean society became more economically prosperous and democratically mature. The power of nationalism still remained strong as the dominant ideology among South Koreans including the working class. However, what had changed was the effect of the persuasive power of the nationalist rhetoric propagated by the state and business elite.

Democratization and the decline of developmental nationalism

As the South Korean economy developed through the 1960s, 1970s, and 1980s, the effect of the nationalist rhetoric propagated by the state and business elite on workers weakened. Now, instead of following the military-led developmental state and the exploitative business elite and conglomerates, South Koreans demanded a more democratic political system and more distributive economic justice. By the late 1980s South Korea became a more democratized country when the military rule was finally ended. Further, in the early 1990s South Korean society became institutionally more democratic as the opposition parties could take power through democratic and peaceful elections. This change came with the growth of the middle class, and in the early 1990s more than 75 percent of South Koreans considered themselves "middle class."

With such changes, the culture of South Korean society also became generally more liberal, open, and democratic. Now, the state would not be able to mobilize or control people with the same ideological and institutional means it had relied on for the last few decades. Workers would not accept such top-down leadership and ideological indoctrination. They would not be controlled or accept the kind of nationalist ideology that the state and business elite used so well in the past. Instead, workers in South Korea became more class conscious and they would even challenge the developmental state and business elite in regard to their legitimacy based on nationalism, the very ideology by which they have been controlled, disciplined, and mobilized.

Here emerged the powerful ideology of "*minjung* nationalism" (民衆民族主義), which emphasizes the legitimacy of "people" (*minjung*) as the most important component of the Korean national community. They claim that the genuine master of the Korean nation is the *minjung* and not the ruling elite. Understanding the fact that South Korean business (especially conglomerates) had collaborated with the Japanese during the colonial period, and also that they had grown rapidly thanks to people's cooperation and sacrifice in the 1960s and the 1970s, workers challenged the hegemony of the country's ruling class. Not only did they demand higher wages, they also legitimized their role as the vanguard of the national community—through their resistance to the Japanese and other foreign powers in the early modern history of Korea. This was evident as South Korea began to see more frequent and violent labor disputes from the mid-1980s. As a matter of fact, the very cause that the business elite (and the developmental state) used, namely nationalism, now served the workers in their demands for better treatment. It showed that people were not just passive objects of ideological manipulation by the developmental state and business elite. People had their own sense of national pride and identity and they desired to correct the wrongdoings of the oppressive state and conglomerates in oppressing and exploiting workers. Their pride as Koreans and their desire to make the nation prosperous allowed them to cooperate with the developmental state and business elite as far as the latter believed that they shared exactly the same goals. Nevertheless, the situation changed after the 1980s with the thaw of the Cold War and the re-evaluated relationship with the United States, and the visible prosperity of conglomerates and other big business. These events awakened the class consciousness of the people.

Such a pattern of industrialization, growth of the middle class, democratization, and labor disputes was rather common in other East Asian countries. After decades of industrialization and economic development, workers in Taiwan, for example, began to resist the rigid regime of the *Kuomintang* and the business elites of the country. With these changes labor disputes were common in both South Korea and Taiwan by the 1980s. In addition, the economic development and democratization also saw the demise of the somewhat paternalistic relationship between the states and business in South Korea. Now the state could not control business as it used to, and the same was true for the control of the labor.

In particular, in South Korea the characteristics of nationalism also changed, and now it has become more civic than ethnic, as it used to be. In particular, after the Asian Financial Crisis in the late 1990s, the "national community" that people used to imagine waned. The communal spirit in the name of the "nation," such as the "nation-as-family" and "corporation-as-family," weakened while society became more individualistic and the level of trust decreased (Kwon 2011). In South Korea the workers would not be swayed easily by any ideological propagation of the state or business elite.

Conclusion

Nationalism or nationalist ideology has played an important role in the industrialization and economic development of East Asian countries. Both South Korean and Taiwanese cases show that nationalist development strategies resulted in rapid economic growth (Desai and Potter 2008: 483). Though the use of nationalism by the state and business elite was not simple, it worked quite well in the case of South Korea. This seems to be true for other East Asian countries including Taiwan, Singapore, and China. Especially in South Korea, the developmental state and business elite utilized the ideology well, controlling, disciplining, and mobilizing people. Nationalistic elements were needed in order to industrialize South Korea and the state utilized them through national campaigns, such as slogans, posters, and pamphlets, to increase people's loyalty and diligence (Kim 2007: 81).

Nationalism may not be the most disciplining ideology, yet nationalism has functioned as a disciplining force in many countries. In particular, where the goal of nationalism was to strengthen the military and to enrich the country, nationalism required more disciplined individuals to achieve its goals. In this case, nationalism was to discipline the masses so that the ruling elite could mobilize the mental and physical energies of the people. Such discipline certainly contributed to the achievement of capitalist industrialization.

The nationalist legitimacy and leadership of the state and especially the business class, nevertheless, met with some serious challenges from the *minjung* populists in the 1980s. Workers resisted the developmental state and business elite in their ideals of nationalism. This was manifested as increasing labor disputes and strong demand for democratization, which eventually were achieved by the early 1990s. By the late 1990s, especially with the Asian financial crisis, the ideological power of the developmental state and the business elite had waned substantially. Accompanying this were the general changes in the social atmosphere and culture of the country: people became more individualistic and there was a decrease of trust among the different classes. The character of Korean nationalism itself has changed from ethnic to more civic. Nationalist ideology, now, would not be able to control, discipline, or mobilize people, not to mention make them sacrifice themselves, for the benefit of the state or business elite.

From the observation of the South Korean case, the power of nationalism in disciplining, controlling, and mobilizing people seems to be effective only in the early stage of industrialization. Such control, discipline, and mobilization of people and resources, however, did not seem to happen in such an effective manner in other Asian countries such as India. There is strong sense of nation and nationalism in other non-East Asian countries as well, but in these countries the state and business elite do not seem to have been able to utilize such popular sentiments for the mobilization of people and resources. This distinguishes the so-called East Asian developmental model from others.

Mobilization of people and resources by the state and ruling elite has been everywhere, but mobilization based on people's voluntary cooperation, as happened in countries such as South Korea in the 1960s and 1970s, does not seem to be common. Although Confucian values and nationalist sentiments were a factor in spurring South Korea's development, it was the strength of the state and the business elite that allowed these to be utilized. The political stability and strong, authoritative nature of the South Korean state, combined with its effective development strategies, provided the means for Confucianism and nationalism to be productively applied to promote industrialization (Kim and Park 2003: 47). Together with the developmental state, the South Korean business elite, although it did not enjoy as much hegemony as its counterpart in Western Europe or Japan, also tactfully utilized the nationalist rhetoric in creating harmonious labor relations.

It is likely that South Korea would not have achieved the level of success it now holds without the dedication of its populace in seeking to improve upon and protect their nation, making nationalism an important aspect of this narrative. Nationalism was and is very important for the development of the South Korean economy as they were able to move on from poverty. Although Park Chung Hee has been criticized for ruling South Korea in a dictator-like fashion, he was a strong leader with massive support. The workers were diligent and worked hard to see their country and their people grow and leave behind the past of hardship. Although the work was not easy during those times of economic development, they worked willingly to help bring their nation to a greater position. Korean nationalism is a very important part of the economic growth in South Korea. Without it, the country would not have united and worked together to rise out of poverty (Yin 2013).

Countries that could achieve such control, discipline, and mobilization of people in the cause of nationalism succeeded in achieving high economic development, as in East Asia. Other countries that could not do so have not been as successful as their counterparts in East Asia. The strategic use of nationalism for economic development, therefore, would be an important factor in distinguishing East Asian countries from others.

Notes

* Acknowledgment: This work was supported by the Academy of Korean Studies Grant funded by the Korean Government (MEST) (AKS-2012-BAA-2101).

1 During the Chosŏn dynasty the state controlled the content of education through the civil examination system. Only Confucian classics were studied since they were the main subjects of the civil examination.

2 In explaining the relationship between the modern state and education, Neo-Marxists view education as an ideological tool of the ruling class, and the purpose of education in capitalist societies is to reproduce the labor force needed by capital and to reproduce such an order for the ruling class (O'Connor 1973: 354). In democratic countries, meanwhile, education tends to be controlled by various social groups including the state. In authoritarian societies education is monopolized or heavily controlled by the state (Spring 1994: 15).

3 Early-morning soccer clubs were encouraged and all public schools opened their playgrounds for these soccer clubs and others who want to exercise.

4 "I pledge, in front of proud Taegeukgi, allegiance to the Republic of Korea for the eternal glory of the country, liberty and justice."

5 Such nationalist (and statist) rituals were common at workplaces, schools, and even on the streets. In 1979 the *National Geographic* reported such a ritual at the World Cup Dinner Theater, a popular restaurant that features dancing, magicians, and Country and Western music (Kim 1979: 794–795).

6 Hegemony is a situation in which the ruling class leads a society, not just with law and force, but with moral and intellectual leadership. It implies stability based on majority consent, and that the people who are ruled positively support the values, ideals, goals, and cultural meanings that bond them to the current power structure. In this situation a group's interests are "generalized" into the interests of the whole society. The hegemony of capitalism has developed as the result of political, economic, and cultural changes over the last 300 years, but the status of capitalism did not become stable until the nineteenth century. Only in the twentieth century, especially with the collapse of the Soviet Union and Eastern European countries, did it seem that a capitalist regime has won out. It can be safely said that right now capitalism has hegemony in the international community (Storey 1993: 17).

7 Nonetheless, at the same time, it also presents Japan as a model to be emulated especially for its hard-working and cooperative working class and harmonious industrial

relations. Finally, it calls attention to the need for national expansion (both through achieving national unification and creating a global pan-Korean community). In so doing, business nationalism envisions the nation's future as a superpower.

8 In the case of China, the official Zhonghua Family (中華大家庭) is frequently used in public discourse.

9 However, the Korean bourgeoisie's "overcoming Japan" discourse contains inherent contradictions. First, it is widely known that Korea is indebted to Japan for today's industrial development. Japan built an extensive infrastructure and numerous industrial facilities in Korea during the colonial period. Many of today's *chaebŏl* in South Korea began under Japanese rule, and it was Japan that provided the funding and technology in the early stages of South Korean industrialization. After the diplomatic normalization between South Korea and Japan in 1965, Japan provided developmental funds, and a symbiotic relationship developed between Japanese and Korean businessmen. Most importantly, South Korea—as well as Taiwan and other Asian Tigers—followed Japanese strategies of development (Scalapino *et al.* 1985; Fukuda 1988; Vogel 1991).

References

Ahmad, N.S.Y., and Eun, K.-S. (2012) "The rise of nationalism among South Korean youth and democracy: An analysis," *Proceedings of World of Academy of Science, Engineering and Technology*, 64: 308–318.

Anderson, B. (1983) *Imagined communities: Reflections on the origins and spread of nationalism*, London: Verso.

Billig, M. (1995) *Banal nationalism*, London: Sage Publications.

Bloom, W. (1990) *Personal identity, national identity and international relations*, Cambridge: Cambridge University Press.

Cumings, B. (1981) *The origins of the Korean War*, Vol. I, Princeton, NJ: Princeton University Press.

Cumings, B. (1997) *Korea's place in the sun: A modern history*, New York: Norton.

Desai, V., and Potter, R.B. (2008) *The companion to development studies*, New York: Routledge.

Eckert, C.J. (1990) "The South Korean bourgeoisie: A class in search of hegemony," *Journal of Korean Studies*, 7: 115–148.

Foucault, M. (1982) "The subject and power," *Critical Inquiry*, 8(4): 777–795.

Fukuda, J.K. (1988) *Japanese-style management transferred: The experience of East Asia*, London: Routledge.

Gellner, E. (1983) *Nations and nationalism*, Ithaca, NY: Cornell University Press.

Greenfeld, L. (1990) "The formation of Russian national identity," *Comparative Studies in Society and History*, 32(3): 549–591.

Greenfeld, L. (1992) *The five roads to modernity*, Boston: Harvard University Press.

Greenfeld, L. (1999) "The formation of the Russian national identity: The road of status insecurity and ressentiment," *Comparative Studies in Society and History*, 32(3): 549–591.

Guibernau, M. (1996). *Nationalism: The nation-state and nationalism in the twentieth century*, Cambridge: Polity Press.

Heo, U., and Roehrig, T. (2010) *South Korea since 1980*, New York: Cambridge University Press.

Hofstede, G., and Bond, M.H. (1988) "The Confucian connection: From cultural roots to economic growth," *Organizational Dynamics*, 16(4): 5–21.

Hoselitz, B.F. (1956) "Nationalism, economic development and democracy," *Annals of the American Academy of Political and Social Science*, 305: 1–11.

Hwang, M.-S. (1993) "Han'guk kyŏngyŏng inyŏm ŭi sajŏk pyŏnch'ŏn" [The change of Korean management ideas], in M.-S. Hwang (eds.), *Han'guk kiŏp kyŏngyŏng ŭi yŏksajŏk sŏnggyŏk [The historical character of Korean corporate management]*, Seoul: Shinyangsa, pp. 171–188.

Johnson, C. (1982) *MITI and the Japanese miracle*, Stanford, CA: Stanford University Press.

Juhn, D.S. (1977) "Nationalism and Korean business under Japanese colonial rule," *Korea Journal*, 17: 4–12.

Kahn, H. (1979) *World economic development: 1979 and beyond*, Boulder, CO: Westview Press.

Kedourie, E. (1993) *Nationalism*, Oxford: Blackwell.

Kim, A.E., and Park, G.-S. (2003) "Nationalism, Confucianism, work ethic and industrialization in South Korea," *Journal of Contemporary Asia*, 33(1): 37–49.

Kim, E.H. (1979) "Seoul: Korean showcase," *National Geographic*, 156(6): 770–797.

Kim, H. (2007) "Cultural and state nationalism: South Korean and Japanese relations with China," PhD dissertation, The American University, Washington, D.C.

Kim, S. (1987) "Korean education: Past and present," *Korea Journal*, 27(4): 4–19.

Kim, Y.-S. (1981) "Kim Yon-su," in Hanguk Ilbosa (ed.), *Chaegye Hoego* (1) *[Memoirs of the business world I]*, Seoul: Hanguk Ilbosa Chulpanguk, pp. 19–276.

Kuznets, P.W. (1988) "An East Asian model of economic development: Japan, Taiwan, and South Korea," *Economic Development and Cultural Change*, 36(3): s11–s43.

Kwon, O.Y. (2011) "Does culture matter for economic development in Korea?" Online: www.akes.or.kr/eng/papers(2011)/31.full.pdf.

Lee, S.H., and Song, H.K. (1994) "The Korean garment industry: From authoritarian patriarchism to industrial paternalism," in E. Bonacich, L. Cheng, N. Chinchilla, N. Hamilton, and P. Ong (eds.), *Global production: The apparel industry in the pacific rim*, Philadelphia, PA: Temple University Press, pp. 147–161.

Nairn, T. (1997) *The break-up of Britain: Crisis and neo-naturalism*, London: New Left Books.

O'Connor, J. (1973) *The fiscal crisis of the state*, New York: St. Martin's Press.

Pak S.-T. (1971) *Kungmin Kyoyuk Honjang ui Sasangjok Paekyong kwa Silchon [The philosophical background and practice of the National Educational Charter]*, Seoul: Kyoyuk Chulpansa.

Park, H.T. (1993) *The decline of mass democracy in South Korea: Personalized politics, state nationalism, political regionalism, and mass democracy*. Ph.D. dissertation, University of Georgia.

Park, J.H. (1998) *The Saemaul Undong: Korea's approach to rural modernization in 1970s*. Seoul: Korea Rural Economic Institute.

Richmond, A.H. (1984) "Ethnic nationalism and post-industrialism," *Ethnic and Racial Studies*, 7(1): 5–16.

Rostow, W.W. (1971) *The stages of economic growth*, Cambridge: Cambridge University Press.

Scalapino, R.A., Sata, S., and Wanandi, J. (1985) *Asian economic development: Present and future*, Berkeley, CA: University of California Press.

Son, C.Y. (2009) *The direction of development and problem about moral and ethics education in elementary and secondary school*, MA Thesis in Education, Wonkwang University, South Korea, pp. 26–27.

Song, C. (2003) "Business elite and the construction of national identity in post-colonial Korea," *Acta Koreana*, 6(2): 55–86.

Song, H.-G. (1994) *Yŏllin sijan tach'in chŏngch'i* [Open market, closed politics], Seoul: Nanam.

Spring, J. (1994) *Wheels in the head: Educational philosophies of authority, freedom, and culture from Socrates to Paulo Freire*, New York: McGraw-Hill.

Storey, J. (1993) *An introduction to cultural theory and popular culture*, Athens: University of Georgia Press.

Ungson, G., Steers, R., and Park, S.-H. (1997) *Korean enterprise: The quest for globalisation*, Boston, MA: Harvard Business School Press.

Vogel, E. (1991) *The four little dragons: The spread of industrialization in East Asia*, Cambridge, MA: Harvard University Press.

Woo, J.-E. (1991) *Race to the swift: State and finance in Korean industrialization*, New York, NY: Columbia University Press.

Woo-Cumings, M. (1999) *The developmental state*, Ithaca, NY: Cornell University Press.

Yi, H.-C. (1993) *Han'guk ŭi kiŏp munhwa [The corporate culture of South Korea]*, Seoul: Pagyŏngsa.

Yin, S.J. (2013) "Pride of the people: South Korea and Korean nationalism." Online: www.isis.org.my/files/IF_2013/IF8/IF8_12.pdf.

Yoshino, K. (1992) *Cultural nationalism in contemporary Japan: A sociological enquiry*, London: Routledge.

4 Democratic development and authoritarian development compared

South Korea*

Hyug Baeg Im

Introduction: Korea as the showcase of testing theses on democracy and economic development

In comparative perspective, South Korea has been the museum of theories of democracy and development. Until the mid-1980s, South Korea was an exemplar case in the Third World countries that showed the incompatibility between capitalist economic development and democracy, i.e., "capitalist development does not promote democracy but rather capitalist development strengthens autocracy or authoritarianism" (O'Donnell 1973). This thesis was the main argument of the so-called "Bureaucratic Authoritarian" (BA) theory, and the Korean experience, together with those of Taiwan and Spain, was often cited as the model case that supported the BA thesis (Im 1987: 231–257). However, since the mid-1980s the successful transition to democracy from authoritarian rule in South Korea has made the modernization thesis stronger than ever before. The main assumption of the modernization thesis is that successful capitalist economic development promotes democratic transition and provides a material base for the consolidation of new, fragile democracies. The spectacular economic growth and ensuing democratic transition in the mid-1980s was often cited as the proving case of Lipset's modernization thesis, which holds a society's level of development to be the critical precondition for democracy (Lipset 1959: 69–105).

Since the democratic transition in 1987, Korea became the exemplar case supporting the exogenous modernization thesis of Adam Przeworski and his associates that although democratic transition may be unrelated to the level of economic development, with regard to the sustainability, durability, or consolidation of new democracies economic development and democracy has a strong causal relationship (Przeworski *et al.* 2000). It is called the neo-modernization thesis because it proves empirically what Lipset said in the same seminal article on "some prerequisites of democracy," i.e., "the more well-to-do a nation, the greater the chances that it will sustain democracy" (Lipset 1959: 69–105). According to Przeworski *et al.*, wealthy democracies with high GDP per capita ($6,055) would avoid slipping back into autocracy.[1] Since the democratic transition in 1987, steady economic growth, the successful overcoming of the East

Asian economic crisis in 1998, and the resumption of economic growth showed that democracy in an affluent society like South Korea would not be subverted to authoritarianism, and the Korean case exactly fit into Przeworski's neo-modernization thesis or "exogenous democratization."[2]

Impressive economic performance and the "compressed completion of democratic consolidation" in just 20 years after the democratic transition in 1987, by-passing the so-called Huntington's "two turnover test" (first by Kim Dae Jung in 1997 and second by current president Lee Myung Bak in 2007), has attracted worldwide scholarly and policy attention. Many tried to learn from Korea as a role model for economic growth with equity, successful export-led industrialization, autochthonous democratization without help from outside forces, endogenous democratization, and exogenous democratization.

In that sense, the last 50 years' experiences of compressed industrialization and democratization provides political scientists and political leaders in the world insights, wisdom, and lessons about democracy and economic development. Until the mid-1980s Korea was an example case that an economically affluent society could not develop a free and competitive liberal democracy, while since 1987 Korea has been applauded as a showcase of the simultaneous development of democracy and capitalist industrialization.

First, democratization in Korea is the model case of "endogenous democratization" in East Asia. The military dictatorship in Korea collapsed neither because of pressure from the United States to democratize nor because of the effects of the end of Cold War, nor due to severe economic crisis, but because military dictators agreed with democratic opponents to hand over power to the winner of a democratic election. It can be called an "endogenous democratization," on the ground that when income per capita crossed a threshold, economic development enabled the transfer of power from the military to democractically elected representatives.

Second, Korea is also a model case for "exogenous democratization" because once established as an affluent democracy in 1987, the new economically developed democracy has never collapsed, nor been subverted, nor overthrown despite the new democracy experiencing external fluctuations such as severe economic and security crises. The new affluent democracy in Korea shows that economic development and affluence makes new democracy stable, sustainable, durable, and resilient.

Finally, democratization in Korea is the model case of "autochthonous democratization" in East Asia because Koreans were not given democracy as a gift from its patron state,[3] the United States, nor as a concession from the incumbent military power holders. Instead, the maximum coalition for democracy among students, intellectuals, workers (including white collar workers), farmers, and the middle class acquired democracy through long struggles for restoring democracy by their own efforts.

This chapter is not about evaluating the characteristics of Korean democratization, but about a comparison between democratic development and authoritarian development. In other words, this chapter tries to test whether democratic governments in Korea have performed better or worse than authoritarian regimes. In this chapter, we will, first, discuss five theoretical models that explain the relationship between a political regime and economic development. Second, we will look into economic development under the authoritarian regime of Park Chung Hee. Third, we will test the so-called "incompetence of democratic governments thesis," contending that the authoritarian regime excelled over the democratic governments in terms of economic performance as measured by GDP growth per capita, export growth, low inflation rate, full employment, and gross fixed capital formation, etc. The tentative conclusion is that the democratic governments did not perform economically worse than the authoritarian governments, but in some areas, democratic governments outperformed authoritarian governments known as the dictatorial government "making the Korean miracle." Finally, we will analyze the reasons why democratic governments in South Korea outshone or at least performed as well as authoritarian governments. In other words, we will look into democratic advantage over authoritarian regimes in terms of economic development.

Theoretical overview: five possible causal relations between democracy and economic development

Until now we have five perspectives that explain the correlations between democracy and development (and vice versa): (1) Modernization Theory: "development first, democracy later"; (2) Praetorianism: economic development, under-institutionalization, hyper-democracy, and praetorian dictatorship; (3) Bureaucratic Authoritarianism: "development does not lead to democracy, but to technocratic authoritarianism"; (4) Democratic Development Theory: "democracy first, development later"; and (5) Agnosticism: "political regime

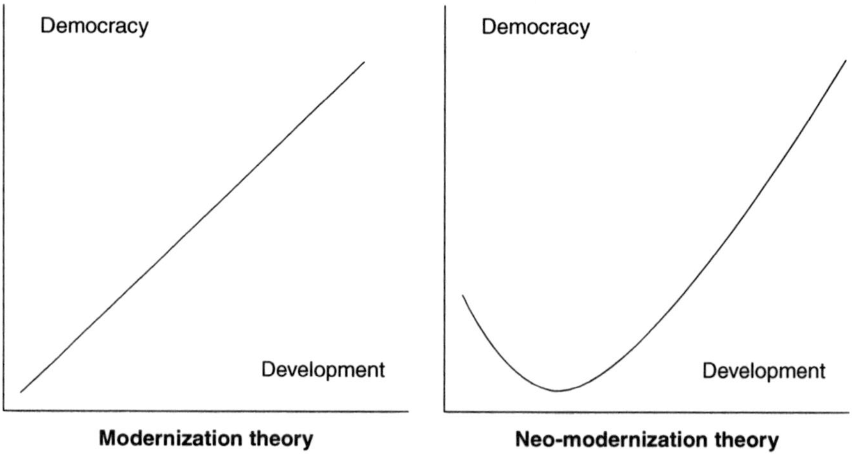

Figure 4.1 Modernization theory and neo-modernization theory (source: Chen 2007).

(democracy or authoritarianism) does not matter in development" (Przeworski and Limongi 1993: 51–69; Chen 2007).

Modernization Theory: "development first, democracy later"

Modernization Theory argues that economic prosperity provides the source of elective affinity between the market economy and democracy. The market economy promotes economic development and thus fosters democracy. Economic prosperity provides rich soil for a democratic political culture laden with tolerance, conciliation, and compromise.[4] De Tocqueville wrote in his *Democracy in America*, Vol. 2, that the development of the market economy fosters democracy by providing "social space within which individuals, groups, and entire institutional complexes can develop independent of state control" (Tocqueville 1945).

The forerunner of Modernization Theory goes back to Aristotle who argues that a large and thick affluent middle class is the backbone of "polity" (Aristotelian democracy in a good sense) (Barker 1995). Later, Barrington Moore Jr. (1966) developed "the Moore's thesis of bourgeoisie democracy," i.e., "No Bourgeoisie, No Democracy," and finally, Seymour Lipset theoretically refined the modernization thesis: "the more well-to-do a nation, the greater the chance that it will sustain democracy," because economic development generates "industrialization, urbanization, high educational standards and a steady increase in the overall wealth of society as a basic condition for sustaining democracy" (Lipset 1959: 75).[5]

Modernization Theory seemed to be discarded as many new democracies with relatively affluent economies in Latin America, Asia, and Africa had been overthrown by military coups in the 1960s. Nonetheless, since the mid-1970s, as many authoritarian countries, like South Korea, Taiwan, and Chile, that achieved successfully market-oriented industrialization finally made the transition to democracy, neo-modernization theory has received strong statistical support. Gabriel Almond, in his article "Capitalism and Democracy," reviews key works of eminent scholars, such as Robert Dahl, Peter Burger, Daniel Lerner, and Karl Deutsch, who demonstrate that statistically there is a correlation between economic development and democratic institutions (Almond 1991: 469; Chen 2007).

Praetorianism: "economic development, under-institutionalization, hyper-democracy, and praetorian dictatorship"

Praetorianism is Huntington's thesis on democracy and development. In contrast to the modernization school, Huntington proposes, in *Political Order in Changing Societies* (1968), an alternative explanation that rapid economic development, an outburst of political participation but without sufficient institutionalization, would lead not to liberal democracy, but to "political decay" and political instability. Faced with the threat of the lower classes and political and social instability, the

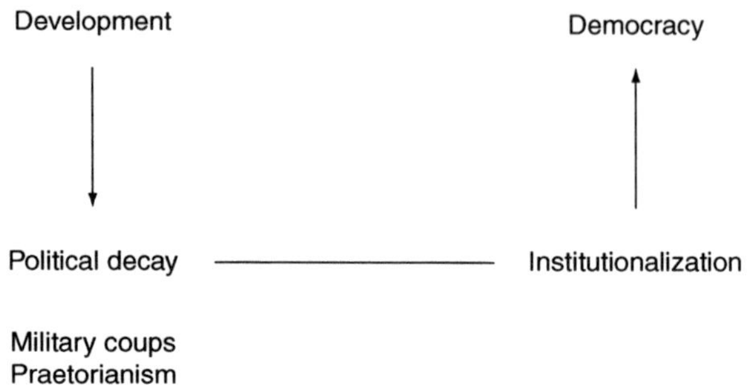

Figure 4.2 Praetorianism.

disenchanted middle class invites praetorian dictators to restore order and stability. While political decay and instability occurred in the early stage of industrialization, Huntington argues, however, that in the later stage, authoritarian regimes move toward democracy through institutionalization.

Huntington developed the logic of the praetorianism thesis into "no easy choice" between democracy and development (Huntington and Nelson 1976). Since socio-economic modernization increases the political participation of citizens without ensuring their demands can be met, economic development is best promoted under conditions of "a high degree" of political stability and order. In a country where the elite lacks "the art of association" and institutions are unable to channel the chaos that accompanies modernization, democracy can be counterproductive because it would likely destroy already fragile political institutions, generate ungovernability caused by an upsurge of popular participation, create division, and encourage consumption at the expense of investment (Sharma 2007: 41).[6]

Huntington's praetorianism thesis meets strong counterfactual evidence in the case of Taiwan. Even though Taiwan had achieved successful industrialization, there was no eruption of political participation of the masses. In addition there was no military intervention in politics; KMT dominance made Taiwanese politics highly institutionalized but there was no democracy until 1996. Because the KMT party was actually a Leninist party, Taiwan had attained strong institutionalization without democratization (Chen 2007).

Bureaucratic Authoritarianism: "development does not lead to democracy"

The third theoretical explanation of the causality between development and democracy is called the Bureaucratic Authoritarianism (BA) thesis, whose main argument is that "development does not lead to democracy." The BA thesis, which was originally developed by Guillermo O'Donnell (1973), runs counter to the modernization thesis that "economic development leads to democracy." Bruce Bueno de Mesquita and George Downs argue that over the past 50 years a

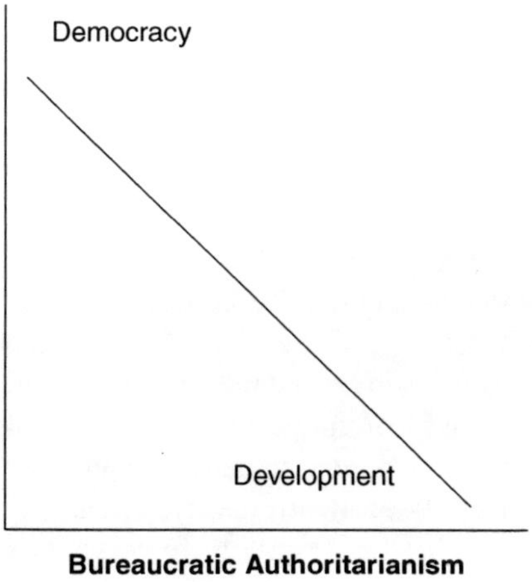

Figure 4.3 Bureaucratic Authoritarianism (source: Chen 2007).

number of authoritarian regimes have experienced dramatic economic development without corresponding political liberalization; in contrast, political elites' power and positions in these countries are more strengthened and more consolidated through the benefits of economic development. Empirically, the cases of China and Russia show that not only can authoritarian regimes generate extensive economic growth, but they also work out "strategies" to avoid political liberalization by distributing portions of the fruits of economic growth to the popular masses (Mesquita and Downs 2005: 77).

In addition, Cardoso's "dependent development thesis" also argues, based on the Latin American experiences especially of Brazil and Argentina under military rule, that economic development does not bring democracy but installs a more repressive but highly technocratic, thus very developmental, dictatorship. There are many theorists of the necessity of authoritarianism for economic development. They claimed an "elective affinity" between authoritarianism and economic development (the core of the authoritarian development thesis) by arguing that rapid industrialization necessitates the discipline and autonomy that only authoritarianism can provide (Sharma 2007: 38). Atul Kohli argued that without effective state capacity, political and economic elites cannot pursue coherent industrialization policies. Kohli cited the regimes of Korea's Park Chung Hee and Taiwan's Chiang Kai-shek as having a relatively high degree of insulation from dominant but parochial interests in society and with its embedded autonomy succeeded in establishing a paternalistic collaboration with powerful chaebols to successfully lead the market-shaping (and market-conforming under Chun Doo Hwan) authoritarian development. According to Kohli, the Park Chung Hee regime was a typical "cohesive-capitalist state" (Kohli 2006; Evans 1995).

Proponents of the authoritarian capitalism thesis draw the main logic for the necessity of authoritarian development from the deficiencies of new emerging democracies after transition in generating economic development. A labor economist, Walter Galenson, and a political economist, Karl de Schweinitz, both argued in 1959 that democracy after democratic transition unleashes pressures for immediate consumption, which occurs at the cost of investment, hence of growth (Schweinitz 1964; Galenson 1959; Przeworski *et al.* 2000: 142). Galenson suggested that "the more democratic a government is,... the greater the diversion of resources from investment to consumption." According to Huntington, "the interest of the voters generally leads parties to give the expansion of personal consumption a higher priority vis-à-vis investment than it would receive in a non-democratic system" (Huntington and Dominguez 1975: 60; Huntington 1968). From this observation, proponents of authoritarian development draw the conclusion that democracy is thus inimical to economic development. In contrast, they argue that authoritarian dictators are better able to force savings and launch economic growth. According to Rao, "economic development is a process for which huge investments in personnel and material are required.... Government must resort to strong measures and they enforce them with iron hand in order to marshal the surpluses needed for investment" (Rao 1984: 75).

Democratic Development Theory: "democracy first, development later"

However, it is not difficult to find arguments in favor of democracy. Democracy better allocates the available resources to productive uses. The theory of the predatory state argues that since authoritarian dictators are not accountable to electorates, they have no incentive to maximize the total output but only their own rents (i.e., predation). Dictatorships are the sources of inefficiency (Barro 1990: 103–125; Findlay 1990: 193–221; Olson 1991; Przeworski 1990).

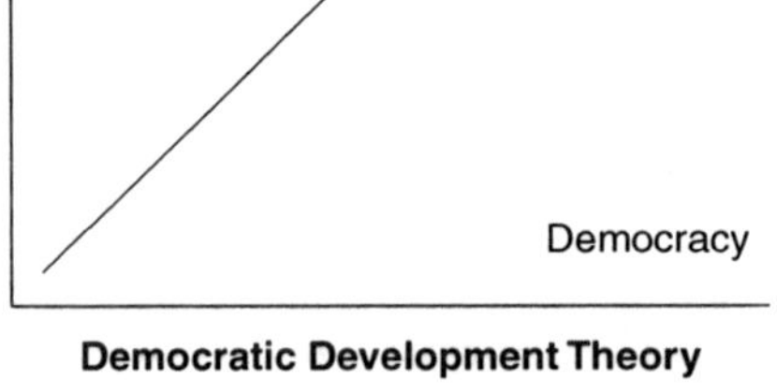

Figure 4.4 Democratic Development Theory.

Dictatorships undersupply or oversupply government activities (Przeworski 1990). Institutionalists note that democracies better protect property rights, thus allowing a longer-term perspective for investors (North 1990: 109; Olson 1991: 153). Democracies permit a free flow of information to improve the quality of economic decisions (Przeworski *et al.* 2000: 144). Recently Rodrik (2000: 22) refuted the BA thesis by saying that "recent empirical studies based on samples of more than 100 countries suggest that there is little reason to believe democracy is conducive to lower growth over long period of time."

The thesis that democracy brings economic development is based on empirical observation that democracies exceed non-democracies in terms of economic growth, standard of living, and the quality of social life (Kolhi 1986; Olson 1993: 567–576). Therefore, "democracy first" theorists recommend that developing countries first promote democracy before they accelerate economic development (Siegel *et al.* 2004: 57–71). This theory argues that democracy and economic development is not the target of "cruel" binomial choice,[7] but they instead argue that democracy and development can co-exist, co-develop, and co-evolve without serious tensions and conflicts (Maravall 1994: 17–31). According to "democracy first" theorists, democracy can efficiently allocate resources, simultaneously pursue economic growth and welfare, and elicit compromise among social groups without hampering political order and social stability.

They argue that democracy should be the precondition for development and promoting democracy is strategically the best way to reach prosperity, development, security, and peace (Siegel *et al.* 2004: 57–71). In fact, the democracy first thesis originates from the institutionalist perspective on economic growth. Democracy first theorists not only argue that "institution matters," but they also further assert that "democracy matters." Joseph Siegle and colleagues, in their paper "Why Democracies Excel," argue that not only do institutions influence states' economic and societal performances, but also, from the perspective of regime type, democracies indeed outperform non-democracies in economic development. Due to regular elections, democratic regimes need to respond to the demands of their citizens and societal groups; the institutional arrangement of elections is the key for democracies' better economic performance. In addition, due to a number of characteristic features of democracy, such as accountability, checks and balances, low corruption, openness, competition, the free flow of information, transparency, and adaptability, democracies usually outperform non-democracies in most indicators of economic and social well-being (Siegel *et al.* 2004: 57–71). Thus, the best strategy to assist developing countries to develop is by promoting democracy, not by promoting economic growth.

According to the "democracy first" thesis, democratic governments are the only governments with some legitimacy. Democratic governments acquire a minimal level of legitimacy from the fact that they are elected by sovereign people and thus represent the will of the majority of the people. With legitimacy or the voluntary compliance from the people, only democratic governments can implement and sustain long-term policies of economic development that may bear high short-term costs.

Democracy has other institutional advantages with regard to making and accelerating economic growth. As Douglass C. North (1990) has argued, democracy has institutional characteristics such as an independent legal system and well-specified and enforced property rights, and these institutional characteristics are the necessary condition for economic growth and for securing political and civil rights; otherwise, arbitrary confiscation is always a threat to political freedom, and thus will hamper sustainable economic growth. Rodrick (2000: 3–31) has argued for democratic advantage in terms of democracy's capacity to limit rent-seeking, the source of economic inefficiency and political corruption, with its system of checks and balances and, in O'Donnell's words, horizontal and vertical accountability (O'Donnell 1994: 55–69). Nobel Laureate Amartya Sen argues that democracies enrich individual lives through the granting of political and civil rights and do a better job in improving the welfare of the poor (Sen 2001; Mesquita *et al.* 2003; Daron and Robinson 2005).

Finally, democracy has the advantage in its high responsiveness to citizens' needs. As Dahl notes, democracies are highly responsive to demands and pressures from the citizenry because the right to rule is derived from the sovereign people (Dahl 1971; Lake and Baum 2001: 587–621).

Exogenous modernization: "democracy does not matter in development"

The last theoretical explanation of the causality between democracy and development is "democracy does not matter in development." Even though politics indeed influences the economy, the impact of regime types, democratic or non-democratic, on states' economic performance is still controversial. After reviewing the arguments that relate regimes to economic growth, focusing on property

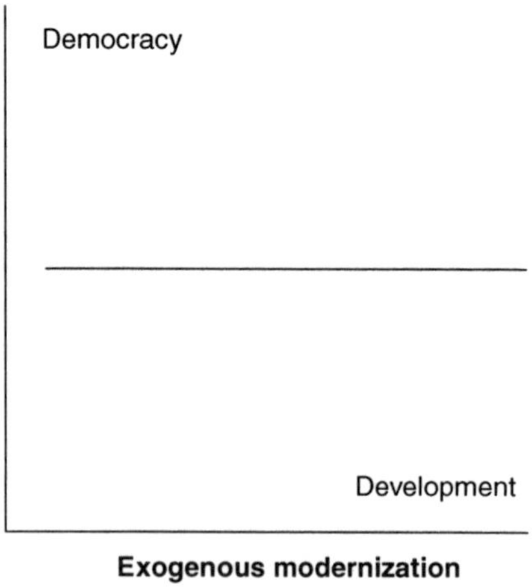

Figure 4.5 Exogenous modernization.

rights, pressures for immediate consumption, and autonomy of dictators, Przeworski and Limongi (1993) summarize that, first, although everyone agrees that the protection of property rights could foster economic growth, there could be a debate on whether democracies or dictatorships better secure citizens' property rights. Second, the primary reason why democracy is considered to hinder economic development is the pressure for immediate consumption under its institution, which leads to reducing investment. Compared with democracies, only dictatorships can resist the pressure for immediate consumption with their repressive institutions and promoting economic development. Third, the primary argument supporting democracy and opposing dictatorship is that the political elites in authoritarian regimes are not interested in maximizing national production and fostering economic growth; in contrast, they try to build up a predatory state to keep their power and positions within the governments and to seek opportunities to prey on the resources of society (Chen 2007). However, democratic regimes would not do that, but instead act to create public wealth and general interest (Przeworski and Limongi 1993: 51). Przeworski and Limongi conclude that politics indeed affects the economy, but people do not know whether democracy fosters or hinders economic growth. The result of the relationship between regime type and economic growth is still inconclusive (Przeworski and Limongi 1993: 51; Seligson 2003; Chen 2007).

In *Democracy and Development* (2000), Przeworski, Alvarez, Cheibub, and Limongi (PACL) investigated the causality between development and democracy, and democracy and development in 135 countries from 1950 to 1990. They found that the factor of regime type has no significant influence on states' economic growth and national income; but in general political instability lowered the level of states' economic development (particularly in autocracies), which implies that in the process of democratization, development declines in the early stage but increases in the later stage (Przeworski *et al.* 1997). The "democracy does not matter in development" thesis that reflects whether development generates democracy or democracy creates development is still controversial.[8]

Democratic interlude and the collapse of the 2nd Republic (1960–1961)

Student revolution opened Korea of the 1960s. However, the 2nd Republic was short-lived, lasting only nine months. Many argued that the emergence of the praetorian society was the main cause of the collapse of the 2nd Republic. After the April 19 Student Revolution, the masses took to the streets but the level of political institutionalization was too low to accommodate their demands in a democratic political process.

The praetorian thesis emphasizes the endogenous character in the downfall of democracy under the 2nd Republic. But the fact of the matter is that the 2nd Republic did not collapse but was overthrown in a military coup led by General Park Chung Hee. "Push factors" originating from the promotion bottlenecks in military officers' groups overwhelmed the "pull factors" that invited military officers to launch a coup from societal forces. On the eve of the coup in May 16, 1961, the economy started to resume growth, the United States promised more economic aid and the economic development plan led by U.S. advisers was under way. More importantly, the praetorian society phenomenon was decreasing in numbers and magnitude. The numbers and the intensity of the street demonstrations had been decreasing since May 1, 1961. The middle class did not invite the military to intervene to protect their property. The main cause of the military coup was internal organizational problems within the military, i.e., bottleneck in promotions and discontent and complaints among alienated military officers including General Park.

Authoritarian development under Park Chung Hee

Myth or reality?

Modernization Theory, the Bureaucratic Authoritarianism thesis, and the Praetorianism thesis all agree that Park Chung Hee's authoritarianism was historically necessary at "the national time" of Korea in the 1960s and 1970s. All three perspectives agree that the authoritarian developmental state was necessary at the initial stage of industrialization on three grounds.

First, it is needed at the initial stage of authoritarian developmental states to squash the reactionary classes (landed elites, according to Barrington Moore Jr.) who oppose and resist modernization and development. Second, it is necessary to have an authoritarian developmental state to repress workers (or popular sectors) that resist the government's policy of constraining consumption for the forced accumulation at the initial stage of industrialization. Third, a developmental authoritarian state is needed to gain autonomy from the external pressures of the world capitalist system.

Nonetheless, in South Korea the necessity of authoritarianism for development in the early stage of industrialization disappeared even before the rise of Park Chung Hee's developmental state. First, the potential reactionary class, the landed elites that resist urban-based industrialization, was "eliminated" as a class by the Korean War and land reform in the 1950s. The resistance of workers (and popular sectors) was resolved not by state repression but by the labor market in the 1960s in which an abundant labor pool in the countryside played the role of "industrial reserve army" to maintain the wage rate at subsistence level without intervention from the state (Im 1987: 231–257). Third, unlike in Latin America, American hegemony toward Korea was "benevolent." The United States provided substantial material benefits to Korea and gave the Korean government autonomous space to choose its own developmental strategy. One of the reasons why Park could choose the developmental state model, which was strongly contrasted with American liberal market model, was due to the relative autonomy of the Korean state with regard to choosing a development model, which in turn emanated from its special position in East Asian geopolitics as a key anti-communist buffer state for the United States.

The argument that the authoritarian developmental state was necessary in the initial stage of industrialization of the 1960s not only cannot stand on firm ground but also cannot be proved empirically. As mentioned above, the facade of liberal democracy was maintained in the Third Republic of the 1960s. It could be counterfactual evidence that every democratic state is not a weak state, but can be a strong and autonomous state that has the autonomy and capacity to formulate and implement economic development policies. If we look into cases that were comparable to Park's developmental authoritarianism, we can find many cases of developmental states that are democratic. Developmental states in Finland, Austria, and Japan successfully implemented statist development under democracy. Park did not establish a dictatorship for pursuing industrialization, but tried to industrialize Korea in order to launch an authoritarian regime.

In addition, the thesis of the historical necessity of developmental dictatorship for industrialization has not been upheld empirically. High economic growth in the 1960s and 1970s was achieved not "because of" developmental dictatorship, but "despite" dictatorship (Sohn 1995). My position is that authoritarian industrialization and liberal industrialization is the matter of choice, not the matter of historical necessity. As Przeworski *et al.* (2000) argue, economic growth can occur under democracy as well as under authoritarianism.

Exogenous growth under Park Chung Hee's authoritarianism

Admirers of Park Chung Hee cite endogenous factors as the key to explain the rapid economic growth in the 1960s and 1970s. They have claimed that the "Korean miracle" was made possible by the optimal strategic choices of Park. Park, at first, chose an import substitution industrialization (ISI) strategy in which rural development and the development of the capital goods industry and ISI industries were emphasized while exports played a secondary role. However, because in the first two years (1962–1963) results in priority areas fell far short of the planned target, but exports increased far above expectations, Park changed the development strategy from ISI to EOI (export-oriented strategy) (Im 1987: 241–242). Park Chung Hee responded to the signal from the internal market that showed the ongoing transition from the classical international division of labor (agricultural and mining exports from colonial economies and manufactured exports from advanced capitalist countries) to the new international division of labor (the feasibility of world market-oriented manufacturing in peripheral countries) (Im 1987: 242; Fröbel *et al.* 1980). Park's Korean miracle was a success story of what Wallerstein called "promotion by invitation." Park promoted the Korean economy from periphery to semi-periphery by responding to the invitation from the capitalist world economy (Wallerstein 1979).

Proponents of authoritarian capitalism have praised the effectiveness, efficiency, and shrewd leadership in the success stories of Park Chung Hee's development strategy. Alice Amsden argues that Park overcame the penalty of "lateness" by state "subsidies" and "getting the relative price deliberately wrong" (Amsden 1990: 5–31). Weiss and Hobson point out the proper strategy of providing "subsidies" by which the subsidies were not provided in the form of giveaway but in exchange for good performances in terms of output, exports, production quality, and investment in training and R&D (Weiss and Hobson 1995). They also emphasize that Park invented big bourgeoisie (chaebol) and nurtured them as "national champions" and "empire builders" that prioritized the long-term interests of expanding market share over the short-term interests of maximizing profits. Seldon and Belton-Jones argue that Park and East Asian states tried to be competitive by changing ahead of the game rather than simply reacting to changes to become sharper in international commerce by combining flexibility, foresight, strategic intervention, and selective planning (Seldon and Belton-Jones 1995: 330). Ha Joon Chang points out that Park pursued the strategy of "flexible rigidities," by which the state created short-run rigidities in order to achieve greater long-term flexibility (Chang 1995: 213).

However, it has turned out that the Korean miracle in the 1960s and 1970s was not made exclusively by optimal economic development strategies and policies that Park chose. There are many exogenous factors that contributed directly and indirectly to rapid economic growth in one of the world's poorest countries. Exogenous factors such as historical legacies, geopolitics, culture, and transmission of ideas were not negligible in determining miraculous economic performance in the Park period.

First, successful industrialization in Korea had been due to the benevolent international environment. The post-World War II Korean state was created by the United States as a crucial anti-communist buffer state. Until the 1970s the main U.S. concern in Korea was political and strategic, not economic. American hegemony toward Korea was benevolent rather than exploitative. As the patron state, it provided financial, economic, technical, and infrastructural aid and assistance to the client states. Among them, land reform imposed by the United States has had a long-lasting impact on urban-based capitalist industrialization. Successful land reform pre-empted the strong bastion of anti-capitalist interests, i.e., the landlord class, and created myriad egalitarian small landholders in the countryside, who had been the political support base for authoritarian regimes and the chief source of labor supply in the early labor-intensive industrialization. In the initial stage of export-oriented industrialization, the United States supported Korean efforts by providing low-interest public loans and by lowering the entry barrier on Korean goods to the U.S. market.

Second, the cultural elements of Confucianism played a crucial role in the rapid economic growth. The Confucian emphasis on education, meritocratic forms of personal advancement, hard work, thrift, goal attainment, filial respect, and respect for one's elders and superiors made it easy for people in Korea to smoothly adjust to market economies. These elements have been transmuted into deference toward managerial authority, high rates of personal and corporate savings, and a commitment to the firm as a collectivity (Appelbaum and Henderson 1992: 16). However, just a few decades ago Confucianism was cited as the main factor for East Asian backwardness: "Confucianism meant deference to authority, resistance to change, respect for the ways of the past, aversion to risk, and other values that inhibit the responsiveness to the market" (Gourevitch 1989: 12). Therefore, the impact of Confucian heritage on East Asian industrialization is a researchable question.[9]

Third, many point out the benevolent effects of the Japanese colonial legacy on postwar industrialization in Korea and Taiwan (Aseniero 1994: 275–336; Cumings 1984; Eckert 1991; McNamara 1990). Eckert argues that many institutions, norms, ideology, and practices of the Korean economic development model, such as state–business relations and oppression of labor, had their origins and foundations in the colonial experiences. For Eckert, the Korean developmental state was the offspring of the Japanese colonial empire (Eckert 1991).[10]

The legacy of Japanese colonialism on postwar Korean economic development should not be overstated. Indeed, Japanese strategic concern predominated over economic concern. It was not bankers and merchants but samurais who made schemes for colonial industrialization projects: the extension of the security front line to the Chinese continent. As a consequence, development in Korea was distorted. Infrastructure was overdeveloped, yet overdeveloped infrastructure had little relationship to the needs of Korean society. Japanese did not nurture the native industrial bourgeoisie. Colonial capitalism was "capitalism without capitalist class." After Liberation in 1945, South Korea was robbed of industrial facilities that had been skewed toward North Korea. The Korean War destroyed most of the infrastructure. Korea had to start from the ashes. The only long-lasting legacy of Japanese colonialism is the idea of authoritarian militaristic development education in a Japanese military academy.

Therefore it is a myth to argue that the Korean miracle was mainly attributed to Park's optimal choice for development strategy and policies. Both endogenous and exogenous factors contributed to the miraculous economic growth in the Park Chung Hee period. To evaluate more properly authoritarian development under Park Chung Hee, we need to debunk the myth that miraculous economic growth in the 1960s and 1970s was mainly attributable to Park's shrewd, wise, and optimal choice of development strategies and instead pay more attention to exogenous factors contributing to economic growth during the period.

Democracy and development since democratic transition in 1987

After the democratic transition in summer 1987, many conservatives demanded "calling the ghost of Park from the grave" to revive high economic growth as disenchantment with the poor performances of democratically elected governments rose and pervaded widely among the masses. Korean ultra-conservatives even argued for the restoration of authoritarianism. They insisted that unbridled behavior in the name of freedom should be disciplined; North Korea, threatening the freedom of South Korean people, should be eliminated; political freedom can be reserved for economic development. They argued that elective affinity between the developmental state and authoritarianism works even after Korea was industrialized. The Park Chung Hee style of developmental dictatorship has been necessary up until now and its feasibility and effectiveness has lasted to the present time (Kim 1995: 208–256).

The strong nostalgia for Park Chung Hee shows that proponents of authoritarian capitalism still remains strong and this could work against the consolidation of democracy in industrialized Korea. Nevertheless, we have abundant evidences that democracy goes well with economic development in the post-democratic transition period and democracy proved better in overcoming economic crisis than authoritarianism.

The record of democratic governments' economic management

The Roh Tae Woo government

Immediately after the democratic breakthrough on June 29, 1987, the worries and warnings of authoritarian developmentalists seemed to be realized. More than 3,000 strikes erupted in the aftermath of June 29. Striking workers demanded higher wages, better working conditions, and right to organize unions. Authoritarian capitalists argued that democracy provided workers the right to demand more consumption, and vote-maximizing democratic politicians tried to satisfy workers' (or low-income masses') demands. As the democratic government tried to transfer to workers by reallocating resources from long-term investment in consumption and welfare, the outcome would be lower profit, less investment, and economic stagnation (Galenson 1959; Schweinitz 1964; Przeworski *et al.* 2000).

However, the dismal prediction of authoritarian capitalists proved to be wrong in the case of Korea. Despite the outbursts of workers in the street, the Korean economy had been doing well. Economic growth in the Roh Tae Woo period was very high compared to advanced industrial countries as well as high-growth East Asian economies. Every new democracy has to pay the costs of transition from authoritarianism to democracy. What new democracies have to do is to minimize transition costs and to remove the danger of authoritarian regression. In that sense President Roh Tae Woo did a good job in managing the transition period. Under the Roh Tae Woo presidency, democracy was not subverted, the economy continued to grow, and the middle class did not invite praetorian dictators.

The Kim Young Sam presidency

Under the Kim Young Sam presidency, Koreans became richer than at any time in history with per capita income of more than $10,000 in 1995 (in 1995, per capita income surpassed $10,000, according to World Databank) and Korea became a member country of the OECD, the club of affluent democratic countries. In Asia, other than Korea, only Japan is a member country of the OECD.

With regard to democracy and development, the distinguishing achievement of the Kim Young Sam presidency was enhancing transparency in politics as well as the economy. President Kim Young Sam, immediately after inauguration, embarked on purging corrupt politicized military officers, politicians, and bureaucrats, and then made institutional reforms for enhancing transparency such as the public disclosure of property of high-ranking officials, a real-name financial transaction system, and the enactment of an ethics law for high-ranking officials. The enhancement of transparency was the key to upgrade the Korean economy to the level of advanced industrial countries. And the transparency reforms worked in favor of Korea becoming a new OECD member.

The Kim Dae Jung presidency: parallel development of democracy and the market economy

The performance of democratic government was shining in the time of crisis. In late 1997 financial crisis erupted, and at the same time there was the first peaceful transfer of power of government in Korea. The peaceful transfer of power to a long-standing opposition leader and democratic activist, Kim Dae Jung, was the first such peaceful democratic transfer in East Asia. But Kim Dae Jung was handed the job of overcoming the unprecedented economic crisis. The crisis in late 1997 took the Korean economy to the brink of state financial default at the end of the year. Korea escaped the crisis by the infusion of emergency stand-by loans from the International Monetary Fund (IMF). The IMF provided Korea an unprecedented $55 billion in exchange for neoliberal structural reform along the lines of the Washington Consensus. The IMF actually demanded Korea discard Park's developmental state model and instead adopt the Anglo-Saxon neoliberal economic model. Kim Dae Jung's solution was "the parallel development of democracy and market economy"; he publicly questioned the efficacy of authoritarian developmental state model. As a result, Park's developmental authoritarianism was downgraded from "historical necessity" to a "historical obstacle" hindering the parallel development of democracy and a market economy (Study Group on Korean Politics 1998; Cho 1997: 46–76).

The election of 1997 and the peaceful transfer of power show the improved accountability of Korean democracy and deepening democratic consolidation. The election demonstrated Korean people's determination to live under democracy regardless of severe external fluctuations like the financial crisis. And the defeat of the ruling party candidate in the election shows that the electoral mechanism of accountability was working since the people blamed the ruling party for generating such profound national economic crisis. Democracy helped Korea to make a comprehensive reform without arousing serious political instability by the institutionalized electoral mechanism for legitimate power change (Haggard 2000; Kim 2001).

The Kim Dae Jung government launched four key structural reforms in the areas of chaebols, financial institutions, the public sector, and labor. In instituting a more flexible labor market, the Kim Dae Jung government, for the first time in Korean history, relied on tripartite compromise, coordination, and agreement among labor, capital, and the state. With the new tripartism, the government persuaded unions to accept the flexible labor market in return for more political and social rights for the workers and made a grand compromise in the "February 6 Social Pact." The tripartite agreement helped Kim Dae Jung to persuade fleeing Wall Street capital to reinvest in Korea and thus to overcome the financial crisis. After overcoming the financial crisis the government founded the IT industry as the future source of growth. The Kim Dae Jung government built up country-wide high-speed Internet infrastructure and nurtured high-tech venture firms and constructed a welfare state for the first time in Korean history, called the "productive welfare system," to compensate market losers and to provide them social safety nets. Under democratic governments, high economic growth continued without victimizing equitable distribution.

The Roh Moo Hyun presidency: neo-nomadic democracy and the digital economy

As the Three Kims (Kim Young Sam, Kim Dae Jung, Kim Jong Pil) Era came to an end, new political phenomena have risen in Korea. The election of Roh Moo Hyun signals an end to the politics of the Three Kims generation. Post-modern and post-materialist political issues such as generational shift, gender equality, environmental protection, peace, and civil society came to the fore of the political agenda. These changes did not occur spontaneously after the exit of the Three Kims who had dominated the Korean political scene. Profound social change acted as the motivating force that pushed the emergence of a new politics. That social change is the rise of what I call "neo-nomadic society" in Korea. South Korea is one of the countries where the IT revolution has been advancing very fast. The number of mobile phone and Internet users and the total amount of Internet use is the highest in East Asia except in city states like Singapore and Hong Kong. More than 30 million Koreans became "netizens" who have everyday access to the Internet. The number of mobile phones exceeds the number of population. South Korea is the only country that has completed country-wide information superhighway infrastructure. The per capita VDSL user is the highest in the world, surpassing the United States. As far as the IT revolution is concerned, South Korea is no longer a country "catching up" with advanced countries, but the frontrunner that leads the revolution.

The nomadic temperament of Koreans has re-emerged with the advent of the digital revolution and globalization. The digital gale in "Teheran Valley,"[11] spectacular growth of mobile phone and Internet users, and phenomenal increase in digital access have been transforming Korean people into virtual nomads. The inflow of foreign workers, flexible labor markets, free trade agreements, and the opening up of the agricultural market by the World Trade Organization has compelled Korean workers and farmers to travel to find jobs for survival and thus become lower-nomads. Affluent people become hyper-nomads who travel all over the world to preoccupy the profitable resources. Thomas Friedman of the *New York Times* points out that Koreans are one of the "cybertribes" of a neo-nomadic world. Equipped with the Internet and connecting with a diaspora community (seven million overseas Koreans) spread out all over the world, the Korean cybertribe can combine speed, creativity, entrepreneurial talent, and global networking, and generate enormous wealth (Friedman 2000).

The rise of neo-nomadic society has been transforming Korean politics toward becoming organizationally smaller, faster, networking-friendly, more open, and tolerant. Neo-nomadic democracy slims down the size of political organization and thus realizes high-efficiency, low-cost politics. Heavy physical materials inconvenience ceaselessly traveling neo-nomads. Neo-nomadic democracy would likely transform Korean politics into a more open, flexible, participatory, and inclusive one (Im 2009).

Neo-nomadic democracy thrives on the neo-nomadic economy. Netizen society power and Internet politics could not have been possible without the development of neo-nomadic industry. And Korea is the frontrunner in the IT industry in terms of IT hardware, software, and systems. And the IT industry became the major source of new economic growth, surpassing heavy and chemical industries and traditional labor-intensive industries. Neo-nomadic democracy goes hand in hand with the neo-nomadic economy and creates a new parallel development of democracy and the market economy in the twenty-first century. Democracy and the market economy found a new source of partnership in the neo-nomadic IT industry.

Performances of democratic governments in comparative perspective: managing sustainable economic growth

After reviewing the performances of authoritarian governments and democratic governments, I came to the conclusion that the performances of authoritarian governments have been overstated while the performances of democratic governments have been underrated. There have been many myths in the thesis of poor performances of democratic governments and public disenchantment with democratic governments. Also, the "miraculous" achievement of authoritarian government has to be demystified because the miraculous achievement was not only attributed to the wise and proper strategic choice of development by dictators (à la Machiavelli, *virtu*) but was also indebted to a large degree of exogenous luck that the dictators were handed from the past, outside forces, and cultural legacies (à la Machiavelli, *fortuna*). Therefore, I can say that the theses of Modernization Theory, Praetorianism, Bureaucratic Authoritarianism, Democratic Developmentalism, and Agnosticism contain only partial truth in explaining the relations between democracy and economic development. Viewed from the present time, I dare to say that Agnosticism will be weakened while Democratic Developmentalism will gain more strength and power to explain the relations between democracy and development.

Table 4.1 IT Index in Roh Moo Hyun Presidency (2007)

Index	*Research organization*	*Ranking*
DOI (Digital Opportunity Index)	World Summit on the Information Society (WSIS)	1/181
Competitiveness of Technology	World Economic Forum (WEF)	7/131
E-Business Index	Economist Intelligence Unit (EIU)	16/69
Competitiveness of IT Industry	Economist Intelligence Unit (EIU)	3/64
E-Government Index	United Nations (UN)	5/191 (2005)
Online Participant Index	United Nations (UN)	2/192 (2008)
National Information Index	National Information Society Agency (Korea)	3/50
Competitiveness of Technology Infrastructure	International Institute for Management Development (IMD)	6/55

Source: National Information Society Agency.

Authoritarian capitalism thesis denied in the development since democratic transition

The economic performances of the democratic governments after the democratic transition in 1987 were strong, robust, and sustainable. Authoritarian capitalists predicted that immediately after the democratic transition workers would protest to demand higher wages to consume; capitalists and governments respond to workers' demands positively because now workers have the organization to solve collective action problems and vote to decide the locus of power. Thus, the firms increased wages and the government transferred income from the rich to the poor through taxes. The outcome, according to authoritarian capitalists, would be economic stagnation as wage increases reduce the profit rate, then firms cut investment and at the same time the government tends to distribute income away from investment by tax, transfer, and less public investment. Hence lowering investment slows down growth (Przeworski *et al.* 2000: 143).

However, in South Korea after the democratic transition in 1987, none of the post-transition syndromes occurred. Of course, workers protested. After the democratic breakthrough in the June 29 Compromise, more than 3,000 strikes erupted between July and August only throughout all industrial workplaces. As authoritarian capitalists predicted, workers demanded higher wages, better working conditions, and rights to organize and collective action. Nonetheless, despite the massive workers' eruption and the sharp rise in wages,[12] firms did not reduce investment: the domestic investment rate in 1987 was 30.8 percent, which was very high compared with that in advanced industrial countries, to say nothing of Latin American new democracies (Figure 4.6); gross fixed capital formation as a percentage of GDP also remained very high at the level of 29 percent compared with 22 percent in advanced industrial countries and 20 percent in Latin American countries (Figure 4.7). As shown in Figure 4.8, the GDP growth rate in 1987 was very high, 11 percent higher than the average GDP growth rate of the whole Park Chung Hee period. Korean capitalists did not reduce investment because of the steep rise in wages because the economy was strong and robust enough to make more profit even with paying higher wages to workers.

The excellence in economic development under democratic governments is not confined to the democratic transition period but extend to the whole democratic consolidation period. Except 1999 when the GDP growth rate dropped to –7 percent from the previous year's 5 percent, the average GDP growth rate in the whole period of democracy after transition (1987–2007) is about 6.28 percent, which is not lower than average GDP growth rate in the whole authoritarian period (1961–1986) (Figure 4.8).

Second, gross fixed capital formation (as a percentage of GDP) during the democratic period has been much higher than the authoritarian "Miracle" period (Figure 4.7). Between 1961 and 1986, average GFCF was 24.54 percent, while that in the democratic period is about twice the GFCF in the authoritarian period.

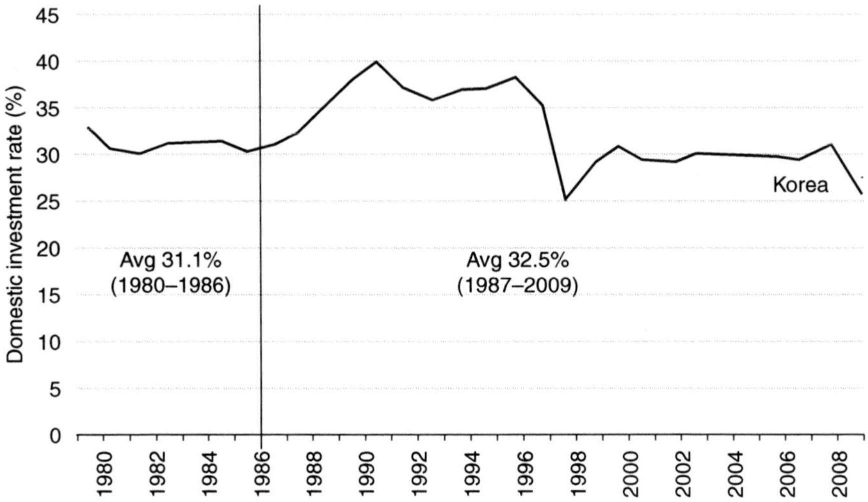

Figure 4.6 Domestic investment rate (source: Korean Statistical Information Service (http://kosis.kr)).

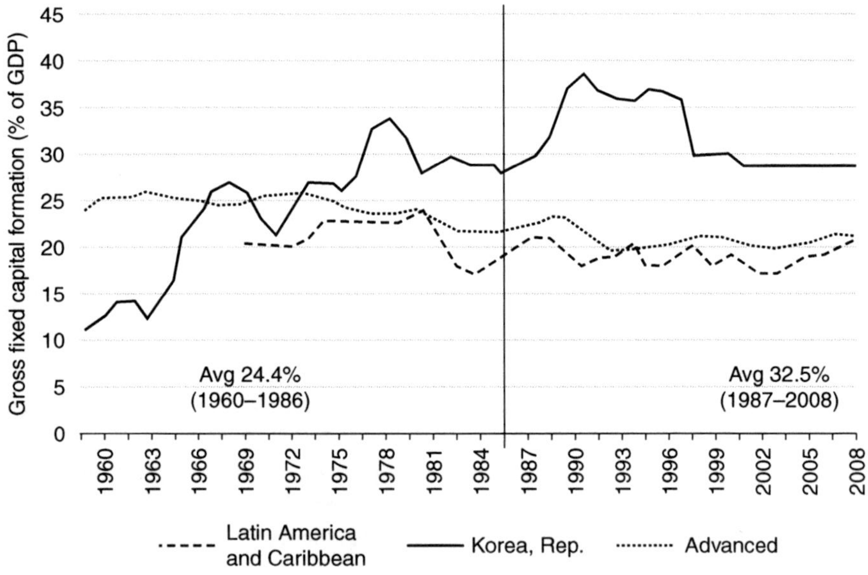

Figure 4.7 Gross fixed capital formation (source: World Databank (http://databank.worldbank.org)).

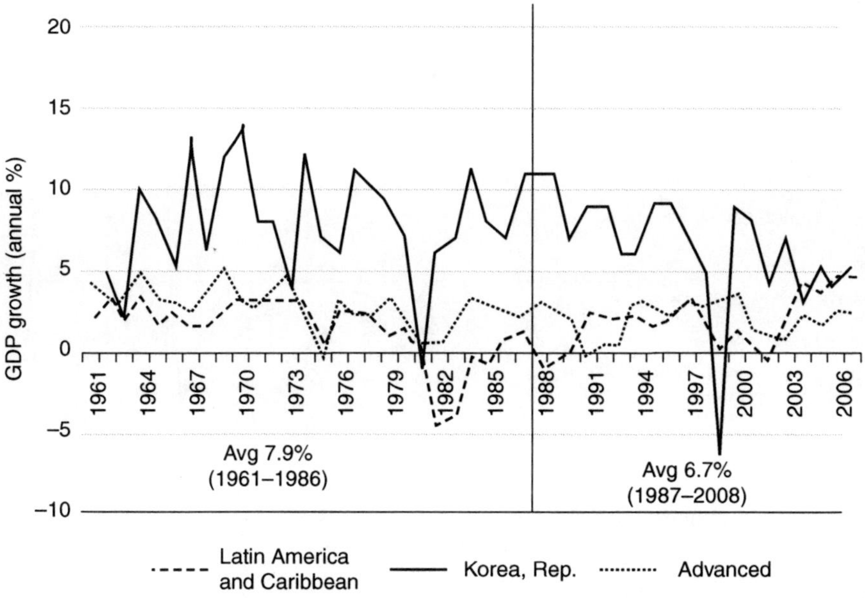

Figure 4.8 GDP growth (source: World Databank (http://databank.worldbank.org)).

Third, democratic governments achieved spectacular economic growth without paying expenses such as high inflation, trade deficit, high unemployment, low wages, and inadequatee provision of social welfare. While during the authoritarian period, the Korean economy suffered the perennial problem of high inflation and a trade deficit, democratic governments in Korea solved the trilemma of high growth, high inflation, and trade deficit. The trade balance in South Korea turned from perennial trade deficit to trade surplus since 1998, except just one year, 2008, the year global financial crisis erupted (Figure 4.9). Since the democratic transition in 1987, the Korean economy emerged from the trilemma of high growth, high inflation, and trade deficit and stabilized a pattern of "high growth with low inflation, trade surplus, good wages, and low unemployment" (Figures 4.10 and 4.11). Korean firms had room for investment even with paying higher wages and taxes without reducing employment.

From this observation, we can conclude that as far as the Korean case is concerned, the need for authoritarianism because of the incompetence of democratic government is not borne out in any aspect of the economy (growth rate, employment, trade balance, investment, gross fixed capital formation). The Korean case shows that democratic governments excel in achieving economic development as well as creating an equitable society with good wages, provision of better social welfare, and, most of all, very low unemployment compared to that in advanced countries.

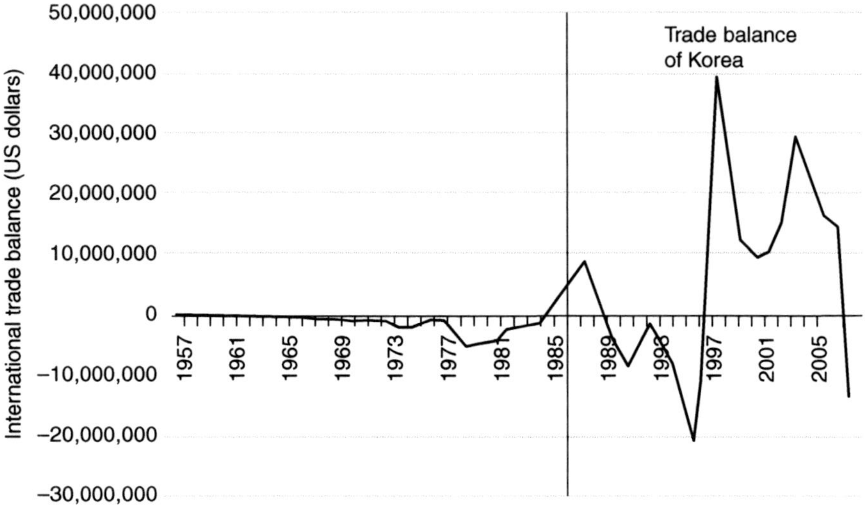

Figure 4.9 International trade balance (source: The Bank of Korea (www.bok or kr)).

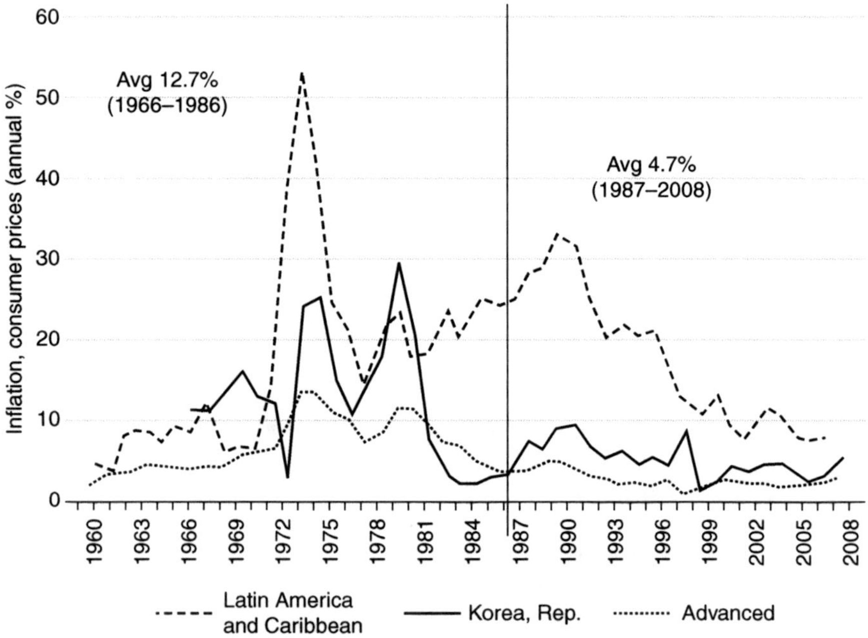

Figure 4.10 Inflation, consumer prices (source: World Databank (http://databank.worldbank.org)).

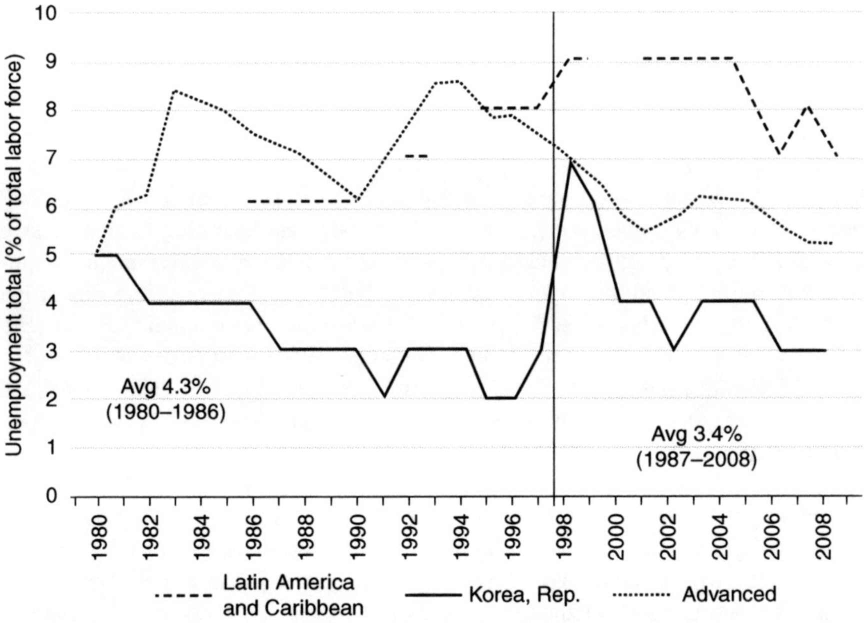

Figure 4.11 Unemployment total (source: World Databank (http://databank.worldbank.org)).

Exogenous factors of growth under democratic governments

Many authoritarian capitalists argue that the spectacular growth under democratic governments has not been achieved by the timely optimal choice of developmental strategy and policies by democratic governments, but by exogenously given good luck such as the timely collapse of socialist countries in Eastern Europe and the Soviet Union, and the end of the Cold War, the emergence of a favorable international economic environment such as the "three lows" economic boom between 1986 and 1988 (low interest rate, low won–dollar rate, and low oil price), the expansion of export markets for Korean goods and services due to economic openness and globalization, and IMF conditionalities imposed by the IMF to carry out economic structural reforms in return for massive IMF loans to Korea at the time of the East Asian financial crisis.

We do not deny that these external or exogenous factors contributed a great deal for sustainable growth under democratic governments. The *fortuna* of the "three lows" from the outside gave ample opportunity to catch "three rabbits" (growth, current account balance, and stabilizing consumer price) with one stone. With the help of these "three lows," exports increased phenomenally; firms invested more in domestic markets as well as global markets; prices stabilized and as a result economy grew at a more than double digit rate. Unfortunately the *fortuna* of the "three lows" was essentially a free gift of global capitalism and was not within the realm of control by Korean governments. The three lows lasted only three years and replaced by "three highs" (high interest rate, high won–dollar rate, and high oil price).

The second exogenous factor contributing to sustainable growth in Korea came from Eastern Europe. The end of the Cold War and the collapse of socialist countries in Eastern Europe relaxed security tensions in East Asia and the Korean Peninsula. The democratic transition in South Korea came at a favorable "world historical time," i.e., the end of the Cold War (Im 2006). The end of the Cold War permitted the new democratic government to cut defense spending to help finance expensive welfare programs and to distribute tax funds for more investment in constructing infrastructure rather than spending for defense. However, the end of the Cold War has not always been favorable to Korean democracy and development. As the Cold War receded in East Asia, the strategic value of South Korea to the United States declined and U.S. hegemony to Korea became less "benevolent." As the Cold War receded, "Washington's major East Asian allies would go from being linchpins of U.S. security in the region to being mere levers to open markets in the region" (De Castro 2000: 201–221). The United States did not give South Korea special treatment in assisting it to overcome financial crisis. Korea, without exception, was subjected to IMF conditionlities, that is, sweeping neoliberal economic restructuring whose rescue package included the typical menu of neoliberal structural reforms such as stabilization, liberalization, financial and corporate restructuring, privatization, and a flexible labor market in return for massive bailout loans from the IMF.

Third, the stretching and expansion of globalization since the end of the Cold War has worked in favor of the Korean economy, which has been heavily reliant on export and foreign investments. While authoritarian regimes persisted with the "developmental state" model of economic growth and protected domestic markets and chaebols in return for their performance in international markets, democratic governments, the Kim Dae Jung government in particular, accepted IMF conditionalities and aggressively pursued comliance with global standards. The Korean case of globalization shows that globalization (or economic openness, in the words of Li and Reuveny 2009) promotes democracy. In other words, globalization promotes economic development, reduces information costs, reduces incentives for dictators to cling to power, intensifies the diffusion of democratic ideas, increases demands for international business for democracy, promotes domestic institutions supporting democracy, and thus, all these facts together work for promoting democracy (Li and Reuveny 2009: 28).[13]

Endogenous factors of growth under democratic governments

Even though we do not deny the contribution of exogenous factors to economic development under democratic governments, we dare to argue that economic development under democratic governments has been due to the rapid completion of the democratic consolidation process and continuous upgrading of the

Table 4.2 Political rights and economic freedom indicators

	1996		*1997*		*1998*		*1999*		*2000*		*2001*		*2002*		*2003*		*2004*		*2005*		*2006*		*2007*		*2008*	
	PR	*CL*	*PR*	*CL*	*PR*	*CL*	*PR*	*CL*	*PR*	*CL*	*PR*	*CL*	*PR*	*CL*	*PR*	*CL*	*PR*	*CL*	*PR*	*CL*	*PR*	*CL*	*PR*	*CL*	*PR*	*CL*
Korea	2	2	2	2	2	2	2	2	2	2	2	2	2	2	2	2	1	2	1	2	1	2	1	2	1	2
Japan	1	2	1	2	1	2	1	2	1	2	1	2	1	2	1	2	1	2	1	2	1	2	1	2	1	2
Taiwan	2	2	2	2	2	2	2	2	1	2	1	2	2	2	2	2	2	1	1	1	2	1	2	1	2	1
Indonesia	7	5	7	5	6	4	4	4	3	4	3	4	3	4	3	4	3	4	2	3	2	3	2	3	2	3
Cambodia	6	6	7	6	6	6	6	6	6	6	6	5	6	5	6	5	6	5	6	5	6	5	6	5	6	5
United States	1	1	1	1	1	1	1	1	1	1	1	1	1	1	1	1	1	1	1	1	1	1	1	1	1	1

Source: Freedom House, “Freedom in the World” (FRW).

Notes
PR: Political Rights/CL: Civil Liberties.
Rating 1–7 (1 → Free, 7 → Not free).

Economic freedom in Korea

Year	*1995*	*1996*	*1997*	*1998*	*1999*	*2000*	*2001*	*2002*	*2003*	*2004*	*2005*	*2006*	*2007*	*2008*	*2009*	*2010*
Economic Freedom Score	72	73	69.8	73.3	69.7	69.7	69.1	69.5	68.3	67.8	66.4	67.5	67.8	68.6	68.1	69.9

Source: 2010 Index of Economic Freedom (www.heritage.org/index).

Notes
Score: 100–80: Free; 79.9–70: Mostly Free; 69.9–60: Moderately Free; 59.9–50: Mostly Unfree; 49.9–0: Repressed.

quality of democracy in Korea (Im 2011). Those are the main components of the endogenous factors of growth under democratic governments since 1987. Since democratic transition in 1987, Korean democracy has completed democratic consolidation and upgraded itself to the group of "Full Democracy." According to the Democracy Index, measured by the EIU (Economic Intelligence Unit), between 2006 and 2008 Korean democracy moved upward from the category of "Flawed Democracy" to "Full Democracy." All East Asian democracies still remain in the category of "Flawed Democracy," including Taiwan.

As a member of "Full Democracy," Korean democracy improved its quality in many partial areas of democracy that are related to economic development under democracy, such as rule of law, voices and accountability, control of corruption, responsiveness, governmental effectiveness, regulatory quality, rule of law, and economic freedom.

Strict application of the rule of law makes democracy better able to protect property rights; democratic accountability either through vertical accountability or horizontal accountability constrains the state from predating or collecting monopoly rents; democracy enriches individual lives through the granting of political rights and civil liberties (Sen 2001); democracy provides political incentives to rulers to respond positively and quickly to the needs and demands of the people (responsiveness); with higher quality of democracy in terms of accountability and responsiveness, democracy can be more effective in policy-making and policy implementation and make sounder state regulation than authoritarianism because democratic governments are subject to popular democratic control and must act as the perfect agent of the people that are their principal.[14]

In South Korea since democratic transition, political rights and civil liberties upgraded to the level of advanced democracies, while voices and accountability improved a little from 0.50 (1996) to 0.75 (2005). So in terms of accountability, Korean democracy has a long way to go. The same can be said of corruption and transparency of politics. According to Governance Matters' "Worldwide Governance Indicators," the corruption index remained at the bottom of OECD countries. Since resuming democratic competition, the responsiveness of the government improved a lot in the area of political stability, absence of terrorism and violence, government effectiveness, and regulatory quality. Especially government effectiveness improved a lot, from 0.90 in 1996 to 1.26 in 2008. Regulatory quality of the government improved from 0.46 in 1996 to 0.88 in 2007 (Table 4.3).

Thus these improvements to democratic quality contributed endogenously to sustaining a high-growth economy by democratic governments. We can say that without democratization, authoritarian Korea could not achieve sustainable growth and could have failed to adjust to the changed environment caused by the end of the Cold War and the spread of globalization. Even though the Korean "developmental state" was the champion of managing economic growth during the 1960s and 1970s, the developmental state became obsolescent with the advent of a unipolar structure after the collapse of socialist countries in Eastern

Table 4.3 Worldwide governance indicators

	1996	*1998*	*2000*	*2002*	*2003*	*2004*	*2005*	*2006*	*2007*	*2008*
Rule of law										
Korea	0.78	0.74	0.80	0.84	0.70	0.75	0.85	0.74	0.90	0.79
Japan	1.48	1.47	1.40	1.25	1.26	1.27	1.29	1.38	1.35	1.40
Taiwan	0.90	0.86	0.90	0.85	0.88	0.86	0.89	0.71	0.69	0.77
Indonesia	–0.31	–0.72	–0.81	–1.01	–0.95	–0.78	–0.84	–0.74	–0.70	–0.66
Cambodia	–1.19	–1.08	–0.97	–1.15	–1.22	–1.25	–1.18	–1.18	–1.10	–1.08
United States	1.68	1.68	1.62	1.53	1.55	1.47	1.51	1.54	1.56	1.65
Voices and accountability										
Korea	0.50	0.62	0.61	0.74	0.75	0.71	0.75	0.61	0.65	0.59
Japan	0.87	0.89	0.87	0.99	1.03	1.01	1.00	0.97	0.97	0.95
Taiwan	0.59	0.82	0.78	0.93	0.97	0.86	0.93	0.66	0.72	0.70
Indonesia	–1.17	–1.04	–0.40	–0.41	–0.41	–0.33	–0.18	–0.18	–0.15	–0.14
Cambodia	–0.96	–0.88	–0.79	–0.73	–0.83	–0.87	–1.00	–0.79	–0.87	–0.94
United States	1.29	1.37	1.37	1.33	1.30	1.34	1.33	1.10	1.09	1.12
Control of corruption										
Korea	0.43	0.21	0.27	0.47	0.4	0.38	0.63	0.39	0.46	0.45
Japan	1.14	1.27	1.31	0.99	1.15	1.16	1.23	1.34	1.17	1.25
Taiwan	0.71	0.86	0.9	0.78	0.8	0.84	0.85	0.67	0.48	0.55
Indonesia	–0.51	–1.16	–0.98	–1.13	–0.97	–0.91	–0.87	–0.77	–0.69	–0.64
Cambodia	–1.17	–1.11	–0.93	–0.98	–0.93	–1.05	–1.18	–1.21	–1.11	–1.14
United States	1.72	1.7	1.73	1.84	1.7	1.73	1.54	1.29	1.4	1.55
Political stability and absence of violence/terrorism										
Korea	0.26	0.14	0.17	0.31	0.33	0.49	0.56	0.41	0.45	0.41
Japan	1.01	1.23	1.11	1.19	1.19	1.08	1.03	1.10	1.03	0.94
Taiwan	1.08	0.88	0.41	0.77	0.75	0.61	0.61	0.60	0.50	0.72
Indonesia	–0.85	–1.39	–1.69	–1.61	–1.99	–1.54	–1.25	–1.21	–1.08	–1.00
Cambodia	–1.37	–1.15	–0.75	–0.72	–0.74	–0.47	–0.50	–0.42	–0.52	–0.27
United States	1.02	1.00	1.20	0.34	0.34	0.17	0.08	0.45	0.37	0.59
Government effectiveness										
Korea	0.90	0.39	0.79	0.96	0.94	0.99	1.03	1.18	1.29	1.26
Japan	1.66	1.01	1.12	1.05	1.18	1.29	1.31	1.56	1.38	1.46
Taiwan	1.57	0.68	0.91	1.08	1.17	1.25	1.16	1.17	1.06	0.88
Indonesia	0.06	–0.85	–0.50	–0.63	–0.56	–0.43	–0.46	–0.37	–0.39	–0.29
Cambodia	–1.02	–0.78	–0.83	–0.81	–0.76	–0.89	–0.92	–0.90	–0.86	–0.81
United States	2.22	1.61	1.91	1.82	1.83	1.85	1.66	1.66	1.64	1.65
Regulatory effectiveness										
Korea	0.46	0.33	0.58	0.77	0.67	0.79	0.79	0.7	0.88	0.73
Japan	0.5	0.65	0.83	0.57	0.99	1.11	1.17	1.19	1.05	1.23
Taiwan	0.85	1.04	0.13	0.99	0.94	1.15	1.08	0.92	0.94	1.07
Indonesia	0.35	–0.27	–0.31	–0.71	–0.65	–0.63	–0.48	–0.31	–0.3	–0.27
Cambodia	0.04	–0.21	–0.17	–0.35	–0.37	–0.52	–0.5	–0.61	–0.51	–0.47
United States	1.26	1.57	1.61	1.49	1.48	1.51	1.54	1.54	1.45	1.58

Source: Governance Matters 2009, "Worldwide Governance Indicators (WGI)."

Europe, globalization, and the IT revolution. Korea can sustain high economic growth with relatively equitable distribution of income just because Korea successfully consolidated its nascent democracy and continuously upgraded its qualities. Therefore, we support the democratic development thesis, i.e., democracy first, economic development later, because economic development followed from good governance made by good democracy.

Notes

* This study is supported by a Korea University grant and the NRF (National Research Foundation of Korea).

1 According to Przeworski *et al.* (2000), affluent democratic countries with per capita income of $6,055 (that is, the income of Argentina in 1976 when the last coup took place) or more were never subverted to authoritarianism (Przeworski *et al.* 2000; also Epstein *et al.* 2006: 552).

2 While "endogenous modernization" is a theory of change from within and contends that autocracies become democracies when per capita income crosses a threshold where dictatorships turned into democracies, "exogenous modernization" is a theory that economic progress makes democracies stable, i.e., a good economy makes a democracy more stable. In the words of Seymour Lipset, "the more well to do a nation, the greater the chances it will sustain democracy" (Lipset 1959; also Przeworski *et al.* 1997: 158). The basis assumption of Przeworski's exogenous democratization is that "democracy is not a byproduct of economic development," its presence or absence "is the result of political actors pursuing their goals" (Przeworski *et al.* 1997: 177; Boix and Stokes 2003).

3 Japan was democratized by General MacArthur's U.S. Military Government; the Philippines dictator Marcos was ousted from power with strong and clear pressure from the United States; without IMF conditionlities, Indonesian dictator did not surrender his power peacefully; Taiwan's democratization was a typical democratization from above in which the ruling KMT controlled the pace, scope, and schedule of democratization by installment.

4 Nineteenth-century British liberals, such as Ricardo, Mckintosh, and J.S. Mill, and Marxists were very skeptical of the compatibility of democracy and capitalism (Przeworski and Limongi 1993; Collini *et al.* 1984).

5 The list of forefathers of Modernization Theory is long: Aristotle, Montesquieu, de Tocqueville, Adam Smith, Kant, and Schumpeter.

6 Kohli calls the similar phenomenon a "cruel choice" between democracy and development (Kohli 1986, 2006); Mancur Olson, in his *Rise and Decline of Nations* (1982), also argued that democracy allows and exacerbates the problem of collective action, i.e., democracy provides strong, organized special-interest groups to influence state policies for advancing their particularistic interests through the wide scope of organization lobbying and thus reduces the flexibility of the economy.

7 Jagdish N. Bhagwati said that "the political economy of development poses a cruel choice between rapid (self-sustained) expansion and democratic process" (Bhagwati 1966: 203–204).

8 Przeworski commented on the draft of this paper that "our thesis [in *Democracy and Development*, 2000] is, in fact, narrower. We claim that democracy does not matter for economic growth but it does matter for the other aspects of development, namely, fertility and mortality."

9 Nobel laureate economist Robert E. Lucas, Jr., indirectly supports the Confucian capitalism thesis by arguing that the accumulation of human capital on the job has been the main engine of economic growth in Korea (Lucas 1993: 270–271).

10 For a critique of Eckert, see Kang (1995: 577–582). According to Kang, the Korean capitalist class was not the offspring of the landed class under Japanese rule and the Korean state had its origins not in Japanese colonialism but in U.S. Cold War policy.

11 The digital area around Teheran Boulevard, Seoul, where IT firms are concentrated.

12 Between 1989 and 1993 inclusive, wage increases in South Korea were 21.1, 18.8, 17.7, 15.2 and 12.2 percent respectively, which were way above the government's wage guidelines. This was in sharp contrast to the years before 1987, when wage increases beyond the guidelines set were suppressed by the government (Park and Lee 1995: 42; Park and Leggett 1998: 284).

13 Eichengreen and Leblanc argue that they found, through a cross-country study, evidence that positive relationships run both ways between globalization and democracy: "globalization (trade openness and financial openness) (FDI, Capital flows to GDP, FDI to GDP) promotes democracy and at the same time democracy promotes globalization (trade openness, liberalization, privatization, capital market opening etc." (Eichengreen and Leblanc 2006).

14 Democracy is a better mechanism to solve principal–agent problem.

References

Acemoglu, Daron, and Robinson, James. (2005). *Economic Origins of Dictatorship and Democracy*, Cambridge: Cambridge University Press.

Almond, Gabriel A. (1991). "Capitalism and Democracy," *Political Science and Politics*, 24(3): 467–474.

Amsden, Alice. (1990). "Third World Industrialization: 'Global Fordism' or a New Model?" *New Left Review*, 182: 5–31.

Appelbaum, Richard P., and Jeffrey Henderson (eds.). (1992). *States and Development in the Asian Pacific Rim*, Newbury Park, CA: Sage.

Aseniero, George. (1994). "South Korean and Taiwanese Development: The Transnational Context," *Review*, 17–336.

Barker, Ernest. (1995). *Aristotle Politics*, trans., rev. and ed. with an Introduction by R.F. Stalley, New York: Oxford University Press.

Barro, Roberto J. (1990). "Government Spending in a Simple Model of Economic Growth," *Journal of Political Economy*, 98(5): 103–125.

Bhagwati, Jagdish N. (1966). *The Economics of Underdeveloped Countries*, London: Weidenfeld & Nicholson.

Boix, Carles, and Susan C. Stokes. (2003). "Endogenous Democratization," *World Politics*, 55(4): 517–549.

Chang, Ha Joon. (1995). "Explaining 'Flexible-Rigidities' in East Asia," in Tony Killick (ed.), *The Flexible Economy: Causes and Consequences of National Economies*, London: Routledge.

Chen, Lisng-chih Evans. (2007). "Development First, Democracy Later? Or Democracy First, Development Later: The Controversy over Development and Democracy," paper presented at the Annual Meeting of the Southern Political Science Association, New Orleans, LA, January 3, 2007.

Cho, Hee Youn. (1997). "Tongasia Palchoroneui Chaegumto" [The Reappraisal of East Asian Developmental Model], *Kyongchewa Saheo [Economy and Society]*, 36: 46–76.

Collini, Stefan, Donald Winch, and John Burrow. (1984). *That Noble Science of Politics: A Study in Nineteenth-Century Intellectual History*, Cambridge: Cambridge University Press.

Cumings, Bruce. (1984). "The Legacy of Japanese Colonialism in Korea," in Ramon Myers and Mark R. Peattie (eds.), *The Japanese Colonial Empire, 1895–1945*, Princeton, NJ: Princeton University Press.

Dahl, R. (1971). *Polyarchy: Participation and Opposition*, New Haven, CT: Yale University Press.

De Castro, Renato Cruz. (2000). "Whither Geoeconomics? Bureaucratic Inertia in the US Post Cold War Foreign Policy toward East Asia," *Asian Affairs*, 26(4): 201–221.

Eckert, Carter J. (1991). *Offspring of Empire: The Koch'ang Kims and the Colonial Origins of Korean Capitalism, 1876–1945*, Seattle: University of Washington Press.

Eichengreen, Barry, and David Leblanc. (2006). "Democracy and Globalization," unpublished paper.

Epstein, David L., Robert Bates, Jack Goldstone, Ida Kristensen, and Sharyn O'Halloran. (2006). "Democratic Transitions," *American Journal of Political Science*, 50(3): 551–569.

Evans, P.B. (1995). *Embedded Autonomy: States and Industrial Transformation*, Princeton, NJ: Princeton University Press.

Findlay, Ronald. (1990). "The New Political Economy: Its Explanatory Power for the LDCs," *Economics and Politics*, 2(2): 193–221.

Friedman, Thomas. (2000). *The Lexus and Olive Tree: Understanding Globalization*, New York: Anchor Books.

Fröbel, F., J. Heinrichs, and O. Kreye. (1980). *The New International Division of Labor*, London: Cambridge University Press.

Galenson, Walter. (1959). *Labor and Economic Development*, New York: Wiley.

Gourevitch, Peter A. (1989). "Pacific Rim: The Current Debates," *The Annals of the American Academy of Political and Social Science*, 505(1): 8–23.

Haggard, Stephan. (2000). *The Political Economy of the Asian Economic Crisis*, Washington, DC: Institute for International Economics.

Huntington, Samuel P. (1968). *Political Order in Changing Societies*, New Haven, CT: Yale University Press.

Huntington, Samuel P. (1991). *The Third Wave: Democratization in the Late Twentieth Century*, Norman and London: University of Oklahoma Press.

Huntington, Samuel P., and Jorge I. Dominguez. (1975). "Political Development," in F.I. Greenstein and N.W. Polsby (eds.), *Handbook of Political Science*, Reading, MA: Addison-Wesley.

Huntington, Samuel P. and Joan M. Nelson. (1976). *No Easy Choice: Political Participation in Developing Countries*, Cambridge, MA: Harvard University Press.

Im, Hyug Baeg. (1987). "The Rise of Bureaucratic Authoritarianism in South Korea," *World Politics*, 39(2): 231–257.

Im, Hyug Baeg. (2006). *Democracy in the Era of Globalization* (in Korean), Seoul: Nanam.

Im, Hyug Baeg. (2009). *Neo-Nomadic Democracy* (in Korean), Seoul: Nanam.

Im, Hyug Baeg. (2011). "Better Democrcacy, Better Economic Growth?" *International Political Science Review*, 32(5): 579–597.

Kang, David. (1995). "South Korean and Taiwanese Development and the New Institutional Economics," *International Organization*, 49(3): 555–587.

Kim, Byung Kook. (2001). "The Public Financial Reform in Korea, Malaysia, Thailand: Does Democracy Matter?" paper presented at Annual Meeting of APSA, San Francisco, August 28–September 2.

Kim, Il Young. (1995). "Parkjunghee cheje 18nyeon, Eutuoge bol gutinga" [How do we view the 18 years of Park Jung Hee regime?], *SaSang*, 27: 208–256.

Kohli, A. (1986). "Democracy and Development," in J.P. Lewis and V. Kallab (eds.), *Development Strategies Reconsidered*, New Brunswick, NJ: Transaction Books.

Kohli, A. (2006). *State-Directed Development*, Cambridge: Cambridge University Press.

Lake, David, and Mathew Baum. (2001). "The Invisible Hand of Democracy: Political Control and the Provision of public Service," *Comparative Political Studies*, 34(6): 587–621.

Li, Quan, and Rafael Reuveny. (2009). *Democracy and Economic Openness in an International System: Complex Transformations*, New York: Cambridge University Press.

Lipset, Seymour M. (1959). "Some Social Prerequisites of Democracy: Economic Development and Political Legitimacy," *American Political Science Review*, 53(1): 69–105.

Lucas, Jr., Robert E. (1993). "Making a Miracle," *Econometrica*, 61(2): 251–272.

McNamara, Dennis L. (1990). *The Colonial Origins of Korean Enterprises, 1910–1945*, Cambridge: Cambridge University Press.

Maravall, Jose Maria. (1994). "The Myth of the Authoritarian Advantage," *Journal of Democracy*, 5(4): 17–31.

Mesquita, B. Bueno de, and George Downs. (2005). "Development and Democracy," *Foreign Affairs*, 84(5): 77.

Mesquita, B. Bueno de, B.A. Smith, R.M. Silverson, and J.D. Morrow. (2003). *The Logic of Political Survival*, Cambridge, MA: MIT Press.

North, Douglass C. (1990). *Institutions, Institutional Change, and Economic Performance*, New York: Cambridge University Press.

O'Donnell, Guillermo. (1973). *Modernization and Bureaucratic-Authoritarianism*, Berkeley: UC Berkeley Press.

O'Donnell, Guillermo. (1994). "Delegative Democracy," *Journal of Democracy*, 5(1): 55–69.

Olson, Mancur. (1982). *The Rise and Decline of Nations: Economic Growth, Stagflation and Social Rigidities*, New Haven, CT: Yale University Press.

Olson, Mancur. (1991). "Autocracy, Democracy and Prosperity," in R.J. Zeckhauser (ed.), *Strategy and Choice*, Cambridge, MA: MIT Press.

Olson, Mancur. (1993). "Dictatorship, Democracy and Development," *American Political Science Review*, 87(3): 567–576.

Park, Y., and M. Lee. (1995). "Economic Development, Globalization and Practices in Industrial Relations and Human Resource Management in Korea," in A. Verma, T. Kochan, and R. Lansbury (eds.), *Employment Relations in the Growing Asian Economies*, London and New York: Routledge, pp. 27–61.

Park, Y., and C. Leggett. (1998). "Employment Relations in Korea," in G. Bamber and R. Lansbury (eds.), *International and Comparative Employment Relations*, 3rd edn., Crows Nest, NSW: Allen & Unwin, pp. 275–293.

Przeworski, Adam. (1990). *The State and Economy under Capitalism*, Chur, Switzerland: Harwood Academic Publishers.

Przeworski, Adam and Fernando Limongi. (1993). "Political Regimes and Economic Growth," *Journal of Economic Perspectives*, 7(3): 51–69.

Przeworski, Adam, Michael E. Alvarez, Jose Antonio Cheibub, Fernando Limongi. (2000). *Democracy and Development: Political Institutions and Well-being in the World 1950–1990*, New York: Cambridge University Press.

Przeworski, Adam, José Antonio Cheibub, and Fernando Limongi. (1997). "Culture and Democracy," in *World Culture Report*, Paris: UNESCO.

Rao, V. (1984). "Democracy and Economic Development," *Studies in Comparative International Development*, 19(4): 67–81.

Rodrik, D. (2000). "Institutions for High-Quality Growth: What They Are and How to Acquire Them," *Studies in Comparative International Development*, 35(3): 3–31.

Schumpeter, Joseph A. (1942). *Capitalism, Socialism, and Democracy*, London: George Allen & Unwin.

Schweinitz, Karl de. (1964). *Industrialization and Democracy: Economic Necessities and Political Possibilities*, New York: Free Press.

Seldon, David and Tim Belton-Jones. (1995). "The Political Determinants of Economic Flexibility, With Special Reference to the East Asian NICs," in Tony Killick (ed.), *The Flexible Economy: Causes and Consequences of the Adaptability of National Economies*, London: Routledge.

Seligson, Mitchell A. (2003). "The Dual Gaps: An Overview of Theory and Research," in Mitchell A. Seligson and John T. Passe-Smith (eds.), *Development and Underdevelopment: The Political Economy of Global Inequality*, 3rd edn., Boulder, CO: Lynne Rienner.

Sen, Amartya. (2001). "Democracy as a Universal Value," in Larry Diamond and Marc Plattner (eds.), *The Global Emergence of Democracy*, Baltimore, MD: Johns Hopkins University Press.

Sharma, S.D. (2007). "Democracy, Good Governance, and Economic Development," *Taiwan Journal of Democracy*, 3(1): 29–62.

Siegle, Joseph T., Michael M. Weinstein, and Morton A. Halperin. (2004). "Why Democracies Excel," *Foreign Affairs*, 83(5): 57–71.

Sohn, Ho Chul. (1995). *HaeBang 50nyeonyui Hangukjungchi [Korean Politics after independence]*, Seoul: Saegil.

Study Group on Korean Politics (ed.). (1998). *Dong Asia Baljunmodeleun Silpaeheatneunga? [Did East Asian developmental model fail?]*, Seoul: Samin.

Tocqueville, Alexis de. (1945). *Democracy in America*, New York: Vintage Books.

Wallerstein, Immanuel. (1979). *The Capitalist World Economy*, Cambridge: Cambridge University Press.

Weiss, Linda, and John Hobson. 1995. *States and Economic Development: A Comparative Historical Analysis*, Cambridge: Polity Press.

5 Japan–South Korea economic ties

Stability and growth through discord

*Terence Roehrig**

Introduction

Japan and South Korea (Republic of Korea—ROK) share a long and often difficult history that has risen up on many occasions to complicate their relationship. Both countries have many common interests as major economic players, democracies, and key U.S. allies in the region. Despite these commonalities, the potential for tension and animosity, even during times of relative calm and good relations, lurks just below the surface.

In fall 2012, Japan–South Korea relations hit an all-time low. Several incidents tied to island disputes and the difficult shared history of these two countries came together to damage what had been a growing relationship. Public opinion surveys in both countries reflected the deteriorating ties. In a November 2012 survey of 3,000 Japanese, 59 percent did not view South Korea on friendly terms, a large increase from 23.7 percent the previous year. In addition, respondents indicating they had an affinity for South Korea dropped from 62.2 percent to 39.2 percent, the first time in 15 years that the sentiment had declined below 40 percent (Schreiber 2012b).

Similar perceptions of Japan are present in South Korea. An August 2012 poll conducted by Gallup Korea showed that 44.1 percent of South Korean respondents ranked Japan as their least favorite country, far more than China at 19.1 percent. Japan was the least favorite country a decade earlier, but then at only 33.4 percent. The Asan Institute, an ROK think tank, conducted a poll that asked ROK respondents to rank country favorability on a scale of one to ten. In 2010, Japan's favorability rating came in at 4.2 but in 2012 and 2013 was 2.7 and 2.57 respectively. Japan's 2012 score ranked it lower than North Korea's 3.3 (Chicago Council on Global Affairs et al. 2012: 3), in large part because the poll was conducted prior to North Korea's December 2012 satellite launch and third nuclear test that occurred in February 2013. In 2013, North Korea returned to a ranking below Japan at 2.37 but a rating that, nonetheless, remained close to the sentiment expressed toward Tokyo (*Chosun Ilbo* 2013). Finally, an April 2013 survey conducted jointly by a South Korean and a Japanese newspaper found that 78 percent of South Koreans thought relations were bad between Seoul and Tokyo, a 14-point increase since the survey was last conducted in 2011. Japanese feelings deteriorated even further for South Korea: 71 percent thought ties with Seoul were bad, a 27 percent increase from 2011 (*Yomiuri Shimbun* 2013).

While political ties frayed between Tokyo and Seoul in the last three months of 2012 and have not improved since, economic ties remained relatively robust. There were some disruptions as nationalism on both sides spilled over into consumer decisions and government actions but, by and large, the strong economic connections between the second and fourth largest economies in Asia remained solid. Both countries have been examples of the "East Asian model" utilizing an export-driven strategy and benefiting from increasing levels of regional economic integration. These realities have helped to tie the Japanese and South Korean economies together in ways that provide a bridge across an often tenuous political and historical divide. Economic factors such as the decreasing value of the yen that has been part of Prime Minister Shinzo Abe's economic plans have altered some business activity but this is not due to the island and history disputes that escalated the previous year. Thus, while the political relationship has taken a beating, Japan–South Korea economic ties have remained relatively strong and provide an important motivation for both sides to better manage their relationship.

Japan–South Korea relations: the problems of history and islands

Japan and South Korea have long had a tempestuous relationship. In the past, Japan's conflicts with others in the region often involved the Korean Peninsula, either as a route to reach China and/or Russia or as a prize in its clashes with these Asian powers. In the late 1500s, Japanese leader Toyotomi Hideyoshi attacked China by going through Korea. Japan quickly overwhelmed Korean forces, moving up the peninsula and close to Pyongyang. Eventually, Korea, along with help from China, halted the Japanese advance and forced them back to a small enclave in the southeast corner of Korea. A few years later, Japanese forces tried again, this time more intent on subduing Korea than on reaching China. However, Korean forces and their Ming Dynasty ally were prepared and beat back the Japanese invasion. Hideyoshi died in 1598, bringing the war to an end along with the complete withdrawal of Japanese forces from Korea. Though Korea was successful in driving Hideyoshi's forces from the peninsula, the war had lasted eight years and wrought severe destruction on the Korean people (Lee 1984: 209–215).

In the late 1800s, China, Japan, and Russia battled for regional hegemony with conflicts that, once again, placed Korea in the middle. For many years, China and Korea had a "big brother–little brother" relationship where Korea provided tribute and loyalty to China in return for protection and leaving Korea alone to handle its own affairs. In the Sino-Japanese War (1894–1895), Japan pulled Korea away from the influence of a crumbling China, "liberating" the peninsula from Chinese suzerainty (Paine 2005). With Chinese dominance over, Japan and Russia continued the struggle for regional supremacy, including control of Korea and Manchuria. Japan emerged the victor in the Russo-Japanese War (1904–1905), becoming the dominant power in all of Asia. Soon after the victory over Russia, Japan pressured Korean leaders to sign a protectorate treaty that gave Tokyo control over Korean trade and foreign policy. The protectorate lasted only five years; in 1910, Japan formally annexed Korea, making the peninsula part of the Japanese empire. From 1910 to the end of World War II, Japan imposed a harsh occupation on Korea where Tokyo sought to assimilate Korea both culturally and linguistically while exploiting the Korean economy (Dudden 2005; Kang 2005). The occupation left a lasting memory in the psyche of the Korean people that has proved difficult to overcome.

After World War II, Japan and South Korea established formal alliances with the United States, yet ties between these allies in the U.S. Cold War security system remained difficult. Tokyo and Seoul normalized relations in 1965 after lengthy and difficult negotiations where Japan provided $800 million in grants, loans, and investment capital as compensation for the occupation (Cumings 1997: 320–321). The injection of capital furnished seed money to help jumpstart the ROK economy and provided the impetus for a growing bilateral economic relationship.

While economic ties began to grow in the 1960s, issues related to history and disputed islets remained with periodic flare-ups that have caused anxiety and tension in South Korea and Japan. During the past few years, these issues have raised their heads once again, creating serious problems in their political relationship with little likelihood of resolution any time soon.

Legacies of history

The legacy of World War II and the occupation of Korea have long been a problem for ROK–Japan relations. Japanese leaders have issued formal apologies for the past. On the occasion of the 50th Anniversary of the end of World War II, Japanese Prime Minister Tomiichi Murayama offered a formal statement that expressed "feelings of deep remorse" and a "heartfelt apology" for Japan's actions during the war along with "feelings of profound mourning for all victims, both at home and abroad" (Ministry of Foreign Affairs, Japan 1995). Later, in August 2010 at a commemoration for the 100th Anniversary of the start of the Japanese occupation of Korea, Prime Minister Naoto Kan declared: "For the enormous damage and suffering caused during this colonial rule, I would like to express once again our deep remorse and heartfelt apology" (Fackler 2010). Despite these formal expressions of regret, resentment and suspicion remains over what Koreans and others perceive as evidence that some corners in Japan have not been completely sincere concerning contrition for the past. In part, some point to the backlash Kan received for the apology from conservatives and others in his own party as evidence. More recently, Prime Minister Abe stirred controversy in April 2013 by declaring that he is "not upholding all of [the Murayama statement] as it is" (Yoshida 2013b). The following day, Abe maintained that the definition of "aggression" has not been "firmly determined" by academia or the global community and that aggression "can be viewed differently" depending on one's position (Yoshida 2013b). Though Abe's Cabinet Secretary Yoshihide Suga later backed away from the statements, the damage had been done (Yoshida 2013c).

History issues have also been problematic in other ways. The periodic release of Japanese textbooks that do not include sensitive events or do not fully examine Japanese actions during World War II, including the occupation of Korea, sex slavery, experimentation with chemical and biological weapons, and the Nanjing Massacre, usually sparks an outcry in South Korea and elsewhere in East Asia to protest what is viewed as Japan's sanitizing of history. History tensions have also flared up whenever Japanese leaders have paid a visit to the Yasukuni shrine. The shrine is located in Tokyo and is a memorial for the souls of the 2.5 million Japanese who perished fighting for the nation. Yasukuni is not a cemetery and the Japanese government does not own or operate the facility, but the list of those enshrined at Yasukuni include 14 Class A war criminals convicted by the Tokyo War Crimes Tribunal following World War II. In addition, on the grounds of the shrine is a memorial museum that many have criticized for its revisionist presentations of Japan's role in World War II. Visits by Japanese leaders are certain to fuel tensions in the region. Prime Minister Yasuhiro Nakasone visited in 1985, and Prime Minister Junichiro Koizumi made the journey on six occasions while in office from 2001 to 2006. Each time Koizumi insisted he was visiting as a private citizen but every trip caused an outpouring of protest in much of East Asia.

For a number of years after Koizumi, Japanese prime ministers did not visit Yasukuni, and President Abe, who began his second term as prime minister in December 2012, also initially refrained from making the trip. In April 2013, a large contingent of Japanese officials decided to visit the shrine, including three of Abe's cabinet members, among them deputy prime minister Taro Aso, along with 168 Diet members, a record number since tallies began to be kept in 1989 (Mie 2013). Though not participating in this visit, Abe did make the trip to Yasukuni on 26 December 2013, generating the expected criticism from South Korea and others in East Asia (BBC 2013).

Following the visit, South Korean Foreign Minister Yun Byung-se remarked that his country

> will continue to keep its resolute stance on the historical awareness issues. Further repercussions on the already tension-ridden relations between South Korea and Japan are inevitable. Given the seriousness of the latest incident, it will be difficult, in my understanding to [hold] high-level diplomatic and security meetings between the two countries down the road.
>
> (*Korea Times* 2013)

Even the U.S. government expressed its concern on the Yasukuni visit, a rare gesture from Washington. A press release from the U.S. Embassy in Japan (2013) stated: "Japan is a valued ally and friend. Nevertheless, the United States is disappointed that Japan's leadership has taken an action that will exacerbate tensions with Japan's neighbors."

Japan–South Korea relations were already sensitive when the issue of sex slavery, known by the euphemism "comfort women," escalated to new levels. During World War II, the Japanese military forced between 200,000 and 400,000 girls and women from Korea, the Philippines, China, and the Netherlands, among others, to serve as sex slaves for soldiers. Approximately 75 percent of the "comfort women" died during their ordeal. In August 2011, the Constitutional Court of Korea ruled by a 6–3 vote that inaction by the South Korean government to settle claims with Japan over the sex slave issue "would not just be confined to the issue of constitutional property rights but would also directly concern the violation of dignity and value as human beings" (Constitutional Court of Korea 2011). In December 2011, a citizens group erected a statue of a young "comfort woman" across the street from the Japanese embassy in Seoul. Since 1992, South Korean protestors, including a number of the surviving "comfort women," gathered weekly in that location to protest the Japanese government's lack of full accountability. Japanese officials maintain they have compensated South Korea through financial considerations that were part of the 1965 Treaty of Normalization. In addition, Chief Cabinet Secretary Yohei Kono issued a statement in 1993 that

> the Government of Japan would like to take this opportunity once again to extend its sincere apologies and remorse to all those, irrespective of place of origin, who suffered immeasurable pain and incurable physical and psychological wounds as comfort women.
>
> (Ministry of Foreign Affairs, Japan 1993)

After the ROK court ruling, negotiators exchanged plans to settle the issue but could not reach agreement. Further complicating the issue, Osaka Mayor Toru Hashimoto remarked, concerning sex slavery during the war, that: "To maintain discipline in the military it must have been necessary at that time" (*Guardian* 2013). Hashimoto had also argued earlier that there was no evidence that women had been forced to be "comfort women." Later, the *Yomiuri Shimbun*, Japan's largest newspaper, published an editorial that questioned if "comfort women" were forced against their will and indicated that the 1993 Kono Statement should be revisited (*Yonhap News* 2013). Soon after, South Korean President Lee Myung-Bak visited a small group of islands and relations worsened.

The island disputes: Dokdo or Takeshima

Another long-simmering source of conflict has been the dispute over a small group of islets that Koreans call Dokdo and Japan refers to as Takeshima. The islets are located approximately equidistant between Japan and South Korea in the East Sea/Sea of Japan. The internationally neutral name for the islets is Liancourt Rocks, a name derived from the French whaling ship that almost ran aground there in 1849. There is little of value on the islets but they are important for fishing and possible offshore deposits of oil and gas. In 1954, South Korea occupied Dokdo and constructed a wharf, lighthouse, and buildings for close to 40 Coast Guard personnel who administer the islets.

Since that time, Seoul and Tokyo have put forth their arguments to demonstrate their respective claims. Though both sides point to evidence prior to 1900 to buttress their claims, the crucial part of the story begins early in the twentieth century. In February 1905, Japan claimed the islets, arguing they were *terra nullius*—belonging to no one. Japanese authorities maintain they acquired the islets before Tokyo established a protectorate over Korea in 1905 and the annexation that followed in 1910. As a result, after World War II when the protectorate and annexation treaties were nullified, Japan's ownership of the islets remained. Moreover, during the U.S. occupation of Japan, U.S. leaders confirmed Tokyo's claims in various documents and in the 1951 San Francisco Treaty that ended World War II. The treaty listed several islands by name for return to Korea but did not mention Dokdo/Takeshima as territory Japan must relinquish to Korea.

South Korea maintains that it had established sovereignty over the islets prior to 1905, so any claim of *terra nullius* along with the incorporation and annexation were illegal. Thus, Japan did not establish sovereignty prior to the protectorate, and any claims to *terra nullius* that are linked to the annexation treaty are null and void since land that is "belonging to no one" would not need to be included in the annexation document (Fern 2005: 86). Regarding the U.S. position during the occupation, many South Korean analysts maintain that Japan was simply better at lobbying U.S. officials but that this is not a reflection on the strength of Japan's claim. Soon after the signing of the San Francisco Treaty, the U.S. position became formally that it takes no position on the sovereignty of the islets and will accept whatever settlement Tokyo and Seoul reach through negotiations, the same position it holds today (Roehrig 2012). More recently, ROK researchers have produced several maps and documents from Japanese sources that support South Korea's claims to the islets (*Chosun Ilbo* 2009, 2010).

In August 2012, relations between Tokyo and Seoul sank to their lowest point in years, in large part over the 10 August visit by President Lee Myung-bak to Dokdo. Lee was the first ROK president to visit the islands and while addressing the police and Coast Guard personnel stationed there, declared: "Dokdo is the end of our territory. Please make sure to defend Dokdo well. Dokdo is indeed our territory and a place worth staking our lives to defend. Let's make sure to safeguard [the islets] with pride" (Chang 2012). Soon after, South Korea defeated Japan 2–0 to win the bronze medal in men's soccer at the London Olympics. At the end of the match, an ecstatic ROK player grabbed a sign from a spectator that stated in Korean "Dokdo is our land," and ran around the field holding the sign up for all to see. The ROK midfielder Park Jong-woo was a hero in South Korea but came close to losing his medal for making a political gesture while on the field. After a lengthy investigation, Park received his medal but he and the South Korean Olympic Committee received a warning for their actions (*Washington Post* 2013).

Japanese leaders were not amused by these events. Prime Minister Yoshihiko Noda fumed that Lee's visit to Takeshima was "unacceptable" and "very regrettable"; "Both historically and by international law, Takeshima belongs to Japan" (Sekiguchi 2012). The Japanese government recalled its ambassador from South Korea and called in South Korea's ambassador for an explanation. Lee made matters worse when, a few days later while meeting with a group of ROK teachers, he demanded that Emperor Akihito apologize sincerely to Korean independence fighters. Lee declared that if the emperor intended to offer only his "deepest regret," a reference to language the emperor used in 1990 to apologize for the past, he need not come to South Korea for a visit (*Japan Times* 2012a; *Yonhap News* 2012a). ROK officials later maintained that Lee had been misunderstood but it was too late and the damage had been done.

Japanese leaders were outraged by the disrespect they believed was shown to the Emperor in Lee's comments. In remarks to Diet members, Noda complained that Lee's statement "considerably deviates from common sense" and he "should apologize for and retract it" (*Mainichi* 2012). Prime Minister Noda sent a letter of protest to the ROK government through the embassy in Seoul but South Korean officials refused to accept the letter. Tokyo also threated to take the matter of Dokdo/Takeshima unilaterally to the International Court of Justice (ICJ), an action Japan had threatened to do twice before in 1954 and 1962. Though Japan might have been able to score political points by taking the issue to the ICJ, the court does not accept cases unless both parties agree to accept the outcome. South Korea will never agree to take the matter to the court as its position is that there is no dispute—the islets belong to South Korea.

In another signal of the likely continuation of the dispute, on February 22, Japan's Shimane Prefecture celebrates Takeshima Day. The local holiday was established in 2005 and is a celebration that has been held every year since to commemorate the day Japan maintains it formally incorporated the islets in 1905. In 2013, prefecture officials invited six cabinet members, including Prime Minister Abe, Foreign Minister Fumio Kishida, and Chief Cabinet Secretary Suga, the first time officials of this high level received invitations (Yoshida 2013a). None of them attended, but Aiko Shimajiri, the parliamentary secretary with the Cabinet Office, did join the event, the first senior government official to do so. Shimajiri remarked during the ceremony that "it goes without saying that Takeshima is Japanese territory," and the dispute is a "very important issue involving sovereignty" (*Japan Times* 2013). The Dokdo/Takeshima dispute will likely remain a serious bone of contention for a long time.

Finally, Japan–ROK relations had also been soured over a problem in summer 2012 with two pending security agreements between Seoul and Tokyo: the General Security of Military Information Agreement (GSOMIA) and an Acquisition and Cross-Servicing Agreement (ACSA). The GSOMIA would have allowed the ROK and Japanese militaries to share intelligence and information capitalizing on South Korea's strength in human intelligence regarding North Korea and Japan's strengths in signals intelligence that would "allow the US to work more effectively with its two allies in the Northeast Asian region, as it would no longer have to withhold intelligence that it received from the other nation" (M. Jun 2012). The Lee Myung-bak administration mishandled the politics of concluding this delicate agreement and, less than an hour before it was to be signed, backed off from the arrangement. Japan has continued to express its willingness to conclude a GSOMIA but South Korea remains opposed.

Japan–South Korea economic ties

Despite the tensions and ongoing difficulties caused by unresolved history and the Dokdo/Takeshima dispute, Japan and South Korea have been able to maintain a robust economic relationship that has endured and often grown in spite of these difficulties (Heo and Roehrig 2014: 88–109). To be sure, the periodic rows between Seoul and Tokyo have caused problems and disruptions in their economies. Yet, there has remained a continuity through economics that has helped create a foundation and motivation for working through and managing these problems, if not always at the government-to-government level, then among businesses. Since these disputes are unlikely to be settled any time soon, managing them and avoiding disruptions in economic sectors will be essential. The remainder of this chapter will examine four areas—trade, investment, pop culture, and tourism—as indicators of continued economic cooperation despite the tensions in ROK–Japan relations.

Trade. The most important economic connection between these two countries is a robust trade relationship that has shown fairly steady growth over the years.

From 1993 to 2013, Japan–South Korea total trade climbed from $31.6 billion to $94.7 billion, almost a 200 percent increase over the two decades (Table 5.1). In 2011, trade totals surpassed the $100 billion mark for the first time. For all those years, trade balances have been in Japan's favor. Throughout the past ten years, Japan has maintained a trade surplus ranging from 19.0 to 36.1 billion.

Japan–ROK trade ties are important for both countries but a bit more so for South Korea. Table 5.2 shows that for Japan in 2012, South Korea was the third largest trade partner at $103.2 billion, behind China at $333.7 billion and the United States at $217.1 billion. For South Korea, Japan ranks as its second largest trade partner behind only China ($215.1 billion).

As adherents of the East Asian Development Model, development based on exports has been a crucial component of their development strategy. Thus, export numbers are important for both countries but significantly more so for South Korea given its dependence on sales abroad to generate economic growth. According to Table 5.3, Japan's reliance on exports as a percentage of gross national product (GDP) has ranged from 13 to 18 percent from 2008 to 2011. For South Korea, those figures have varied from 50 to 56 percent during that period, making it far more vulnerable to decreases in exports.

In addition to these numbers, there are other important trends evident in Japan–South Korea trade relations. First there has been an expansion of South Korea's exports to Japan that has helped push down Japan's trade surplus in the

Table 5.1 Japan–South Korea trade (1993–2013) (US$ billions)

Year	*Imports from Korea*	*Exports to Korea*	*Total trade*	*Japan surplus*	*% increase in total trade*
1993	11.6	20.0	31.6	8.5	–
1994	13.5	25.4	38.9	11.9	23.0
1995	17.1	32.6	49.7	15.6	27.8
1996	15.8	31.4	47.2	15.7	–5.0
1997	14.8	27.9	42.7	13.1	–9.5
1998	12.2	16.8	29.1	4.6	–31.9
1999	15.9	24.1	40.0	8.3	37.5
2000	20.5	31.8	52.3	11.3	30.8
2001	16.5	26.6	43.1	10.1	–17.6
2002	15.1	29.9	45.0	14.7	1.9
2003	17.3	36.3	53.6	19.0	8.6
2004	21.7	46.1	67.8	24.4	26.5
2005	24.0	48.4	72.4	24.4	6.8
2006	26.5	51.9	78.4	25.4	8.4
2007	26.4	56.3	82.7	29.9	5.2
2008	28.3	61.0	89.2	32.7	8.0
2009	21.8	49.4	71.2	27.7	–20.2
2010	28.2	64.3	92.5	36.1	30.0
2011	39.7	68.3	108.0	28.6	16.8
2012	38.8	64.4	103.2	25.6	–4.4
2013	34.7	60.0	94.7	25.3	–8.2

Source: Korea Customs Service.

past few years. After the tsunami and Fukushima disaster in March 2011, supply chains were disrupted and Japanese producers had to develop new ties with ROK suppliers. Other factors increasing South Korean exports include increased purchases of South Korean smartphones, and fashions and accessories through online outlets. South Korean producers such as LG and Samsung have also made a greater effort to pursue Japanese markets (Mukoyama 2012: 13–14). As a result, according to Hidehiko Mukoyama (2012: 13–14) from the Japan Research Institute, South Korean companies “have become increasingly important to Japanese companies as customers for parts, raw materials, manufacturing equipment and other items.”

Table 5.2 Japan and South Korea: 2012 largest trade partners (US$ billions)

Japan's largest trade partners	*2012 Total trade*	*South Korea's largest trade partners*	*2012 total trade*
China	333.7	China	215.1
United States	217.1	Japan	103.2
South Korea	103.2	United States	101.8

Source: JETRO and Korean Customs Service.

Table 5.3 Exports of goods and services as percentage of GDP

	Japan	*South Korea*
2008	18	53
2009	13	50
2010	15	52
2011	15	56

Source: World Bank (2012).

Japan–Korea trade flows in 2013 were impacted by another issue, but one that was not tied to history or territory disputes. In December 2012, Shinzo Abe became Japan's new prime minister with a plan to weaken the yen through a massive monetary stimulus program. Lowering the value of the yen would make Japanese exports more attractive and help to bring its economy out of the doldrums that has lasted for years. As a result of these policies, the yen's value has fallen more than 30 percent over the past two years (*Star Online* 2014), and in early January 2014 the yen hit a five-year low compared to the South Korean won and a 15-year low compared to the Chinese yuan (Jang and Lee 2013). Consequently, Korean exports are more costly in Japan, but despite the potential impact on trade in the future, the ROK government's response has been somewhat reserved. President Park Geun-hye noted that "the weaker yen is a burden for Korea but crisis can be turned into opportunity," calling for rebalancing the economy toward domestic consumption away from exports to reduce risk in the future (Song 2014).

One of the casualties of sour relations between Tokyo and Seoul has been a continued delay in the resumption of free trade agreement (FTA) talks. Japan and South Korea began FTA negotiations in December 2003 and held six rounds before stopping in November 2004 over a number of unresolved issues. Specifically, Japan was reluctant to open its agriculture and fishing markets to South Korean producers, while South Korea feared opening its markets for automobiles, capital goods, and machinery to Japan. Seoul was also unhappy with the chronic trade deficit it had with Tokyo and wanted the agreement to address certain non-tariff barriers. Yet, the joint statement of the 43rd Japan–Korea Business Conference (as quoted in Mukoyama 2012: 20) in September 2011 maintained that:

> Business people in Japan and South Korea believe that the formation of a single economic zone within which people, goods and money can move freely is essential to the economic prosperity of Japan and South Korea and the evolution of their relationship as partners, and that for East Asia to function as an axis of stability for the world economy, it will be necessary to build a predictable integrated economic zone with stable systems based on market mechanisms that will not be disrupted by external factors, such as financial crises.

The statement might have also included island and history disputes as other potential external factors that an FTA could alleviate.

In fall 2011, Japan and South Korea signed an agreement to increase their currency swap arrangement from $13 billion to $70 billion out of concern for impending trouble in Europe (Oliver and Whipp 2011). During this meeting, representatives indicated a desire to resume FTA negotiations but nothing came of it. In spring 2012, signs arose again that the talks may resume, in part due to fears in Seoul of a bilateral FTA between China and Japan. A researcher from the Samsung Economic Research Institute in South Korea noted that "The pursuit of the China–Japan free trade agreement that excludes Korea is the most uncomfortable situation in the landscape of East Asia's economic integration" (*Dong-A Ilbo* 2012). Despite these signs, it soon became clear that ROK President Lee was not enthusiastic to restart talks. In June 2012, during a session with international media outlets, Lee acknowledged that "when we look at exchanges between businesses and people, [Japan] is the country with which South Korea has the biggest ties," but Japan would have to cut its persistent trade surplus with South Korea before talks could resume (Ue 2012). Lee also raised concerns over non-tariff barriers, remarking that "Japan is a country that traditionally has strong non-tariff barriers. If a country with the world's highest competitiveness has non-tariff barriers, even if it opens its market with an FTA, it will effectively remain closed" (*Yonhap News* 2012b). With the likelihood of talks restarting already dim, the Dokdo/Takeshima dispute sealed its fate for the time being. At a briefing on August 27, 2012 by South Korea's lead trade negotiator, Choi Kyung Lim stated that "Soured relations between Korea and Japan pose a difficulty for us. It is difficult to decide whether we will resume the talks unless these problems are resolved" (Kim 2012). The Park administration has shown little inclination to restart talks either.

South Korea and Japan have a strong and growing trade relationship, despite the regular flare-ups over history and territory. In some sectors, their economies are complementary and in others, they are competitors that produce the expected levels of competition and cooperation. Moreover, while there have been fluctuations in trade flows, much of this is due to the ebb and flow of economic factors and less to do with political tensions. Though the strains in relations between Tokyo and Seoul have been palpable, economics often has a momentum that continues in spite of other problem areas.

Investment. An important dimension of Japan–South Korea economic ties is the flow of foreign direct investment (FDI). For South Korea, 2012 brought a sharp increase in Japanese investment in its economy with a first ever peak of close to $4 billion, a 62.6 percent rise from the previous year's total of $2.44 billion.

Japanese investment in 2012 ranked first among foreign investors in South Korea, accounting for 28 percent of its total FDI, followed by the United States ($3.6 billion), Hong Kong ($1.6 billion), Singapore ($1.4 billion), and China ($730 million) (KBS World 2013). For the first three-quarters of 2013, Japanese investment has been substantial but is running behind the previous year's totals.

Table 5.4 Japanese investment in South Korea (2010–2012) (US$ millions)

Year	*FDI*	*Percentage increase*
1995	347	–
1996	405	16.7
1997	172	–57.5
1998	421	144.8
1999	383	–9.0
2000	1,074	180.4
2001	650	–39.5
2002	437	–32.8
2003	333	–23.8
2004	771	131.5
2005	1,736	125.2
2006	1,517	–12.6
2007	1,302	–14.2
2008	2,369	82.0
2009	1,077	–54.5
2010	1,085	1
2011	2,439	125
2012	3,966	62.6
2013	*3,286	–17.1

Source: JETRO *provisional.

In addition to impacting trade, Abe's efforts to devalue the yen have also had an impact on foreign investment. Much of the increase in Japanese FDI prior to Abe's economic policies came from the strong value of the yen relative to the South Korean won, making ROK investments a good deal for Japanese capital. Moreover, when the won was relatively low compared to the yen, exports from Japan were pricey. Japanese firms that operated in South Korea lowered the cost of their goods to ROK consumers.

Abe's efforts to drive down the value of the yen has reduced investment flows. Though Japanese investment may decrease, Han Ki-won, Commissioner of the Korea Trade-Investment Promotion Agency's foreign investment division, argued that, "As many Japanese investors come to Korea with a long-term view, which has little to do with the fluctuations of the foreign exchange rate, I think we will be able to achieve the goal if we continue to do our utmost" (Kim 2013). In fact, Japanese FDI in South Korea has remained strong despite the political tensions and the devalued yen.

The value of the yen, up or down, is only part of the explanation for Japanese FDI in South Korea. Given the strength of key ROK producers, Japanese firms are seeing that it is increasingly beneficial to move production facilities to South Korea. With production facilities there, Japanese firms supplying key component parts and raw materials are closer to their ROK customers. For example, four Japanese material manufacturers—Teijin, Toray, Ibiden, and Sumitomo Chemical—are growing their presence in South Korea to produce lithium-ion batteries and carbon fiber, among other items, to be closer to ROK manufacturers. The move to South Korea is also an effort to address what economic analysts in Japan call the Six Hardships: high corporate taxes; high electricity rates and supply restrictions; environmental regulations; delayed trade liberalization; an over-regulated labor market; and, prior to Abe's election, the high yen. In spite of the devalued yen, moving production to South Korea avoids most of these issues (*Nikkei Business* 2012). Indeed, the South Korean government has built industrial parks to attract Japanese investment that will create a stable supply chain and reduce the country's trade deficit with Tokyo. Japanese producers relocating to South Korea also benefit from South Korea's aggressive pursuit of FTAs. With the U.S. and E.U. FTAs, manufacturing in South Korea also gives Japanese companies these tariff advantages (Mukoyama 2012: 13–14).

The inward flow of FDI from South Korea to Japan has been growing steadily but is far less in the aggregate compared with Japanese investment in South Korea. As shown in Table 5.5, FDI flows have fluctuated since 2004 but have increased from $251 million to a 2012 total of $559 million.

At the time of this writing, the data for 2013 was provisional but based on these numbers, there was a significant drop in ROK investment in Japan for the year. In this category, politics may have played a role. In addition, despite the increased buying power of the Korean won, investments in Japan dropped, possibly because investing in Japan remains a pricey proposition.

Table 5.5 FDI flows from South Korea to Japan

Year	*FDI flow from South Korea to Japan (millions US$)*	*Annual increase (%)*
1995	117	–
1996	56	–52
1997	81	45
1998	19	–77
1999	49	158
2000	48	–2
2001	38	–21
2002	63	66
2003	101	60
2004	251	149
2005	31	–88
2006	108	248
2007	221	105
2008	279	26
2009	255	–0.9
2010	274	7.5
2011	197	–28
2012	559	184
2013	47*	–91.6

Source: Japan External Trade Organization *provisional data.

Pop culture. Another dimension of Japan–South Korea economic ties is the popularity of the Korean Wave, or *hallyu*, in Japan. The Korean Wave began in 2003 with the introduction of the Korean television drama *Winter Sonata* by the Japanese station NHK. The show was a smash hit and was soon followed by other television dramas, K-Pop (teen music, singers and groups that drew a huge youth fanbase), and Korean movies. Adoring Korean Wave fans in Japan generated 70–80 percent of the revenue for South Korean performers. The Japanese fan base for K-Pop is particularly lucrative, producing $5.99 billion annually compared to the $396.5 million in the South Korean market (*Chosun Ilbo* 2012). In 2012, a Korean drama produced by the Korean Broadcasting System (KBS) titled *Love Rain* sold for $10 million to a Japanese station, the second highest price ever for a KBS show (Kwon 2013).

The popularity of the Korean Wave in Japan has declined in the past year or so, in part due to the increasing tension between the two countries. In particular, the events of fall 2012 may have had an impact on Japan's interest in Korean music and drama. According to Park Sung-hyun, a researcher at the Korea Foundation for International Culture Exchange:

> We researched last year how many Japanese people believed *hallyu* was no longer culturally relevant in their country. In March [2012], 15 percent of the 400 people surveyed answered *hallyu* was already moving toward its end. That percentage jumped to 41 percent by November. We interpreted this result as to be linked with President Lee's demand in August last year for the Japanese Emperor to apologize. It seems that historical and political issues can have detrimental effects on the consumption of Korean cultural products abroad.
>
> (Yun 2013)

Lee's actions sparked anti-Korean rallies in Japan calling for the removal of Korean programming from Japanese television stations. Another high-profile incident involved South Korean actor Song Il-guk. On August 15, 2012, the popular actor joined a swim relay to Dokdo to commemorate the end of Japan's occupation after World War II. Song was scheduled to begin filming two police dramas in which he was the lead. However, the Japanese government refused permission for him to enter the country and the project was delayed (Schreiber 2012a). Yamaguchi Tsuyoshi, Vice Minister of Foreign Affairs, told reporters: "Unfortunately, it will not be easy for him to come to Japan from now on" (*Chosun Ilbo* 2012). Finally, at the end of 2012, K-Pop artists were snubbed at one of Japan's largest music events. To celebrate the New Year, NHK hosts Kōhaku Uta Gassen, an annual music competition on New Year's Eve featuring many of the year's most popular singers and bands. South Korean performers have been regular participants in the event but this time, no South Koreans participated. When NHK announced the line-up of individuals and groups to perform, it noted that Korean Wave musicians were not included "considering public opinion and [their] activities this year" (*Japan Times* 2012b), a veiled reference to the support some of these performers have demonstrated for South Korea's position on Dokdo and history. These actions were likely a cautious response by NHK to political tensions of the time and its fears of a viewer backlash if South Korean performers participated. No South Koreans participated in the 2013 Kōhaku Uta Gassen either.

Some of the declining fan base may not be due to politics. It has been ten years since the Korean Wave began in Japan and sustaining popularity for over a decade is difficult in the entertainment business. According to one South Korean analyst, the popularity of *hallyu* may be impacted by the one-way flow of pop culture from Korea to Japan with little moving in the other direction. As result, "too much Korean content could have offended the Japanese when theirs didn't affect Korea" (Yun 2013). Regarding the quality of South Korean entertainment,

> the content of *hallyu* is becoming less impressive than when it first began. The K-pop groups that enter the Japanese market are quite similar and they might be boring Japanese consumers. K-pop is still popular but Korean TV dramas became less popular due to their same old melodramatic storyline.
>
> (Yun 2013)

Another assessment, from a CEO of a managing agency, argued that

> K-Pop has become oversaturated with many idol dance groups advancing into the country. There are too many groups with similar concepts holding the same fan meets and concerts, which will inevitably make the market tired and bored in just a few years.
>
> (*All KPop* 2013)

The declining value of the yen hurts sales of K-Pop music and merchandise as well. One media report noted in June 2013 that

> it wasn't so long ago that everywhere you looked in Japan there were ads for Korean pop groups, cosmetics and health drinks. More people than ever were snapping up Korean language textbooks and, despite territorial squabbles and a few extreme-right noise makers, Japan was positively leaping on anything prefixed by the letter "K."
>
> (Kendall 2013)

Due largely to the decreasing value of the yen, S.M. Entertainment, a major South Korean record company and talent agency, reported losses of more than 70 percent for 2012, a huge drop considering the share of revenue that is generated from overseas markets. According to the editor of a Japan-based Korean entertainment magazine, "some 70 percent of S.M.'s profits come from overseas, with Japan making up close to 50 percent of that. It's only natural that, having relied on the [previously] strong yen so much, the company should take a hit now" (Kendall 2013). Japanese fans simply have less buying power to support K-Pop.

Tourism. Finally, the two countries have a strong economic connection through tourism. In 2011, Japanese tourists were the number one group of visitors to South Korea, spending $800.5 million, a 31.1 percent increase from the previous year's total of $610.6 million. The United States and China came in far behind Japan in second and third place, spending $402.2 million and $149.4 million respectively. Approximately 3.2 million Japanese visited South Korea in 2011, with much of their spending going on entertainment, shopping, and accommodation (VISA 2012: 2–3). South Korean tour companies have assembled packages that appeal to Japanese fans of Korean television dramas, K-Pop, and cooking. The K-Pop tours have included learning the newest dance moves since Japan made dance a mandatory part of the physical education curriculum in middle schools in 2012 (Shin 2012). In addition, 120,000 of these visitors were medical tourists in large part seeking plastic surgery. However, the number of Chinese tourists is increasing rapidly and in July 2012 China surpassed Japan as the number one source of tourist traffic, with 322,917 Chinese visiting South Korea compared to 299,477 tourists from Japan. Both of these numbers are increasing but Chinese visitors have been climbing at a much quicker pace. In August 2012, Chinese visitors rose by 30 percent while Japanese tourists increased by a more modest 6.5 percent (K. Jun 2012). Chinese visitors are also considerably more enthusiastic consumers, spending on average $2,154 compared to the overall tourist average of $1,530 (*Chosun Ilbo* 2014).

For Japan, South Koreans are the second largest source of tourist income behind the United States but the largest source of tourists. In 2010, ROK tourists spent $396.8 million in Japan. The figure dropped in 2011 to $297.6 million in large part due to the March 2011 tsunami and Fukushima nuclear disaster. Despite the row over Takeshima/Dokdo, South Korean tourists to Japan continued to rise for the remainder of that year with 168,138 in October 2012, 183,600 in November, and 199,900 in December 2012, a 20 percent increase over these three months from a year earlier (Japan Tourism Marketing 2013).

In 2013, tourism remained relatively stable and some of the fluctuation can be explained more by economic factors than political ones. As shown in Table 5.6, South Korean tourism during these three months in fall 2013 remained steady with increases in two of the three months and only a modest decline of 5.9 percent in October compared to the same month the previous year. In

Table 5.6 2013 Japan–South Korea tourism: August, September, and October

Japanese tourists to S. Korea			*S. Korean tourists to Japan*		
Month	*Total tourists*	*Percentage change (%)*	*Month*	*Total tourists*	*Percentage change (%)*
August	270,582	–22.0	August	215,498	6.8
September	246,926	–20.1	September	164,500	12.9
October	245,021	–9.2	October	158,300	–5.9

Source: JETRO.

contrast, Japanese tourism showed some decline, including drops of 20 percent or more during two of the three months. While politics may be part of the answer, similar to declines in foreign investment, the decline of the yen may be the more persuasive explanation. Traveling to South Korea has simply become more expensive for Japanese and visiting Japan has become a better bargain for ROK tourists.

Conclusion

The disputes over history and Takeshima/Dokdo are likely to continue for many years. The solutions and leadership necessary for a final solution are difficult to see any time soon. These issues may eventually calm down and recede into the background but if the past is any indicator, it is only a matter of time before some aspect of these disputes once again raises its head and disrupts relations.

Despite the likelihood of periodic disruptions of South Korea–Japan ties, economic relations have continued to grow. Indeed, the realization of what is at stake at the business-to-business and, perhaps, government-to-government level has helped to restrain some of the effects of ROK–Japan animosity and provide a foundation for the relationship to persevere the many difficulties that have occurred and will likely occur in the future. Both countries have built their success in part on following the East Asian Economic Model that depends heavily on exports and economic integration. The growth of Japan–South Korea economic relations has its roots in this model and continues to provide a basis for these two Asian economic leaders to weather the political and historical storms ahead. Economic ties are no guarantee that the two countries will be able to manage these disputes and indeed, governments often have incentives to play up the rows for domestic political benefit. But so long as Japan and South Korea remain close economic partners, these ties will help provide the motivation for leaders in Seoul and Tokyo to manage their differences while they struggle to find long-term solutions to their disagreements.

Note

* The views expressed here are the author's alone and do not represent the official position of the Navy, the U.S. Department of Defense, or the U.S. government.

References

All KPop (2013) "Can the Hallyu wave last another 10 years in Japan?" February 10. Online. Available at: http://forums.allkpop.com/threads/can-the-hallyu-wave-last-another-10-years-in-japan.143504 (accessed February 13, 2013).

BBC (2013) "Japan PM Shinzo Abe visits Yasukuni WW2 shrine," December 26. Online. Available at: www.bbc.co.uk/news/world-asia-25517205 (accessed March 10, 2014).

Chang, J. (2012) "Lee's surprise visit to Dokdo raises tensions with Japan," *Yonhap News*, August 10. Online. Available at: http://english.yonhapnews.co.kr/national/2012/08/10/32/0301000000AEN20120810006451315F.HTML (accessed March 10, 2014).

Chicago Council on Global Affairs, Asan Institute, and the Korea Economic Institute (2012) "Working Paper on the U.S.–ROK alliance." Online. Available at: www.thechicagocouncil.org/UserFiles/File/Task%20Force%20Reports/2012_CCS_US-ROK ConferenceReport.pdf (accessed March 11, 2014).

Chosun Ilbo (2009) "Japan must give up false claims to Dokdo," January 5. Online. Available at: english.chosun.com/site/data/html_dir/2009/01/05/2009010561031.html (accessed March 11, 2014).

Chosun Ilbo (2010) "More maps weaken Japan's claim to Dokdo," February 18. Online. Available at: english.chosun.com/site/data/html_dir/2010/02/18/2010021800465.html (accessed March 11, 2014).

Chosun Ilbo (2012) "Korean stars in Japan in bind over Dokdo," August 27. Online. Available at: english.chosun.com/site/data/html_dir/2012/08/27/2012082701139.html (accessed March 11, 2014).

Chosun Ilbo (2013) "S. Koreans like Japan no better than N. Korea," December 23. Online. Available at: english.chosun.com/site/data/html_dir/2013/12/23/2013122301937.html (accessed March 11, 2014).

Chosun Ilbo (2014) "Many Chinese tourists disappointed by Koreans," January 16. Online. Available at: english.chosun.com/site/data/html_dir/2014/01/16/2014011601657.html (accessed March 11, 2014).

CIA (2013) *World Factbook*. Online. Available at: www.cia.gov/library/publications/the-world-factbook (accessed June 12, 2013).

Constitutional Court of Korea (2011) "Challenge against Act of Omission involving Article 3 of [the Constitution]," August 30. Online. Available at: http://english.ccourt.go.kr/home/english/decisions/rcnt_decision_view.jsp?seq=844&pg=3&sch_sel=&sch_txt=&nScale=15&sch_code=9&actype= (accessed March 11, 2014).

Cumings, B. (1997) *Korea's place in the sun: A modern history*, New York: W.W. Norton.

Dong-A Ilbo (2012) "Korea–Japan free trade talks to resume in year's 2nd half," May 16. Online. Available at: http://english.donga.com/srv/service.php3?biid=2012051640878 (accessed March 11, 2014).

Dudden, A. (2005) *Japan's colonization of Korea: Discourse and power*, Honolulu: University of Hawaii Press.

Fackler, M. (2010) "Japan apologizes to South Korea on colonization," *New York Times*, August 10. Online. Available at: www.nytimes.com/2010/08/11/world/asia/11japan.html?_r=0 (accessed March 11, 2014).

Fern, S. (2005) "Tokdo or Takeshima? The International Law of Territorial Acquistion in Japan–Korea island dispute," *Stanford Journal of East Asian Affairs*, 5(1): 78–89.

Guardian (2013) "Japanese mayor says Second World War 'comfort women' were necessary," May 14. Online. Available at: www.theguardian.com/world/2013/may/14/japanese-mayor-comfort-women (accessed March 11, 2014).

Heo, U. and Roehrig, T. (2014) *South Korea's Rise: Economic Development, Power, and Foreign Relations*, Cambridge: Cambridge University Press.

Jang, J. and Lee, S. (2013) "China, South Korea alarmed as yen slide threatens exporters," *Reuters*, December 30. Online. Available at: www.reuters.com/article/2013/12/30/us-asia-currency-idUSBRE9BT03A20131230 (accessed March 11, 2014).

Japan Times (2012a) "Japanese Emperor must apologize for colonial rule: S. Korean president," August 15. Online. Available at: www.japantimes.co.jp/news/2012/08/15/national/japanese-emperor-must-apologize-for-colonial-rule-s-korean-president (accessed March 11, 2014).

Japan Times (2012b) "Korean singers dropped from yearend NHK music show," November 28. Online. Available at: www.japantimes.co.jp/news/2012/11/28/national/korean-singers-dropped-from-yearend-nhk-music-show/#.UtgP95WA3IU (accessed March 11, 2014).

Japan Times (2013) "Seoul hits senior official's Takeshima Day presence," February 22. Online. Available at: www.japantimes.co.jp/news/2013/02/23/national/seoul-hits-senior-officials-takeshima-day-presence (accessed March 11, 2014).

Japan Tourism Marketing (2013) "Tourism statistics," February. Online. Available at: www.tourism.jp/en/statistics (accessed March 11, 2014).

Jun, K. (2012) "Japanese tourists are no longer no. 1," *Wall Street Journal*, September 27. Online. Available at: http://blogs.wsj.com/korearealtime/2012/09/27/japanese-tourists-are-no-longer-no-1 (accessed March 11, 2014).

Jun, M. (2012) "History intrudes on Korea–Japan security cooperation," Stimson Center, July 13. Online. Available at: www.stimson.org/spotlight/history-intrudes-on-Korea-Japan-security-cooperation (accessed March 11, 2014).

Kang, H. (2005) *Under the black umbrella: Voices from colonial Korea, 1910–1945*, Ithaca, NY: Cornell University Press.

KBS World (2013) "Japan's foreign direct investment in Korea doubles in 2012," February 19. Online. Available at: http://world.kbs.co.kr/english/news/news_Ec_detail.htm?No=96874.

Kendall, P. (2013) "Has Japan's K-Pop bubble burst? Weakening yen hits major Korean record label hard," *Japan Today*, July 13. Online. Available at: www.japantoday.com/category/entertainment/view/has-japans-k-pop-bubble-burst-weakening-yen-hits-major-korean-record-label-hard (accessed March 12, 2014).

Kim, C. (2012) "S. Korea says Japan free trade talks 'difficult' due to tensions," *Bloomberg*, August 27. Online. Available at: www.bloomberg.com/news/2012-08-27/s-korea-says-japan-free-trade-talks-difficult-due-to-tensions.html (accessed March 12, 2014).

Kim, T. (2013) "Invest Korea head behind surging investment from Japan," *Korea Times*, February 20. Online. Available at: www.koreatimes.co.kr/www/news/people/2013/02/178_130846.html (accessed March 12, 2014).

Korea Times (2013) "S. Korea vows stern reaction to Abe's shrine visit," December 30. Online. Available at: http://koreatimes.co.kr/www/news/nation/2013/12/113_148821.html (accessed March 12, 2014).

Kwon, M. (2013) "K-pop stars dominate TV dramas," *Korea Times*, March 3. Online. Available at: www.koreatimes.co.kr/www/news/culture/2013/03/201_131417.html (accessed March 12, 2014).

Lee, K. (1984) *A New History of Korea*, Seoul: Ilchokak Publishers.

Mainichi (2012) "S. Korean president should apologize for remark on emperor: Noda," August 24. Online. Available at: http://mainichi.jp/english/english/newsselect/news/20120824p2g00m0dm024000c.html (accessed March 12, 2014).

Mie, A. (2013) "Record 168 lawmakers visit Yasukuni," Japan Times, April 24. Online. Available at: www.japantimes.co.jp/news/2013/04/24/national/record-168-lawmakers-visit-yasukuni/#.UyMsavldV-4 (accessed March 14, 2014).

Ministry of Foreign Affairs, Japan (1993) "Statement by the Chief Cabinet Secretary Yohei Kono on the result of the study on the issue of 'comfort women'," August 4. Online. Available at: www.mofa.go.jp/policy/women/fund/state9308.html (accessed February 4, 2013).

Ministry of Foreign Affairs, Japan (1995) "Statement by Prime Minister Tomiichi Murayama: 'On the occasion of the 50th anniversary of the war's end'," August 15.

Online. Available at: www.mofa.go.jp/announce/press/pm/murayama/9508.html (accessed February 1, 2013).

Mukoyama, H. (2012) "Japan–South Korea economic relations grow stronger in a globalized environment," *RIM: Pacific Business and Industries*, 12(43): 13–14.

Nikkei Business (2012) "Japanese firms intensify investment in South Korea," March 12. Online. Available at: http://business.nikkeibp.co.jp/article/eng/20120312/229700 (accessed March 12, 2014.

Oliver, C. and Whipp, L. (2011) "S Korea and Japan boost currency swap deal," *Financial Times*, October 19. Online. Available at: www.ft.com/cms/s/0/f57b8216-fa3c-11e0-b70d-00144feab49a.html#axzz2MroloSe7 (accessed March 12, 2014).

Paine, S.C.M. (2005) *The Sino-Japanese War of 1894–1895: Perceptions, power, and primacy*, Cambridge: Cambridge University Press.

Reuters (2012) "FOREX: Yen falls sharply as Japan's Abe vows to weaken it," December 26. Online. Available at: www.reuters.com/article/2012/12/26/markets-forex-idUSL1E8NQ7TI20121226 (accessed March 12, 2014).

Roehrig, T. (2012) "The Dokdo/Takeshima dispute: Caught between two allies," unpublished conference paper.

Schreiber, M. (2012a) "Will the Takeshima dispute break the Korean Wave?" *Japan Times*, September 2. Online. Available at: www.japantimes.co.jp/news/2012/09/02/national/will-the-takeshima-dispute-break-the-korean-wave (accessed March 12, 2014).

Schreiber, M. (2012b) "Japan loses its cool as South Korea heats up," *Japan Times*, December 16. Online. Available at: www.japantimes.co.jp/news/2012/12/16/national/japan-loses-its-cool-as-south-korea-heats-up (accessed March 12, 2014).

Sekiguchi, T. (2012) "Japan PM Noda: Lee visit to Takeshima unacceptable," *Wall Street Journal*, August 10. Online. Available at: http://online.wsj.com/article/BT-CO-20120810-705088.html (accessed March 1, 2013).

Shin, S. (2012) "Notable changes in the trend of Japanese tourists," *Korea Focus*, May 29. Online. Available at: www.koreafocus.or.kr/design2/layout/content_print.asp?group_id=104121 (accessed March 12, 2014).

Song, J. (2014) "Park Geun-hye warns South Korean companies on weaker yen," *Financial Times*, January 6. Available online (subscription required).

Star Online (2014) "Seoul non-committal on action over yen depreciation," January 6. Online. Available at: www.thestar.com.my/Business/Business-News/2014/01/06/Seoul-noncommittal-on-yen-depreciation (accessed March 12, 2014).

Ue, I. (2012) "Lee: Onus on Japan to restart FTA talks," *Daily Yomiuri*, June 13. Online. Available at: www.yomiuri.co.jp/dy/world/T120612005299.htm (accessed March 12, 2014).

United States Embassy—Tokyo, Japan (2013) "Statement on Prime Minister Abe's December 26 visit to Yasukuni Shrine," December 26. Online. Available at: http://japan.usembassy.gov/e/p/tp-20131226-01.html (accessed January 14, 2014).

VISA (2012) "Tourism outlook: South Korea," May. Online. Available at: http://usa.visa.com/download/corporate/_media/south-korea-tourism-outlook-english.pdf (accessed March 12, 2014).

Washington Post (2013) "South Korean soccer player Park Jong-woo to get Olympic medal despite political banner," February 12. Online. Available at: http://articles.washingtonpost.com/2013-02-12/sports/37049136_1_south-korean-soccer-player-park-jong-woo-ioc-executive-board (accessed March 13, 2014).

World Bank (2012) "Exports of goods and services (% of GDP)." Online. Available at: http://data.worldbank.org/indicator/NE.EXP.GNFS.ZS (accessed March 14, 2014).

Yomiuri Shimbun (2013) "71% consider relations with S. Korea 'bad'," April 7.

Yonhap News (2012a) "Lee: Japan's emperor should apologize if he wants to visit S. Korea," August 14. Online. Available at: http://english.yonhapnews.co.kr/national/2012/08/14/53/0301000000AEN20120814008100315F.HTML (accessed March 14, 2014).

Yonhap News (2012b) "Lee urges Japan to make concessions on non-tariff barriers in FTA talks," June 13. Online. Available at: http://english.yonhapnews.co.kr/national/2012/06/13/28/0301000000AEN20120613005600315F.HTML (accessed March 14, 2014).

Yonhap News (2013) "Japan's major newspaper suggests revisit of the Kono Declaration … denies enforcement on comfort women," August 1 [in Korean]. Online. Available at:www.yonhapnews.co.kr/bulletin/2013/08/01/0200000000AKR20130801047800073.html.

Yoshida, R. (2013a) "Takeshima ceremony to draw 18 lawmakers," *Japan Times*, February 19. Online. Available at: www.japantimes.co.jp/news/2013/02/19/national/takeshima-ceremony-to-draw-18-lawmakers (accessed March 14, 2014).

Yoshida, R. (2013b), "Buoyant Abe's true colors emerging," *Japan Times*, April 26. Online. Available at: www.japantimes.co.jp/news/2013/04/26/national/buoyant-abes-true-colors-emerging/#.UrhjCfRDt-4 (accessed March 14, 2014).

Yoshida, R. (2013c) "Suga: Abe not in denial over 'wars of aggression' stance," *Japan Times*, May 11. Online. Available at: www.japantimes.co.jp/news/2013/05/11/national/suga-abe-not-in-denial-over-wars-of-aggression-stance/#.UrhkLPRDt-4 (accessed March 14, 2014).

Yun, S. (2013) "'Hallyu' in Japan at a fork," *Korea Times*, February 12. Online. Available at: www.koreatimes.co.kr/www/news/culture/2013/02/386_130378.html (accessed March 14, 2014).

Part III

Japan

6 The development of Japan's developmental state

Stages of growth and the social costs of energy and export promotion policies

Brian Woodall

Social costs and stages of growth[1]

Japanese economic policy-making is perplexing. For instance, one might have expected that the triple disasters of March 2011—particularly the Fukushima nuclear crisis—would have dictated a restructuring of the nation's energy supply mix, which is critically important to economic prosperity. Yet changes to date have been mostly incremental (Woodall 2013). Likewise, what should have been an innocuous spat over Japanese textile exports in the late 1960s nearly precipitated all-out trade war with the United States, the country's most important trading partner and the guarantor of its national security (Destler *et al.* 1979). On the surface such behavior is puzzling, but it begins to make sense when seen as a side-effect of Japan's *developmental state* approach to industrialization. This helps to explain why state actors and the captains of industry resisted efforts to deviate from a time-tested strategy that capitalizes on sunk investment in energy infrastructure to drive an economy primarily powered by imported fossil fuels and nuclear power. It also provides clues as to why policy-makers and business leaders, who were convinced that resource-deficient Japan must "export or die," went to the brink of trade war to resist limits on textile exports.

The central argument advanced in this chapter is that much of what is puzzling about Japanese economic policy-making derives from institutional hangover, structural rigidities, and path dependence that are by-products of a *developmental state* approach. "In states that were late to industrialize," explains Chalmers Johnson who pioneered the field of study, "the state itself led the industrialization drive, that is, it took on developmental functions" (1982: 19). This contrasts with the primarily regulatory role of the typical "Western" state, and its single-minded drive to promote export-led growth differs from the import-substitution strategy employed in many developing countries. Yet more than three decades after the publication of Johnson's *MITI and the Japanese Miracle* ignited debate over the role of industrial policy in economic growth, the developmental state remains enormously controversial. Reported sightings of developmental states in South Korea,

Taiwan, Singapore, Hong Kong, Malaysia, Thailand, China, Indonesia, and Vietnam have only added fuel to the fire (e.g., Deyo 1987; Wade 1990; Amsden 1992; Evans 1995; Fields 1995; Akyuz *et al.* 1998; Chibber 1999; Doner *et al.* 2005; Lin *et al.* 1996; Vu 2007; and Knight and Ding 2012).[2] If there really is an "East Asian model," then it is essential to understand the Japanese archetype, which has changed in form and function with the passage of time. The analysis that follows aims to explain the causes and consequences of this largely unexplored metamorphosis, laden as it is with theoretical and policy implications.

In the pages that follow, I explain how dynamic tension generated by the social costs of institutional choices punctuated the transformation of Japan's developmental state into four *stages* of progression. For empirical support, I focus intensively on the consequences of institutional choices in two sets of critically important, and inextricably interconnected, policy domains. Providing a stable, inexpensive energy supply is essential to the success of the developmental state's export-led industrialization, especially in the initial stages when the focus is on nurturing heavy and petrochemical industries. With a preferred private sector given an implicit license to pollute, *energy* choices produce inevitable and predictable *environmental* consequences. In other words, just as the developmental state is a "paradise for big industrialists" (Woo-Cumings 1999: 17), it is purgatory for environmentalists. The inextricable interconnectedness of these two policy domains is summed up in former British prime minister Tony Blair's famous quip that they are "two sides of the same coin" (Watt 2006). Likewise, rightly or wrongly, politicians and business leaders in trading partner countries blame job losses and current account deficits on the developmental state's "adversarial" trade practices. In other words, the developmental state's obsessive quest to promote *export-led growth* inevitably invites *strained relations* with major trading partners.

In the section that follows, I outline the essential components of Japan's developmental state approach and propose a dynamic model of institutional change. I then employ a modified case study method to illustrate how the social costs of institutional choices generate tension that drives change in the strategies and structures of the developmental state. By exploring the consequences of institutional choices in two sets of *linked* policy domains—*energy/environmental* and *export promotion/trade* policies—I hope to shed light on the forces that drive the punctuated evolution of the developmental state. Although other cases could have been selected, I chose to analyze these particular linked pairs because they provide exceptional insights into the *domestic* and *international* tensions that drive institutional change. In making this assessment, I examine time-series indices of economic growth (e.g., real growth in gross domestic product, income distribution), energy use (e.g., energy mix, energy efficiency), environmental pollution (e.g., levels of airborne pollutants, CO_2 emissions), and trade flows (e.g., balance of trade, levels of intra-industry trade, export concentration).[3] I summarize my findings and their implications in a brief concluding section.

Elements of the developmental state model

In the immediate aftermath of World War II, Japanese state actors and key industrialists—with an assist from American occupation planners—began assembling the institutional scaffolding for nurturing strategically important export-oriented industries. The anointed industries were those of significant size to permit the achievement of further comparative advantage as the relative supplies and costs of factors of production changed and as learning-curve economies were realized (Yoshikawa and Woodall 1985: 695–696). State actors also considered the costs associated with importing essential materials and transporting finished manufactures to foreign markets. As a result, manufacturers focused their efforts on a narrow set of relatively high value-added exports (Lincoln 1990: 30). Yet the apparent success of these efforts should not be taken to imply omniscience on the part of the state actors who helped devise the high-growth policies; indeed, clearly they were mortal beings (Weinstein and Beason 1996). Moreover, it is essential to understand that "market-oriented private-sector calculations"—*not* government policies in and of themselves—propelled growth (Calder 1993: 16). However, as Dani Rodrik explains, mistakes are inevitable and necessary to good industrial policy, which relies on a "set of mechanisms that recognizes errors and revises policies accordingly" (Rodrick 2013: 4–5). In the final analysis, therefore, the central issue is whether or not the Japanese economic miracle would have been even more resplendent had the state *not* intervened heavily and for an extended period.

What is crucial for the present study is that, in their obsessive quest to promote growth, Japan's developmental state actors chose to ignore the social costs of their institutional choices. This is why unrestrained industrialization was permitted to produce a dangerously polluted domestic environment, and "concentrated downpourings of exports" (*shūchū gōu-teki yushutsu*) and perpetual current account surpluses led to ongoing trade friction. When the social costs of these institutional choices became intolerable, disadvantaged interests rose up to demand that the offending institutions be reformed. As a result, many of the policy tools that transformed Japan into an economic juggernaut were gradually—and, for the most part, grudgingly—decommissioned. Nevertheless, deeply entrenched institutional arrangements do not break down easily and, however illogical, can be a "long time in dying" (Braudel 1982: 32). Hence, institutional hangover accounts for some measure of the developmental coalition's reluctance to fundamentally rethink energy policy in the wake of the March 2011 triple disasters. It also helps to make sense of the interminably conflict-ridden state of Japan's foreign economic relations; although, in recent years, China's rise has shifted the spotlight.

To function properly, the Japanese developmental state requires the fulfillment of three broad conditions. First, a stable policy environment is *sine qua non* to ensure sustained, coherent state-led guidance to a market-driven *capitalist* economy. Crucial to this is an economic bureaucracy staffed by the "best managerial talent available in the system" with the wherewithal to hold the preferred private sector to performance requirements (Johnson 1982: 315). During Japan's high-growth era, the Ministry of International Trade and Industry (today's Ministry of Economy, Trade and Industry) played the role of pilot planning agency, while the perpetually dominant Liberal Democratic Party (LDP) deflected interest group demands that threatened to derail the growth train. Second, broad interaction and intensive bargaining between state actors and the preferred private sector fosters "reciprocal consent" that helps to open "institutionalized channels for the continual negotiation and renegotiation of goals and policies" (Samuels 1987: 260; Evans 1995: 12). Conflict of goals is avoided by the absence of any commitment to social welfare—at least in the early stages of growth—and the exclusion of labor from the political process (Onis 1991: 111, 117). And, third, the success of the developmental state is not realized overnight, and, to endure the hardships of forced march industrialization, it is essential to have the ongoing support of the vast majority of citizens. In Japan's case, the relatively equal income distribution that accompanied the high-speed growth era helped to foster social quiescence that provided critical support for the developmental state (Johnson 1995: 29).

The developmental state is constructed out of institutions, which are, in Douglass North's classic words, "the rules of the game in a society or … humanly devised constraints that shape interaction" (1990: 3). Yet, as James Mahoney and Kathleen Thelen explain, institutions also contain "dynamic tensions and pressure for change" as a result of the unequal distributions of resources and burdens they dictate (2010: 7, 14). By fusing these two views, the dynamic tension produced by the "social costs" of institutional choices becomes clear. Indeed, choices concerning the rules of the game in any given institutional arena inevitably dictate an unequal distribution of costs that may affect interests—domestic or foreign—in adjoining policy domains. "[B]y shifting part of the costs of production to third persons or to the community at large," explains K. William Kapp, private interests are "able to appropriate a larger share of the national product than they would otherwise be able to do" (1978: 15; also Swaney and Evers 1989: 10). In this way, the developmental state's social costs include all direct and indirect losses incurred by domestic and foreign interests as a result of growth-at-all-costs policies.

Stages of growth for Japan's developmental state

Tension generated by the social costs of institutional choices has driven the progression of Japan's developmental state through what, paraphrasing W.W. Rostow, is best understood as a "*sequence of stages* rather than merely a continuum" (Rostow 1959: 2; italics added). During *Stage 1*, a developmental coalition coalesced and set about erecting the *institutional scaffolding* for nurturing strategically important export-oriented industries.[4] These efforts paved the way for *Stage 2*, when *export-led growth* generated by heavy and petrochemical industries produced predictable social costs, including a badly degraded environment and contentious trade relations. As a result, during *Stage 3*, the developmental coalition was obliged to *decelerate* the high-growth machine and *liberalize* some of its more blatantly mercantilist components. When the Japanese developmental state arrived at the frontier of technological and economic advancement—and, in so doing, crossed the threshold into *Stage 4*—state actors were forced to confront the challenges of *globalization* and *sustainable* development. Focusing on the dynamic tension generated by the social costs of institutional choices in the aforementioned linked policy domains, I trace the development of Japan's developmental state and draw attention to the tipping points and critical junctures that preceded each stage in the progression.

Stage 1: Scaffolding for strategic growth, 1945–1954

At the time of Japan's surrender in September 1945, much of the country lay in ruins and it was not clear that resources could be mustered to feed and clothe an exhausted and demoralized citizenry. The ravages of 14 continuous years of war had reduced the country's GNP to a level not seen since the 1920s. Sixty-six major cities had been heavily bombed, destroying between one-quarter and one-third of the nation's wealth. This produced a state of affairs so dismal that it would require nearly two decades for Japan to claw its way out of the ranks of the World Bank's list of "less developed countries" (Dower 1999: 45). Of necessity, therefore, economic recovery became the paramount objective of the economic bureaucrats, industrialists, and U.S. occupation planners who began *erecting the institutional scaffolding* for a developmental state. In so doing, they combined pre-existing institutions and structures with novel departures to create a powerful alternative to the Anglo-American "free enterprise" model of industrialization (Johnson 1985: 64).[5]

Without trying to so do, American occupation authorities played an important part in laying the institutional foundation for a Japanese developmental state. The "New Deal" orientation of many occupation authorities allowed them to tolerate an autonomous state, and, by redistributing the vast holdings of prewar landlords to legions of small-scale farmers, an American-inspired land reform helped foster social harmony. The social quiescence thus produced was further assured by the fact that all Japanese were equally impoverished at war's end. Fatefully, the Americans decided to exempt almost all civil bureaucrats from a purge of militarists, while declaring almost all senior military officials and most prewar cabinet ministers ineligible for public office. This meant that many of the technocrats who were in charge of wartime economic planning remained at their desks (Dower 1999: 325; Johnson 1982: 40–41). In so doing the Americans unwittingly enhanced the influence of an already elite central state bureaucracy, which boasted the country's best and largest source of experienced administrative talent.

Two days before the occupation began, Japanese authorities took it upon themselves to do what the American occupiers would have done anyway, that is, abolish the Ministry of Munitions, the cockpit of wartime state planning and resource mobilization. In its place, they restored the Ministry of Commerce and Industry, which, in 1949, morphed into the Ministry of International Trade and Industry. This is significant in that it suggests that the Japanese economy was "mobilized for war but never demobilized during peacetime" (Johnson 1999: 41). As with all central state officials, bureaucrats at "notorious MITI"—as the ministry came to be known—were required to pass a meritocratic upper civil service examination, and many were alumni of the country's most prestigious universities (Johnson 1982: 283; Koh 1989: 89). These elite bureaucrats locked arms with officials of the former *zaibatsu*—industrial and financial business conglomerates, now reconstituted as bank-centric *keiretsu* groups—which had dominated significant parts of the prewar economy. This preferred private sector made its collective voice heard through the Federation of Economic Organizations (Nippon Keizai Dantai Rengōkai, or Keidanren), a "peak" umbrella organization for industry associations and big business.

American foreign-policy-makers were willing to indulge state-led capitalism in Japan as long as the end result was a vibrant capitalist economy to help "contain" creeping communism. As part of this plan, the U.S. government encouraged large Western companies to provide technology, training, and capital to their Japanese counterparts. In a system akin to the Marshall Plan for Europe, the Americans set aside funds to provide low-cost loans to key Japanese industries such as coal, iron, shipbuilding, fertilizer, and electric power (Schlei 1995: 1). At the same time, Japanese manufactured exports flowed freely into U.S. and other markets, while barriers were allowed to remain in place impeding access to Japan's protected domestic markets. Nevertheless, during this first postwar decade Japan ran a trade surplus only once, that being in 1950 as a result of Korean War procurement.

With rebuilding under way, state actors could now concentrate on forging developmental institutions. Institutional devices were created to channel scarce investment capital into the construction of transportation systems, power plants, schools, and public buildings. In 1947, the Economic Stabilization Board initiated a "Priority Production System" (*Keisha seisan hōshiki*) to marshal critical resources needed for the production of iron and steel, electric power, shipbuilding, and other sectors deemed critical to long-term recovery (Sasada 2012: 124). The developmental coalition was aided in its efforts to plot long-term strategy by the predictability afforded by a fixed exchange rate of 360 yen to the dollar and balanced national budgets. These institutional devices had been adopted upon the recommendation of Detroit banker Joseph Dodge, who visited Tokyo in February 1949 to explore ways to stabilize Japan's economy (Calder 1988: 79; Pempel 1998: 104). Beginning in June 1950, the outbreak of the Korean War set loose a "procurement boom" (*tokuju būmu*) that drove up demand for Japanese manufactures. At the same time, the strategically important sectors were targeted for loans from the Reconstruction Finance Bank and Export-Import Bank, special depreciation for equipment investment, tariff protection, and other policy benefits (Inoue *et al.* 1993: 3–4).

By 1952, when sovereignty was restored, bustling industrial centers had sprouted up around energy and transportation infrastructure in heavily populated—and soon-to-be heavily polluted—urban areas. In the immediate aftermath of Japan's surrender, hydroelectric plants—which had largely escaped Allied bombing—provided 97 percent of electric power generated. By 1954, however, electric power generated at thermal plants accounted for 20 percent of the total. Although official pronouncements continued to assure the continued primacy of domestically produced coal, it soon became clear that imported oil would be the fuel of preference (Hein 1990: 60–61). Not surprisingly, little attention was given to the environmental consequences of rapid industrialization, even though sporadic protests against industrial pollution popped up in prewar times (McKean 1981: 35–42). On the contrary, firms in the favored private sector were, in effect, given an implicit license to pollute, which they set about doing with gusto. When, in 1953, Ministry of Health and Welfare bureaucrats proposed an environmental protection bill, MITI and big business deftly torpedoed the plan (Reich 1984: 381, 383).

Behind the scenes, resentment was festering against institutional arrangements adopted under the U.S. occupation. Prime Minister Yoshida Shigeru was singled out as the principal domestic collaborator in imposing these arrangements, symbolized in the 1947 "Peace Constitution" and the United States–Japan Mutual Security Treaty. In 1954, an "anti-Yoshida alliance" ousted the man who had held the premiership eight-and-a-half years. When the left and right branches of the socialist movement merged in October 1955, Keidanren and other business interests—fearful that the return of a leftist government might sidetrack economic growth—threatened to withhold campaign funding unless the major conservative parties united. With vivid memories of an earlier Socialist-led cabinet's temporary nationalization of the coal industry, business leaders were keen to avoid the return of a leftist government. And so it was that, on November 15, 1955, the Liberal and Democratic parties finally managed to patch over longstanding differences to form a dominant pro-business party whose perpetual dominance would ensure political stability and policy consistency (Okimoto 1989: 181).

Stage 2: Export-led industrialization, 1955–1970

With the basic institutional scaffolding in place and the hegemonic ruling Liberal Democratic Party on guard to deflect unwanted interest group demands, *rapid, export-led industrialization* ensued. In December 1960, Prime Minister Ikeda Hayato announced a plan to double national income (*shotoku baizō keikaku*) by the end of the decade, and the economy responded by growing at an average annual rate of 10.44 percent while per capita GDP ballooned from $564 to $2,004. At this frenetic pace, it took less than seven years to achieve Ikeda's goal, which was supported by a broad-based national consensus of business interests and a citizenry that found joy in the relatively equitable distribution of income that accompanied rising standards of living (Wang 2011: 2). Economic bureaucrats piloted the growth machine, while former government officials assumed key ministerial and political posts and others descended into "second careers" in the private sector. This intermingling of the developmental coalition fostered interaction and communication that helped keep key stakeholders in lock step when it came to plotting economic strategy.

Government and private-sector leaders worked together to identify prospective "sunrise" industries, which, in these years, included the automotive sector, synthetic fibers, shipbuilding, petrochemicals, machinery and parts, and electric equipment. A variety of policy tools was employed, including tax and tariff breaks, import permits for foreign technology, waivers from anti-trust law, and "administrative guidance" through which MITI could "make life thoroughly miserable for any company that defied its wishes" (Johnson 1982: 265, 1999: 48). By steering funds to large-scale industrial borrowers through "policy loans"—with the government serving as "guarantor of last resort"—MITI ensured that the growth industries were supplied with low-cost capital (Zysman 1983; Yoshikawa and Woodall 1985: 695–696). In most cases, these efforts produced a handful of manufacturing giants in a limited number of strategic export-oriented industries and sectors. "Concentrated downpourings of exports" were inevitable by-products of this arrangement, and the trade friction it produced was exacerbated by protected domestic markets and strong bonds among firms in the bank-centric *keiretsu* groups. Taken together, these factors ensured that, as a general rule, Japanese did *not* buy goods they produced themselves, injecting additional tension in relations with trading partners (Lincoln 1990).

Energy policy continued to play a critical role in Japan's economic strategy. In 1956, the Energy Subcommittee of MITI's Industrial Rationalization Council called for the construction of a fleet of large oil tankers to transport fuel for a rapidly expanding industrial plant. As a result, between 1955 and 1970, Japan's reliance on oil surged from 17 percent to 70 percent of the total supply of primary energy, while coal's contribution plunged from 48 percent to 21 percent. This "fluid revolution" was driven by the heat control advantages of oil-fired power plants, the falling price of fuel oil, and fears of unrest by unionized mine workers (Kobori 2009: 2). On this score, the bloody suppression of a labor strike at the Mitsui Company's Miike mine in 1959 and 1960 essentially sealed the demise of domestic coal. And, with most of the easily accessible dam sites already taken, increased reliance on hydropower was not a viable alternative. Thus, by the end of the 1960s, thermal power plants supplied three-quarters of generated electricity.

At the time, few questioned the prudence of a strategy that gambled the nation's energy security on what, in hindsight, was the risky assumption of an unimpeded supply of cheap imported oil. As Arisawa Hiromi, one of the brains behind the Priority Production System, explained: "providing cheap energy engenders immense economic benefit for the nation … [and] interruption of supply is a rare danger. We cannot, because of such a small possibility of danger, demote this cardinal principle of cheap energy to a secondary position" (quoted in Murota and Yano 1993: 103). In the *unlikely* event that shipments of imported oil were to be disrupted, low-cost nuclear power would ensure an adequate energy supply. This option was made possible by the Diet's passage of the

Atomic Energy Basic Law of 1955, paving the way for construction of the country's first nuclear reactor, a research plant that began operations in 1963. The first commercial reactor came on line in 1966, and, within four years, nuclear power plants were supplying 1 percent of the country's electricity. And so it was that state actors and the business community poured enormous investments into building a world-class infrastructure for generating electricity in large centralized thermal and nuclear power plants.

Largely as a consequence of energy policy choices, by the mid-1960s Japan was the world's most polluted country (McKean 1981: 17). In fact, air quality was so bad "that vendors sold oxygen on Tokyo streets, and children wore masks on their way to school in a futile attempt to protect their young lungs" (Schreurs 2002: 36). At the same time, the tragic plight of victims of the "four great pollution diseases"—Minamata and Niigata Minamata Disease, Itai-Itai Disease, and Yokkaichi Asthma—elicited worldwide attention. In a particularly embarrassing moment for the Japanese government, Minamata victims made an emotional appearance at the 1972 Stockholm Conference on the Environment (Mason 1999: 201). Although climate change had yet to become a hot button issue, between 1960 and 1973 per capita carbon dioxide emissions grew by 365 percent, placing Japan in the top tier of the world's emitters of greenhouse gases.

Yet the developmental coalition refused to acknowledge a causal link between industrial pollution and horrific afflictions such as Minamata Disease. In fact, Japanese scientists confirmed in 1956 that that dreaded disease was caused by methyl mercury, which, for decades, had been dumped into the waterways. With no sympathy for the cause within the perpetually ruling party, a grassroots movement burst forth and pressed its demands outside established channels. The movement was buoyed by extensive media coverage and victim-friendly court rulings. After progressive local governments enacted anti-pollution measures and opposition parties in the Diet embraced the environmental cause, the LDP government took note and abruptly reversed course, hoping to co-opt the issue. Yet business interests insisted that the LDP-sponsored 1967 Basic Law for Environmental Pollution Control include a "harmony clause" stipulating that pollution control must not impede economic growth (McKean 1981: 20; Rosenbluth and Thies 2002: 11). When these and other token gestures did not extinguish the protests, the LDP took meaningful action by sponsoring 14 environmental protection laws in what came to be known as the "Pollution Diet" of 1970. One of those laws established a cabinet-level Environment Agency.

Meanwhile, it was only a matter of time before Japan's export promotion policies—including perpetual bilateral trade surpluses with the United States—produced frayed foreign economic relations.[6] That time arrived in the mid-1950s, when resentment in the textile-producing states of Alabama, South Carolina, and Georgia against Japanese-made "one dollar blouses" reached boiling point (Mettler 2010: 214–215; McClenahan 1991: 183). In 1957, despite opposition from MITI and domestic manufacturers, the Japanese government acquiesced to U.S. demands for a five-year voluntary export restraint of cotton textile exports (McClenahan 1991: 183). Yet Japanese textile exports continued to find their way to American markets, and, during the 1968 presidential campaign, candidate Richard M. Nixon promised southeastern textile makers that, if elected, he would remedy the problem. The following year, now President Nixon obtained what he thought was a promise from Prime Minister Satō Eisaku to accept comprehensive export limits on Japanese textiles. Satō later claimed that he made no such promise, but had merely agreed to do his best to honor Nixon's request (Destler *et al.* 1979: 134–135). In fact, MITI and domestic business interests were loath to accept export limits of any kind for fear of unleashing a feeding frenzy that would spill over into other sectors. Thus, the "textile wrangle" became the first major salvo in a series of trade skirmishes.

Stage 3: Deceleration and liberalization, 1971–1989

In August 1971, President Nixon unilaterally removed the dollar from the gold standard, thereby dictating a floating exchange rate for the Japanese yen and other foreign currencies. Then, in October 1973, the Organization of the Petroleum Exporting Countries (OPEC) abruptly raised the producer price of oil and threatened an embargo against America and its allies for supporting Israel in the Yom Kippur War. A U.S. ally with a heavy addiction to imported oil, Japan was stunned by OPEC's action. Coming on top of environmental protests and the LDP's electoral woes, the "Nixon" and "oil" shocks brought an end to high-speed growth, unleashing a scrum among rival domestic groups for a slice of a now static budgetary pie. Moreover, although, at least for the time being, nine out of ten Japanese categorized themselves as "middle class," and the gap between rich and poor was beginning to expand (Murakami 1982: 33).

Having labored in the shadows of elite ex-bureaucrats—such as Ikeda Hayato and Satō Eisaku, both of whom descended from the pinnacle of government officialdom into second careers in politics—the LDP's expanding contingent of "career politicians" eagerly took the helm (Woodall 2014). Their first order of business was increase pork barrel and social welfare spending, which quickly brought an end to the fiscal responsibility and balanced budgets that became policy under the "Dodge Line." Prime Minister Tanaka Kakuei epitomized this new breed of political leader. His plan to "remodel" the Japanese archipelago through a bonanza of highways, island-linking bridges, and other public works projects captivated the nation; until, that is, inflation and exposés of dirty dealing crashed the party. Having endured decades of hardship so that their country could climb the ladder of world economic power, citizens now demanded quality-of-life improvements, including a safe, clean environment. Meanwhile, trading partners grew frustrated with what they perceived to be "unfair" trade practices, including perpetual trade surpluses, export concentration, low levels of intra-industry trade, and barriers to import penetration (Lincoln 1990). In this changed and charged milieu, the developmental coalition was obliged to find ways to *decelerate* the high-growth machine and *liberalize* insulated markets.

In May 1973, the government proclaimed that the economy was "100 percent liberalized," although the credibility of the claim was questioned when it became known that 22 industries were to be "exempted" and would, therefore, continue to receive preferential treatment. With Japanese industry at the technological cutting edge, the preferred private sector now came to view MITI's "guidance" as unwanted meddling by government bureaucrats suffering from a nasty case of institutional hangover. Although a MITI-sponsored high-tech consortium produced excellent results in the Very-Large-Scale Integrated (VLSI) semiconductor program, similar success stories in microelectronics and other advanced sectors were uncommon (Borrus *et al.* 1982; Callon 1995). Meanwhile, the United States and other frustrated trading partners assailed an assortment of allegedly unfair trade practices in Japanese textiles and clothing, telecommunications equipment, steel, machine tools, computers, color televisions, and consumer electronics. Yet the most volatile disputes involved American demands for "local content" in Japanese-made passenger cars, and voluntary export restraints in exports of automobiles and semiconductors (Levinsohn 1997; Prestowitz 1988). These sector-specific disputes further inflamed bilateral relations, which were already strained owing to perpetual Japanese trade surpluses—topping $50 billion per year in the late 1980s—that accounted for about half of America's total deficit.

In a long-term plan issued in 1974, MITI called for efforts to decouple pollution control and economic growth. As a result of this and other efforts, the annual average of sulfur dioxide in the air was cut from 0.034 parts per million to 0.006 ppm between 1970 and 1985. Significant reductions were also realized in nitrogen oxides, carbon monoxide, and suspended particulate matter. Although Japan remained a major emitter of greenhouses gases, per capita emissions remained essentially unchanged even as the economy continued to grow. A second oil shock that accompanied the 1979 Iranian Revolution sent petroleum prices soaring to record levels. In response, the Japanese government sponsored the Energy Conservation Act of 1979 to further encourage the rational use of energy. As a result, the country transformed itself into an energy efficiency "superpower," and, in an ironic twist, Japanese companies became world leaders in the production of pollution-control devices (Stewart and Wilczewski 2009; Pempel 1982: 232).

The oil shocks dictated efforts to diversify Japan's energy supply, even as overall consumption increased by nearly 50 percent. This resulted in a sharp reduction in dependence on oil, whose share of the total energy supply dropped from 72 percent in 1971 to 57 percent in 1989. The resulting void was filled by expanded reliance on liquefied petroleum (LP) gas and nuclear power, whose respective shares of total supply leapt from 1 percent to the 9–10 percent range. Although increased reliance on LP gas did not reduce Japan's dependence on energy imports, it provided an environmentally friendlier fossil fuel alternative to fuel oil. Similarly, although nuclear power produced few airborne pollutants and greenhouse gasses, it came with obvious risks and challenges of its own, especially in a seismically challenged country like Japan. By the close of the 1980s, nuclear power supplied 26 percent of electricity generated (up from only 2 percent in the early 1970s), while reliance on thermal and hydroelectric power declined.

The LDP-led government's deft co-optation of the pollution issue helped to ensure that no green party would appear, as was the case in Germany and elsewhere (Schreurs 2002: 69, 89). This left the environmental movement without a center of gravity, and, therefore, easily marginalized in policy-making debates and elections. Moreover, although the Environment Agency's Director General occupied a seat at cabinet meetings, the Agency remained "institutionally weak" and had to share authority over pollution control with other more powerful ministries (Rosenbluth and Thies 2002: 13). Nevertheless, the 1972 U.N. Conference on the Environment brought international attention to environmental protection, and Japanese leaders took note. Under pressure from the United States to shoulder a bigger share of the burden for the maintenance of the international order, Japan's government grudgingly agreed to become party to the 1987 Montreal Protocol to address stratospheric ozone depletion (Schreurs 2002: 138–139).

Although the economy grew at a modest 4 percent clip—a sharp drop-off from the pre-1973 figure—Japan rebounded from the first oil shock more quickly than other advanced countries. Under the shadow of a perpetual trade surplus with the United States, however, bilateral relations were marred by a series of trade disputes, many of which centered on the manufactures of export-oriented industries nurtured under the developmental state. As part of a larger effort to remedy a perpetual trade deficit, the United States pressed Japan to increase domestic demand (*naiju kakudai*), threatening sanctions if protected domestic markets in agricultural commodities and forestry products, telecommunications equipment, and construction services were not promptly opened (Woodall 1996: 1).

By the mid-1980s, "Japan bashing" (*Nihon tataki*) was *en vogue*, with the most cacophonous cries coming from the United States, then laboring under the expanding weight of "triple deficits" in trade, current accounts, and national budget. At a September 1985 meeting convened in New York's Plaza Hotel, finance ministers of the G-5 countries agreed to devalue the dollar in relation to the yen and other currencies. Almost overnight the value of Japanese assets began appreciating wildly. In late 1989, when the resulting "bubble economy" (*baburu keizai*) reached its hyper-inflated peak, the Nikkei stock index stood at more than three times its value at the time of the Plaza Accord. Similarly, the estimated value of Japanese land ballooned to quadruple that of the entire United States, a country more than 25 times larger in size (Woodall 1992: 115). The United States and other foreign governments mobilized to demand that Japan dismantle "structural impediments"—such as a Byzantine distribution system and cross-shareholding within *keiretsu* groups—impeding efforts on the part of foreign firms to heed the Sirens' calls to establish a presence in Japan's now fantastically lucrative domestic markets (Schoppa 1997).

Stage 4: Sustainable globalization, 1990 and beyond

Just as the "bubble economy" was bursting, the fall of the Berlin Wall dispelled much of the ideological and institutional gridlock that had characterized the Cold

War, clearing the way for countries to focus on cross-border challenges. For Japan to prosper in an increasingly interdependent world economy, state actors understood that they had to create incentives for innovation and investment, and enhance the quality of life for citizens empowered by social media and other digital technology. They also had to search for ways to maintain economic prosperity while addressing global threats such as climate change, which soared to the top of world leaders' to-do lists following the 1992 "Earth Summit" in Rio de Janeiro. Inasmuch as the finite supply and environmental consequences of fossil fuels had been long understood, the eventual need for countries like Japan to embrace sustainable development was both predictable and capable of deduction (Smil 1994: 217). With Japan in the upper echelon of the world's CO_2 emitters, a smattering of domestic voices called for action to confront global warming. In this altered context, Japan's developmental state actors now found themselves casting about for ways to address the challenges of *globalization* and *sustainable development*.

Unfortunately, the institutions and structures that transformed Japan into the world's second richest economy had rigidified, and a once unwavering political system was now beset with instability and immobilism. Although, as Steven K. Vogel convincingly demonstrates, deregulation produced "no net loss of government control," the perception on the street was that Japan's economic bureaucracy had lost some of its vigor (1996:2). However, a series of incidents involving ineptitude and corruption *did* strip away the fig leaf concealing the reality that lay beneath the myth of bureaucratic infallibility. As a consequence, it became more difficult for ministries to recruit the best and brightest university graduates. Whereas, until the early 1990s, nearly 200 graduates each year from Tokyo University's prestigious Faculty of Law elected to become career bureaucrats, in 2006 only 68 did (Nariai 2007). Meanwhile, a succession of ephemeral governments proved unable to right a badly listing economic ship, as companies struggled to compete with foreign competitors not burdened with a workforce guaranteed lifetime employment. In addition, powerful politicians known as "policy specialists" (*zoku giin*) came to play the part of feudal lords in rent-seeking subgovernments—such as the "postal lobby" and rice farmers—that ferociously guarded their fief-like sources of profit and privilege in a now hopelessly fragmented policy-making environment (Woodall 2014). As a result, Japan drifted aimlessly through consecutive "lost decades" (*ushinawareta jūdai*) of political instability and economic malaise, with average annual growth below the 1 percent level.

The September 11th terrorist attacks sent oil prices skyrocketing and refocused attention on a national energy strategy that relied heavily on fossil fuels imported from politically unstable regions. This sparked efforts to diversify supply by expanding imports of Russian oil and natural gas, and upped the ante in the territorial dispute with China over control of potential energy reserves near the Senkaku (Diaoyu) Islands. Nevertheless, no serious thought was applied to giving renewables a significant role in the fuel mix, as was happening in Denmark and the European Union (Nygard 2013; Huberty 2013). Although

Japan's 2010 Basic Energy Plan envisioned a somewhat expanded reliance on renewables (from 6 to 13 percent of the energy mix), it projected a much bigger role for nuclear power (from 10 to 24 percent) to be realized through the construction of 14 new nuclear plants (Duffield and Woodall 2011: 3743). While the Fukushima crisis postponed plans for new plant construction, the immediate response to the loss of nuclear power from the crisis and the subsequent shutdown of all remaining reactors was to increase reliance on oil and LP gas. This meant that fossil fuels and nuclear power continued to supply about 94 percent of domestic primary energy, and, even as the economy languished, energy consumption expanded by 13 percent between 1990 and 2010.

The lost decades did see some meaningful developments in environmental policy. On the international front, the government directed official development assistance to China to curb acid rain, and the country hosted the 1997 negotiations for the Kyoto Protocol that produced a binding international agreement to reduce greenhouse gas emissions. Domestically, the Diet passed the 1993 Basic Law on the Environment and the Special Measures Law for Renewable Energy, which took effect in July 2012. The latter created a feed-in tariff requiring utility companies to purchase energy generated by solar, wind, geothermal, and other renewable sources at above-market rates. In 2001, the Environment *Agency* became the Environment *Ministry* as part of a reorganization of government organs, signaling, at least symbolically, the elevated status of ecological concerns in the hierarchy of government priorities (Woodall 2014). Meanwhile, Japanese automakers came to dominate a rapidly expanding market for hybrid vehicles, and the innovative "Rooftop Program" became the world's first large-scale development of photovoltaic technology. In September 2009, shortly after his Democratic Party of Japan temporarily unseated the LDP, Prime Minister Hatoyama Yukio boldly pledged that Japan would reduce greenhouse gas emissions to 75 percent of 1990 levels by 2020.

Yet, at the end of the day, the lost decades stalled efforts to address the challenges of globalization and sustainable development. Some saw the prolonged economic malaise and political instability as indisputable proof of the defectiveness of the developmental state model and the superiority of the "Washington Consensus" with its calls for trade liberalization, privatization, and other neoclassical prescriptions (e.g., Williamson 2004). This view even gained currency on the domestic front, where expanding income inequality threatened to explode the shared perception of Japan as one giant middle class (Murakami 1982; Satō 2000). Although much of the raw edge had been taken off Japanese trade practices, multilateral and bilateral negotiations continued, leading to a partial opening of the long-protected rice market, abolition of the Large Retail Stores Law, and further deregulation in government procurement, automobiles, and semiconductors. While the bilateral trade surplus with the United States continued to grow—averaging $66 billion per annum from 1991 through 2013—the principal object of American ire now became China.

Even as world leaders applauded Prime Minister Hatoyama's bold pledge, key domestic stakeholders described it as "unrealistic" and a "burden on the people" (Ryall 2009). Business leaders warned that increased reliance on renewables would force manufacturers to move operations overseas, while utility companies instructed their employees to fill seats at hearings to discuss restarting nuclear power plants and to send emails expressing support for atomic power. Although the Fukushima crisis generated calls to replace nuclear energy with a greatly enhanced reliance on renewables, the environmental movement and anti-nuclear interests remained hopelessly divided. This state of affairs paved the way for the LDP's return to power in the December 2012 elections. A similar outcome was seen in the February 2014 Tokyo gubernatorial election, in which the LDP-endorsed candidate prevailed, in part, because his two main rivals split the anti-nuclear vote. Following the Tokyo gubernatorial triumph, the government of Prime Minister Abe Shinzō renewed efforts to restore nuclear power as "a base-load power source" by reactivating idle reactors upon confirmation of their safety by the Nuclear Regulation Authority (Government Energy Policy 2014).

The development of the developmental state

Many puzzling aspects of Japanese economic policy-making are, in fact, by-products of a developmental state approach to industrialization. During the early postwar decades, the developmental coalition that served as the board of directors for "Japan, Incorporated" ruthlessly subordinated all other objectives "to the singular pursuit of increased production, increased exports, and national wealth" (Rosenbluth and Thies 2002: 2). Yet long after the dream of an economic miracle became reality, many elements of Japan's high-growth system remained in operation. By the late 1980s, it was clear that new tools would have to be found to steer an economy driven by cutting-edge high-technology industry. However, novel departures in economic strategy were impeded by institutional hangover, structural rigidities, and path dependence that had accumulated over the course of decades.

Numerous studies have shown that, once established, institutions are "sticky" and difficult to change. Yet Japan's developmental state has been transformed over time. This transformation was punctuated by periodic bursts of institutional reform enacted by the developmental coalition in response to pressure from disadvantaged interests, such as those displayed in the linked domains of *energy/environmental* and *export promotion/trade* policies. As a result, Japan's developmental state has progressed through four stages, each with its own challenges, institutional adaptations, and consequences. During *Stage 1*, a developmental coalition coalesced and erected the institutional scaffolding to foster export-led growth. This set the stage for *Stage 2* in which miraculous rates of growth persisted until exogenous "shocks" created an opening that was seized by environmentalists and frustrated trading partners to force state actors to undertake institutional reform. In *Stage 3*, although government and industry took the lead in decoupling pollution control from economic growth, Japan's leaders struggled to cope with the panoply of problems created by a hyper-inflated economy. In the early 1990s, just as the bubble burst, state actors were beginning to contemplate the challenges of globalization and sustainable development. It is unclear whether or not post-March 2011 institutional adaptations will re-start Japan's progression through *Stage 4*, where it has remained stalled amidst immobilist politics and rudderless leadership since the onset of the lost decades.

Writing in 1950, Kapp observed that the "political history of the [previous] 150 years can be interpreted as a revolt of large masses of people ... against social costs" (1978: 15–16). Similarly, the history of Japan's developmental state over the past seven decades can be interpreted as a series of uprisings by domestic and foreign interests disadvantaged under the existing institutional arrangements. Clearly, therefore, the nexus between social costs and institutional change deserves deeper inquiry over a wide range of policy cases and time periods. Understanding the evolution of the developmental state is critically important for the East Asian states that have adapted the model to suit local conditions, especially South Korea and China, which are progressing through stages that broadly resemble those traversed by the Japanese state at comparable levels of economic attainment (Woodall and Han 2014). If so, leaders of these countries ought to take heed of the Japanese experience to prepare for what may lie ahead, while Japanese leaders could take lessons from what their East Asian neighbors are doing. In any event, it would be foolish for world leaders to dismiss the possibility that an East Asian *model*—whose archetype was "made in Japan"—might represent an alternative to the free-market system peddled by proponents of the Washington Consensus.

Notes

1 I am grateful to Meg McKean, Penny Prime, Fei-ling Wang, Shiping Hua, and Siqi Han for their comments and suggestions on various incarnations of this chapter.

2 Routley (2012) provides a quite thorough review of the vast literature on the developmental state approach, while Uriu (2013) explores its rise, fall, and rebound.

3 Data used in this study were primarily drawn from the following sources: Ministry of Internal Affairs and Communications (MIAC), "Historical Statistics of Japan" (www.stat.go.jp/english/data/chouki); MIAC, "Japan Statistical Yearbook 2014" (www.stat.go.jp/english/data/nenkan/index.htm); U.S. Census Bureau, "Trade in Goods with Japan" (www.census.gov/foreign-trade/balance/c5880.html); U.S. Energy Information Administration, "International Energy Statistics" (www.eia.gov); and the World Bank's "World Development Indicators" (http://data.worldbank.org/indicator).

4 It is beyond the scope of the present study to consider the *preconditions* for the emergence of Japan's developmental state. Indeed, the "democratic" post-1945 capitalist developmental state was forged in a crucible fashioned in a "hard authoritarian" prewar milieu in which state actors and their private-sector allies (officials of the *zaibatsu*) dominated the economy. The important role of preconditions, timing, contingency, and path dependence in shaping the Japanese, Korean, and Chinese developmental states is explored in Woodall (forthcoming 2015).

5 Johnson (1982) traces the roots of the developmental state back to the 1926 founding of the Ministry of Commerce and Industry. However, the case could be made that it originated in the state-led effort to "catch up with and surpass the Western countries" (*ōbei ni oitsuke oikose*) that guided policy following the 1868 Meiji Restoration.

6 Between 1965 and 2010, imports from the United States exceeded exports only twice, in 1967 and 1975.

References

Agency for Natural Resources and Energy (Japan) (2010) *Energy in Japan 2010*. Tokyo: Ministry of Economy, Trade, and Industry.

Akyuz, Yilmaz, Ha-Joon Chang, and Richard Kozul-Wright (1998) "New Perspectives on East Asian Development," *Journal of Development Studies*, 34 (6), 4–36.

Amsden, Alice (1992) *Asia's Next Giant: South Korea and Late Industrialization*. New York: Oxford University Press.

Borrus, Michael, James Millstein, and John Zysman (1982) *U.S.–Japanese Competition in the Semi-Conductor Industry*. Berkeley: Institute of International Studies Press.

Braudel, Fernand (1982) *On History* (translated by Sarah Matthews). Chicago: University of Chicago Press.

Broadbent, Jeffrey (1998) *Environmental Politics in Japan: Networks of Power and Protest*. New York: Cambridge University Press.

Calder, Kent E. (1988) *Crisis and Compensation: Public Policy and Political Stability in Japan, 1949–1986*. Princeton, NJ: Princeton University Press.

Calder, Kent E. (1993) *Strategic Capitalism, Private Business and Public Purpose in Japanese Industrial Finance*. Princeton, NJ: Princeton University Press.

Callon, Scott (1995) *Divided Sun: MITI and the Breakdown of Japanese High-tech Industrial Policy, 1975–1993*. Stanford, CA: Stanford University Press.

Chibber, Vivek (1999) "Building a Developmental State, The Korean Case Reconsidered," *Politics and Society*, 27 (3), 309–346.

Destler, I.M., Haruhiro Fukui, and Hideo Satō (1979) *The Textile Wrangle: Conflict in Japanese–American Relations, 1969–1971*. Ithaca, NY: Cornell University Press.

Deyo, Fredric (ed.) (1987) *The Political Economy of the New Asian Industrialism*. Ithaca, NY: Cornell University Press.

Doner, Richard F., Bryan Ritchie, and Daniel Slater (2005) "Systemic Vulnerability and the Origins of the Developmental State, Northeast and Southeast Asia in Comparative Perspective," *International Organization*, 59, 327–361.

Dower, John W. (1999) *Embracing Defeat, Japan in the Wake of World War II*. New York: W.W. Norton.

Duffield, John S., and Brian Woodall (2011) "Japan's New Basic Energy Plan," *Energy Policy*, 39 (April), 3741–3749.

Evans, Peter B. (1995) *Embedded Autonomy: States and Industrial Transformation*. Princeton, NJ: Princeton University Press.

Fields, Karl J. (1995) *Enterprise and the State in Korea and Taiwan*. Ithaca, NY: Cornell University Press.

"Government Energy Policy to Have Nuclear Base" (2014) *Yomiuri Shimbun*, February 11.

Hein, Laura E. (1990) *Fueling Growth: The Energy Revolution and Economic Policy in Postwar Japan*. Cambridge, MA: Harvard East Asian Monographs.

Huberty, Mark (2013) "The European Union, Green Growth without Borders, Transnational Energy Systems and the Politics of Transformation." In John Zysman and Mark Huberty (eds.), *Can Green Sustain Growth? From the Religion to the Reality of Sustainable Prosperity*. Stanford, CA: Stanford University Press, pp. 107–124.

Inoue, Ryuichiro, Hiromasa Kohama, and Shujiro Urata (1993) *Industrial Policy in East Asia*. Tokyo: JETRO.

Johnson, Chalmers (1982) *MITI and the Japanese Miracle: The Growth of Industrial Policy, 1925–1975*. Stanford, CA: Stanford University Press.

Johnson, Chalmers (1985) "Political Institutions and Economic Performance: The Government–Business Relationship in Japan, South Korea, and Taiwan." In Robert A. Scalapino, Seizaburo Sato, and Jusuf Wanandi (eds.), *Asian Economic Development: Present and Future*. Berkeley: Institute of East Asian Studies, University of California at Berkeley, pp. 63–89.

Johnson, Chalmers (1995) *Japan: Who Governs? The Rise of the Developmental State*. New York: W.W. Norton.

Johnson, Chalmers (1999) "The Developmental State, Odyssey of a Concept." In Meredith Woo-Cumings (ed.), *The Developmental State*. Ithaca, NY: Cornell University Press, pp. 32–60.

Kapp, K. William (1978 [1950]) *The Social Costs of Business Enterprise*. Nottingham: Spokesman.

Knight, John, and Sai Ding (2012) *China's Remarkable Economic Growth*. Oxford: Oxford University Press.

Kobori Satoru (2009) "Japan's Energy Policy During the 1950s: Reasons for the Rapid Switch from Coal to Oil." Paper presented at the Asia-Pacific Economic and Business History Conference. Available at: http://apebhconference.files.wordpress.com/2009/09/kobori1.pdf (accessed September 15, 2014).

Koh, B.C. (1989) *Japan's Administrative Elite*. Berkeley: University of California Press.

Kushida, Kenji E. (2012) *Japan's Fukushima Nuclear Disaster: Narrative, Analysis, and Recommendations*. Stanford, CA: Stanford University, Shorenstein APARC Working Paper Series.

Levinsohn, James (1997) "Carwars: Trying to Make Sense of U.S.–Japan Trade Frictions in the Automobile and Automobile Parts Markets." In Robert C. Feenstra (ed.), *The Effects of U.S. Trade Protection*. Chicago: University of Chicago Press.

Lin, Justin Yifu, Fang Cai, and Zhou Li (1996) *The China Miracle: Development Strategy and Economic Reform*. Hong Kong: The Chinese University Press of Hong Kong.

Lincoln, Edward J. (1990) *Japan's Unequal Trade*. Washington, DC: The Brookings Institution.

McClenahan, William (1991) "The Growth of Voluntary Export Restraints and American Foreign Economic Policy, 1956–1969," *Business and Economic History*, 20, 180–190.

McKean, Margaret A. (1981) *Environmental Protest and Citizen Politics in Japan*. Berkeley: University of California Press.

Mahoney, James, and Kathleen Thelen (2010) "A Theory of Gradual Institutional Change." In James Mahoney and Kathleen A. Thelen (eds.), *Explaining Institutional Change, Ambiguity, Agency, and Power*. Cambridge: Cambridge University Press, pp. 1–37.

Mason, Robert T. (1999) "Whither Japan's Environmental Movement? As Assessment of Problems and Prospects at the National Level," *Pacific Affairs*, 72 (2, Summer), 187–207.

Mettler, Meghan Warner (2010) "Gimcracks, Dollar Blouses, and Transistors: American Reactions to Imported Japanese Products, 1945–1964," *Pacific Historical Review*, 79, 202–230.

Murakami, Yasusuke (1982) "The Age of New Middle Mass Politics: The Case of Japan," *Journal of Japanese Studies*, 8 (1), 29–72.

Murota, Y., and Y. Yano (1993) "Japan's Policy on Energy and the Environment," *Annual Review of Energy and the Environment*, 18, 89–135.

Nariai Osamu (2007) "A New Business Model for the Civil Service," *Japan Echo*, 34. Available at www.japanecho.com/sum/2007/340507.html (accessed February 1, 2014).

North, Douglass C. (1990) *Institutions, Institutional Change, and Economic Performance*. Cambridge: Cambridge University Press.

Nygard, Jakob Riiskjaer (2013) "Denmark, Country Case Analysis." In John Zysman and Mark Huberty (eds.), *Can Green Sustain Growth? From the Religion to the Reality of Sustainable Prosperity*. Stanford, CA: Stanford University Press, pp. 89–106.

Okimoto, Daniel I. (1989) *Between MITI and the Market: Japanese Industrial Policy for High Technology*. Stanford, CA: Stanford University Press.

Onis, Ziya (1991) "The Logic of the Developmental State," *Comparative Politics*, 24 (1), 109–126.

Pempel, T.J. (1982) *Policy and Politics in Japan: Creative Conservatism*. Philadelphia, PA: Temple University Press.

Pempel, T.J. (1998) *Regime Shift: Comparative Dynamics of the Japanese Political Economy*. Ithaca, NY: Cornell University Press.

Prestowitz, Clyde V. (1988) *Trading Places: How We Are Giving Our Future to Japan and How to Reclaim It*. New York: Basic Books.

Reich, Michael R. (1984) "Mobilizing for Environmental Policy in Italy and Japan," *Comparative Politics*, 16 (4), 379–402.

Rodrik, Dani (2013) "Green Industrial Policy." Unpublished paper. School of Social Science, Institute of Advanced Study, Princeton University. Available at www.sss.ias.edu/publications/economicsworking (accessed January 28, 2014).

Rosenbluth, Frances M., and Michael F. Thies (2002) "The Political Economy of Japanese Pollution Regulation," *American Asian Review*, 20 (1), 1–32.

Rostow, W.W. (1959) "The Stages of Economic Growth," *The Economic History Review*, 12 (1), 1–16.

Routley, Laura (2012) "Developmental States, A Review of the Literature," *ESID Working Paper No. 3*. Available at www.effective-states.org/_assets/documents/esid_wp_03_routley.pdf.

Ryall, Julian (2009) "New Japanese PM Pledges Deep Greenhouse Gas Cuts," *The Telegraph*, September 7. Available at: www.telegraph.co.uk/earth/earthnews/6148559/New-Japanese-PM-pledges-deep-greenhouse-gas-cuts.html (accessed November 14, 2013).

Samuels, Richard J. (1987) *The Business of the Japanese State: Energy Markets in Comparative and Historical Perspective*. Ithaca, NY: Cornell University Press.

Samuels, Richard J. (2013) *3.11: Disaster and Change in Japan*. Ithaca, NY: Cornell University Press.

Sasada Hisanori (2012) *The Evolution of the Japanese Developmental State: Institutions Locked in by Ideas*. London: Routledge.

Satō Toshiki (2000) *Fubyōdō shakai Nihon, sayonara sōchūryū [Japan's Unequal Society, Farewell to One Big Middle Class]*. Tokyo: Chūō kōron shinsha.

Schlei, Norbert A. (1995) "Japan's 'M-Fund' Memorandum, January 7, 1991," *Japan Policy Research Institute Working Paper No 11*. Available at: www.jpri.org (accessed February 2, 2014).

Schoppa, Leonard J. (1997) *Bargaining with Japan: What American Pressure Can and Cannot Do*. New York: Columbia University Press.

Schreurs, Miranda A. (2002) *Environmental Politics in Japan, Germany, and the United States*. Cambridge: Cambridge University Press.

Smil, Vaclav (1994) *Energy in World History*. Boulder, CO: Westview Press.

Stewart, Devin T., and Warren Wilczewski (2009) "How Japan Became an Efficiency Superpower: Lessons for U.S. Energy Policy under Obama," *Policy Innovations* (February 3).

Swaney, James A., and Martin A. Evers (1989) "The Social Cost Concepts of K. William Kapp and Karl Polanyi," *Journal of Economic Issues*, 23 (1), 7–33.
Uriu, Robert (2013) "Idea Wars: The Rise, Fall, and Rebound of the East Asia Challenge to Development Orthodoxy." Paper presented at the 3rd Annual Lang Seminar, "The Japanese Political Economy," University of Louisville (March 23).
Vogel, Steven K. (1996) *Freer Markets, More Rules: Regulatory Reform in Advanced Industrial Countries*. Ithaca, NY: Cornell University Press.
Vu, Tuong (2007) "State Formation and the Origins of Developmental States in South Korea and Indonesia," *Studies in Comparative International Development*, 41 (4), 27–56.
Wade, Robert (1990) *Governing the Market, Economic Theory and the Role of Government in East Asian Industrialization*. Princeton, NJ: Princeton University Press.
Wang, Feng (2011) "The End of 'Growth with Equity'? Economic Growth and Income Inequality in East Asia," *Analysis from the East-West Center No. 101* (July).
Watt, Nicholas (2006) "Blair Warns of Climate Change 'Tipping Points'," *The Guardian*, October 20.
Weinstein, David E., and Dick Beason (1996) "Growth, Economies of Scale, and Targeting in Japan (1955–1990)," *Review of Economics and Statistics*, 78 (2), 286–295.
Williamson, John (2004) "A Short History of the Washington Consensus." Paper commissioned by Fundación CIDOB for the conference, "From the Washington Consensus towards a new Global Governance," Barcelona, September 24–25. Available at www.iie.com/publications/papers/williamson0904-2.pdf (accessed February 11, 2014).
Woo-Cumings, Meredith (1999) "Introduction: Chalmers Johnson and the Politics of Nationalism and Development." In Meredith Woo-Cumings (ed.), *The Developmental State*. Ithaca, NY: Cornell University Press, pp. 1–31.
Woodall, Brian (1992) "The Politics of Land in Japan's Dual Political Economy." In John O. Haley and Kozo Yamamura (eds.), *Land Issues in Japan: A Policy Failure?* Seattle: The Society for Japanese Studies, pp. 113–148.
Woodall, Brian (1996) *Japan under Construction: Corruption, Politics, and Public Works*. Berkeley: University of California Press.
Woodall, Brian (2013) "Japan, Energy Efficiency Paragon, Green Growth Laggard." In John Zysman and Mark Huberty (eds.), *Can Green Sustain Growth? From the Religion to the Reality of Sustainable Prosperity*. Stanford, CA: Stanford University Press, pp. 150–169.
Woodall, Brian (2014) *Growing Democracy in Japan: The Parliamentary Cabinet System Since 1868*. Lexington: University of Kentucky Press.
Woodall, Brian (2015) *The Development of the East Asian Developmental State: The Politics of Energy and Environmental Policy in Japan, South Korea, and China*. Forthcoming.
Woodall, Brian, and Siqi Han (2014) "Stages of Growth in the Developmental State, Social Costs and Change in Japan, South Korea, and China." Paper presented at the Annual Meeting of the Southeast Conference of the Association for Asian Studies, Duke University, Durham, NC, January 18.
Yoshikawa, Akihiro, and Brian Woodall (1985) "The Venture Boom and Japanese Industrial Policy: Promoting the Neglected Winners," *Asian Survey*, 25 (June), 692–714.
Zysman, John (1983) *Governments, Markets, and Growth: Financial Systems and Politics of Industrial Change*. Ithaca, NY: Cornell University Press.

7 A tale of two capitalisms

Developmentalism, neoliberalism, and the Japanese postal system

Patricia L. Maclachlan

For many years, the postal system has served as a battleground of sorts between the proponents of two competing visions of Japan's economic future. On one side stands a diverse and loosely organized network of conservative politicians, economists, and business leaders who view the postal services as an impediment to financial and political reform and, in turn, Japan's effective integration into the global economic order. Arrayed against them is a more tightly knit alliance of politicians, bureaucrats, and vested interests that vigorously defends the post office as an invaluable vestige of Japan's distinctive model of economic development. By the mid-2000s, the battle for the post office grew so intense that it threatened to bring down the government of the day. Today, the conflict still simmers—and in ways that speak volumes about the tenacity of "traditional" economic values and political institutions in twenty-first century Japan.

In this chapter, I analyze the politics of postal reform as a case study of the broader clash between developmentalism and neoliberal economics in contemporary Japan. What role did the postal services play in the context of state-led economic development? How can we explain the staying power of interest groups that evolved out of the services—and that remain a significant brake on neoliberal reform? How, moreover, has the political system negotiated conflict between vested interests connected to the postal services and advocates for neoliberal change, and how have the results of those conflicts been reflected in public policy? In answering these and related questions, I provide a snapshot of the postal services not only as a contributor to and reflection of the country's distinctive approach to development, but also as one of contemporary Japan's "stickiest" sets of political-economic institutions.

The postal services and the developmental state

The scope of the postal system's contributions to the evolution and accomplishments of Japanese developmentalism has never been fully understood. While scholars have long acknowledged the significance of the postal financial services in empowering the state to fulfill many of its developmental goals (see, e.g., Calder 1990; Cargill and Yoshino 2003; Johnson 1982; Rosenbluth 1989), less well known has been the postal system's overall impact on the development of Japan's activist state, the private sector, and even social welfare objectives.

If any one dimension of the postal system stands out as integral to developmentalism, it is the postal savings system. Established in 1875, several years before the appearance of a viable commercial banking system, the postal savings system offered ordinary Japanese the nation's first safe—deposits were backed by a government guarantee—and convenient haven for their hard-earned cash. In so doing, the system helped instill the virtues of saving and thrift into the population (Garon 2011), values that were at the heart of the high savings rates that enabled bank-financed corporate development.

Together with the postal insurance system, postal savings served as the main source of funds for what in 1953 became formally known as the Fiscal Investment and Loan Program (FILP), or Japan's "second budget." As Park explains, the FILP functioned as a vast reservoir of funds that the state could invest more or less at its discretion without significantly raising taxes or straining the official budget (Park 2011: 4). From the late Meiji period (1868–1912) through the end of World War II, the government invested postal funds in a variety of projects geared toward the expansion of strategic industries and the country's military infrastructure. After the American occupation (1945–1952), funds were redirected toward the reconstruction of coal mining, iron and steel, and shipbuilding. During the rapid growth era (*c.*1960–1973), FILP funds were focused on the development of potential growth industries that would help Japan "catch up" to the West: oil refining, machine tools, nuclear power generation, and the like (see Maclachlan 2011: 163; Scher and Yoshino 2004: 126). As such, FILP investments were key to the effective fulfillment of the state's various industrial policies.

The postal system contributed to developmentalism in a number of other ways, including modern state building. During the early Meiji period, state officials looked to the rapid expansion of the postal network as a mechanism for consolidating Japanese territory and extending the state's reach to the very grassroots level of society (Hunter 1976: 116–118; Maclachlan 2011: 58; Yūseishō 1971: 132). To pull this off, the state recruited well-known local "men of influence" (*meibōka*) to administer—without pay, before 1945—postal services at the local level. These "special" or "commissioned" postmasters (*tokutei yūbinkyokuchō*) went on to become important intermediaries between the people and the state. Although no hard data is available to support this point, the local postmaster's status, like that of other *meibōka*, as a *respected* personage with deep roots in his community no doubt fueled popular identification with and trust in centralized state authority (Maclachlan 2004, 2011: 61–63; Westney 1987). And since it was the local postmaster who collected the bulk of funds in the postal savings and insurance systems, he can also be credited for contributing to the high savings rates that were so essential to the state's pursuit of developmental goals.

The postal system also promoted private-sector firms. Along with the postal savings system, the Meiji post office introduced a money order service and a host of other financial services that nurtured local entrepreneurship and facilitated interregional commercial transactions; a century later, funds from the postal savings and insurance services were being channeled through the FILP as loans to local small and medium enterprises, many of which had trouble securing loans from the commercial banks, which primarily serviced large firms (Park 2011: 73–74). The Meiji government helped launch Japan's internationally competitive merchant marine via the postal system by transferring ownership of 13 ships to the Mitsubishi corporation in return for carrying the mail to points both at home and abroad (Wray 1984). The mail service effectively "contracted out" a number of other services to private-sector firms, including overland parcel deliveries. These "public–private partnerships" resembled the broader strategic alliances between the state and private firms that went on to become a major hallmark of Japan's particular brand of economic development.

Last but not least, the postal system contributed to social welfare goals. Much has been written in recent years about the state's relatively weak social safety net and its devolution of numerous welfare responsibilities to private firms (see, e.g., Estévez-Abe 2008). But the postal system also picked up some of the slack, in both formal and informal ways. In the absence of a viable private-sector alternative, the postal life insurance system grew steadily in popularity among ordinary Japanese following its introduction in 1916. And it continued to outperform its private-sector competitors by a significant margin during the remainder of the century, thanks to its broad accessibility and comparatively low premiums. The postal system also ran a small-scale (and widely accessible) pension plan. Perhaps more famously, many post offices in declining rural areas introduced informal programs for elderly residents known as *himawari* (sunflower) services. Mail carriers on their rounds would routinely check in on their elderly clients, offering at-home banking services and taking orders for groceries and pharmaceuticals that would then be filled by participating local businesses and/or community welfare groups (Maclachlan 2011: 128–129). Although their quality tended to vary from locality to locality, these programs helped reinforce the postal system's reputation as a truly *public* institution that prioritized the community and consumer well-being over profit.

And therein lay the secret to the postal system's popular appeal. If postwar developmentalism was ultimately defined by rapid industrial growth led by an activist state and the prioritization of producer interests in the political economy, the post office and its many supporting institutions not only helped finance that ambitious agenda but also gave practical expression to many of the values and objectives of the broad social contract that buttressed it. The state may have imposed low wages and high prices on consumers, but the post office helped soften the blow through the provision of savings vehicles that promised safety, convenience, and competitive interest rates, and of life insurance policies that were accessible even to low-income groups and the elderly. Meanwhile, postal employees established close, very personal relationships with their clients and built reputations for themselves as community servants. And as Japan reached economic maturity, FILP investments increasingly targeted projects designed to advance the quality of life of ordinary Japanese, from local public works projects that helped develop local communities and boost employment rates to public housing efforts. The postal system, in short, functioned as a complement to Japan's relentless pursuit of economic growth in its prioritization of stability, security, and service over competition and profits.

The postal lobby

As it went about the business of advancing postwar Japan's economic and social agendas, the postal system produced one of the country's most powerful vested interests: the proud, socially cohesive, and extraordinarily well-organized postmasters. Thanks to the overtures of Tanaka Kakuei, the Liberal Democratic Party's (LDP) consummate political broker and the prime minister from 1972 to 1974, the postmasters by the late 1950s were firmly ensconced in a mutually beneficial exchange relationship with the newly formed party. In return for a host of particularistic favors, including, in those early years, protection from the increasingly militant postal workers' union (Zentei), the postmasters performed local electoral services for the party, including recruiting new party and *kōenkai* members and gathering the vote at election time. By the early 1980s, Zentoku, the postmasters' voluntary organization (*nin'i dantai*), along with affiliated organizations, were delivering more than one million votes behind individual candidates in the national tier of upper house elections. They also stood out as the most vocal opponents of mounting calls for postal reform.

In their defense of the postal status quo, the postmasters were supported by a wide array of groups that were both directly and indirectly connected to the now massive state-owned postal system. These included Ministry of Posts and Telecommunications (MPT) bureaucrats at both the regional and national level; networks of private firms that serviced the postal system; special corporations (*tokushu hōjin*) that provided welfare and other services both for postal employees and the general public and that implemented specialized postal programs; government financial institutions and special corporations that either dispensed or received FILP funds; and even, by the late 1980s, the postal workers, who now feared the expanding postal reform movement more than they did the postmasters. And at the heart of this "postal lobby" (or the Postal Family, *yūsei ikka*, as it was sometimes called) was the electoral partnership between the postmasters and the LDP, most notably politicians within Tanaka Kakuei's powerful faction and other members of the postal *zoku* (policy tribe), the nerve center of LDP—and hence governmental—policy-making in the postal sphere (see Maclachlan 2011: 167–176).

From the early 1980s, the postal lobby had good reason to feel anxious. For a number of years, economists and not a few LDP politicians had been arguing that the postal savings and insurance systems were growing too large, that they enjoyed unfair legal and tax advantages, and that both had become barriers to much-needed financial liberalization (Maclachlan 2011: 181; Matsubara 1996: 221). A mature economy like Japan's no longer needed a postal savings system—or a FILP; the country would be far better off channeling household savings directly into private-sector markets. These arguments gained enough traction for Prime Minister Nakasone Yasuhiro (1982–1987) to target the postal financial institutions for privatization, along with Nippon Telegraph and Telephone (NTT), Japan National Railways (JNR), and Japan Tobacco (JT). Faced with overwhelming opposition from the postal lobby, Nakasone was quick to abandon postal privatization as a political non-starter. But his efforts provided impetus to a reformist movement that grew steadily over the years, culminating in Prime Minister Koizumi Jun'ichirō's dramatic passage of postal reform legislation in 2005.

It was Koizumi and his privatization "czar," the Keio University economist Takenaka Heizō, who most famously articulated the neoliberal argument in favor of postal privatization. Koizumi had come to power in 2001 determined to cut government spending and slash the FILP, revive the beleaguered banking system, and reform the nation's inefficient network of public and semi-public corporations. As he and Takenaka saw it, the first step toward any of these reforms was privatizing the postal financial services—the primary source of funds for both the FILP and, by extension, many of Japan's special corporations, not to mention an "unfair" competitor of the banks (see Takenaka 2005; Koizumi 1999). By bundling postal privatization with other much-needed economic and financial reforms, Koizumi hoped to invigorate the private financial system, jump-start economic growth, and ultimately increase the tax base so that the government could be better equipped to address the many demands of Japan's rapidly aging society. It was a recipe for reform that privileged market forces, competition, risk-taking, and profitmaking.

As Koizumi embarked on his ambitious plan to "let the market do what the market can do," his opponents launched a concerted counterattack. In a spate of books and other publications, the postal lobby and sympathetic social critics looked into a future with a privatized postal system and predicted disaster: the collapse of uncompetitive rural post offices, the loss of the postal savings system's slight competitive edge, the deterioration of the post office's informal social welfare programs, rising unemployment among postal employees, an influx of (unwanted) foreign investment in the postal system, and an outflow of what remained of postal savings and insurance proceeds to destinations abroad (see e.g., Arai 2003). These predictions may have been overstated, but against the backdrop of rising unemployment, the middle class's rapid decline, and the depopulation and infrastructural decay of rural communities, they struck a responsive chord among many Japanese. Koizumi, many concluded, was sacrificing the best of Japan's traditional economic institutions and values at the altar of cutthroat, American-style capitalism.

Koizumi's crusade

The successful passage of postal privatization legislation in 2005 was primarily the result of three interrelated factors: a small but significant precedent for postal reform that had been set during the late 1990s; new institutional opportunities for proactive leadership; and Koizumi's leadership style.

Although postal reform simmered on the political backburner for years following Nakasone's ill-fated attempt to tackle the issue, it was not until Hashimoto Ryūtarō 1996 ascension to the prime ministership that the issue was effectively revived. On the heels of introducing a spate of sweeping reforms known as the "Financial Big Bang," Hashimoto turned to the privatization of postal savings and insurance as the final—and most daunting—frontier of Japanese public-sector financial reform. Supported by Koizumi, who served as Hashimoto's Minister of Health and Welfare, postal privatization looked like it had a fighting chance—at least for a while. But it was not to be. Led by anti-reformist LDP politicians, the postal lobby launched an aggressive offensive that nearly killed any hope for change. It was Koizumi who ultimately put reform back on the agenda by threatening to resign his cabinet position and bring down the government if progress were not made. The ruse worked. Within a few short weeks, the two sides of the debate worked out a compromise plan that transformed the state-owned postal system into an independent government agency, eliminated the requirement that proceeds from the postal savings and insurance systems be funneled into the FILP, and required subsequent governments to transform the postal system into a public corporation by 2003 (Maclachlan 2011: 207–220).

Although critics scoffed at the Hashimoto postal reforms as mere window dressing, the stage had been set for future, more radical reform. No longer could naysayers argue that postal privatization would hurt Japan by destroying an important source of government debt (the FILP was a major investor in government bonds), for the formal delinking of the postal financial services from the FILP was carried out in 2001 with nary a hitch (in part because the postal system opted to *voluntarily* channel its funds into the FILP, which continued to buy up government debt). Furthermore, the government's partial retreat from the postal system through the creation of a Postal Services Agency weakened the opposition of postal authorities to postal reform not only by demonstrating that reform could actually enhance the efficiency of the postal services but also by building expectations for even more change (Maclachlan 2011: 230). By the time Prime Minister Koizumi took up the mantle of postal reform, the political balance of power between the forces for and against postal privatization had shifted slightly in his favor.

The political system that Koizumi inherited was also much different from the one Nakasone—and even Hashimoto—operated in. Thanks largely to Hashimoto's passage of the 1998 Basic Law for the Reform of Central Ministries and Agencies, a number of institutions had been introduced that empowered the prime minister within the policy-making system. The Cabinet Secretariat (Naikaku Kanbō) was expanded in ways that enhanced the prime minister's policy coordination authority. Provisions were now in place for the establishment of issue-specific ad hoc cabinet positions; Koizumi went on to create one such position for Takenaka Heizō, the other leading figure in the postal privatization saga. New advisory councils had been set up that were directly accountable to the prime minister; one of these, the Council on Economic and Fiscal Policy, oversaw the policy formulation and legislative drafting processes—processes that in years past would have been delegated to the (anti-reformist) Ministry of Posts and Telecommunications. Together, these and related institutional innovations reduced bureaucratic control over policy-making and narrowed opportunities for special interests to veto policies they did not like (see Estévez-Abe 2006; Mulgan 2002). Without these reforms, Koizumi's autumn 2004 postal privatization blueprint—the most radical postal reform proposal Japan had ever seen—never would have materialized.

The Hashimoto reforms may have enabled Koizumi to hammer his neoliberal ideas into a concrete postal privatization plan, but they proved powerless once that plan reached the Diet in summer 2005. Angry LDP politicians were outnumbered in the lower house, which passed the bills by a five-vote margin in July, but ruled the day in the upper house, which defeated the bills the following month. Undaunted, the innovative Koizumi implemented an unprecedented political strategy that gave full expression to the heretofore unfulfilled lower house electoral reforms of 1994—reforms that were supposed to privilege policies that served the common good, rather than the public interest. He called a snap lower house election for September 11, 2005 and then refused the party's endorsement of candidates who had voted against his privatization legislation in July. He subsequently cast the election as a veritable referendum on neoliberal reform and postal privatization, thus drawing a line in the sand between the LDP, which now stood for reform, and the more reactionary opposition parties. In so doing, Koizumi severed the LDP's long-standing exchange relationship with the postmasters. The conservative party went on to clinch an overwhelming victory, and Koizumi's postal privatization legislation sailed through the Diet the following month (Maclachlan 2011).

By mid-autumn 2005, Japan's political-economic landscape appeared transformed. The postal privatization process was slated to begin in October 2007 and the postmasters and other members of the postal lobby had been relegated to the margins of the decision-making system. Koizumi and his neoliberal allies, it seemed, had scored a major victory against one of the last institutional vestiges of developmentalism.

Backtracking

With the benefit of hindsight, we now know that postal privatization—and Koizumi's neoliberal reform agenda—was in trouble from the start. This turn of events, which culminated in the 2012 passage of another set of postal reform bills that restored several of the key features of the "developmentalist" postal services, can be largely attributed to the re-emergence of the postmasters in Japanese electoral politics and the effects of increasing competition between the LDP and the Democratic Party of Japan (DPJ) for their allegiance.

In one of the biggest threats to Koizumi's legacy, the postmasters quickly re-established themselves after fall 2005 as a significant political force. They first focused their energies on leveraging concessions from postal authorities that would ensure their survival as a distinctive occupation. But as the months unfolded, they also grew adept at currying favors from the parties.

The LDP was quick to recognize the postmasters' continuing political significance. In fall 2006, shortly after Koizumi stepped down as prime minister, his successor, Abe Shinzō, readmitted 11 politicians into the LDP who had been expelled during the 2005 election campaign (the "postal rebels"). Although the rebels were required to pledge their support for postal privatization as the cost of readmission, the party was far more interested by this time in how these rebels could help it win elections: with the dreaded 2007 upper house election just months away, the LDP viewed the rebels as their best hope for a renewed electoral exchange relationship with the postmasters.

Unfortunately for the postmasters, however, the LDP was tied to its 2005 electoral mandate to uphold Koizumi's privatization legislation and was therefore not able to grant them what they wanted most in return for their electoral support: an end to postal privatization. But the DPJ and the People's New Party (PNP), a tiny party established in 2005 by the postal rebels, were subject to no such restrictions; led by DPJ general secretary Ozawa Ichirō, the two parties made exactly the sorts of promises that the postmasters wanted to hear. In 2007, the postmasters threw their organizational heft behind the two parties, performing the same electoral tasks they had once carried out for the LDP. And they repeated this performance during the 2009 lower house election, thus helping the DPJ ascend to power in coalition with the PNP (and the Social Democratic Party of Japan).

The DPJ-led government immediately set out to make good on its promises to the postmasters by appointing the PNP's Kamei Shizuka minister of postal privatization. An avowed enemy of Koizumi and of the neoliberal principles he espoused (see Ōshita 2010), Kamei hammered out a series of radical postal reform bills that would have destroyed much of Koizumi's handiwork. But with the cabinet's unexpected collapse in summer 2010, the bills were shelved. Two years later, the DPJ backed a series of watered-down versions of the bills, which, surprisingly, passed with the support of not only the Kōmeitō but also the LDP, which had been released by its 2009 electoral defeat from its commitment to uphold the tenets of Koizumi's privatization blueprint.

Now that the LDP had re-established its bona fides on postal reform, the postmasters loosened their electoral commitment to the increasingly unpopular DPJ. In the lead-up to the 2012 lower house election, leaders of the postmasters associations officially adopted a multi-partisan stance, instructing their local chapters to endorse whichever candidates in the single-member districts of their jurisdictions were most committed to protecting the postmasters and promoting the postal services (*Asahi shimbun*, November 28 and December 3, 12 and 14). Following the LDP's victory and return to power, the postmasters threw in their lot with their former patrons. In early 2013, a former head of Zentoku, Tsuge Yoshifumi, met with the current Zentoku head and Ishiba Shigeru, general secretary of the LDP, in a show of mutual support (*Tsūshin bunka* 2013). The postmasters pledged to back the LDP in upcoming elections in return for the LDP's commitment to actively support new business ventures by the postal services. In July 2013, Tsuge clinched a seat in the upper house election with 429,002 votes, by far the highest vote yield among LDP politicians running as individual candidates in the national proportional representation (PR) tier (*Asahi shimbun* 2013).

As the unfolding saga of Japanese postal reform attests, the DPJ and the LDP have begun to *compete* for the electoral allegiance of the postmasters (as well as other vested interests), and in ways that are breathing new life into the anti-reformist elements of those parties. How can we explain this development?

One explanation is that the parties face electoral incentives to court the organized vote. In the PR districts of upper house elections, politicians who run as individual candidates must capture fairly large proportions of the popular vote in order to secure a seat; reaching out to organized interests that can deliver predictable numbers of votes is a logical step toward that goal. Even in the single-member districts (SMD) of the lower house, which are supposed to encourage electoral competition along programmatic policy lines, few candidates can afford to appeal solely to the fickle independent (or floating) voter—particularly given Japan's prohibitively short official campaign period. Also significant has been the so-called dual candidate system, in which incumbents whose SMD seats are insecure are allowed to run simultaneously in the lower house PR tier; since seats in the latter are doled out according to the proportion of the popular vote secured in the SMD district, candidates have good reason to solicit the backing of organized interests—even when victory in the SMD seems hopeless (Bawn and Thies 2003: 22; Koellner 2009: 131).

While electoral incentives may *push* candidates to court organized groups like the postmasters, the organizational structure of the groups themselves helps *pull* them into these exchange relationships. Zentoku and Taiju, the association of retired postmasters and the spouses of active postmasters, are multi-tiered, hierarchically organized entities that stretch from the national level to the local level. These organizational structures enable these groups to establish linkages to local society that the LDP and the DPJ, with their top-heavy organizations, sorely lack. They are thus in a position to co-opt certain electoral functions from the parties: they tap into their local social networks to mobilize the vote behind individual candidates; they have the organizational presence at the regional and national levels to coordinate vote-gathering across electoral districts; and they can even *self-monitor* these functions, thanks to the hierarchical structure of their organizations.

In other words, the postmasters associations remain in a position to electorally *compensate* the parties for their organizational handicaps—particularly at the local level. The LDP and the DPJ, for their own part, will likely continue depending on organized interests like the postmasters for such services for as long as their organizational handicaps continue, they remain vulnerable to intra-party factionalism, they are peopled by second-, third-, and even-fourth generation incumbents who came to power on the backs of special interests, and they lack overarching ideological identities that would position them to compete more effectively with one another along programmatic lines. And for as long as DPJ and LDP dependence on interest groups continues, we should expect the parties to send lukewarm and even conflicting signals on neoliberal reforms like postal privatization.

Whither the post office?

As a result of the twists and turns of many years of political deal making, the Japanese postal system is now a hybrid of the old state-run system and Koizumi's neoliberal vision.

For Japan, Koizumi's neoliberal vision was most certainly a radical one. Koizumi's 2005 privatization legislation broke up Japan Post, the public corporation established in 2003, into five separate companies: one each for the mail, savings, and insurance systems, one for the network of post offices, and a government-owned holding company. Between 2011 and 2017, the government was required to divest its shares in the holding company and the holding company its shares in the two financial firms. Many of the perquisites that had advantaged the postal services relative to their private competitors, like the government guarantee of postal savings deposits and insurance premiums and the services' various tax exemptions, were to be immediately eliminated or gradually phased out. In the meantime, it was expected that the volume of postal savings deposits and insurance policies would shrink, thus creating a leaner and more efficient system that competed on a more level playing field with private-sector firms.

That was the plan, but on close scrutiny it is clear that even Koizumi's "radical" privatization legislation contained loopholes that in practice made it not so radical after all—loopholes that the government grudgingly endorsed in return for the backing of conservative politicians who were still wary of reform (see Maclachlan 2011). Whereas Koizumi and Takenaka had pushed for the breakup of Japan Post Bank into regional institutions in order to help level the playing field with city and regional banks, their opponents insisted that it remain national in scope. So much for "fair competition." In a move that appeased local postal employees who feared post office closures following privatization, Koizumi and Takenaka agreed to preserve the massive postal network of approximately 24,000 post offices by promising at least "one post office for every village." And in response to local fears that profit-sensitive rural post offices would abandon their informal social welfare programs, the government agreed to channel some of the proceeds from the sale of shares in the postal savings and insurance systems into a special fund that would both prop up struggling post offices and enable them to carry out *himawari* and other services. The size of that fund expanded from one to two trillion yen during the final stages of the legislative process. So much for "letting the market do what the market can do." Finally, the government was given the option to buy back as much as one-third of its shares in the financial services after 2017. It also agreed to a two-year transition period before the official start of the privatization process, during which the services were more or less free to introduce a number of new products; since the postal services were still wholly owned by the government during this time, these innovations had the support of a de facto government guarantee. So much for drastically reducing governmental control over the services.

By the time the DPJ-coalition government came to power in 2009, Koizumi's "compromise" legislation was all but doomed. Problems with the corporate structure of the new postal system helped seal its fate. Postal employees and their customers complained of long line-ups as local post offices struggled to adapt to the separation of services into discrete firms and the mountain of new regulations that the privatization process had produced. The mail service grappled with declining revenue. And local residents in rural and semi-rural areas mourned the decline of *himawari* services. At this time, Japan was feeling the effects of the 2008 financial crisis, which had simply magnified public concerns about the rapid decline of the middle class and the widening gaps (*kakusa*) between rural and urban areas. During the 2009 election campaign, soon-to-be Prime Minister Hatoyama Yukio attributed these problems to the neoliberal principles of economic globalization as he railed against "American-style capitalism," "market fundamentalism" (*shijō genrishugi*), and the evils of "vulture capitalism," and called for a resurrection of values and institutions that had supported the old developmental social contract (Maclachlan 2011: 320). Once the new government was in power, Minister of Postal Privatization Kamei Shizuka set out to reverse the damage that the "laws of the jungle" had wrought on the post office (www.kamei-shizuka.net, accessed October 28, 2009).

Toward the end of the year, the government passed legislation to freeze the divestiture of shares in the postal financial services, thus giving Kamei a space in which to draft his controversial bills. Although the bills ultimately failed, their contents and that of supporting policies warrant scrutiny for what they tell us about the tenacity of political support for retaining the postal system as a vehicle for achieving social goals. The government promised to "grow" the financial services relative to their private competitors by dramatically raising the ceilings on postal savings deposits and insurance payouts. The network and mail firms were to be merged with Japan Post Holdings, and the financial firms reorganized as subsidiaries of that new entity; this would have enabled the government to extend a "universal service" requirement to the financial firms.[1] The government pledged to hire as many as 100,000 postal employees as a (partial) corrective to high unemployment rates in the countryside. And it required future governments to retain at least one-third of its shares in the postal savings and insurance services, a move that would have guaranteed a continued government presence in their future growth. If passed, the Kamei plan would have marked a major step toward the status quo ante—one that in all likelihood would have inflicted major losses on the postal system.

For nearly two years, postal reform languished on the political backburner as Japan grappled with political instability and then the repercussions of the massive earthquake, tsunami, and nuclear disasters that befell the Tohoku region in March 2011. Ironically, it was recognition that the postal services might help fuel the reconstruction of the beleaguered region that ultimately revived the issue. By this time, the services were still "frozen" under the 2009 legislation. With the passage of DPJ Prime Minister Noda Yoshiko's reform bills in spring 2012, that freeze was lifted and the government prepared to begin divesting shares in the postal financial services. A portion of the proceeds from the divestiture process is to be channeled into post-earthquake reconstruction.

Noda's reform legislation struck a more workable balance between neoliberal and developmental principles than Kamei's blueprint. Gone was the pledge to hire tens of thousands of new postal employees and to raise the ceilings on postal savings deposits and insurance payouts. But the mail and network firms are to be merged and the two financial firms subjected to the universal service principle—an unprecedented requirement in the history of international postal savings systems that will guarantee the system's long-term survival. Also noteworthy is the requirement that the government retain at least one-third ownership of shares in those firms—a goal that is likely to be exceeded since the new legislation does not set a firm deadline for the completion of the divestiture of shares in these services. The Noda government may not have completely reversed Koizumi's postal privatization plan, but it did restore a significant government presence within the services in ways that will clearly advantage them relative to their private sector competitors.

With the passage of the 2012 postal reform legislation, Japanese policy-makers turned their attention to other issues and priorities. But behind the scenes, advocates of the postal system are warily tracking a new set of potential threats: Prime Minister Abe Shinzō's economic reform agenda ("Abenomics"). As of this writing, the Abe government is focused on the so-called "third arrow" of structural reform, which includes a commitment to trade liberalization. The postmasters, the postal workers, and many within the network of Japan Post firms are particularly concerned about Abe's determination to join the Trans-Pacific Partnership (TPP), a proposed free trade zone of 12 countries bordering the Pacific Rim that aims not only to eliminate all remaining tariffs on traded goods but also to liberalize cross-national investments and the flow of financial services. Advocates view the TPP as Japan's best hope for an enduring economic recovery. The postal lobby, by contrast, is worried that the TPP will intensify pressures on the Japanese government to retreat from the postal sector, increase the number of foreign firms in Japan that will compete with postal banking, insurance and mail services, and open the door to foreign investment in the postal network and services (see, e.g., Higashitani 2012). As such, it will give Japan no choice but to adapt to the many unwanted values of American-style "market fundamentalism." It appears, in short, that the battle over the Japanese post office is poised to move from the domestic political arena to the international stage.

Conclusion

By the time Japan embarked on its postwar quest for rapid economic growth, the postal system had logged several decades not only as the nation's most ubiquitous institutional network and the center of communications, but also as an activist branch of the state that performed essential financial and other functions. Thus, the postal system was supremely positioned after World War II to facilitate the fulfillment of the state's developmental goals. The postal financial services became a vehicle for the implementation of Japanese industrial policy by generating much of the funds for state investment in strategic "growth industries." But as we have seen, the postal system also assumed a variety of functions that supported the implicit social contract or political bargain that helped bind ordinary Japanese to the state's developmental agenda. Serving hard-working consumers and struggling small firms over profitable big businesses, those functions were at the heart of the postal system's reputation as a deeply traditional institution that embodied Japan's distinctive capitalist style.

When combined with the powerful vested interests that developed out of the postal services over the years, the post office's centrality to the economic, financial, social, and, yes, political history of Japan all but guaranteed that pressures for postal reform would quickly develop into high politics. As this chapter has illustrated, the battle over the post office has become a metaphor of sorts for the ongoing conflict between developmentalism and neoliberalism—between the proponents of a growth model that values state paternalism, safety, security, and community and those who believe that the ticket to future economic recovery and prosperity lies with the prioritization of market forces and a smaller government, risk-taking, competition, profit-making, and free trade. Although the forces in favor of neoliberal reform continue to expand, the survival of vested interests like the postmasters and their ongoing political importance to the parties will ensure that deep-seated compromise continues to inform Japan's reformist agenda.

Note

1 The "universal service" principle normally applies to mail services. It requires postal systems to service all communities within a given territory at uniform rates.

References

Arai Hiroyuki. 2003. *Yūbinkyoku o Amerika ni uriwatsu na: yūsei min'eika o nerau gurōburizumu no wana [Don't Sell out the Post Office to America: The Globalization Trap of Postal Privatization]*. Tokyo: Asuka shinsha.

Asahi shimbun. 2013. "Shoshikihyō fukkatsu no kizashi" [Signs of a Revival of the Organized Vote], July 22. Online: www.asahi.com/senkyo/senkyo2013/news/TKY201307220283.html.

Bawn, Kathleen, and Michael F. Thies. 2003. "A Comparative Theory of Electoral Incentives: Representing the Unorganized under PR, Plurality and Mixed-Member Electoral Systems." *Journal of Theoretical Politics* 15, no. 5: 5–32.

Calder, Kent E. 1990. "Linking Welfare and the Developmental State: Postal Savings in Japan." *Journal of Japanese Studies* 16, no. 1: 31–59.

Cargill, Thomas F. and Naoyuki Yoshino. 2003. *Postal Savings and Fiscal Investment in Japan: The Postal Savings System and the FILP*. Oxford: Oxford University Press.

Estévez-Abe, Margarita. 2008. *Welfare and Capitalism in Postwar Japan: Party, Bureaucracy and Business*. Cambridge and New York: Cambridge University Press.

Estévez-Abe, Margarita. 2006. "Japan's Shift Toward a Westminster System: A Structural Analysis of the 2005 Lower House Election and Its Aftermath." *Asian Survey* 46, no. 4 (July–August): 632–651.

Garon, Sheldon. 2011. *Beyond Our Means: Why America Spends While the World Saves*. Princeton, NJ: Princeton University Press.

Higashitani Satoshi. 2012. *Yūsei hōkai to TPP [Postal Collapse and the TPP]*. Tokyo: Bunshun shinsho.

Hunter, Janet E. 1976. "A Study of the Career of Maejima Hisoka, 1935–1919." PhD diss., St. Antony's College, University of Oxford.

Isao Iijima. 2006. *Koizumi kantei hiroku [Secret Records of the Koizumi Administration]*. Tokyo: Nihon keizai shinbunsha.

Johnson, Chalmers. 1982. *MITI and the Japanese Miracle*. Stanford, CA: Stanford University Press.

Koellner, Patrick. 2009. "Japanese Lower House Campaigns in Transition: Manifest Changes or Fleeting Fads?" *Journal of East Asian Studies* 9: 121–149.

Koizumi Jun'ichirō. 1999. "Foreword." In Koizumi Jun'ichirō and Matsuzawa Shigefumi (eds.), *Yūsei min'eika ron: Nihon saisei no daikaikaku! [The Postal Privatization Debate: The Biggest Reform for the Rebirth of Japan!]*. Tokyo: PHP kenkyūjo, pp. 1–4.

Maclachlan, Patricia L. 2004. "Post Office Politics in Modern Japan: The Postmasters, Iron Triangles, and the Limits of Reform." *Journal of Japanese Studies* 30, no. 2 (Summer): 281–313.

Maclachlan, Patricia L. 2011. *The People's Post Office: The History and Politics of the Japanese Postal System, 1871–2010*. Cambridge, MA: Harvard University East Asia Center.

Matsubara Satoru. 1996. *Gendai no yūsei jigyō [The Contemporary Postal Services]*. Tokyo: Nihon hyōronsha.

Mulgan, Aurelia George. 2002. *Japan's Failed Revolution: Koizumi and the Politics of Economic Reform*. Canberra: Asia Pacific Press, Asia Pacific School of Economics and Management.

Ōshita Eiji. 2010. *Kamei Shizuka: tenbakū o yuku [Kamei Shizuka: Flights of Fancy]*. Tokyo: Tokuma shoten.

Park, Gene. 2011. *Spending Without Taxation: FILP and the Politics of Public Finance*. Palo Alto, CA: Stanford University Press.

Rosenbluth, Frances McCall. 1989. *Financial Politics in Contemporary Japan*. Ithaca, NY: Cornell University Press.

Scher, Mark J. and Naoyuki Yoshino. 2004. "Policy Challenges and the Reform of Postal Savings in Japan." In Mark J. Scher and Naoyuki Yoshino (eds.), *Small Savings Mobilization and Asian Economic Development: The Role of Postal Financial Services*. Armonk, NY: M.E. Sharp, pp. 121–145.

Takenaka Heizō. 2005. *Yūsei min'eika: chiisa na seifu e no shikinseki [Postal Privatization: The Litmus Test for a Small Government]*. Tokyo: PHP kenkyūjo.

Tsūshin bunka. 2013. "Yūsei seisaku ni kanshi gōi: Zentoku Jimin, Wadakamari o kokufukusuru" [An Agreement on Postal Policy; Zentoku and the LDP Overcome Their Grudge], March 11. Online: www.tsushin-bunka.co.jp/backnumber/detail.php?sub_content_id=225.

Westney, D. Eleanor. 1987. *Imitation and Innovation: The Transfer of Western Organizational Patterns to Meiji Japan.* Cambridge, MA: Harvard University Press.

Wray, William D. 1984. *Mitsubishi and the N.Y.K., 1870–1914: Business Strategy in the Japanese Shipping Industry.* Cambridge, MA: Harvard University Asia Center.

Yūseishō, ed. 1971. *Yūsei 100-nen no ayumi [A History of the Postal System's 100 Years].* Tokyo: Teishin kyōkai.

8 The political economy of digital television transition in Japan and the United States

How well can a coordinated market economy solve a coordination problem?

Henry Laurence

Introduction

Scholars have long been divided about the effectiveness of the Japanese state in managing its economy. Many in the tradition of the developmental state see a network of highly trained, politically independent technocrats rising above the pleading of special interests to craft successful national policies (Johnson 1982). Health care and mobile telephony have been cited recently as policy issues on which Japan has outperformed the United States, even in the so-called "lost decades" after the crash of 1990 (Reid 2010; Bleha 2005). Recent scholarship in the literature on varieties of capitalism sees Japan—like other coordinated market economies (CMEs) such as Germany and Sweden—as having institutional structures yielding positive policy outcomes in terms of income equality without necessarily sacrificing overall economic performance (Hall and Soskice 2001). Other scholars (Tabuchi 2012; Grimes 2001) see in Japan a corrupt pattern of cozy relations between big business and captured regulators, resulting in policies that are ineffective at best (e.g., fiscal policy) and disastrous at worst (e.g., nuclear power). Ellen Immergut, Ikuo Kume, and colleagues (2006) see Japan as responding far less effectively to the "crises of governance" in industrial relations, banking, economic policy, and electoral reform than either Sweden or Germany. What has become clear, though, is that the effectiveness of the Japanese state in addressing policy challenges varies considerably from issue to issue.

This chapter explores how well the Japanese state makes policy on the issue of information technology (IT) development, by way of a comparative study of how Japan and the United States approached the challenge of accomplishing the transition from analog to digital transmission of television. This issue is substantively very important since it involves the economically vital IT sector and the building of a key element in the infrastructure for a digital economy. The case is also of considerable theoretical interest to political economists, for it allows us to compare the effectiveness, in terms of resolving a common collective-action problem, of two countries thought to have paradigmatically different approaches to economic policy-making.

The chapter asks three closely related sets of questions. First, what strategies did policymakers in Japan and the United States adopt to accomplish digital transition? Second, how and why did they vary, and do these cross-national differences correspond with conventional wisdom among comparative political economists? Finally, how successful were policymakers in either country at achieving the goals they set out to accomplish?

Digital television transmission as a coordination problem

Traditional "over the air" television transmissions are possible only across a limited segment of the spectrum ("the airwaves"). Moreover, signals on close frequencies interfere with each other.[1] Electromagnetic spectrum can therefore be regarded a common-pool resource: like a forest or a fishery, it is characterized by low excludability (anyone can in theory transmit a signal) and high depletability (too many broadcasts cause chronic interference). As such, spectrum is susceptible to the "tragedy of the commons," in which individually rational decisions to exploit the resource result in the collectively irrational outcome of destructive overuse (Olson 1965; Hardin 1968). Government management or regulation of the resource is a standard solution, and ever since public radio transmissions proliferated in the 1920s, governments have regulated spectrum use.[2]

In 1990 the U.S. firm General Instrument developed a digital transmission format for television to replace the traditional analog format. Unlike analog broadcasting, in which a particular channel takes up a specific frequency, digital compression allows multiple broadcasts along a single frequency.

Digital television (DTV) is technically superior to analog broadcasting in three respects. Most important from a public policy perspective, digital transmissions take up much less spectrum space; in the early 1990s the bandwidth of one analog TV channel could accommodate four to six digital channels. Second, it allows for interactivity with other digital formats, such as computers, mobile phones, or cameras, and for viewer interactivity, such as voting for *American Idol* contestants, shopping from home, or using e-government websites. As such, it offered the possibility of bridging the "digital divide" by bringing Internet access to less wealthy citizens, substantial numbers of whom could not afford computer access. Third, from the viewers' standpoint, DTV provides far better visual quality. DTV was therefore seen as highly desirable, and governments in all advanced industrial democracies committed to switching from analog to digital transmission by deadlines ranging from 2006 to 2022.[3]

However, digital transition has significant up-front costs that loomed large in the early stages of the process. Broadcasters must invest in new transmission and production facilities. Electronics manufacturers must invest in new product lines for which there is no proven market. Most important from a political perspective, viewers need to buy new televisions, or at least convert boxes, because analog TV sets cannot receive digital signals and thus become utterly obsolete after digital transition. The cheapest way for viewers to receive DTV is with a set-top box converter (STB), which enables an analog set to receive digital channels, but will not upgrade picture quality. STBs are cheap (initially less than around $100), but a separate converter is required for each TV set.[4] The full benefits of interactive and high-definition digital programming can be realized with an integrated digital TV set (iDTV). In the late 1990s these could cost around $4,000 or $5,000 in the United States, with high-end models costing well above $10,000.

All the relevant actors—broadcasters, electronics manufacturers, and viewers—faced the first-mover risk of investing in the new technology only to lose out if others did not follow suit. The result was a catch-22. Viewers were reluctant to upgrade to expensive new equipment without tangible benefits such as more channels or improved programming. Broadcasters, however, were reluctant to invest in such services in the absence of a ready audience of digital-capable viewers. Eventually, as the supply of digital programming increased, demand for digital televisions rose and set prices began to fall.[5] Initially, though, all three groups showed great reluctance to make the switch, each waiting for the other to move first in a classic collective-action problem. The transition to DTV might eventually have happened if left entirely to market forces, but that might have taken decades if it happened at all.[6] In short, democratic governments all wanted a swift transition to digital transmission, but they wanted to avoid the politically toxic outcome of analog switch-off in the face of large numbers of viewers who had only analog TVs. They therefore faced a coordination problem.

Coordination problems and state capacity

The literature on collective action makes a distinction between competition problems, such as the classic prisoner's dilemma, and coordination problems. In the former, while the actors may reach an initial bargain easily enough, compliance is hindered by self-interested defection (e.g., as in a price cartel or an international agreement on CO_2 emissions, such as the Kyoto Protocol). Coordination problems, by contrast, occur when actors disagree over the initial bargain but have strong incentives not to defect once agreement is struck (e.g., as in an international agreement on technical standards for electronics equipment). In such cases, initial agreement is hard to accomplish, but compliance is self-reinforcing.[7]

Gregory Noble (1998: 21) notes that the distinction is important because both the strategies and the governmental capacities necessary to overcome these problems will be different in each case. Coordination problems, as he points out, have obstacles to agreement in the form of uncertainty and recalcitrance among the different actors. These obstacles are best solved with mechanisms to reduce uncertainty and promote trust. State skills at mediation and providing information are therefore essential.[8] Also helpful is a political culture in which private corporate actors accept the legitimacy of state mediation, and in which state–business relations are generally cooperative rather than contractual and arm's-length. As Noble observes, "specific policy tools … [are] less important than networks of communication and negotiation" (1998: 9). He argues that Japan is well endowed with both the state capacities needed to mediate coordination problems, and the willingness of firms to accept state mediation. Hence, he writes, "collective action in the form of enhancing cooperation among competing capitalist firms has been a significant and growing part of Japanese industrial policy" (1998: 26).

Noble's findings about Japan's high capacity to resolve coordination problems should be expected in light of the literature on varieties of capitalism. Scholars such as Hall and Soskice (2001) observe systematic institutional differences in government–business relations between liberal market economies (LMEs) such as the United States and coordinated market economies (CMEs) such as Japan. The former are said to resolve collective-action problems through decentralized, arm's-length, market-based relations, while the latter rely more on information sharing and willingness to collaborate on the part of private corporate actors. We might therefore expect CMEs to be more effective at resolving coordination problems such as digital transition.

Comparing Japan to the United States therefore makes sense in shedding light on how two wealthy countries with very different political economies tackle a common problem. Of course, many factors unique to each country influence broadcasting policy, so the comparison is not exact. Broadcasting and television markets are strongly influenced by geography, with cable TV more popular in densely populated urban areas, and terrestrial or satellite TV more appropriate for rural areas. The challenge for U.S. broadcasters and policymakers has been to provide coverage to vast, sparsely populated rural regions. Japan is smaller but relatively more mountainous, with tens of thousands of relay substations necessary to retransmit terrestrial broadcasts to isolated households. However, both the United States and Japan had well-developed commercial cable and satellite TV markets. Since the mid-1990s a majority of viewers in both countries subscribed to some form of cable or satellite service, and also received the free-to-air commercial and public terrestrial broadcasts. TV viewing is very popular in both countries, with the average citizen of each watching 4.5 hours of TV per day.[9] Perhaps the most significant difference between the two countries was the presence in Japan of the very well-funded public broadcaster Nippon Hôsô Kyôkai (NHK), the Japan Broadcasting Corporation. NHK was required by law to serve all households in the country, no matter how remote, and Japan therefore had a well-developed transmission infrastructure in place for households dependent on terrestrial TV. However, while the two countries began the transition with somewhat different geographic challenges and market structures, their situations were sufficiently similar to warrant comparison.

In light of the literature on varieties of capitalism, we might expect the following: (1) Japan and the United States should adopt different strategies to solve the coordination problem of digital switchover. In Japan, one might expect close cooperation between private economic actors and the state, with the bureaucracy playing a mediating role, providing guidance, and sharing information, and the private actors accepting the legitimacy of such intervention. We might further expect the extensive use of subsidies, given the degree to which successive Japanese governments have employed public works spending. On the other hand, we would expect the U.S. state to play a less central role, allowing market forces and private actors to take the lead. Relations between policymakers and firms should be arm's-length, and we should similarly not expect to see collusive cooperation between rival firms. Finally, we might not expect to see extensive use of public subsidies for private actors and individuals.

(2) The second hypothesis is that Japan should be more successful at managing the transition than the United States since Japan is said to possess, in greater degree than the United States, state skills at mediation and an institutional structure facilitating networks of cooperation. "Success"—that is, policy effectiveness—is somewhat subjective and indeterminate, but there are at least three crude measures of effectiveness: (a) Speed of implementation. When did each country achieve switchover and therefore begin to derive the "digital dividend" of freed-up spectrum? (b) Household penetration of DTV. How quickly and extensively did viewers adopt the DTV technology? (c) Cost. To what extent did each government rely on taxpayer-funded subsidies or other incentives to encourage the various private actors to make the transition?

The next two sections examine how digital transition policy was handled in each country.

Digital transition policy in Japan

Japan's transition to digital TV started relatively later than elsewhere because of the ill-fated pursuit of the Hi-Vision/MUSE analog high-definition television (HDTV) system in the late 1980s (Krauss 2000: 185–196). Hi-Vision had been developed and promoted by the public broadcaster NHK, in collaboration with the Ministry of Posts and Telecommunications (MPT),[10] the Ministry of International Trade and Industry (MITI), and the major consumer electronics manufacturers. So, just as the idea of digital broadcasting was taking hold in the United States and Europe, the Japanese were heavily invested in an analog system that none of the major players wanted to abandon. There was also no important constituency pushing for digital transition. The great economic slowdown had only just begun, the explosion of public debt had not yet become a policy issue, and there was no pressing need for the revenue benefits of spectrum auction. Moreover, as Noble (2000: 88) notes, the national character of Japanese television and the restrictions on political advertising on TV meant that few Japanese politicians took much day-to-day interest in broadcasting policy. Finally, as in the United States, the viewing public showed little awareness of, let alone demand for, technical changes in the mechanics of broadcast transmissions (*Financial Times* 1996).

The MPT began to call for all-digital broadcasting in 1994 (MPT 1995). At first this was bitterly opposed by the electronics manufacturers, who still hoped that sales of the MUSE system would pick up. A representative of Matsushita TV, which controlled 25 percent of the TV market, went so far as to call the

MPT's support for digital television "stupid" (Krause 1994). But by then it was becoming abundantly clear that Hi-Vision/MUSE was an expensive and obsolete failure, with few domestic subscribers and no international prospects, once the United States and Europe had refused to adopt it as the global transmission standard. The MPT was under intense pressure to rejuvenate Japan's information and communications sectors[11] and saw digital conversion as a means to do so, with revenues for related industries calculated at ¥212 trillion over ten years (Nakamoto 1999). The Ministry also saw tremendous commercial potential for Japan's world-beating creative industries in the field of digital content such as anime, toys, and software (MPT 2000a). As a side benefit, the MPT saw the move as a way of winning control of a key new technology from their bureaucratic rivals at MITI (J. Hart 1998: 233). In 1998 the MPT's Advisory Committee on Digital Terrestrial Broadcasting called for a complete switch to digital transmission by July 2011, with analog broadcasting to continue concurrently until then (MPT 1998).

DTV was particularly attractive in Japan because it offered a solution to the problems created by the relatively small size of houses and apartments. There was much appeal in promoting a single appliance that could serve as a TV, web browser, and personal computer. In the words of the 2002 White Paper by Japan's Ministry of Public Management, Home Affairs, Posts, and Telecommunications (MPHPT),

> The digitization of terrestrial broadcasting is aimed at replacing television receivers, which are disseminated in almost all households in Japan, with a simple advanced information and communications terminal that can be used at home, and as such it will play an important role as a gateway to an advanced information and communications network society.
>
> (MPHPT 2002: 11)

Some policymakers even believed that slow Internet usage was caused by the difficulty of inputting Japanese characters onto a conventional keyboard designed for the Western alphabet. Many Japanese, the thinking went, would prefer to surf the Internet by thumb-scrolling a TV remote control than by typing at a computer monitor.[12]

By the late 1990s NHK had also accepted digitization (Krauss 2000: 196). The appointment in 1997 of Chairman Ebisawa Katsuji had been a key turning point, since Ebisawa, a close and well-connected ally of the powerful Takeshita faction of the Liberal Democratic Party (LDP), was an enthusiastic supporter of the digital project (*Gekkan Nyûmedia Henshûbu* 2000). The public broadcaster had enormous financial resources, state-of-the-art research facilities, and the freedom from short-term commercial pressures to take a leadership role in developing new technology. Ebisawa was also well aware of the political capital to be made by supporting national infrastructure projects. NHK finally threw their corporate resources into selling digital TV to a skeptical public.

The Japan Electronics and Information Technology Industry Association (JEITIA) also came to see DTV as the next big "must-have" product, driving sales growth for years to come (*Nihon Keizai Shimbun* 2002). This view was strongly held by Tokyo's investment banking community, which was pushing electronics stocks hard in the mid- and late 1990s.[13] The appeal of digitization as a boost for the electronics industry was closely tied to the strategy the MPT used to sell DTV to an apathetic public. In the United States and the United Kingdom, where more channels and interactive TV were key selling points, Japanese consumers were wooed with greater picture quality (Hara 2003). The MPT had decided in 1997 to adopt the ISDB-T (Integrated Services Digital Broadcasting—Terrestrial) transmission standard, which differed significantly from the ATSC (Advanced Television Systems Committee) standard in the United States. The American system was simpler and cheaper, but with worse audiovisual quality (Pollack 2001). Thus, the MPT and the electronics manufacturers did all they could to play up the superior visuals of HDTV. They were successful: in 2002, 65 percent of Japanese viewers said that high-quality pictures were what they most expected from DTV, compared with 20 percent who cited interactive programming or data broadcasting (Wakasugi 2003). Of course, this decision greatly benefited the Japanese electronics manufacturers of the high-priced digital televisions needed to take advantage of the great visuals.

The LDP had been slow to back DTV, but by the late 1990s it had become a key part of the party's vision for an advanced information society. Politicians saw its potential to facilitate e-government at a time when few households (19 percent in 1999) had Internet access (MPT 2000b, 10). In November 2000 Prime Minister Mori Yoshiro announced the adoption of a national IT strategy, the goal of which was to turn Japan into the world's most advanced country in the field of IT within five years (*Japan Times* 2000). This "e-Japan" initiative was greeted with initial skepticism, perhaps because of widely circulating rumors that Mori and many of his cabinet were so technologically inept they could not manage their own e-mail accounts.[14] Nevertheless, adoption of the project showed the degree of seriousness with which the LDP and the MPT were taking IT. An MPT advisory group concluded in 2002 that DTV would be an effective way to provide local government services such as reserving public facilities or checking information, especially for the elderly (*Kyodo News Service* 2002a). In short, by 2003 DTV was seen by most in Tokyo as "the engine for the construction of an information-oriented society."[15]

The main opponents of digitization were the commercial broadcasters. Naturally, they were not pleased that a multichannel digital world would encroach on the hitherto protected and highly lucrative advertising market (*Financial Times* 1996). Their publicly stated objection was the high cost of transmission conversion, estimated at over ¥1,000 billion (*Financial Times* 1996). Costs were high partly because Japan's mountainous geography necessitates a very high number of relay stations to rebroadcast signals (*Asahi Shimbun* 2002a). The broadcasters wanted the government to either help pay for the costs of transition or slow the aggressive timetable for transmission (*Kyodo News Service* 1999). Said Machida

Kazuo of Minpororen (the Japan Federation of Commercial Broadcast Workers' Unions), "Digitalization is important, but there is little enthusiasm for investing. It is almost impossible to meet the government's schedule … we believe that this is a national policy which the government is forcing on us" (Nakamoto 1999).

Minpororen also called for the plan to be put on hold (*Kyodo News Service* 2002b). In addition, Keidanren, the powerful Federation of Economic Organizations, joined the broadcasters in arguing that the costs were too high for the private sector to bear alone (*Jiji Press* 2000a).

The LDP immediately agreed to subsidize the broadcasters. In April 1999 the Diet revised Japan's broadcast law to allow for additional services on the existing TV licenses. In the same year, the Advanced Television Broadcasting Facility Development Promotion Temporary Measures Law allowed the government to use tax incentives or low-interest loans to assist broadcasters in the switch. In April 2000 the Joint Study Committee Concerning Digital Terrestrial Broadcasting drew up a draft channel-allotment plan, which estimated ¥85 billion in costs for continuing analog broadcasting when the digital terrestrial television (DTT) system began in 2003. These costs were about ¥54 billion on the receiver side and ¥31 billion on the transmission side. The LDP's Communications Division promptly agreed the government should pay all the costs. In return, the LDP demanded that the private broadcasters and NHK shoulder more than ¥1 trillion in other costs of digitalization (*Jiji Press* 2000b).

The MIC sweetened the deal for commercial broadcasters by granting them exclusive rights to the spectrum and refusing to allow any new entrants into the terrestrial broadcasting market. This, added to the fact that the MIC encouraged the broadcasters to utilize spectrum-greedy HDTV rather than standard-definition broadcasts, meant that there was no increase in the number of terrestrial TV channels as a result of digitization (Kumabe 2012: 350). The MIC allocated ¥12.3 billion for fiscal 2001 and ¥12.2 billion for 2002 for reallocating existing analog frequencies prior to switch-off. They used radio utilization fees, made possible by a revision of the Radio Law in 2001 (MPHPT 2002: 61).

These measures placated the broadcasters, and in 2001 the LDP-dominated Diet passed the law requiring analog switch-off in 2011. The cost of the subsidies aroused considerable criticism, particularly since there was little evidence of support for digitization among viewers.[16] One 2002 poll found that only 18 percent of viewers were even aware of the planned launch of DTT in 2003 (*Asahi Shimbun* 2002b). But LDP Minister of Telecommunications Katayama Toranosuke was determined "to launch digital broadcasting as scheduled at any cost" (*Kyodo News Service* 2002b).

In December 2000 NHK and the five big networks had launched digital satellite services, but while NHK was promoting DTV with a convert's fervor, the commercial stations put few resources into their digital satellite services (Herskovitz 2000). The MPT had set a target of reaching ten million subscribers in 1,000 days, but the uptake was much slower. The fact that the MIC's strategy resulted in no greater channel choice for viewers, and required them to buy expensive digital sets to enjoy the greater HD visual quality, no doubt contributed to consumer reluctance. By the 2003 target date, only 4.2 million households had subscribed, and the commercial channels were all operating at losses (*Kyodo News Service* 2003a). NHK Chairman Ebisawa blamed the slow take-up on the high costs of reception equipment: at the time, the cost of a set-top converter box was around ¥60,000. But a 2003 poll found only 1 percent of viewers to be "fully aware" of the digital revolution, and 58 percent to be at "limited" or "vague" levels of awareness (Osaki 2003). Critics suggested that the government was to blame for failing to educate the public on the benefits of DTV (*Kyodo News Service* 2003a).

DTT was launched in Tokyo, Nagoya, and Osaka in December 2003, by which time the state had invested the equivalent of an estimated ¥200 billion (about $2 billion) into the project (*Asahi Shimbun* 2003). According to plan, the coverage of DTT services was extended gradually until late 2006, when DTT transmissions were available in all 47 prefectures, although to only 84 percent of all households. However, viewer interest lagged behind, and in particular viewers were reluctant to buy digital TV sets (i.e., those who could receive DTT transmissions on their own, as opposed to digital-compatible TVs, which needed a converter) (Katori 2006). By 2008 consumer interest was still low, with only 43 percent of households ready for DTT. Worried, the MPT followed the U.S. Congress's lead and established a ¥220 billion ($2.1 billion) program to subsidize the transition, including stepped-up consumer awareness campaigns, the establishment of 51 "Audience Support Centers" nationwide, and the provision of free converter boxes to the 2.6 million low-income households receiving welfare (*Kyodo News Service* 2008; see also Kumabe 2010). Subsidies were also given for those (mostly urban) dwellings with shared antennae. A year later digital TVs were included in the government's new "eco-points" scheme, which gave cash paybacks for the purchase of certain environmentally friendly products (Takeishi 2009).[17] With these subsidies in place and the 2011 deadline getting closer, digital penetration increased to 60 percent of households by July 2009 (Suzuki 2009). NHK led the way, announcing in May 2010 that it would end analog satellite broadcasting four months ahead of schedule (*Kyodo News Service* 2010).

Digital transition policy in the United States

Since the 1934 Communications Act, the National Association of Broadcasters (NAB) had come to see its access to spectrum as a right, but during the mid-1980s mobile radio and phone companies such as Motorola began lobbying the Federal Communications Commission (FCC) for more spectrum, especially in the less-used ultra-high frequency (UHF) bandwidth. The NAB fought back with an aggressive campaign to assert an alternative use of this spectrum. They argued that they needed space to develop a domestic version of Japan's HDTV technology. The consumer electronics industry also voiced concern that failing to develop an indigenous HDTV system would damage their competitiveness. The NAB's claims were calculated to resonate with policymakers who feared further Japanese domination of high-tech industries. Following a demonstration of Japanese HDTV on Capitol Hill in October 1987, Representative Don Ritter (R-PA) commented, "We're talking about immense markets with billions of dollars in manufacturing and potentially tens of thousands of jobs.... We are talking about the next revolution in television and right now we are just not a player" (Burgess 1987).

In 1987 such concerns prompted the FCC to establish an Advisory Committee on Advanced Television Service (ACATS), and in 1990 the FCC announced its intention to develop an HDTV system, allowing the NAB to keep the spectrum in return for promises to develop HDTV. But although General Instrument's development of a digital HDTV system in 1991 rendered moot any concerns about the competitive threat from NHK's analog system, the bargain between the NAB and the FCC stuck. In 1993 the Digital HDTV Grand Alliance was chartered to develop an industry standard for DTV broadcasting.[18] The Alliance persuaded the FCC to license the UHF bandwidth for digital HDTV programming to run concurrently with traditional analog broadcasts. This "simulcasting" would provide consumers with ample time to switch from analog to digital sets and was intended to make the driving force behind conversion the supply of attractive HDTV programming offered by broadcasters. The NAB successfully demanded that those licenses be limited to incumbent broadcasters. They also insisted on "spectrum flexibility"—that is, the choice of whether or not to offer the HDTV programming that they had claimed was vital to their long-term competitiveness only a few years earlier. The FCC, in short, agreed to allocate the incumbent broadcasters double the spectrum they already controlled, with an estimated value of up to $70 billion, for a period of at least ten years.

Many observers doubted that the deal served the public interest. Senator Robert Dole (R-KS) lamented, "This is a big, big corporate welfare project ... Here we're cutting Medicaid and doing all the painful things while we lend them [the NAB] the spectrum for 12 years. Why shouldn't they pay for it?" (Safire 1996).

Some suggested auctioning off the spectrum, a scheme similar to the one later championed by the British, which would at least have forced the commercial broadcasters to pay for their privileges. But the NAB lobbied hard and successfully against the idea, exploiting its best political weapon—its own TV broadcasts—to scare the public. NAB lobbyist Jim May admitted, "I want to create an environment where Congress understands that auctions will have a devastating effect on free, over-the-air TV" (Fahri 1996). The NAB even set up a call station complete with operators to warn callers, "Congress wants to pass a law.... All the shows you see, they want you to pay for it. If this passes, the networks would send you a bill each month, just like cable" (Fahri 1996). The Grand Alliance also invoked the old theme of national competitiveness in 1996 comments by Robert K. Graves before the Commerce Committee Subcommittee on Telecommunications and Finance: "Up-front auctions would delay HDTV generally, and render it stillborn for free over-the-air TV. This would throw away America's technological lead, threaten jobs and global competitiveness, and thwart the delivery of valuable services" (*HDTV Magazine* 2005).

Congress proved easily swayed, not least because of the desire of almost all members of Congress to keep good relations with the television industry, which held such a central role in shaping public opinion (Mintz and Farhi 1997). The Telecommunications Act of 1996 (47 U.S.C. 336(a)) contained several provisions very favorable to broadcasters—for example, giving incumbent broadcasters first refusal on any additional spectrum allocations for new television services (Galperin 2004: 98). Implicit in the bill's provisions was the belief that broadcasters had a right to spectrum access, although it also authorized the FCC to condition this right by requiring a minimum amount of HDTV broadcasting hours per day.

Six months later, in 1997, the Balanced Budget Act was before Congress. By then the FCC had set an aggressive timetable for the return of the analog spectrum by 2006. The NAB feared this accelerated schedule and sought to insert a provision into the Act that would allow them to keep the analog stations longer. They found an advocate in Representative W.J. "Billy" Tauzin (R-LA), who drafted a provision that would have allowed broadcasters to keep their analog stations until 95 percent of the viewers in their market were able to receive digital signals. Senator John McCain (R-AZ) successfully lowered this digital penetration threshold to 85 percent (Mintz and Farhi 1997).

But the broadcasters defeated other proposals requiring them to earn their newly awarded spectrum and ten-year protection from competition. Senator McCain had led efforts to require the commercial broadcasters to provide more public-interest services such as educational programming or mandatory prime airtime for political candidates during elections. This last proposal was a particularly hot issue in the debate over campaign finance, and McCain expressed his frustration at its defeat:

> Broadcasters pulled off one of the greatest scams in American history by getting billions of dollars in free digital TV licenses. It's outrageous that they now refuse to act in the public interest and give a mere five minutes of air time for candidate discourse while they rake in billions of political ad dollars.
>
> (Turegano 2000)

The idea behind loaning second channels to the networks was to enable them to promote consumer interest in DTV while maintaining their regular schedules in analog. But the broadcasters showed little urgency in meeting the deadline of December 31, 2006, because by law the switch-off could occur only when digital penetration reached 85 percent. Unhurried, the networks used the spectrum to transmit extra analog channels rather than HDTV or digital offerings (Labaton 2002). By 2005, one year before the 2006 deadline for analog switch-off, just 3 percent of households had digital TVs. Around 80 percent could receive digital signals through cable or satellite, but any analog TV not hooked directly to the signal input would be obsolete after transition.

In 2005, faced with the prospect that the looming 2006 deadline for analog switch-off would leave at least 20 percent of the country without any TV, and with hundreds of millions of useless analog sets even in digital households, Congress extended the deadline to February 2009. Congress also authorized up to $1.5 billion in subsidies for coupons to help pay for set-top converters (a maximum of two $40 coupons per household, with converters then starting at about $60) (Labaton 2005). The FCC reinvigorated its public awareness campaign, using thousands of employees and volunteers to staff over 500 walk-in advice centers, provide call-in services, or make house calls to install converters (FCC 2009).

Even so, the February 2009 deadline was extended again, at the very last minute, by newly elected President Barack Obama. Over 6.5 million households were still analog-only, and disproportionately poor and non-English-speaking. The converter-box subsidy program had been confusing, underfunded, and poorly managed, with more than 3.7 million households still on a waiting list for coupons (K. Hart 2009). The coupon program was refinanced as part of Obama's massive stimulus package, the FCC dealt with a last-minute rush of inquiries, and switch-off went off relatively smoothly in June 2009. Although 2.8 million households (about 2.5 percent, and disproportionately African-American and Hispanic) were still analog-only, that figure continued to fall dramatically to 1.2 million households (1.1 percent) by July 2009 (Nielsen Company 2009). The entire transition had been estimated to cost $2.15 billion and had raised $19.6 billion from the 2008 auctions of freed-up spectrum (Huck 2009).

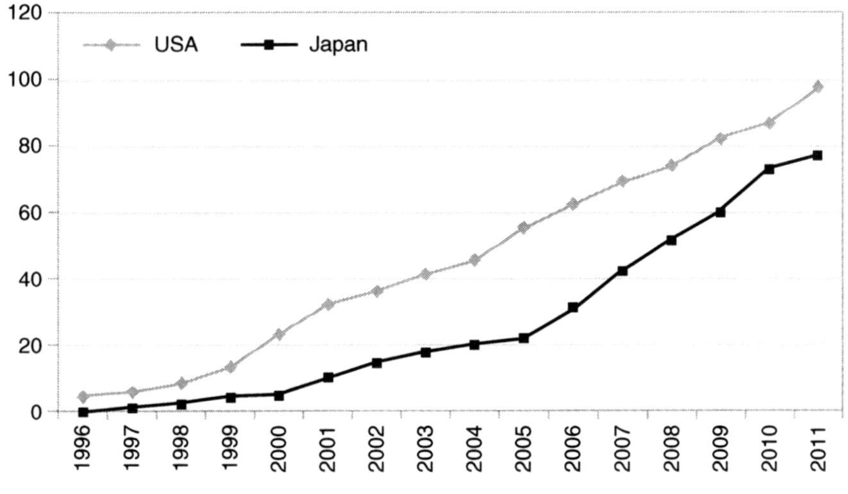

Figure 8.1 Digital television households: percentage penetration rates (sources: Ofcom 2012; MPHPT 2002; FCC 2009).

Table 8.1 National strategies for digital TV transition

	Japan	*United States*
Launch	1994	1993
First b'cast (Sat/C)	1996	1994
First b'cast (DTT)	2003	1998
Transition	2011	2009
Transmission format	ISDB-T higher audiovisual quality, more expensive	ATSC cheaper, more flexible
New spectrum allocation	Incumbents	Incumbents
Subsidies to broadcasters	Grants and tax breaks for conversion costs	Free spectrum 2x existing allocation
Subsidies to consumers	$2 billion in converter boxes, eco-coupons, etc	$1.5 billion in converter box coupons
Last-minute panic measures	Publicity campaigns Helplines Call centers Antennae assistance	Publicity campaigns Helplines Call centers Antennae assistance
DTV penetration (% households) in 2011	77%	89%

Table 8.2 Diffusion of digital television in selected countries

Country	*Transition from analog to digital broadcasts*	*DTV households in 2011 (%)*
Netherlands	2006	68
Sweden	2007	63
Germany	2009	66
United States	2009	89
Spain	2010	100
Japan	2011	77
Canada	2011	78
France	2011	97
United Kingdom	2012	99
Italy	2012	93
Australia	2013	83
New Zealand	2013	70

Sources: Ofcom (2012); European Commission (2006); Syfret (2004); Ofcom (2010).

Conclusion

This chapter has three main findings. (1) The Japanese state was no more effective than the U.S. government at managing digital transition. Indeed, if anything, the United States outperformed Japan, which started the process of transition later, completed it later, and achieved consistently lower rates of DTV penetration. (2) Despite the expectations of the literature on varieties of capitalism, there was little *systematic* difference in the strategies both countries adopted. Both American and Japanese policymakers employed a mix of market-friendly and state-directed carrots and sticks to accomplish transition. In both countries, relationships between state and market actors were sometimes antagonistic, at other times cooperative—and both the Japanese and the Americans provided handsome subsidies to both broadcasters and viewers. (3) Japanese policy favored the consumer electronics industry. In contrast, U.S. policy favored the commercial broadcasters and, to a lesser extent, the viewers, for whom greater channel choice resulted, albeit often with lower audiovisual quality.

Notes

1 The exact frequencies for TV broadcasting vary from country to country, but typically use the very high frequency (VHF) and ultra-high frequency (UHF) bandwidths. A full technical explanation is beyond the scope of this chapter. The reader is instead referred to the explanations found at the website of the Federal Communications Commission, FCC.gov.

2 Recent work by Ostrom and others (1994) notes that institutional solutions to common-pool resource problems may also be devised privately under certain favorable conditions, such as the very close social ties that allow the "lobster gangs of Maine" to enforce informal rules against overfishing (Acheson 1988). Such conditions have not generally applied to spectrum use, and this chapter is therefore concerned with formal state regulation.

3 Three books stand out in telling the full story; see J. Hart (2004), Galperin (2004), and Starks (2007).
4 In the United States around 75 percent of households own more than one set, and around 43 percent own three or more. In Britain the average is three TVs and one VCR per household.
5 In Britain STB prices fell from around $600 in 1998 to around $150 or less in 2004.
6 The switch from black-and-white to color TV took at least 15 years.
7 The neatest example of a cooperation game with a self-reinforcing compliance mechanism is reaching agreement over which side of the road to drive on (Noble 1998).
8 By contrast, competition problems are best solved by strong institutional mechanisms to enforce compliance.
9 In 2008; the figure has declined only marginally with the increased popularity of the Internet.
10 The Ministry of Posts and Telecommunications (MPT) (Yûseishô) was to become in 2001 the Ministry of Public Management, Home Affairs, Posts, and Telecommunications (MPHPT) as a result of a major reorganization and consolidation of ministries in 2001. It was renamed the Ministry of Internal Affairs and Communications (MIC) (Sômushô) in 2004.
11 Confidential interview with MPT official, Tokyo, August 2001.
12 Interview with NHK staffer, Tokyo, October 2000.
13 Interviews with investment analysts, Tokyo, August 2001.
14 Interview with political journalist, Tokyo, December 2000.
15 In the words of Fukuoka Toru (quoted in *Yomiuri Shimbun* 2003).
16 A February 2002 poll conducted by NHK discovered that 61 percent of the viewing public had never heard of terrestrial digital broadcasting, and only 9 percent had a clear idea of what it involved (*Asahi Shimbun* 2002a).
17 A 32-inch liquid crystal digital TV would receive a ¥12,000 (about $130) rebate. As with the U.S. coupon system of refunds for set-top box converters, the degree of confusion and hassle involved was apparently high enough to deter many consumers from taking advantage.
18 The Alliance included representatives from AT&T, General Instrument Corp., MIT, Philips Consumer Electronics, Thomson Consumer Electronics, Zenith Electronics Corp., and the David Sarnoff Research Center.

References

Acheson, James. 1988. *The Lobster Gangs of Maine*. Hanover, NH: University Press of New England.

Asahi Shimbun. 2002a. "Cost Overruns and Other Delays Slow the Shift." May 22.

Asahi Shimbun. 2002b. "Government Should Explain New Technology." November 25.

Asahi Shimbun. 2003. "Digital Broadcasting on a TV Near You." December 2.

Bleha, Thomas. 2005. "Down to the Wire." *Foreign Affairs* 84 (May/June): 111–124.

Burgess, John. 1987. "Chances Are High TV Breakthrough Is in the Air; U.S. Industry Looks for Its Place in the Picture Even Though Japanese Have Head Start." *Washington Post*, October 11.

European Commission. 2006. "The European Commission's Approach to Digital Interactive Television: Frequently Asked Questions." Online: http://europa.eu/rapid/press-release_MEMO-06-60_en.htm.

Fahri, Paul. 1996. "TV Claims Congress Could Steal Show; Digital-Auction Advocates Dispute Ad's Scare Tactics." *Washington Post*, March 20, p. D1.

FCC (Federal Communications Commission). 2009. *FY 2009 Annual Performance Report*. Online: http://transition.fcc.gov/Reports/ar2009.pdf.

Financial Times. 1996. "Japanese TV Loses Cosy Glow in Digital World." October 10, p. 33.

Galperin, Hernan. 2004. *New Television, Old Politics: The Transition to Digital TV in the United States and Britain*. New York: Cambridge University Press.

Gekkan Nyûmedia Henshûbu [New Media Monthly], eds. 2000. *Dijitaru kôkyô hôsôron: NHK Kaicho Ebisawa Katsuji ga kataru* [Digital Public Broadcasting: NHK Chairman Ebisawa Katsuji Speaks]. Tokyo: New Media Company.

Grimes, William. 2001. *Unmaking the Japanese Miracle: Macroeconomic Politics 1985–2000*. Ithaca, NY: Cornell University Press.

Hall, Peter, and David Soskice, eds. 2001. *Varieties of Capitalism: The Institutional Foundations of Comparative Advantage*. Oxford: Oxford University Press.

Hara, Yoshiko. 2003. "Japan Tunes in to Digital TV." *Electronic Engineering Times*, June 16.

Hardin, Garrett. 1968. "The Tragedy of the Commons." *Science* 13 (December): 1336–1337.

Hart, Jeffrey. 1998. "Digital Television in Europe and Japan." *Prometheus* 16 (2): 217–237.

Hart, Jeffrey. 2004. *Technology, Television, and Competition: The Politics of Digital TV*. Cambridge: Cambridge University Press.

Hart, Kim. 2009. "Congress Delays Troubled Switch to Digital TV." *Washington Post*, February 5, p. A1.

HDTV Magazine. 2005. "Oral Statement of Robert K. Graves before the Commerce Committee Subcommittee on Telecommunications and Finance, United States House of Representatives, March 21, 1996." Last modified March 25. Online: www.hdtvmagazine.com/archives/graves.html.

Herskovitz, Jon. 2000. "Japan Nears Digital Age." *Variety*, April 3, p. M34.

Huck, Peter. 2009. "The Day America Changed Channels." *Guardian* (London), June 17, Technology section, p. 3.

Immergut, Ellen, and Ikuo Kume, eds. 2006. "A Crisis of Governance in Japan and Europe." Special issue, *Governance* 19 (1) (January).

Japan Times. 2000. "State Adopts IT National Strategy." November 28, p. 1.

Jiji Press. 2000a. "Keidanren Urges Government to Pay for Digital Terrestrial TV." *Jiji Ticker Service*, August 16.

Jiji Press. 2000b. "LDP OK's Government Shouldering Digital Broadcast Costs." *Jiji Ticker Service*, April 25.

Johnson, Chalmers. 1982. *MITI and the Japanese Economic Miracle*. Stanford, CA: Stanford University Press.

Katori, Naotake. 2006. "Digital TV Sales Static as Off-Air Date Looms." *Daily Yomiuri*, December 5, p. 4.

Krause, Reinhardt. 1994. "Japan's Strategy Shifts to ISDB." *Electronic News* 40 (2015), May 23.

Krauss, Ellis. 2000. *Broadcasting Politics in Japan*. Ithaca, NY: Cornell University Press.

Kumabe, Norio. 2010. "Preparations for Digital Switchover in Japan: An Update." *International Journal of Digital Television* 1 (1): 85–87.

Kumabe, Norio. 2012. "Challenges of Television after Digital Switchover in Japan." *International Journal of Digital Television* 3 (3): 349–355.

Kyodo News Service. 1999. "Government Urged to Tolerate Delay in Upgrade to Digital TV." *Japan Economic Newswire*, September 14.

Kyodo News Service. 2002a. "Government Sets up Digital TV Study Group." September 13.

Kyodo News Service. 2002b. "Viewer Understanding Key to Success of Digitization." *Japan Economic Newswire*, April 24.

Kyodo News Service. 2003a. "Little to Celebrate as Digital Satellite TV Marks 1,000th Day." September 22.

Kyodo News Service. 2003b. "Terrestrial Digital TV Trial Broadcasts to Begin." August 5.

Kyodo News Service. 2008. "Government Strives for Smooth Transition to Digital TV." July 18.

Kyodo News Service. 2010. "Japan's NHK to Bring Forward End of Analog Satellite Broadcasting." May 30.

Labaton, Stephen. 2002. "Most Commercial Broadcasters Will Miss Deadline for Digital Television." *New York Times*, April 29, p. C6.

Labaton, Stephen. 2005. "Transition to Digital Gets Closer." *New York Times*, December 20, p. C1.

Mintz, John, and Paul Farhi. 1997. *Washington Post*, July 20.

MPHPT (Ministry of Public Management, Home Affairs, Posts, and Telecommunications). 2002. *Information and Communications in Japan: White Paper 2002*. Tokyo: MPHPT.

MPT (Ministry of Posts and Telecommunications [Yûseishô]). 1995. *Broadcasting System in the Multimedia Age*. Tokyo: MPT.

MPT. 1998. Digital Terrestrial Broadcasting Advisory Committee [Chijô dijitaru hôsô kondankai]. *Shin dijitaru chijô hôsô shisutemu no keisei* [Shaping the New Digital Broadcasting System]. Tokyo: MPT.

MPT. 2000a. *Maruchimedia hakusho 2000: Kontentsu-komasu ni mukete* [Multimedia White Paper 2000: Towards Contents-Commerce]. Tokyo: MPT.

MPT. 2000b. *Tsushin Hakusho Heisei 12* [MPT Communications White Paper 2000]. Tokyo: MPT.

Nakamoto, Michiyo. 1999. "Digital TV Causes Divisions and Heart-Searching in Japan." *Financial Times*, April 28, p. 7.

Nielsen Company. 2009. "98.9% of American Homes Able to Receive DTV." *Nielsen Newswire*, July 29. Online: www.nielsen.com/us/en/newswire/2009/989-of-american-homes-able-to-receive-dtv.html.

Nihon Keizai Shimbun. 2002. "Manufacturers Have High Expectations for Digital TV Sets." July 18.

Noble, Gregory. 1998. *Collective Action in East Asia: How Ruling Parties Shape Industrial Policy*. Ithaca, NY: Cornell University Press.

Noble, Gregory. 2000. "Let a Hundred Channels Contend: Technological Change, Political Opening, and Bureaucratic Priorities in Japanese Television Broadcasting." *Journal of Japanese Studies* 26 (1): 79–109.

Ofcom. 2010. *International Communications Review*, 117.

Ofcom. 2012. "Spain Has the Highest Proportion of Digital Television (DTV) Homes per 100 TV Households, with the UK in Second Place." Online: http://stakeholders.ofcom.org.uk/market-data-research/market-data/communications-market-reports/cmr12/international/1.08.

Olson, Mancur. 1965. *The Logic of Collective Action: Public Goods and the Theory of Groups*. Cambridge, MA: Harvard University Press.

Osaki, Tad. 2003. "Nervous Energy: Digital TV Is Nigh in Japan." *Television Asia* (November).

Ostrom, Elinor, Roy Gardner, and James Walker. 1994. *Rules, Games, and Common-Pool Resources*. Ann Arbor: University of Michigan Press.

Pollack, Andrew. 2001. "Japan Says It Will Move up Introduction of Digital Television." *New York Times*, March 11, p. D6.

Reid, T.R. 2010. *The Healing of America.* London: Penguin Books.

Safire, William. 1996. *Times Picayune*, January 6.

Starks, Michael. 2007. *Switching to Digital Television: UK Public Policy and the Market.* Bristol, UK: Intellect.

Suzuki, Yoshikazu. 2009. "Viewers Lag in Digital TV Prep." *Daily Yomiuri*, July 25, p. 4.

Syfret, Toby. 2004. "European DTV Trends 2003–2005." *Enders Analysis* (January).

Tabuchi, Hiroki. 2012. "Inquiry Declares Fukushima a Man-Made Disaster." *New York Times*, July 7.

Takeishi, Masahiro. 2009. "Demystifying Eco-Points System." *Daily Yomiuri*, May 18, p. 7.

Turegano, Preston. 2000. "Critics Press Local Stations to Air Issues." *San Diego Union-Tribune*, October 2.

Wakasugi, Mariko. 2003. "Shift to Digital TV: Will It Benefit Japan's Techs?" *Jiji Press*, December 10.

Yomiuri Shimbun. 2003. "Launch of Digital Terrestrial TV Broadcasting to Face Difficult Tasks." October 31.

Part IV

The People's Republic of China

9 The Beijing consensus, the world capitalist system, and the limits of globalization

Peter Moody

The 2008 financial crisis encouraged some rethinking about the way the world works. With the general collapse of the world communist movement after 1989, many thought liberal democracy, coupled with a liberal market economy, was the only way the world possibly could be organized (Fukuyama 1992). What used to be pejoratively called the world capitalist system had defeated all plausible rivals, allowing the free movement of goods, services, and capital across the globe, unimpeded by narrow national or cultural obstacles, creating the conditions for enduring prosperity.

Hardly by coincidence, this vision had its greatest currency when the United States dominated the world militarily, politically, economically, and even morally. The economic vision was summed up under the name "Washington consensus," a tacit program for a globalized liberal market economy.[1] Whether or not there was really a consensus, "Washington" set the rules everyone had to abide by.

Those rules, however, seemed less compelling after the near-collapse of the U.S. economy in 2008; a consequence, some asserted, of inadequate political regulation of economic activity. Among the major powers, China seemed to weather the global storm the best, and for a time it became fashionable to postulate a "Beijing consensus" to replace that of Washington (Rambo, 2004).[2] This supposed alternative included a drive for innovation directed and protected by the state; self-determination, meaning the ability of the state to set for itself the terms on which it interacted with the world outside; a concern for maintaining social and political stability; and state action to ensure a relatively even distribution of the benefits of growth, avoiding gross disparities of wealth and income.

Chinese elites were loath explicitly to adopt the notion of a Beijing consensus, at least until the Xi Jinping era. And an equitable distribution of wealth and income has hardly been a prominent feature of post-Mao development. The oohing and aahing over Chinese ways may be an instance of 多驚少怪, much marveling over something not very strange. As described, the Beijing consensus or model seems much like the old Asian (or Japanese) model that so amazed the world in the last quarter of the twentieth century,[3] a model that supposedly crashed and burned in 1997. On the other hand, the Chinese way seemed to be prospering under the conditions in which the older Asian model seemed to have failed.

The Washington Consensus and the East Asian Tigers

Globalization, the flattening of the world into a single integrated market, has a close family resemblance to Lenin's version of imperialism, the highest stage of capitalism; although the current version lacks the promise of anything better to come, should capitalism collapse. The current U.S.-centered imperialism, if we can call it that, is based more on access than on control of territory (Huntington 1973). A generalized free access should in principle work to allow the fullest play of comparative advantage and so foster the maximum possible wealth and productivity for the world as a whole. Sovereign rulers, however, wish to control access to the territory supposedly under their jurisdiction; and while free access may in principle benefit everyone as a whole, it can impose unwanted costs on particular social or economic interests. Also, while free trade may make the best use of comparative advantage, it also reinforces existing patterns of comparative advantage, and ruling elites may wish to shift the set. Historically it has been the politically and economically dominant countries that have most vigorously promoted free trade (Lake 1988). And under certain circumstances these hegemonic powers may be willing, for strategic or other reasons, to allow others a free ride—as England did the United States during the nineteenth century.

Globalization in its current phase may foster industrialization in poor countries, that is, as rich areas transfer manufacturing to areas where wages are low (Mittelman 1999: 226). Globalization is also often thought to weaken the power of the state. There are disputes concerning just how true this is. It does not necessarily weaken the coercive power of the state over the weaker part of those subject to it; a free trade regime does limit the ability of rulers to control economic activity within their scope of sovereignty.[4] A major function of the state is to protect those subject to it—against foreigners and thieves, but also, in contemporary times, against undue economic hardship. State intervention to give preference to domestic industries or welfare benefits to ordinary people disrupts the logic of comparative advantage. These interventions often have the actual consequence of themselves imposing unnecessary hardship on the people and limiting productive potential: so by the 1980s the Chinese rulers had concluded they were better served by linking to the world capitalist system rather than by isolating themselves from it or seeking to overthrow it. But they wished as much as possible to link up on their own terms, and not be left helpless before it.

Any "consensus" on the virtues of the market is relatively recent or, maybe more accurately, a now-passing phase in a recurring cycle. The more general sense in the decades following World War II was that the state had to take an active interest in popular welfare, even at the expense of market efficiency. In the 1950s there was much discussion of a mixed economy, of the need for planning, of the obsolescence, impracticality, inhumanity of the "untrammeled" market, of the convergence of capitalist and socialist systems.

As the economically dominant power, in the postwar years the United States was committed in principle to a universal free trade system (many considered the global turn to economic nationalism in the 1930s to have exacerbated the depression, which in its turn contributed to the rise of aggressive totalitarian regimes); and the American economy was generally open to the outside, at least to what Americans considered the free world. At the same time, however, the United States was caught up in a political and strategic rivalry with the Soviet Union and the communist bloc generally. After the collapse of the European colonial empires Americans feared that these new states might "go communist" unless they were able to develop economically, and the theories of economic development at the time were friendly to programs of state intervention to foster growth (Rostow 1971). In Asia the Americans had a particular interest in the prosperity of Japan. Japan developed its own impressive growth strategy, but one condition for its effectiveness was Japanese access to the American market and American forbearance in allowing Japan to keep its own market closed.

Chalmers Johnson's (1982) classic summary of the Japanese growth model credits the old Ministry of International Trade and Industry (formerly the Ministry of Munitions) as a kind of economic general staff guiding state and industrial policy: "just as a nation mobilized for war needs a military general staff, so a nation mobilized for economic development needs an economic general staff" (Johnson 1982: 241). The Japanese economy was *effective*, but not efficient in the macroeconomic sense. It tolerated a highly wasteful agricultural program geared to maintain a class of small landowners, and put obstacles in the way of developing large retail outlets, keeping alive mom-and-pop stores forced to charge high prices for consumer goods: farmers and shopkeepers voted for the Liberal Democratic Party, which rubber-stamped the policies favored by MITI and the rest of the professional civil service. Japan was not "market rational" but "plan rational." Unlike the Soviet Union or China at the time, the state did not own or directly control the means of production, but provided administrative guidance—setting down regulations and suggestions that business could follow to its benefit or violate to its cost. While governmental bureaucracy and private businessmen (mainly salaried employees) communicated frequently and interacted intensely, it was the bureaucracy that set the rules and had the final say.

The "tiger economies" of the 1980s[5] were variations on the Japanese pattern, and some of this pattern spilled over into the "second string" tigers later on (Malaysia, Indonesia, Thailand). Japan and the tigers proper were all "Confucian" (or, better, "post-Confucian") societies, although mainstream analysts have come generally to shy away from explanations stressing culture. Structurally, all were ruled by a state that was both strong (able to enforce its writ upon society) and autonomous (relatively insulated from particular social interests), the ruling elite "representing" mainly itself, not some segment of society. None were functionally democratic: Taiwan and South Korea were outright police states; Hong Kong was a colony without genuine representative institutions; Japan and Singapore were democratic in form, but worked in a way that guaranteed that the same people would always win. The motive of the ruling elite was the perpetuation of their status—for Taiwan and South Korea in the face of genuine external threat—rather than wealth as such (although individual members of the elite were not necessarily averse to skimming off generous helpings). Economic development helped buffer social discontents while enhancing state capacity. In contrast to the somewhat similar bureaucratic authoritarianism of Latin America (O'Donnell 1981),[6] the Asian model embodied growth with equity: typically as an economy grows, so do disparities of income and wealth; but the Asian states were becoming more egalitarian. None of the governments followed an explicitly redistributionist policy: equality was a by-product of the general strategy—of land reform and the increased rural standard of living as a way to avoid peasant discontent; perhaps a fear of nurturing an overly powerful cohesive moneyed class.

Japan and the tigers encouraged production for export, with the United States as the main target for exports.[7] The East Asian states were tied into the world economy, with the states strong enough to keep control of the terms of that connection, avoiding the Latin American pattern of dependency. These economies also remained relatively closed to goods and services from the outside, combining export promotion with import substitution (here meaning mainly Japan, Taiwan, and Korea).

An "exogenous" background condition for this, however, was American willingness to put up with it, a reflection of the overwhelming size of the American economy and American strategic competition with the Soviet Union. American patience grew shorter as the relative difference between the United States and the rest of the world shrank, as the dollar lost value as a result of government spending on welfare and warfare, the withering of comparative advantage in key industries, and the diminishing sense of threat from the Soviets.

Especially as the perception of threat from the Soviets diminished, so did any American impulse to indulge Asian allies. American policy began pushing its East Asian friends to open their economies—threatening a dilution of state strength—and, a little less consistently, to open up their political systems, diluting state autonomy.

Globalization and the limits of the Asian model

The Asian countries were successful in their export policy because they could produce high-quality goods at economical prices, and perhaps the ultimate reason they could do this was that they followed a sound economic program backed by a healthy society and, alas, rather repressive politics. But another necessary condition for the success of the model was the willingness of foreign markets to absorb Asian products without demanding reciprocity. By the late 1970s the American economy was losing its traditional areas of comparative advantage, especially in industrial manufacturing. These sectors employed large numbers of people who had a certain amount of political clout, and this led to pressures either to open up Asian markets to allow American products to enter or to restrict Asian imports.

Restricting imports would go against the larger American global strategy; and, while Asian markets were certainly closed, opening them to American products was unlikely to create much of a demand for American goods—the

Japanese forte was in making high-quality goods at relatively cheap prices, something the United States was no longer as good at. But a substantial school of scholarship also focused on the way the Japanese government worked to foster Japanese sales: the "competition" with Japan was unfair because the Japanese government, directed by the formidable MITI, was fully behind Japanese industry, whereas the American government remained indifferent or even hostile to American industrial strength. By the late 1980s the animus against Japan, a democracy and an ally, was more vehement than any twenty-first-century grousings about the growing strength of China.[8]

While the American lead goose[9] was flagging, the Soviet threat was also receding, detracting from any American incentive to humor its Asian allies. The United States had tolerated both what many of its citizens considered an uneven economic playing field tilted in favor of the allies, but also the repressive, often harsh regimes that ruled some of the Asian states, with the idea that this was required for the fight against communism. Effective popular resistance to autocracy began in the Philippines (hardly an example of the Asian model), but soon spread to Taiwan and South Korea, the process gaining the full backing of the United States. As ultimate authority came to require an ability to win votes in competitive elections, the autonomy of the state declined, the balance shifting toward those with the means to finance elections. American pressures to open up markets reduced the ability of the state apparatus to control the domestic economy. The old connections between government and economy remained, but the advantage had moved toward those with money rather than governmental office. American policy was operating under its own as-it-were ideology of globalization: universal human happiness is assured by free enterprise, free trade, and political democracy. History had come to an end.[10]

By the 1990s the relationship between America and its traditional Asian friends was testy. Some of the Asian elites, with varying degrees of intensity and seriousness, deployed the concept of Asian values as a counter to American universalism, China joining in this with the more conservative Asian states. The idea was that the Western notion of universal rights was in actuality not universal but a product of a particular set of historical and social conditions, and that democracy and human rights now functioned as a tool to allow America (or America-centered capital) to dominate the globe. "Asian" societies, on the other hand, eschewed "extreme individualism" in favor of the common good and kept a strong sense of family, as opposed to "western" (meaning mainly American) hedonism, characterized by promiscuity, illegitimacy, divorce, crime, perversion—not to mention sloth and envy (of superior Asian performance).

Whatever the validity of "Asian" appreciations of American decadence, the conditions that had sustained the Asian model no longer held and the Asian economies proved weaker than they appeared to be. The Japanese economy went into a seemingly endless sag in the early 1990s: the money flowing into the country had few outlets beyond speculation in stocks and real estate and bribes to politicians—and increasingly to civil servants, who previously had been considered to be scrupulously honest. The result was a bubble, with its inevitable deflation.

The general Asian collapse came in 1997. During the 1990s the old tigers' and their southeast Asian neighbors' economies began to be undercut by Chinese competition, forcing them to push down prices and lowering profits. Globalization opened Asian firms to international competition and allowed mobile foreign capital access to the local economy. In the face of international exposure, the politicians and bureaucrats lost the ability to control economic activity, and the old state–society partnership devolved into "crony capitalism."[11] The state, or its functionaries, who were no doubt duly rewarded, remained sufficiently entangled in economic activity to allow the political elites to direct favors and finance toward the firms of their unprofitable cronies, shielding those cronies from the need to behave in an economically responsible way.

As the firms' profitability fell their debts piled up, but governmental functionaries could protect their business cronies against banks' demands for repayment. But foreigners now had substantial funds in local banks, and began to withdraw them because of what they perceived to be the banks' untenable economic position. The various states responded by devaluing their currencies (enhancing the local value of foreign-denominated bank deposits). The process began in Thailand but soon spread throughout the region in a race to the bottom.[12] U.S.-led globalization was the main beneficiary: indeed the Asian right and left wings both agree that the crash was deliberately engineered by global capitalists, particularly the insidious George Soros.[13] The Asian economies were "bailed out" by the International Monetary Fund, in effect giving the United States, and presumably its financial circles, ever greater control over how the Asian economies should be managed.[14] The 1997 crisis seemed to mark the end of the Asian model, and certainly to chatter about Asian values.

America's comeuppance, of course, came a little more than a decade later, with the collapse of the housing bubble in 2008 and the subsequent financial crisis. Now it was the "Washington consensus" that came to seem pretty pathetic. In the meantime, China had coped well with the 1997 crisis—indeed, it had served as a stabilizing force—and, with a few more rough spots, the 2008 crisis as well. Maybe there was a new lead goose, a new king of the hill.

China as number one

In 2010 China surpassed Japan, becoming in gross terms the world's second largest economy. The United States was still much larger, but there was also a general sense that America was on the decline and China was on the rise (few apparently remembering how a generation earlier there was a similar sense about Japan). A blogger writing from France, Song Luzheng (2013),[15] in an essay carried by the official Chinese media, described a Japan permanently sunk in recession, an India failing to meet earlier developmental promises, America beset by economic crisis and political paralysis, and a Europe stubbornly continuing to live beyond its means. China evidently had both the best economic and the best political system in the entire world. "China has developed a new and completely successful model ... Obviously, when western elites have begun to lose their self confidence, China is welcoming its own return to self-respect." The inexplicably influential *New York Times* columnist Thomas Friedman (2009) had earlier conceded that while "one-party autocracy has its drawbacks," China's system allows its rulers better to cope with the problems of contemporary governance than America's dysfunctional democracy.

Friedman asserted that the Republican Party, responding to the "have-nots of globalized America" (who, unlike the "have-nots of the recession," apparently should reconcile themselves to the trash-heap of history), had become a purely negative force, standing in the way of the ruling class's progressive initiatives on climate, energy, immigration, health care, whatnot. The progressive Chinese ruling class does not have to worry about anyone effectively representing China's globalized have-nots (for example, the poor peasants and workers whom Chairman Mao affected to be so concerned for), but can unimpeded enforce policies in the public good, whether society wants them or not.[16]

Those impressed by a "Beijing consensus" seem to imagine China's rulers, like the mythical old Asian miracle elites, are a set of Platonic guardians unencumbered by a need to pander either to reactionary social forces or to selfish special interests (Bell 2006). This misses the actual political dynamic in China and the earlier tigers. The driving force was not the common good as such but the preservation of the existing structure of power and privilege. In China, however, the nature of state autonomy is a little different from that of the other post-Confucian societies, with the ruling elite now more organically entwined with Big Money.

China was not really sheltered by the American security system, except insofar as the rapprochement between the two powers in the 1970s resulted from common fear of the Soviet Union. The two economies did, however, become interdependent, and so, as Kenneth Waltz (1979: 205, 222) points out, mutually vulnerable, this vulnerability helping to feed strategic differences of interests, something not really an issue between Japan and the United States. China's declaratory policy dilated on how China did not threaten American hegemony over the globalized system: China merely wanted its proper place in that system. But China's military planning, as far as one could glean from open sources, centered on fighting and winning a localized war against the United States.

A strong and autonomous state was a necessary but not sufficient condition for the older Asian model. The Maoist state was generally strong and certainly not subservient to any social interests, but also aspired to control all human activities, including economic activities. By the time Mao Zedong died, this radical politicization was perceived not only as insupportably repressive and gratuitously cruel, but as economically unproductive, perpetuating an artificially low standard of living.

Deng Xiaoping assumed that socialism was supposed to make things better, not worse, and the way to make things better was to allow the economy, through the market, to operate according to its own rationale. Economic liberalization encouraged demands for social, cultural, and, most dangerously, political liberalization. Deng made it clear early on that any liberalization was to remain within certain "cardinal principles," most especially the unchallenged ruling position of the Communist Party.

The logic of reform, however, undermined the rationale for Party supremacy. The earliest reform slogan was that practice was the sole criterion of truth: Marxism, as both Lenin and Mao readily asserted, was not an abstract set of dogmas but a guide to action, to be tested in practice and adjusted accordingly. So, unlike during the Cultural Revolution, the Thought of Mao was not itself the standard of truth: the Thought was followed because it had proved itself in practice. The catch here, though, is that if practice is sufficient to reveal proper policy, then the leadership of the Communist Party is judged according to practice: and, anyway, since anyone can judge whether something works in practice, what is the need for Party leadership in the first place? As Deng himself once said: white cat, yellow cat: who cares?—if it catches mice it's a good cat. Socialism, capitalism—who cares, as long as it delivers the goods? The content of socialism had become ambiguous, and the ideological rationale for Party leadership was vitiated (forcing the ideologues into sophisms about the need for "correct" practice and the like).

In spite of these tensions, the 1980s is probably contemporary China's golden age: living standards rose and life became more varied and more free. But the perpetual bugbears of the reform era also emerged: corruption and inflation—ominous to a generation that still had living memories of the last years of the KMT rule. Inflation resulted from the freeing up of prices that had remained frozen since the 1950s, compounded by poorly chosen methods to combat it.[17] Corruption (in the common pecuniary sense) had been relatively rare in the early days of the PRC.[18] The introduction of the market economy—and the accompanying greater circulation of cash—coupled with the very uneven depoliticization of the economy, meant that those in positions giving them material control over goods and services now had expanded opportunities to make real money from those positions. "Rent seeking"—the ability of those in office to profit from an ability to foster or block economic transactions without adding any value to the transaction—pervaded the economy (Hu 1995).

Corruption, inflation, and the economic and personal insecurities entailed by the pull-back from total control fed the social discontent that culminated in the democracy movement of 1989. The movement and its violent suppression showed that reform of the system had reached the limit it could without spilling over into a reform of the system itself.

The repression, however, changed the parameters. True political liberalization was now off the table. The repression also undermined what legitimacy there was left in the system. The only things the regime had going for it were the ability to inflict pain on those who did not go along and the ability to nurture a rising standard of living. Hardliners saw the reforms themselves as the cause of unrest and would have tightened up the social and economic controls: but this threatened to harm the economy. The regime and people reached what amounted to a new tacit social contract, symbolized by Deng Xiaoping's 1992 "southern tour": the people would not challenge the Party's hold on power and the Party would allow the people to get rich if they could and otherwise live pretty much as they pleased. During the 1990s the economy really took off, and the regime reacquired at least a passive legitimacy.

The Chinese state is strong and autonomous, but only in a qualified sense. It is able to keep the general population in line, although sometimes only by the use of violence or extra-legal coercion. The center can generally control the localities, but not always in fine detail: the higher-ups have their policies, and we have our responses, as the saying goes. The prevalence of corruption shows that the "state" (as an abstract entity) has limited control over the behavior of its functionaries, and this is a form of state weakness.

In classic Marxist theory, the state is the executive committee of the ruling class: under capitalism it does what the bourgeoisie wants, while after the revolution it defers to the proletariat. In the Asian model and the Mao-era PRC, however, there was not really a ruling class as such. The political-bureaucratic-military elite ran the system presumably in its own interests, but without being deeply beholden to any particular interest in the wider society. During the reform era in China, this system broke down, with the de facto merger of the economic elites and the party-state apparatus, or the transformation of the political elite into the economic elite (McGregor 2010). Private capital functions at the sufferance of the political elite and political power has become a means for economic gain. An epitome of the process is in Jiang Zemin's redefinition of the role of the Party in the Three Represents. Classically, the Party represents the proletariat (in alliance with other segments of the "laboring people"). In the "new conditions," the Party represents society's "advanced productive forces," including business leaders, or, in the common parlance, millionaires.[19] Less has been heard of the Represents since Jiang left office, but the reality remains.

The Chinese elite seems to agree about the nature and scope of the system's problems; this has been the object of constant talk since at least the mid-1980s. But at the same time, everyone whose opinion counts has had a vested interest in keeping the system as it is: everyone accepts the need for change in the abstract, but no one has an incentive to do anything in particular.[20] Some even purport to fear that if these tensions are not confronted, the outcome will be turmoil, economic collapse, and a new revolution. On the other hand, in gross terms China is doing just fine and may well continue to do so. But the Beijing model, if that is the proper term for it, has the political costs of the old Asian model but without the social advantages.

Tensions and contradictions of the Beijing model

In the early 1990s there was a debate among some exiled Chinese scholars over whether China's pattern of growth approximated that of Latin America more than the Asian tigers. Whereas the tigers were noted for "growth with equity," Latin America, despite or because of high rates of GDP growth, experienced growing gaps between rich and poor: one of the few economic ills absent from Maoist China. There may be cultural factors that made this inequity even more demoralizing in China than elsewhere: Confucius himself had commented that inequality is more likely to lead to turmoil than is simple scarcity (*Analects* 16:1). The impression in the early days of fast growth was that the ordinary person did not resent the wealth of others as such: if one got rich by dint of greater effort, skill, intelligence, propensity to take risks, or even luck, there was no problem. It became a problem when the general perception was that wealth came by dirty ways, through swindles, favoritism, connections, pull. This perception was strengthened as the years rolled by and money and power became ever more intimately entangled.

While the urban–rural gap may have shrunk in the first years following the agricultural reforms, by the mid-1990s it was widening again. The Mao-era policies regarding household registration and grain rationing were designed to keep the rural population in place. By the 1990s younger peasants, perceiving the possibility of greater opportunities in the cities and the growing tacit official tolerance for what one analyst, citing Marx, called a "reserve army of labor," fed a "blind flow" toward the cities. This helped keep labor costs, and the costs of production generally, low, and enhanced China's competitive position in the globalized economy. The migrants undermined the security of established urban workers and were perceived by the local population as a source of crime and vice. While migration was tolerated or even encouraged by the authorities, basically the old regulations remained in place, dooming the migrants to a marginal existence, vulnerable to exploitation and abuse. In the meantime many rural villages were left without a labor force, populated by small children and the aged.

Prior to reform the urban sector was organized into "work units," *gongzuo danwei*. The workplace provided not only wages or salary, in effect for a lifetime, but also subsidized housing, education, medical care, pensions, travel arrangements, even movie tickets. As China moved into a market economy, especially one aspiring to become globally competitive, the state-owned firms were strapped to keep up with their welfare burdens. But there was no general system of state-provided social welfare to replace the benefits provided by the work unit. Many workers, bred to expect a low but secure standard of living, now had to shift for themselves in a market economy that was increasingly becoming a market society as well (Zhang 1998).

Especially around the turn of the century there was great discontent among the newly insecure state-owned enterprise (SOE) employees. Later the more visible discontent has been in the countryside. Since the 1950s the ownership of land has been vested in the commune or other level of collective. With reform, households became able to rent from the collective for long periods of time, 30 to 50 years, and even were allowed to sublease. In most respects this was tantamount to a return to private farming. But since the family technically did not own the land, ultimate control remained with the collective, or, concretely, the local party-state apparatus.

It has become hard in China as elsewhere to make a living by subsistence farming, and the push of rural poverty complemented the pull of city lights in feeding the blind flow. Land "ownership" has become more concentrated, leading to something like a return to pre-Liberation patterns of stratification. In the early 2000s, the center acted to limit the imposition of arbitrary taxes by local authorities, leaving the localities short of income and encouraging the imposition of arbitrary fees to take the place of the lost arbitrary taxes. The local authorities are also tempted to confiscate farmland and sell it to outside developers, who would normally offer those same local authorities a generous share of the cut. The peasants may try to take the local cadres to court, but the courts, of course, remain under the leadership of the Party.[21] Since the early 2000s there has been a proliferation of "mass incidents" (the official preferred term for riots and demonstrations) (Yu 2009). Higher authorities may intervene in favor of the discounted if the demonstrations become too visible, illegal or extra-legal action by the public serving as a means whereby the higher-ups control their underlings.

Writing toward the end of the 1990s, the commentator He Qinglian noted that those left behind by the reform, and specifically by China's impending entry into the WTO, included industrial workers and poor peasants—China's equivalents of the have-nots of globalization and also the specific supposed social base of the communist revolution (He 1998). Although these have even less political clout than their American counterparts, there is evidence that the ruling elite fears the discontent generated by the social and economic changes. In 2001 the Organization Department circulated a long document detailing "new contradictions among the people." The document claimed that the public has become divided into diverse interest groupings: farmers against workers; "mental workers" versus manual workers; workers in private firms against workers in state firms; center against locality; firms against their own workers; employed versus unemployed; locality against locality; on and on. Some of these differences are reflected within the Party itself and between Party members. The benefits of reform are distributed unevenly; among those left behind there has been a deterioration of access to health care and education and to life chances generally. Social order is endangered by crime, with criminals in cahoots with political authorities; ethnic and religious particularism; hostile subversion:

> Contradictions among the people have become increasingly interwoven with other kinds of contradictions. In recent years various gang-style social formations have colluded with those in authority at the local level and have become a means of social control ... Another prominent manifestation is the use of contradictions among the people such as ethnic or religious problems ... by internal and external enemies to ... cause public unrest and turn it to their advantage.
>
> (Central Organization Department 2001)

The document reflected a sense that during the Deng Xiaoping era policy had focused too narrowly on economic growth for its own sake without attention to the side-effects of growth. Growth should be supplemented with proper social and political measures. Government action should "adjust the relations of advantage," particularly toward narrowing the gap between the rich and the poor. Development programs should give attention to small towns and rural areas. Public administration should be more efficient and transparent, with more supervision and participation by the general public. Cadres should be better educated and better behaved. Government should act within the limits of the law, and both cadres and "masses" should become better aware of what the law entails. And so forth. The document also proposes that the Party organization in neighborhoods be revitalized and that it be extended to non-state firms—a proposal that would possibly facilitate greater social control, but not do much to relieve popular discontent.

The document was drawn up under the general aegis of Zeng Qinghong, consigliere to Jiang Zemin and in those days in overall charge of Party organization. Its proposals and others like them are implied in Hu Jintao's uninspiring slogans concerning a Scientific Development Concept and a Harmonious Society, and remain a part of Xi Jinping's China Dream. That is, all sectors of the elite agree generally on what should be done: and the problems continue decade upon decade.

Of course, it is always fairly easy to point out what is wrong, and proposed solutions are likely to be impossible to implement and, when implemented, ineffective and generative of new problems of their own. But the other consideration is that addressing the political and social problems requires political reform, and the consequences of political reform are uncertain and threaten to disrupt the equilibrium of political forces that ruled throughout the first decade of the twenty-first century, damaging the interests of those who, when all is said and done, benefit from things as they are. Everyone knows that change is needed, but each is motivated to block initiatives taken by others.

The late Tang Tsou (1995) of the University of Chicago, criticizing theories of Chinese politics based on factionalism, argued instead that the process is a winner-take-all one. Any seeming accommodation between rivals is only a temporary expedient born of an inability to consolidate a decisive victory. But if this kind of deadlock persists too long, however, it may become institutionalized: the "game to win all" may become too risky and there may be greater expected value in remaining content with partial and shared victories. China seems to have evolved during the 1990s an alternative balance of power system in which the victors both refrain from attempting to eliminate their rivals and even share some of the power with them. It is too much to say this is fully institutionalized: we might infer that Xi Jinping hoped to move back to winner-take-all; but for at least two decades it shaped the Chinese political process.

The political scientist Cheng Li (2009) identifies a kind of "two-faction" system. One "faction" is a congeries of Jiang Zemin's "Shanghai Gang" (cadres who worked with Jiang in Shanghai prior to 1989—although perhaps not all of these, since Zhu Rongji was probably not part of that Gang) and the so-called "princelings" (*tai zi dang*),[22] children of high-ranking leaders of the PRC's founding generation. The key figure was Zeng Qinghong, both a princeling and a member of the Shanghai Gang. The "rival" group was rooted in those cadres who had once served in the Communist Youth League under its one-time head, Hu Jintao (who in his turn had, amazingly, been designated by Deng Xiaoping as Jiang Zemin's successor in the early 1990s). Li identifies these groupings with particular policy tendencies—the Shanghai crowd were "elitists," given to a technocratic and free-market approach to issues, while the League faction was "populist," favoring broader political participation and greater equality of result. It is probably an error to attempt to identify the groupings with approaches to policy, however: it is more likely there are few if any systematic differences of opinion between the groups.[23] The groupings are, rather, more nearly loose guanxi networks, not hard and fast disciplined factions. The bitterest political battle of 2012 was centered within the princelings' network; and the specific constellation of power Li describes is unlikely to endure over the coming years.

During the 1990s there seems to have evolved a consensus, whether implicit or explicit, that offices will be shared between the two groupings. There were limits on how long anyone could hold high office: cadres should not be reappointed if they were over the age of 70 at the expiration of their current term (although in 1997 Jiang Zemin managed to get around this through what his peers probably considered a slimy maneuver), and the tenure for the top position, General Secretary, would be limited to two five-year terms.[24] Also, since the 1990s there has been a back-and-forth between the two groupings: so when Jiang Zemin was boss, Zeng Qinghong kept the second seat warm until he reached 70 and then passed on the real crown princedom to Hu Jintao; Hu's crown prince was the princeling Xi Jinping; and Xi's crown prince, it is assumed, was Li Keqiang or Wang Yang, one-time vassals of Hu Jintao's.

Xi Jinping does not show an abstract commitment to these rules, and if there is any consensus it is far from fully institutionalized. Its original form is unlikely to survive the lifespans of the current cohort of high-ranking cadres. Ambitious persons impatient for their turn or fearful their turn will never come have an incentive to try to break the pattern, constrained only by the risk the attempt would damage the system, bringing themselves down with everyone else. What was expected to be a smooth transition in 2012, well planned five years in advance, became instead a vicious underground power struggle.

While there has been a general consensus on policy—mainly, to talk about what is wrong but don't do anything about it—in recent years there have been two well-publicized differences of approach in what *might* be done about it: the so-called Guangdong and Chongqing models (Zheng 2013). The Guangdong model is associated with Wang Yang, who was Party boss of that province until 2012, when he was promoted to the Politburo and made a vice-premier of the State Council with a general responsibility for poverty alleviation and economic development. Prior to coming to Guangdong in 2007 he had been First Party Secretary of Chongqing municipality. Wang had previously served in the apparatus of the Communist Youth League under Hu Jintao. The Guangdong model stressed the free market with less state involvement in economic activity and expanded democratic procedures at the local level. The model addresses the core problem of corruption by holding local officials more directly accountable to those they rule and, by weakening the ties between state and economic activity, reducing the opportunities to translate power and position into money.

The somewhat more famous Chongqing model is associated with Bo Xilai, son of the late Party elder Bo Yibo. Bo followed Wang as Party boss in Chongqing. His approach stressed a certain reliance on SOEs conditioned to respond to market signals, cooperation between the state and private business, active measures to alleviate differences between the rich and the poor, severe police repression against corruption, and the organized inculcation of mass patriotism and morality. These last two measures are epitomized in the slogan *chang hong da hei*: sing of the Red and smash the Black (black societies, mafias). Police boss Wang Lijun (2011) wrote, or signed, a good summary of the Chongqing approach in 2011, addressing the pathologies of social change, identified as an intermeshing of political authority and organized crime, and its consequence, a loss of any sense of social solidarity.

Wang's focus, as might be expected, is on smashing the Black. But his discussion goes beyond that, since "the field of law and order is the meeting place for all contradictions in society." He traces analogies between the development of capitalism and of organized crime. Gangs, he says, evolve from primitive violence to more sophisticated forms of activity. At the highest level of development they leave raw violence behind and organize themselves as companies or firms, "using a legal cover to mask their illegal goals." "They put their own representatives into the organs of public authority … They will use their influence to affect the government and judicial activities."

The "hotbed" for organized crime is rapid social change. The government loses "its sense of what is going on at the lower levels of society." There are local breakdowns of public order, providing space for crime to move into. Social change brings cultural conflict, unemployment, and social mobility, with the "mobile population" (here meaning rural migrants living a semi-legal existence in the cities) providing a "reserve army for organized crime."

Wang identifies the strength of organized crime in its connections with government and business. To overcome crime, government must become "more transparent." "The state must have absolute power of social management in order to keep a firm grip on all that relates to the people's welfare." "We must strictly supervise companies and firms to see that they do not depart from the proper track." The state must promote economic development, but also work to eliminate disparities of wealth. But at the same time it must also assure equality of opportunity in addition to fairness of outcome. "The key is to strengthen grassroots governmental authority, keeping a firm hold on the management of society at the base level, rooting out the sprouts of organized crime."

"Virtue grows from a solid root when it is irrigated by culture from within. We must hold firmly to the construction of a core socialist value system" (the rationale for singing the Red). "We must broaden controls over mass media and the cultural market place, preventing the spread of corrupt and reactionary cultural products."

In practice the model included an embarrassingly overt exaltation of Bo Xilai as a person and a ruler.[25] Bo thus violated the rule of thumb in the leadership consensus: blend into the background, keep your mouth shut, and wait your turn. Bo and Wang Yang were, of course, political rivals, and much of Bo's anti-crime activity in Chongqing is credibly alleged to have been directed against Wang's clients in that municipality. But Wang was hardly the most potent rival, and in 2012 Bo was brought down.

The Bo Xilai saga is intrinsically and pruriently fascinating—involving murder, adultery, foreign intrigue, you name it—but it is out of place to try to trace it here (*Financial Times* 2012). Bo may in fact have been a vicious and corrupt thug, but his real crime was that he threatened the delicately balanced political order. Bo and heir-apparent Xi Jinping were both "princes," and in 2012 it was the turn of a prince to take over the top leadership: so Bo threatened Xi more than Wang Yang or any of the other Youth Leaguers. His campaign against crime was directed not only against Wang Yang but at the economic and criminal connections of any potential rivals; and at the same time he used the spoils to reward his own cronies and induce others to sign up. He also, all the propaganda aside, was genuinely popular, able to talk with ordinary people as an equal and on their own terms. His "charisma" threatened a system that might have been designed to weed out any trace of that quality.

The novelist and social critic Wang Lixiong (2012), accepting the model of two quasi-factional groups alternating in power, argued that Bo's fall did not indicate a crisis in the existing system but, rather, its "mechanization"—机器化—perhaps meaning something like institutionalization, but without the implication of orderly process and capacity for evolutionary change that the second term implies. Wang speculates that had Bo succeeded in his drive to the top, or at least to the Politburo Standing Committee, that would not have been good—but only because of the kind of person Bo is and the methods he uses. But it also would have broken the deadlock, putting some motion into the political machine that for decades has been mainly spinning its wheels.

The ruling coalition is interested in preserving the system that keeps it where it is. Each member individually may want to push himself ahead of the others, but too much energy toward this end undermines the structure itself and provokes action against the would-be insurgent.[26] A strong and systematic attempt to redress the system's pathologies, whether from the left or right, also endangers the structure and disturbs the tranquility of the whole. None of this means the system is unstable—more nearly, the reverse—nor does it mean that China's growth is headed for collapse. But it may imply some major differences between the "Asian model" and the pattern most relevant to China.

Some reflections

The political-economic system is sustained by a particular structure of political power. That structure has prevented major initiatives toward reform, and the general drift is likely to continue as long as the structure is in place. Everyone may agree in principle on the need for political reform, but no one has an incentive to allow anyone else to move toward structural reform.

On the other hand, the structure itself is at best only partly institutionalized, and in its specific composition relies on a particular cast of characters, something that inevitably will change over time. Wang's interpretation may be too pessimistic. While the existing system may be "mechanized" and self-sustaining, that does not mean that those who are a part of it may not try to change it if they think they can get away with it. In the fall of 2013 the new boss, Xi Jinping, seemed to wish to introduce an array of liberalizing economic reforms: cutting red tape, making greater use of the market, curbing some of the privileges of the SOEs. Together with the apparent straight-shooter Wang Qishan, head of the Party disciplinary system, a person with no obvious entangled connections with either of the "factions," he seemed to be rooting out corruption at high levels. The targets of the corruption investigations had their connections in the SOEs, particularly the energy sector, and in the Shanghai/princes group, Xi's own guanxi base.[27] These measures were combined with repression of independent thought (including repression of ordinary people who took it upon themselves to expose official corruption), a verbal return to certain Maoist themes (the "mass line"), and the inculcation of patriotism and conventional morality. Actually, Xi's program may share much with Bo Xilai's "Chongqing model."[28] At the same time, and perhaps worrisomely, Xi seemed to be moving away from the pattern of collective leadership, concentrating power in himself. As General Secretary he would already have the main say in matters pertaining to Party life, the military, and foreign policy; and he seemed intent as well in taking personal control of economic matters and the political police. A single strong ruler might be able to cut through the morass of vested interests, although at least equally likely the result would be to favor one particular collection of interests while alienating the rest.[29] But there may actually have been the possibility that the old post-Deng pattern of political alliances was changing, for better and for worse.[30]

The Chinese pattern and the Asian model share a family resemblance: a state–business "partnership" with the state in the senior position, and a free ride on the globalized economy, the "world capitalist system." More intense globalization combined with shifting American interests strained the old Asian model, and China has perhaps handled globalization better than its erstwhile role models. Given the huge potential domestic demand and relative abundance of natural resources, continent-sized China is also in principle better placed to handle possible retrenchments of globalization and the shrinking of foreign markets—although either of these developments would disaccommodate some in the existing balance of power and privilege.

A major difference is that China presented huge opportunities for rent-seeking. In the Asian model the state regulated and even directed the economy. State functionaries no doubt helped themselves to some of the spoils, but the thrust of the control was to enhance the power of the state, not to enrich the bureaucrats. Corruption was left mainly to businessmen themselves and to elected politicians, not to those who really controlled the direction of things. China, however, retained many of the structures of the old Soviet-style socialist economy. Given a market orientation, this does not hinder economic growth, but it pushes the fruits of growth onto the "red capitalists," the intermixed Party–economic elite. This produces social and morale problems that the earlier tigers were generally free of, at least prior to democratization.

With all of this there was apparently a genuine, if not necessarily well-founded, fear of revolution among some of the elite should political reform not take place. In the aftermath of the 18th Congress there was a curious interest, most notably on the part of corruption-buster Wang Qishan, in a new translation of Alexis de Tocqueville's 1856 classic, *The Old Regime and Revolution* (Tocqueville, 1992–1998). Readers found striking similarities between France prior to 1789 and China today. Peking University professor Guo Yi (2013) notes that during the reign of Louis XVI France was more prosperous than it ever had been. Revolution, Tocqueville said, does not occur when people are thoroughly miserable but, rather, when things have been getting better and there are indications that these good times might not last. The French bourgeoisie had been accumulating greater wealth and influence, and this provoked a reaction by the traditional aristocracy fearful for their power and status. Also, intellectuals had greater opportunities than before to comment on political affairs but not freedom actually to participate in politics; and they were always at risk of sporadic and arbitrary persecution for their commentary. Guo traces the violence and fanaticism of the revolution, when it did come, to the seizure of power by these intellectuals, claiming to speak in the name of the people: the revolutionary politicians were full of political ideals and utterly void of practical political experience. Guo offers his "personal opinion": "First, the privileged class should not focus all attention on preserving their privileged position. Second, the central government should not strive to limit the political freedom of citizens."

The analogies with China are clear, however debatable their relevance. The "bourgeoisie" are like the new private business class and the politicized "intellectuals" are like the multitude of bloggers and other users of the new social media. The "privileged class," of course, is the Party elite. The flaw in the prescription offered by Guo is that there is still little beyond exhortation to induce this privileged class to back down a notch or two in clinging to its privileges. Will a strong dictator serve the turn? Will the system still tolerate a strong dictator?

Fear of revolution may motivate change, but the fear is probably not well founded. In the early twentieth century the battle between KMT and CPC armies was a fair fight. No organization comparable to the CPC could develop in China today; and any band of rebels, whatever the logic of asymmetric conflict, could match the PLA regulars. Even if there are would-be Robespierres among the intellectuals and new "middle class" itching to chop off a few over-privileged heads, there are many more in the same situation who will stick with the way things are for the plausible reason that the alternative would be worse. Those dispossessed by the system, Thomas Friedman's rejects of globalization, whatever their hurts, indignities, and injustices, have little leverage to bring about change. The Chinese "model" has so far been successful, but it is not necessarily something others would deliberately choose to emulate.

Notes

1 The term was apparently coined by John Williamson, an English economist (Williamson 1990).
2 And for an extended discourse on the superiority of Chinese ways, see Arrighi (2007).
3 The literature on this is voluminous. For the general notion, see Johnson (1982), Calder and Hofheinz (1982).
4 That is, the state may act to impose policies suitable to the needs of the global investors. Mittelman (1999: 55). Garreton (1989) argues with respect to Pinochet's Chile that a strong authoritarian state (unresponsive to demands from society) was required to impose a free-market economy.
5 Taiwan, South Korea, Hong Kong, and Singapore; see Calder and Hofheinz (1992).
6 Im (1987) argues for the application of the concept to the Korean military dictatorship; but I think the analogy is valid only to a certain extent, inasmuch as the Korean class structure was very different from that of Latin America.
7 Korea and Taiwan turned to an emphasis on export as a means to acquire hard currency after the cut-off of American economic aid in 1965.
8 For a feel of the times, see Crichton (1992), and the 1999 movie of that novel; for an academic-journalistic account, see Woronoff (1986).
9 The reference is to the "flying geese paradigm," a common Japanese metaphor to describe the international dimensions of economic development (see Akamatsu 1962).
10 To echo Sellar and Yeatman (1935). The more solemn reference is to Fukuyama (1992).
11 The term was widely used as an explanation for the 1997 crisis, but I think it first came into use applied to the business–politics relations in the Philippines under Marcos. As indicated earlier, the Philippines was not one of the Asian miracle economies—in part just because the business–government relationship did take the form of crony capitalism.
12 Korea was the hardest hit of the original tigers, although Hong Kong also suffered, probably because of its position as a financial center. The Korean weakness may have been because that country, like Japan, tended to rely on loans to finance business ventures, rather than direct foreign investment.
13 A more academic version is that the predominant interpretation of the crisis constituted a self-serving western "construct" (Hall 2003).
14 Thus, Korea elected a leftist administration a few months after the crisis, but the new rulers had little choice but to follow the austerity program demanded by the foreigners.
15 The structure of the name suggests this might actually be a "gang of three."
16 Friedman's real intention was to pronounce on the United States, so his comments about China (for example, his curious impression that China's rulers have dealt effectively with environmental pollution) are perhaps not intended seriously.
17 Thus, in the early days, bonuses were issued to state employees—factory workers, but not peasants—to make up for inflation, and the bonuses were not tied to productivity.
18 And, given the paucity of ready cash in the system, it tended to take the form of clumsy exchanges of tangible goods for political favors (Liu Binyan 1983: 11–68).
19 Generally speaking, though, it is less that millionaires are flocking to join the Party than that those in the Party now have the opportunity to become millionaires. In effect, the Party elite functions like the "traditional elites" that supposedly stood in the way of healthy social development in bureaucratic-authoritarian Latin America.
20 This particular generalization *may* need to be qualified in view of the outcome of the Third Plenum of the 18th Party Congress, held in November 2013. See below—but we should not hold our breath.

21 There have been cases where the peasants have been able successfully to appeal to higher courts, but these decisions are often ignored by the cadres affected, who may then treat the suit-seeking peasants to a broken leg or two as a souvenir of the experience.
22 The Chinese could easily be rendered princes' group or faction, but the English translations always gratuitously add the pejorative diminutive suffix *-lings*.
23 Zeng Qinghong's 2001 program was fairly populist in tone, and the most colorful proponent of populist programs was Prince Bo Xilai during his reign in Chongqing. The godfather of the rival "Guangdong model," Wang Yang, is a Youth Leaguer and a strong proponent of market economics.
24 Song (2013) considers this "rotation in office" a source of the superiority of the Chinese system over the personalistic dictatorships of the Middle East and the democratic systems of the West: it allows new faces without the bother and uncertainty of competitive elections.
25 See www.youtube.com/watch?v=6QzSe6-m3Lg.
26 Supposedly a reporter visited Hu Jintao's hometown shortly after Hu's 2002 elevation and interviewed one of his elderly aunts. The old lady remembered Jintao as a nice little boy, one who respected his elders and never had to be spanked. Exactly.
27 The ultimate target seemed to be Zhou Yongkang, until his retirement in 2012 the head of the political police system and possibly an ally of Bo Xilai. Xi also seemed to aspire to concentrate in his own person ultimate authority over the police system.
28 His method of operation may also follow the classical Stalinist tactic: unite with the left to purge the right; join with the remnants of the right to purge the left; and when both have been weakened, crunch them together and destroy them both.
29 There may be a comparison with the Philippines under Ferdinand Marcos's martial law. The pre-1972 democracy was dominated by shifting alliances of oligarchical plutocrats, and one of Marcos's rationales for imposing dictatorship was to override these oligarchs. But the result was that he favored his own cronies and made enemies of the rest, making rigid what had been a flexible balance of power system.
30 It must still be remembered that economic liberalization and drives against corruption have been commonplace since the 1980s, so it may also be the same old same old. Also, Xi's early moves against corruption fit the familiar pattern, corruption having replaced the Maoist theme of ideological heterodoxy as a stick with which to beat your opponents.

References

Akamatsu, K. "A Historical Pattern of Economic Growth in Developing Countries," *Journal of Developing Economies*, 1, 1962, 3–25.

Arrighi, Giovanni. *Adam Smith in Beijing: Lineages of the Twenty-First Century*. New York: Verso, 2007.

Bell, Daniel. *Beyond Liberal Democracy: Political Theory for an East Asian Context*. Princeton, NJ: Princeton University Press, 2006.

Calder, Kent, and Roy Hofheinz. *The Eastasia Edge*. New York: Basic Books, 1982.

Central Organization Department. "Correctly Recognize and Handle the New Contradictions among the People under the New Social Situation," *Xin Hua Wenzhai*, July 2001.

Crichton, Michael. *Rising Sun*. New York: Knopf, 1992.

Financial Times, ed. *The Bo Xilai Scandal: Power, Death, and Politics in China*. London: Penguin, 2012.

Friedman, Thomas L. "Our One-Party Democracy," *New York Times*, September 8, 2009.

Fukuyama, Francis. *The End of History and the Last Man*. New York: Free Press, 1992.

Garreton, Manuel. *The Chilean Political Process*. Boston: Unwin Hyman, 1989.

Guo Yi. "What Do We Learn from the Old Regime and Revolution?" *Xin Hua Wenzhai*, May 5, 2013.

Hall, Rodney Bruce. "The Discursive Demolition of the Asian Development Model," *International Studies Quarterly*, 47, 2003, 71–99.

He Qinglian. *Xiandaihua di Xianjing* [Pitfalls of Modernization]. Beijing: Zhongguo Jinri Chubanshe, 1998. [This is a slightly expurgated edition of the original, published in Hong Kong under the title of *China's Pitfalls*].

Hu Angang. "Eradicating Corruption by Means of Creating a New System." *Hu Angang Ji* [Works of Hu Angang]. Harbin: Heilongjiang Jiaoyu Chubanshe, 1995, 441–470.

Huntington, Samuel P. "Transnational Organizations in World Politics." *World Politics*, 25, 1973, 333–368.

Im, Hyug Baeg. "The Rise of Bureaucratic Authoritarianism in South Korea." *World Politics*, 39, 1987, 231–257.

Johnson, Chalmers. *MITI and the Japanese Miracle: The Growth of Industrial Policy, 1925–1975*. Stanford, CA: Stanford University Press, 1982.

Lake, David Power. *Protection, and Free Trade: International Sources of US Commercial Policy, 1887–1939*. Ithaca, NY: Cornell University Press, 1988.

Li, Cheng. "China's Team of Rivals," *Foreign Affairs*, 154, 2009, 88–93.

Liu Binyan. *People or Monsters*. Bloomington: Indiana University Press, 1983, 11–68.

McGregor, Richard. *The Party: The Secret World of Chinese Communist Rulers*. New York: HarperCollins, 2010.

Mittelman, James H. *The Globalization Syndrome: Transformation and Resistance*. Princeton, NJ: Princeton University Press, 1999.

O'Donnell, Guillermo. *Bureaucratic Authoritarianism: Argentina, 1966–1973 in Comparative Perspective*. Berkeley: University of California Press, 1981.

Rambo, Joshua Cooper. "The Beijing Consensus," Foreign Policy Centre, 2004.

Rostow, W.W. *Politics and the Stages of Growth*. Cambridge: Cambridge University Press, 1971.

Sellar, Walter and Robert Yeatman, *1066 and All That*. London: Methuen, 1935.

Song Luzheng. "We Can See the Future Only by Looking at China," *Hong Qi*, 3, 2013.

Tocqueville, Alexis de. *Jiu Zhidu yu Da Geming* [The Old Regime and Revolution]. Shanghai: Shangwu Yinshuguan, 1992–1998.

Tsou, Tang. "Chinese Politics at the Top: Factionalism or Informal Politics? Balance of Power Politics or a Game to Win All?" *China Journal*, 34, 1995, 95–156.

Waltz, Kenneth. *Theory of International Politics*. New York: Random House, 1979.

Wang Lijun. "Combatting and Managing Organized Crime by the Black Societies," May 15, 2011, in *Xin Hua Wenzhai*, August 5, 2011.

Wang Lixiong. "Bo Xilai and the 'Mechanization' of the CPC," *Boxun*, May 3, 2012.

Williamson, John. "What Washington Means by Policy Reform." In Williamson, John, *Latin American Adjustment: How Much Has Happened*. Washington, D.C.: Institute for Economic Studies, 1990, ch. 2.

Woronoff, Jan. *The Japan Syndrome: Symptoms, Ailments, Remedies*. New Brunswick, NJ: Transaction Books, 1986.

Yu Jianrong. "Preserve the Common Denominator for Social Stability: Speech at the Beijing Lawyers Association," December 29, 2009. Online: www.chinaelections.org/printnews. Asp?newsid=169507.

Zhang Pingli. "From 'Unit Man' to 'Social Man': A Slanted View of Chinese Social Development," *Renmin Ribao* (Overseas edition), August 14, 1998.

Zheng, Yongnian. "China in 2012," *Asian Survey*, 53, 2013, 162–175.

10 China's development path

Joys and worries

Weixing (Mark) Chen

China's economic success over the last three decades has made many people wonder whether there is a Chinese model of development. By any standard, China's economic reform is a great success. Given its chaotic past since 1949 before the economic reform, China is certainly a model for itself to emulate, because for the first time since 1949 the Chinese Communist Party (CCP) sets its priority on economic growth and development. Since the economic reform, China has become the second largest economy in the world, the Chinese standard of living has improved significantly, and millions of Chinese have been lifted out of poverty. A country with 1.3 billion people or 19 percent of the world's population on less than 7 percent of the world's arable land has achieved what no other country has. However, could China sustain its economic growth in the years to come and effectively address the pressing issues that have accompanied China's economic success under the framework of "socialism with capitalism" or "socialism with Chinese characteristics"? At what cost has China achieved its economic success? More importantly, has China's economic success so far made China a model to be emulated by others in their development? In addressing these questions, this chapter analyzes China's economic success in the first part, examines China's development from the perspectives of the three generations of Chinese leaders after Deng, and discusses what China has become after three decades of economic reform in the third part, followed by a conclusion.

China's economic success

Only a few years after China started its economic reform, Harry Harding claimed that China's economic reform is "China's Second Revolution" (Harding 1987: ix). Indeed, it is, given both the magnitude of change and the profound transformation that the CCP, Chinese society, and Chinese people have undergone in the process.

Based on two decisions passed at the Third Plenum of the CCP Central Committee in December 1978 (Decision on Some Questions Concerning the Acceleration of Agricultural Development and Resolution on work in Rural People's Communes), China started its economic reform in 1978 by implementing a Household Responsibility System (HRS) in its rural areas. The HRS was basically a land-lease system between the village (state) and peasants that did not change land ownership but established a direct link between work and reward. It was partly the outcome of an unorganized movement in Anhui Province endorsed by the CCP. It declared the end of the Maoist model of development and led to broader reforms in all fields of Chinese society (Chen 1999: 47). The significance of the HRS is threefold. First, it indicates a relaxation of political control by the state over Chinese peasants. Second, peasants were given relative autonomy and freedom to manage their economic affairs. Third, an emphasis was placed on market mechanism and individual incentives (Tsou 1988: 189).

Many factors have contributed to China's economic success, but the following could be emphasized.

First, "politics of politics" during the Mao years before the economic reform was being replaced by "politics of economics," and the ideological fever of the previous decades was replaced by pragmatism. With the shift of priority by the CCP in the late 1970s and early 1980s from ideology and politics to economic growth, both state–society and central–local relationships changed and social mobility increased significantly. With more emphasis placed on individual incentives and the newly created space and freedom within Chinese society, a new environment and opportunity for individual entrepreneurship, innovation, and economic initiatives and activities across the nation were created and new enthusiasm for a better life surged. With the official endorsement of capitalist practice by the CCP following the 1992 Deng Xiaoping "*nanxun*" (tour of the South),[1] the fear of recurrence of political campaigns of the past was gone, which ushered in a new phase of economic reform and growth.

Second, the behavior of the Chinese and institutions all changed in the process. China's hierarchical political structure remained intact despite the policy change and economic reform as the CCP is the sponsor of China's economic reform and remains at the helm of China's economic reform from the beginning. China's economic success benefited from this hierarchical political structure in the short run, because it allowed the CCP to mobilize and organize the whole Party and society, and concentrate all resources and energy on economic growth and development. As economic growth and development became the new criterion for evaluating the performance of the party and government officials and the revenues of local governments hinged more upon economic performance and growth of their localities, local Party and government organizations and officials must actively promote local economic and industrial development. Mobilizing investment funds, targeting enterprises and industries for growth, gathering and providing information about market opportunities, acting as brokers for contracts, and engaging in making development plans, local government officials behaved like corporation CEOs (Oi 1995: 1144–1146). Local governments as economic actors prove to be indispensable to China's economic growth (Walder 1998: 16–17) in the beginning phase of China's economic reform in the 1980s.

Third, Chinese people are certainly the engines of China's fast economic growth. With the relaxation of control by the government, it is the Chinese "characteristics" of saving, hard work, thrift, self-motivation, family values, discipline, loyalty, individual entrepreneurship, and respect for scholarship and learning that led to the immediate and sustained economic success over the last 37 years. Such "characteristics" were harshly suppressed in the Mao era when the Chinese were tightly controlled ideologically with intensive ideological indoctrination, physically with the household registration and ration systems, and politically with tight organizational control. Such "characteristics" were revived in the new environment. To provide for their families and improve their and their families' standards of living are the strongest incentives for Chinese to work hard and find ways to make money in the new environment. Preoccupied with making money individually, the Chinese have collectively created the fastest-growing economy in the world for over three decades, a Chinese economic miracle.

Fourth, state-owned enterprises (SOEs) and the development of the real estate business have made important contributions to China's economic success and are therefore part of China's success story. The dominance of SOEs in the major sectors of the economy, such as banking, media, communications, transportation, aviation, energy, construction, steel, oil, etc., is a major feature of the Chinese economy. These large SOEs were an outcome of restructure and reorganization, while the less important SOEs and almost all collective enterprises were allowed to go bankrupt, or were leased or "privatized." The emergence of real estate in China since the 1980s was a welcome addition to the Chinese economy. It generated large amounts of money for governments at different levels for land-lease deals with developers and created many jobs and economic opportunities for many industries and businesses. Even though China's SOEs and the development of real estate have their own problems, which will be discussed in the third section of this chapter, they are an important part of China's "socialism with Chinese characteristics."

Fifth, Chinese peasants' contribution to China's economic success is indispensable. The successful implementation of the HRS in the rural area resulted in an unprecedented increase of agricultural production and productivity, and it also resulted in huge surplus labor in rural areas. With their newly gained mobility, millions upon millions of Chinese peasants looking for new economic opportunities became migrant workers, thus providing the necessary and badly needed cheap labor in urban areas, especially along the east coast, and playing their part in the development of China's labor-intensive export-oriented economic strategy and in China becoming the world's processing center. China had a lot of unskilled labor and was technologically undeveloped with low incomes when it first started its economic reform, and the development of its labor-intensive export strategy and becoming the processing center of the world met both the needs of millions of Chinese peasants looking for jobs and the needs of a global economy that was emerging with the end of the Cold War.

Sixth, from a policy perspective, the establishment of "specialized zones"[2] in many provinces and regions across the nation certainly served as "models" of capitalist practices in China, and they were instrumental to China's becoming the world's processing center and the development of a labor-intensive export strategy through world-wide Chinese networks. As "specialized zones" were less restricted for economic initiatives and activities, they could better correspond with the needs of a global economy on the one hand and served as testing grounds for economic initiatives and activities on the other. Both the labor-intensive and export-oriented economy and China's becoming the world's processing center were a result of such initiatives and activities, and they were not necessarily an outcome of a top-down national strategy.

In retrospect, China's economic success over the last 37 years was a result of many factors. The differences between China and other East Asian countries in development are obvious. First, China is a Party-state while other East Asian countries are democracies. With one-Party rule and the hierarchical political structure in China, the state is more powerful than those in other East Asian countries both in terms of control and in terms of planning and mobilization. Second, China is much bigger than any other East Asian country. Does size matter? Yes, it does, because size poses different challenges for governing and makes it more difficult to set priorities and balance economic growth with social and other developments. Third, China is certainly more diverse in terms of ethnicity and regional differences, which often produce tensions that other East Asian societies do not have to face. Fourth, China has a large peasant population, about 700 million, which poses daunting challenges in development that other East Asian countries also do not have to deal with. Finally, no other East Asian country has gone through such political turmoil over the two decades before the economic reform since 1949 as China has: land reform of 1950; the Three-Anti campaigns of 1951; the Five-Anti campaigns of 1952; the Great Leap Forward of 1958–1960; the Four-Clean-ups movement of 1963–1966; and the Cultural Revolution of 1966–1976.[3] No other East Asian country has seen the ideological fever during the ten years of the Cultural Revolution as China had just before the economic reform, with the exception of North Korea, but North Korea is excluded from this comparison. These differences make comparative analysis challenging, as every country is unique in its own development. There are, however, a few comparison that are worth noting between China and other East Asian countries in their respective developments.[4]

First, the state played an important role in all East Asian countries' development, more actively involved in planning, resource allocation, and other economic activities in East Asia than in the West, which is one way to distinguish the Western model of development from the East Asian model of development. The Chinese government is even more involved in China's economic development than those in other East Asian countries, because China's economic reform is sponsored and supervised by the state. Second, China's economy, like some of the East Asian countries in their early development, is also export-oriented and labor-intensive, because exports based on labor-intensive products to the Western markets met the domestic needs of those East Asian countries and the demands of Western societies. It provided an opportunity for East Asian countries to become newly industrialized nations as a later comer. Finally, East

Asians do share certain cultural similarities. In a conversation with Fareed Zakaria, Lee Kuan Yew noted the following that distinguishes, he believes, East Asian societies from other societies: the belief that the individual exists in the context of his family and the government does not try to provide for a person what the family best provides; the belief in thrift, hard work, filial discipline, piety, and loyalty; and the respect for scholarship and learning (Zakaria 1994: 113–114). In terms of the role of individuals and their relationships in the society, Lee emphasized an old Chinese maxim: "Xiushen qijia zhiguo ping-tianxia." Xiushen means "cultivate and look after yourself and do everything to make yourself useful"; qijia: "look after your family"; zhiguo: "look after your country"; pingtianxia: "all is peaceful under heaven" (Zakaria 1994: 113–114) Only when individuals cultivate themselves and make themselves useful can they look after their family and country, and when all individuals can look after themselves, family and country, all is peaceful in the world. Francis Fukuyama also points out that

> just as surely the cultural heritage of those Far Eastern societies, the ethic of work and saving and family, a religious heritage that does not, like Islam, place restrictions on certain forms of economic behavior, and other deeply ingrained moral qualities, are equally important in explaining their economic performance.
>
> (Fukuyama 2013: 10)

If the economic success of East Asian countries is associated with their cultural heritage, it could be said that China's economic success is also to a certain extent like other East Asian countries.

From the perspective of governance and "model," development is more than just economic growth and cultural heritage can hardly be transferred. What are Chinese leaders' visions for Chinese development, and how have they responded to the problems that have accompanied China's economic growth?

Development from the perspective of Chinese leaderships since Deng Xiaoping

Did Deng Xiaoping know what development path China was taking and what China would become when he started China's economic reform? Deng clearly knew from the very start of China's economic reform that it would be carried out under the leadership of the CCP and it was not aimed at dismantling the CCP. But Deng was probably not sure himself what China would become. Deng's pragmatism is reflected in his famous sayings that have served as guidelines for China's reform for different periods, such as "black cat or white cat, it is a good cat as long as it catches mice," "let few people get rich first," and "crossing the river by groping the way." Such pragmatism is responsible for both China's economic success and its problems. Would Deng Xiaoping be happy with where China is today? He would have been happy with China's economic growth, but not with the ills that have accompanied China's economic success. Surely, economic growth has not made governance or development easier for leaderships after Deng.

The three generations of Chinese leaderships after Deng each have developed their visions for development, which are reflected in the Party doctrines under each generation. To put these Party doctrines in perspective, it is clear that the CCP, to a large extent, has been fighting itself as it blazes its trails of reform and development, because the one-Party political system is both a reason for China's success and a cause of China's problems. What all the three generations of Chinese leadership since Deng are preoccupied with is to muddle through between political control and market and between economic growth and social development and justice for legitimacy and survival. An analysis of each generation's perspective for development would give us a good glimpse of the struggle. The CCP as the only political party in a hierarchical political structure must be sensitive and responsive to problems in Chinese society and challenges to its rule as the CCP, being the only party in power, is to blame for all the problems, many of which are often unsolvable under the current political system. The CCP must perform and respond, because it concerns China's stability and the CCP's own legitimacy and leadership. Survival through performance and problem-solving can only prolong life a little bit but not indefinitely. Creating a "model" of development may be a by-product in the end but definitely one of the last things in the minds of Chinese leaders, despite the fact that they all hope to leave their political legacies.

While economic growth has indeed improved the material well-being of the Chinese since the economic reform, it has been accompanied by problems, which include but are not limited to income disparity and the wealth gap between the rich and the poor, uneven development between the east and west and between urban and rural areas, rampant corruption, widespread resentment among the population, high unemployment rate, lack of social insurance and social safety net, no access for many to human services such as education, health care and housing, environmental deterioration, accountability issues involving both government agencies and state-owned enterprises (SOEs), private property rights, and the issue of rural development. These problems and issues under one-Party rule in the absence of rule of law in a commercial environment pose serious questions about sustainable development, social justice, social and political stability, and governance. Some of the problems are problems of development while others are related to the one-Party rule political system. In fact, one of the major challenges for the CCP leadership in post-Deng China is governance (Perkins 1997: 29), which has not changed since the 16th Party Congress. Legitimizing the power and leadership of the CCP has, to a large extent, become the essence of Chinese politics in post-Deng China. Responses by each generation of Chinese leadership after Deng reflect the leaderships' perspectives for development in China and their doses of medicine to the ills and endeavor to balance development.

All three generations of Chinese leadership after Deng have been confronted with unprecedented challenges of governance for a number of reasons. First,

Chinese leaders after Deng are no longer revolutionaries but technocrats, and "the era of Communist ideology and charismatic leaders came to an end with the death of Deng Xiaoping" (Chen and Zhong 2005: 5). For technocrats, their legitimacy is based more on their performance than ideology or charisma. Second, facilitated both by the Communication Revolution and changed state–society and central–local relations since the economic reform, Chinese society has become more diverse and vocal. Media is still tightly controlled in China but the Internet has created unprecedented platforms and avenues for individuals and groups. Third, institutionalization since the economic reform has made coalition building both within the CCP and in Chinese society a necessity as diverse interests have already made unity in the pursuit of interest impossible. Finally, order and stability, which can no longer be taken for granted, override any other concerns.

Confronted with unprecedented challenges of governance, Jiang Zemin's vision and response were to build a *xiaokang shehui* (comfortable society) in China, which aims at bringing prosperity to the majority of the Chinese population and making it a reality for the majority of Chinese to live a comfortable life. It seems to be a natural next step to Deng's "let few individuals get rich first" and a response to the huge wealth gap created since the 1980s, for few individuals indeed got rich, extremely rich, while the majority have not been so fortunate. The new rich are all well connected with the CCP apparatus, including many government officials, former government officials, their children and family members, and CEOs and managers of SOEs. Yet, the majority, especially many former urban workers and most peasants in rural areas, was left behind despite China's high economic growth rates for decades. Improving the standard of living and social status of the majority of the Chinese population through policies of redistribution and resource allocation seemed to be a natural function of the Party and state in China since the CCP claims to represent all the people in China. The vision of *xiaokang shehui* places emphasis on redistributing wealth through growth. It propounds the notion that everybody could eventually attain at least a comfortable standard of living (*xiaokang shehui*). This, in large measure, was an attempt by the third generation of the Chinese leadership to appeal to the population about their resentment over the wealth gap and widespread corruption. It also reflects the leadership's increasing concern with social stability. *Xiaokang shehui* conveys the concept of "middle class," but the term "middle class" is never used because it is inextricably linked to Western liberal democracy. The rejection of the use of "middle class" does indicate that China intends to chart its own political development path (Zheng 2005: 28).

Economic growth was still the top priority for the third generation of leadership under Jiang, because economic growth itself was becoming the new basis of CCP legitimacy and the CCP would be safe and sound when the majority of Chinese could live a comfortable, or *xiaokang*, life. Life would go on as long as the economy continued to grow and a majority of Chinese still had opportunities to improve their standard of living. Politically, it is important for the Jiang leadership to stress politics, political study, and political moral spirit (*sanjiang* or "three stresses") in response to de-politicization, loss of the CCP's ideological appeals, and rampant corruption within the CCP. The Jiang leadership also reformulates what the CCP really represents after almost two decades of economic reform in response to the diversification of interests within the Party and in Chinese society and for the need for sustained economic growth. To maintain sustained economic growth, the CCP cannot try to expand the private arena on one hand and keep "capitalists" out of the political order on the other. According to the new formulation, the CCP represents "advanced culture," "advanced forces of production" that include Chinese "capitalists," and "the interests of the majority of the Chinese population" (the three represents), and these "three represents" were later written into the CCP Constitution at the 16th CCP National Congress.

The "three represents" and *xiaokang* society constitute the main part of Jiang's political legacy and represent Jiang leadership's vision of development for China. Unfortunately, many of the problems that the Jiang administration tried to address were unresolved and got worse, and a *xiaokang shehui* was still an ideal for many Chinese. To Jiang's credit, however, the significant political transition for China from the era of charismatic leaders to technocrats went smoothly under Jiang and China's economy continued to grow even though the population's resentment also continued to increase.

The fourth generation of Chinese leadership under Hu Jintao put forth the concept of "scientific development" and "harmonious society" (an extension of "scientific development concept"), which was enshrined as the new Party doctrine and eventually written into the Party Constitution at the 18th Party Congress in 2012 when Hu stepped down. "Scientific development" and "harmonious society" represent the Hu leadership's vision of development. Both "scientific development" and "harmonious society," a centuries-old concept, stress balanced development, because balance is "scientific" and balance means harmony. What was not scientific with China's development and what was displaced in Chinese society that would require responses emphasizing balance or "scientific development" and "harmonious society"? Obviously, social solidarity was further eroding and Chinese society was not harmonious because of lack of balance when the fourth generation under Hu came to power. First, "scientific development" placed emphasis on "people as the primary beneficiaries of economic growth" because Chinese peasants and many in urban areas had not been the primary beneficiaries of China's economic growth. Second, it also emphasizes "sustainable development." Economic growth had provided and would continue to provide legitimacy for the CCP. A balance between human development and its environment must be maintained for sustained development and a balance between government and the people must be found as the existence of disharmony had resulted from the resentment of the population and distrust of governments by the people, the conflicts between the central government and local governments, and the tensions between the rich and the poor, between urban and rural residents, between money-making enterprises and consumers, and between humankind and its environment. "Scientific development" and "harmonious society," if achieved, would represent a model of development.

For over two decades, the development strategy under two generations of Chinese leadership, Deng Xiaoping and Jiang Zemin, was to promote economic growth at all costs. Due to "unscientific development" and lack of harmony, the fourth generation of Chinese leadership under Hu tried to project a pro-people image in response to the population's resentment and distrust. By advocating the "scientific development concept" and making "building a harmonious society" a goal of development, the fourth generation of Chinese leadership under Hu tried to address all these issues: rampant corruption, wealth gap, enormous waste and unfair practices by the government, government's sporadic approaches to problems, and injustice in Chinese society.

"Harmonious society" placed top priority on reducing disparities, establishing a social safety net, and providing basic public health care, which were the sources of disharmony in recent years in Chinese society. The trouble in China was not just the issues and problems, but also people's perceptions of them. These perceptions matter more in Chinese politics, because the CCP is the only Party to blame. There is simply no exit for the Party. Economic opportunities have been serving as temporary exits, because people are not preoccupied with politics as long as they have opportunities to make money despite their complaints and grievances. When problems were piling up and people were unhappy, pressures would build up on the Party. While Party doctrines may vary between leaderships, they all aim at addressing the pressing issues and challenges facing the CCP. The shift in the source and legitimacy of the Chinese leadership requires the CCP's commitment to economic growth. Economic growth itself, however, would not be able to provide all the answers to development when economic growth had not resulted in balanced development on which the CCP's legitimacy is based. As a consequence, the CCP leaderships' vision for development is more driven by the need for legitimizing the power and leadership of the CCP, the essence of Chinese politics in post-Deng China, than by development strategy. The Hu–Wen administration fell far short of expectations in both. To their credit, however, they did start the first step in the right direction on the issue of Chinese peasants.

About 60 percent of the Chinese population still live in rural areas, and the rural situation had been a trouble spot for years. Rural problems are often summarized as *san nong wenti* (three rural issues): *nongmin wenti* (referring to peasants' declining income, poor living conditions, and problems resulting from them), *nongye wenti* (referring to low profitability of agricultural products, low agricultural technology levels, and scarce agricultural land use), and *nongcun wenti* (referring to instability and potential chaos in China's rural areas resulting from *nongmin wenti* and *nongcun wenti*) (Zhong 2003: 183). China's old family-based agriculture had collapsed and Chinese agriculture was no longer able to support such a huge rural population. It is estimated that there are about 700 million laborers in China's rural areas and only 100 million are needed. Rural businesses and enterprises employ about 250 million. There are about 350 million surplus laborers in rural areas. The CCP 17th Central Committee passed a resolution regarding China's rural areas on October 12, 2008 at its Third

Plenum. It reconfirms that the terms of the land lease with the state by peasants would not change for a long time and emphasizes the urgency and importance of the transition of agriculture toward technology, and support for professional and special cooperatives even though the fundamental issue of property rights underlying the *san nong wenti* was not addressed directly. It did get rid of many of the fees imposed on Chinese peasants.

Xi Jinping and Li Keqiang were confirmed as the fifth generation of Chinese leadership at the 18th Party Congress in late 2012. As the next ten years will be crucial for China and the CCP, the fifth generation's vision and response will, to a greater extent, help determine China's development path and the CCP's fate. About one year after the 18th CCP National Congress, the "Decision on Many Important Issues Regarding All-Round Deeper Reform" (the "Decision" hereafter) was passed at the Third Plenum of the 18th CCP Central Committee. The Decision has been viewed as a comprehensive blueprint for "deeper reforms" for the next ten years since its passage. It covers politics, economics, society, culture, Party building, environment, and defense. If the Decision on Some Questions Concerning the Acceleration of Agricultural Development and the Resolution on Work in Rural People's Communes, passed at the Third Plenum of the 13th CCP Central Committee, started China's reform and Deng Xiaoping's Nanxun in 1992 officially endorsed capitalist practice in China's economic reform, the Decision passed at the Third Plenum in 2013 marks another important phase of China's economic reform, a phase of "storming heavily fortified positions" and "the area of deep water," according to the Decision. "Fortified positions" and "deep water" refer to all the tough issues that have not been resolved and are hard to resolve within the current framework of "socialism with capitalism" and the successful resolution of these issues would require reform of the current political system. What is clear to the Xi leadership is that failure to effectively address the serious issues in China's development would have irreversible consequences for China and the CCP.

How will the fifth generation of Chinese leadership try to manage the incompatible combination of free market economy and one party rule to maintain the dominance and leadership of the CCP, on the one hand, and sustained economic growth and balanced development, on the other, in the years ahead? How will it respond to the rising popular pressure and resentment against corruption and the widening wealth gap, and increase the state's ability to maintain equitable economic growth and its redistributive capacity? How will the Chinese leadership try to meet the increasing demands of citizens and groups? Bolder and more comprehensive reforms seem to be the answer. To conquer the "heavily fortified positions" and get out of "the area of deeper water" concerns the survival of the CCP and the prosperity of China. The Decision touches on many of the pressing issues that have not been effectively addressed by the previous two generations of Chinese leadership. The Decision is therefore timely and important, but the devil is always in the details and implementation. A number of things are definitely worth noticing with regard to the Decision.

Since the Decision is such a comprehensive document, different people would emphasize different things in their interpretation. Related to the theme of the book and this chapter, I would emphasize the following. First, economic growth and development will still be the top priority as the legitimacy of the CCP continues to depend on economic growth, but economic growth in the political context of China seems to be a Pandora's Box. Even though the political leadership of the CCP could not be marginalized for "deeper reforms," it is important to clearly define the relationship between market and the state in order to maintain sustained economic growth. Second, in response to the ever-widening wealth gap and growing resentment and grievances in Chinese society today, improving the quality of life for the large majority of the Chinese and promoting social justice would have to be two of the immediate goals of China's economic growth. The former is in tone with Jiang's *xiaokang shehui* and Hu's concept of "scientific development," while the latter on the promotion of social justice in the Decision is new. To achieve both, a series of reforms in the following areas are necessary: income distribution or redistribution, provision of public services and benefits including social security and health care, household registration, and social justice and equal opportunities and treatment for everybody. Third, property rights, one of the most important economic rights, which has significant implications for China's sustained economic growth, is emphasized for the first time in the Decision. According to the Decision, both public and private property rights are sacred, and peasants' property rights should be protected. It stresses the necessity of reforming SOEs and defining and protecting both public and private property rights. Fourth, in response to the changed central–local relations and the diversification of interests across regions and provinces, the Decision recognizes the importance of the autonomy and independence of local governments, especially in social development. Politically, federalism may not work in China, but given the size of China and differences between regions, local government will have to be granted more autonomy and power in managing their own affairs. Politics is local in many ways in China today. Fifth, institutionalization, rule of law, process and standard operating procedures, basic-level democracy, transparency, and supervision by the people are all mentioned and emphasized in the Decision. Many of these are concepts related to democracy, which is also a first. It also stresses the importance and necessity of judicial reform and rule of law and the leadership's determination to fight corruption. Sixth, developing new ways and mechanisms, institutional or otherwise, to prevent and dissolve social tensions and conflicts is emphasized. The Decision touches upon state–society relations and points out the importance of promoting the activity of societal organizations and the independence of society. Seventh, it announces that a new National Security Council and a National Leading Group for "deeper reforms" will be established (*People's Daily Overseas Edition* 2013). The National Security Council would strengthen the power of Xi in the wake of unprecedented development of interest groups and opinion groups within the CCP and Chinese society, and the Leading Group will exercise centralized leadership in addressing and coordinating the dysfunction of institutions, the relationship between market and government, property rights of the peasants, the redistribution structure in regards to income, taxation, social security/pension and health care, governance ability, political reform, and judicial reform concerning rule of law.

In comparison with the previous two generations of Chinese leadership under Jiang and Hu, the Xi administration seems, as indicated by the Decision, to be more determined to tackle the long-overdue problems in China's reform and influence the direction of China's development. The outcome of "deeper reforms" concerns sustainable economic growth, the legitimacy of the CCP, the stability of Chinese society, and the prospect of China's reform. The effective implementation of the Decision in practice could help determine the Chinese path of development.

Desire for a model

There has always been a desire and search for a "model" from Georg Wilhelm Friedrich Hegel's "absolute moment" and Karl Marx's "communism" to Francis Fukuyama's "end of history." There is nothing unnatural about a Chinese model of development. The political appeal of a Chinese model of development is obvious, because it could provide legitimacy for the CCP at home and an alternative to the Western model of development characterized by the "free market and democracy" abroad, which could be politically convenient for many authoritarian developing countries. Political appeal aside, a model of development should be a balanced one that would result in the improvement of the overall quality of life and well-being of the overwhelming majority of the population and the promotion of social development and justice. Economic growth is a necessary condition but does not guarantee the improvement of the overall quality of life and well-being of the overwhelming majority of the population and the promotion of social development and justice.

There are two basic economic systems in the world: c apitalism and socialism. Since there is no pure capitalism or socialism in the world and all economic systems are mixed, it has always been a point of discussion where the balance should be. Idealistically, a model of development is a balanced one that combines the good elements of both systems. What has China become after 37 years of economic reform? The CCP and official media of China describe China's development path as "socialism with Chinese Characteristics." If "socialism" refers to the CCP one-Party rule and the CCP's role in economic activities and society, "Chinese characteristics" would mean capitalist practices in a market economy on the one hand and whatever China does successfully in promoting economic growth in practice on the other. Is China developing "state capitalism"? According to Ian Bremmer, state capitalism has four primary actors: national oil corporations, state-owned enterprises, privately owned national champions, and sovereign wealth funds (SWFs) (Bremmer 2009: 41). China seems to fit the description and definition. Whether state capitalism or "socialism with Chinese characteristics," it is clear that China needs to work hard on several fronts.

The combination of one-Party rule with a market economy has resulted in unprecedented economic growth but also led to rampant corruption and a huge wealth gap that are threatening the CCP and China. The rampant corruption and huge wealth gap have significant economic, social, and political ramifications for China and the CCP. Disharmony in terms of various relationships also exists in different forms in Chinese society. The dominance of SOEs in China's economy is both a reason for China's economic success and a potential threat to China's sustainable economic growth. It is surely a source of corruption. The lack of constitutional protection for private property rights has already cast a shadow on China's economy. With the collapse of work-unit socialism for most Chinese in urban areas and no safety net for Chinese peasants, it is a matter of urgency to develop a sound and effective safety net for the majority of the Chinese population. As China's economy continues to grow, institutional avenues and channels need to be provided both for citizen participation and for the pursuit of interests by diverse groups and organizations. All these need to be effectively addressed in a timely fashion. A Chinese model of development could very well be a by-product of successful resolution to these issues.

Rule of law is essential to China's transition to a complete market economy. A market economy must also be a legal economy. In the absence of the rule of law, predictability for economic transactions could not be guaranteed, private disputes could not be fairly resolved, the powers of officialdom could not be restrained, and the transfer of political power could not be regulated (Hendley 1996: 12). Economic growth requires a government that can provide the needed infrastructure for development, including stable and supportive policy and a stable legal environment for private or public investors (Perkins 1997: 29). At present, the rule of law in the Chinese political context is secondary to the Party, and the legislature, the National People's Congress, is also secondary to the Party. A sound market economy is impossible unless there is a level competition ground, which requires a high degree of regularity, predictability, and transparency. The heavy reliance on policies and individuals would not satisfy the needs of a market economy and will only feed corruption. The market would require strong laws, and Chinese leaderships in post-Deng China have expressed their wishes to strengthen legal-rational authority[5] and institutionalization. No leader in post-Deng China can resort to charismatic authority like Mao or Deng. China has moved into a new era of modernization since Jiang, and the authority of leaders is to be based more on legal-rational legitimacy, while legal-rational authority will promote China's efforts in building a more democratic and civilized country. The rule of law is also essential in addressing the rampant corruption in Chinese society, which has affected the image, reputation, and legitimacy of the CCP. China's corruption is a result of the bad combination of market greed and monopoly of political power in a one-Party political system. Corruption cannot be resolved by political campaigns or the CCP's Disciplinary Inspection Committees even though the fifth generation of Chinese leadership under Xi is more determined than previous leaderships to crack down on corruption. Rule by law in the context of one-Party rule has been part of the problem so far. The transition from rule by law to the rule of law, however, would represent a significant departure from current CCP politics.

China's economy has been dominated by SOEs, which in turn serve as the economic base for the CCP's one-party rule. SOEs control and dominate the following: media, banks, energy and oil, telecommunications, transportation, petrochemicals, power generation, mining, iron and steel production, port management and shipping, weapons manufacturing, cars, heavy machinery, and aviation. There is no level ground for competition in all these fields and areas, but SOEs are in general characterized by huge waste, inefficiency, and rampant corruption. What is more troubling is who are the real owners of these SOEs, to whom are the SOEs are accountable, and who should benefit from their "profits"? The CEOs of state-owned enterprises are appointed by the CCP, and very often they are either Party officials or closely connected to the CCP. The reform of SOEs is a "must."

After 37 years of economic reform, state–society relations have changed dramatically, and different voices from many socioeconomic groups can be heard openly. Ideas such as citizenship, human rights, transparency, and political accountability are taking form in political life. The Internet has definitely facilitated civil society activities by offering new possibilities for citizen participation (Yang 2006: 303). Individuals and groups, whether they are elites or vulnerable individuals or social groups, are more cognizant of how to protect and advance their interests and rights, which would require further reform of the institutions linking state to society within the general parameters of maintaining stability (Burns 1999: 594) and increased structural differentiation, more regularized decision-making processes, and more society autonomy from the state (Dittmer and Liu 2006: 13). The traditional venues, still tightly controlled by the CCP, need to open up and new institutional venues need to be created for the society.

Lieberthal and Oksenberg once argued that the interests of social groups are articulated not through autonomous interest groups but through bureaucratic organizations (1988: 396–401). It is true, but with the changed state–society relationship after 37 years of economic reform, the diversification of the Chinese economy has created favorable conditions for diverse interests and interest representations. The imperative for sustained economic growth, the consensus among top Chinese leaders on the top priority of stability, and the necessity of creating more institutional outlets for grievances to alleviate social tensions and pressures (Chen 2009: 267) are driving diverse interest representations within the Party and in Chinese society. Institutional channels for the articulation and aggregation of the interests of entrepreneurs, businesses, and other social-economic groups would demand more representation in the Party and government. Since order and stability override any other concerns, which is a consensus among top Chinese leaders across factions within the Party, more diversity in the Party and government would have to be allowed. With ever-increasing resentment, institutional outlets in various forms for such resentments and protests are necessary to alleviate social tensions and pressures. With more space and freedom, innovative ideas and entrepreneurship will flourish, which is also essential to sustained economic growth.

The People's Congress system will have to be strengthened, making it more independent and representative. Democracy may not be the objective, but it does promote the process of democratization in doing so. A case in point is the village election. The introduction and promotion of village elections are not to promote democracy in China but to serve specific purposes. First, reorganizing peasants through elections after the collapse of the Commune system would help maintain stability and order without negative economic consequences. Second, only when peasants were organized in whatever form could state policies be carried out and state laws enforced in the rural area. Third, village elections would create opportunities for capable villagers who could develop and promote the village economy and increase the accountability of village leaders at the same time, which would help improve relations between village leaders and villagers (Chen and Liu 2005: 63). However, the village election itself is a process of democratization. What is different today from when village elections were introduced in China's rural areas is that (1) it is difficult to see the leadership's effort simply as a top-down process, and (2) it cannot be limited to rural areas. All these seem to point to the direction of democratization in terms of institutionalization and rule of law in China, which is the ultimate challenge for the Chinese leadership in the twenty-first century. In the end, the outcome will be determined by the political skills of the Chinese leadership in the short run and by their courage, wisdom, and willingness to meet the demands of citizen-masses in the long run.

China's socialism before the economic reform was basically "work-unit socialism." Socialist services and benefits were all associated with one's work-unit, whether it be pension, health care, education, or services. Individuals without a work-unit would not be able to enjoy socialist benefits and services, and Chinese peasants never had the same access to benefits and services provided by the state through work-units because villages were not viewed as work-units. Work-unit socialism has been undergoing a transformation. Government agencies and institutions of education remain "socialist" in many ways in terms of access to benefits and services such as pension, health care, subsidized housing, etc. Those reorganized and restructured SOEs are still privileged in many ways, and their full-time employees enjoy many of the same benefits and services as employees of government agencies and institutions of education. SOEs' key personnel are appointed by the Party/state. Millions upon millions of former SOE workers were laid off when those SOEs went bankrupt. Many were symbolically compensated for the loss of their jobs, but with the loss of their jobs they also lost their access to the "socialist services and benefits" they used to enjoy. A new safety net has not been established in the wake of such transformation. Millions upon millions of collective enterprise (*jiti*) employees had the same fate as the laid-off SOE employees. There were at least health clinics and barefoot doctors and schools in almost every village before the economic reform, and they were gone with the reform. Many in China have lost the old "socialist benefits" and have not tasted any benefit of "socialism with capitalism." Instead, it is wealth gaps, corruption, lack of individual freedom and protection of any kind, and lack of access to health care and education. Education has become less accessible to rural children especially since the economic reform. In many ways, U.S. and European countries are more "socialist" than China in areas such as provision of health care, access to education, and redistribution of wealth through taxation and other programs to help the poor, sick, elderly, and handicapped. China surely has lost many of its "socialist features" over the course of reform and is more capitalistic in many ways than U.S. and European countries in terms of provision and protection of public goods, equality of opportunities, fair competition, wealth distribution, anti-privileges and corruption, and responsible use of public assets. Yet, the Chinese do not enjoy individual freedom as do those in the West. The CCP claims that it is a socialist country, but the fact that the CCP is in total control in China does not make China socialist. In some ways, China represents some of the bad elements of both capitalism and socialism at this point.

Finally, China's economic growth has inflicted severe damage on its environment: air and water pollution, deforestation, degradation of agricultural land, greenhouse warming, and stratospheric ozone depletion. *Wumai*, or smog, is spreading across the whole of China from north to south, and seven of the world's ten most polluted cities are in China (*Beijing Review* 2014). These are often "characterized as large-scale human-induced problems, with long-term and often irreversible consequences" (Homer-Dixon 2013: 619). Other East Asian countries are done with environment as the cost of economic growth but China is not yet.

Conclusion

China's economic success could be attributed to a lot of factors, many of which are unique to the Chinese political, social, and cultural contexts and can hardly be transplanted. China's political ideology, system, and culture are different from those in the United States and the West, and China is also different from other East Asian countries in that it achieved its economic success under the framework of one-Party rule with capitalism. Has China adopted the good elements of capitalism and retained the good elements of socialism over the course of reform and thus become a model of good combination? Or has China rejected the good elements of socialism and adopted the bad elements of capitalism over the course of reform and thus become a model of bad combination? There are no easy answers to these questions. China has been able to muddle through between market economy and political control with good economic results. All three generations of Chinese leadership very well understand the dangers in China's development but are all restricted to finding responses and solutions within the system to prolong life. As China moves forward, it is becoming more and more difficult to muddle through. The Decision is timely and important not only because it touches upon all the important issues and problems that the CCP and China must tackle but also because it is pointing in a new direction and hopefully will trail-blaze some of the political boundaries.

The Chinese path of development so far has both joys and worries. As China is still groping for its way in development, it is definitely premature to define a Chinese model of development. What is important for China at this point is to find solutions to the pressing issues and become a model that is uniquely Chinese and for the Chinese.

Notes

1 Deng Xiaoping toured the South in the aftermath of 1989 Tiananmen Incident and rallied the Party to endorse capitalist practices in China's economic development.

2 Economic initiatives and entrepreneurship were less restrained in these designated specialized zones and many of the practices during the early phase of China's economic reform in these specialized zones were emulated nationwide later.

3 The Land Reform of 1950 was a political campaign to redistribute lands taken from landlords to peasants in rural area. The Three-Anti Campaign of 1951 was a political campaign against corruption, waste, and bureaucratism within the Party and government. The Five-Anti Campaign of 1952 was a political campaign against bribery, tax evasion, theft of public property, cheating, and theft of national economic intelligence by business people. The Great Leap Forward of 1958–1960 was an economic campaign resulting in famine and deaths estimated at over 26 million people. The Four-Clean-up Movement of 1963–1966 was part of the "socialist education" political campaign. The Cultural Revolution of 1966–1976 was a comprehensive ideological and political campaign that resulted in serious consequences.

4 North Korea is excluded in the comparison here because the focus of analysis is on economic growth and development, which has not started yet in North Korea.

5 According to Max Weber, there are three types of authority patterns: traditional, charismatic, and legal-rational legitimacy. See Weber (1983: 111–112).

References

Beijing Review (2014) "China's Top New Words," January 23.

Bremmer, I. (2009) "State Capitalism Comes of Age: The End of the Free Market," *Foreign Affairs*, 88(3): 40–55.

Burns, J. (1999) "The People's Republic of China at 50: National Political Reform," *The China Quarterly*, 159(3): 580–594.

Chen, W. (1999) *The Political Economy of Rural Development in China, 1978–1999*, Westport, CT: Praeger.

Chen, W. (2009) "Political Leadership in China in the Twenty-First Century," in J. Masciulli, M.A. Molchanov, and W.A. Knight (eds.), *Political Leadership*, Burlington, VT: Ashgate, pp. 259–268.

Chen, W. and Zhong, Y. (2005) *Leadership in a Changing China*, New York: Palgrave.

Chen, W. and Liu, G. (2005) "Building a New Political Order in China: Interpreting the New Directions in Chinese Politics," in W. Chen and Y. Zhong (eds.), *Leadership in a Changing China*, New York: Palgrave, pp. 57–80.

Dittmer, L. and Liu, G. (2006) *China's Deep Reform*, New York: Rowman & Littlefield.

Fukuyama, F. (2013) "The End of History?" in Richard Betts (ed.), *Conflict after the Cold War*, Boston: Pearson, pp. 6–17.

Harding, H. (1987) *China's Second Revolution: Reform after Mao*, Washington, DC: Brookings Institution Press.

Hendley, K. (1996) *Trying to Make Law Matter*, Ann Arbor: University of Michigan Press.

Homer-Dixon, T.F. (2013) "Environmental Changes as Causes of Acute Conflict," in R. Betts (ed.), *Conflict after the Cold War*, Boston: Pearson, pp. 614–628.

Lieberthal, K. and Oksenberg, M. (1988) *Policy Making in China: Leaders, Structures, and Processes*, Princeton, NJ: Princeton University Press.

Oi, J.C. (1995) "Role of the Local State in China's Transitional Economy," *The China Quarterly*, 144(4): 1132–1149.

People's Daily Overseas Edition (2013) "The Decision on Many Important Issues Regarding All-Round Deeper Reform," November 16. Online. Available at: http://finance.haiwainet.cn/n/2013/1121/c352345-19953711-21.html and http://finance.haiwainet.cn/n/2013/1121/c352345-19953711-24.html.

Perkins, D.H. (1997) "History, Politics, and the Sources of Economic Growth: China and the East Asian Way of Growth," in F. Itoh (ed.), *China in the Twenty-First Century: Politics, Economics, and Society*, Tokyo: United Nations University Press, pp. 25–41.

Tsou, T. (1988) *The Cultural Revolution and Post-Mao Reforms*, Chicago: The University of Chicago Press.

Walder, A. (1998) *Zouping in Transition*, Cambridge, MA: Harvard University Press.

Weber, M. (1983) "Politics as a Vocation," in D. Held *et al.* (eds.), *States and Societies*, New York: New York University Press.

Yang, G. (2006) "The Internet and Civil Society in China," in L. Dittmer and G. Liu (eds.), *China's Deep Reform*, New York: Rowman & Littlefield, pp. 303–318.

Zakaria, F. (1994) "Culture is Destiny: A Conversation with Lee Kuan Yew," *Foreign Affairs*, 73(2): 109–127.

Zheng, Y. (2005) "The 16th National Congress of the Chinese Communist Party: Institutionalization of Succession Politics," in W. Chen and Y. Zhou (eds.), *Leadership in a Changing China*, New York: Palgrave, pp. 15–36.

Zhong, Y. (2003) *Local Government and Politics in China*, Armonk, NY: M.E. Sharpe.

11 Two models of economic development in China

Kate Zhou and Stephen Zierak

Introduction

The rapid rise of the Chinese economy has led scholars to conclude that China is just another state-led development model in East Asia (Xu 2011; Park 2012). One of the most important scholars for East Asian developmental models is Chalmers Johnson, who defined the developmental state as a state that is focused on economic development and takes necessary policy measures to accomplish that objective. He argued that Japan's economic development had much to do with far-sighted intervention by bureaucrats, particularly those in the Ministry of International Trade and Industry (Johnson 1982). McNulty and Lee (2003) attribute Korean economic success to the state smart strategies. Recently, this view has been challenged by several scholars. China is not another East Asian Model. As Huang (2008) argues, the "[e]volution of capitalism in China is a function of a political balance between two Chinas—the entrepreneurial, market-driven rural China vis-à-vis the state-led urban China."

This chapter will examine the two models of post-Mao economic reform: market capitalism developed from the bottom up in China's countryside; and the state capitalism directed from the top down by party-state leadership. However, it is worthwhile first to review Mao's legacy. What was it, how was it achieved, and what were its results for Chinese economic development?

Mao was a highly committed ideologue, willing to pay any price to gain a fully communist society, where the state owned and operated all means of production and distribution of goods and services. When the Chinese Communist Party came to power in 1949, it built goodwill in the countryside by redistributing the property of landlords and "rich" peasants to poor peasants. In the cities, first the military and then civilian party cadres occupied private enterprises and enforced state planning. Those who knew how to do things were initially left in place, but by 1957 the state had taken ownership of all city businesses. Meanwhile the farms were increasingly collectivized, and by the time of the Great Leap Forward in 1958 they were reorganized into 26,000 people's communes, each with an average of 4,600 peasant households and about 6,700 workers (Maddison 2007: 72). Private plots were no longer allowed. Rural markets were ended, and rural enterprises were either closed or integrated into the communes. In less than a decade of transition, all private enterprise was gone from China.

In 1949, China was even more of an agrarian society than the Soviet Union had been at the time of its revolution. China's rural residents were close to 90 percent of the total population in the early years of the party-state, and still exceeded 80 percent of the total population at Mao's death. Mao's plan was to use surplus from the farms to fund growth in heavy industry. Peasants would sell to the state at low prices for sale to people in urban areas at similarly low prices. Industrial wages would be kept low enough that sales of industrial product would furnish capital for investment in further industrialization. Peasants would be attached to the farms through the *hukou* registration system, and city workers would be assigned to permanent jobs in state-owned enterprises (SOEs) where they would be controlled by the *danwei* system (dossiers on each worker, kept by workplace cadres, available for state review, and documenting permissions and benefits provided each worker). Both international trade and foreign direct investment (FDI) were discouraged, as Mao pursued a policy of Chinese self-reliance. Goods needed for industrialization were obtained from other communist states. The Soviet Union was a source of aid and assistance until relations soured in the early 1960s.

The Great Leap Forward (GLF; 1959–1961) was to be the culmination of the transition to pure communism. Mao was not only hostile to capitalism; he was also suspicious of centralized party-state bureaucracy, such as that found in the planning functions. Mao often governed through local party cadres in various campaigns to purify society. The GLF would mobilize the countryside, allowing use of "underutilized" labor to expand harvests while at the same time contributing to rural industrialization. This was the time of the backyard iron smelter. In 1957, agricultural employment was 80 percent of total employment, producing 54 percent of China's GDP. Due to resource diversion, agricultural employment had fallen to 71 percent of total by 1961 (end of the GLF), and had dipped as low as 68 percent of total in 1958.[1] This diversion of labor resources created much poorly made and unusable industrial production. It also resulted in a major famine in the countryside. Mao had abandoned central planning, replacing it with ambitious goals, and making rural cadres responsible for meeting and exceeding those goals. The cadres vastly overreported food production, and food was provided to the cities while the residual production was insufficient to feed the people in the countryside. By 1961 the agricultural share of GDP had fallen to 43 percent, not because of a sudden shift in the economic structure, but because of falling output from the communes. Yang (2010) attributes responsibility for the deaths of 36 million to China's totalitarian system and the refusal of officials at every level to value human life over ideology and self-interest. Frank Dikötter (2010), a scholar at both the University of Hong Kong and the University of London, has estimated that at least 45 million rural people died as a result of the famine. It was a brutal time when a peasant could be executed for stealing a potato. Even with all the misreporting of agricultural production, Mao must have become aware of what was happening. He allowed the situation to continue for what he considered the greater good of better establishing a communist society. Mao's later Cultural Revolution (1966–1976) was a similar attempt to remake Chinese society and purge "deviationist" forces. It too was based on a campaign model to purify society by empowering cadres at the expense of economic planners. During the first half of the period the Statistical Department was closed, and no official statistics were kept. This was also a period of state terrorism and routine murders. As it ran its course, the schools were closed and students sent to the country for "reeducation." All this had deleterious effects on the Chinese economy.

While there was economic growth in the pre-reform period, largely due to bringing more women into the labor force and increasing hours of work, it was quite modest compared to the growth in the rest of the world during these years. From 1952 to 1978, GDP per capita grew at an average annual rate of 2.3 percent. Meanwhile, India, Japan, and the Tigers were growing in excess of 5 percent. Even mature economies such as France and Germany were growing at around 4 percent. China would only begin to take advantage of its backwardness (operating well under the production possibility frontier) with reform (Chow 2002). Between 1978 and 2003, GDP per capita in China grew at an average annual rate of 6.6 percent, by far the best result among the nations of the world (Maddison 2007: table 3.4). In 1952, China had 22.5 percent of the world population, and 4.6 percent of world GDP. In 1978, China had 22.3 percent of world population, and 4.9 percent of world GDP. In 2003, China's share of world population had fallen to 20.5 percent, due largely to the one child policy after 1972, but GDP share had risen to 15.1 percent (Maddison 2007: table 2.2).

Picking up the pieces after Mao

The problems facing the Chinese economy in the late 1970s were not unusual in communist societies. The Soviet Union and the Eastern European satellite countries had also experienced the shortages, shoddy production, and lack of consumer choices endemic to planned economies. China had the additional burden of "campaign economics," leading to even greater economic dislocations than those faced elsewhere among the communist states. Many communist societies were searching for reform methods that would improve economic productivity while maintaining the political control of the Communist Party. For example, Eastern European economists such as Janos Kornai (1993) of Hungary promoted the idea of "market socialism" in the 1950s as a way of using market forces to discipline the economy while maintaining public ownership and party political monopoly.

As early as the Fourth National Party Congress in early 1975, Zhou Enlai put forward his "four modernizations": the need for comprehensive modernization of agriculture, industry, national defense, and science/technology. At the same time, Deng Xiaoping was recommending ideas that accorded with some of the principles of market socialism: strong management and production controls at the enterprise level, pursuit of economic and financial norms, responsibility systems for managers and workers with the use of economic incentives, importation of advanced technology paid for with national resource exports, and the use of long-term foreign credits to build China's export capacity. These were all "capitalist road" ideas to Mao. Deng Xiaoping disappeared from view after Zhou Enlai's death in early 1976, and it was Hua Guofeng who assumed the leadership after Mao's death. In the immediate post-Mao period, city people began returning from the countryside, and unemployment of young people in the cities began to become a problem. There was a certain schizophrenia in the center. Hua commonly used the rhetoric of the Cultural Revolution while simultaneously calling for Zhou's four modernizations, codification of rational rules and regulations, and improved economic management. Enterprise management was passed back and forth from the center to the provinces, ending up with some enterprises controlled by the center and others controlled by the provincial governments. The Party well understood that it would be necessary to build a better economy if it was to maintain its legitimacy in the absence of its charismatic leader. Deng Xiaoping had re-emerged by late 1978, and he was much more open to economic reform.[2]

Meanwhile there had been some interesting developments in rural China. After the disaster of the GLF, the center knew something would have to be done to motivate increased agricultural production. Small private plots were authorized, and prices were raised for the crops produced. Some provincial governments went further, experimenting with a responsibility system, *zerentian*. The *zerentian* system allowed incentive payments for contracted production above state quotas, with distribution to farmers at the brigade level within the commune, and also placed farming decisions at either the brigade or team level. Interestingly, field management became the responsibility of individual households. These changes were pioneered in Anhui Province, but also spread to other provinces. They saved agriculture in China from its downward spiral. Nevertheless, Mao leveled an attack on *zerentian* at the Beidaihe Conference in July 1962, and launched the Socialist Education Movement (1962–1965) to eradicate the *zerentian* system.

In the early years of the Cultural Revolution, agricultural production again stagnated. Some farmers tried to take advantage of chaotic times to practice household responsibility and to market above-quota crops in nearby cities (still illegal). In order to increase production, the party-state introduced modern technology to the communes in the early 1970s. With the death of Mao, the farmers were emboldened to establish a household responsibility system (*baochan daohu*) within the communes. Farmers learned they could bribe local cadres to allow households to take responsibility for farming a given part of commune land, then unofficially contract to provide state quota, to provide a percentage of crops to the cadre, and to keep the rest for sale on the market. The household would decide what to plant and what methods to use. Equipment was shared among the households. This was a radical step that essentially privatized the communes (viewing state share and cadre share as similar to a lease of the land), and it was accomplished not through a mass movement, but through the unorganized spread of a good idea from commune to commune, province to province. It certainly was not approved by the party-state at the time of its establishment.

At the Third Plenum of the Eleventh Party Congress in December 1978, the government agreed to give commune work teams more decision authority, to raise agricultural prices, and to allow sideline family production. However, the 1978 resolution specified that *baochan daohu* was illegal. It was not until early 1983, after Deng and his reform leadership saw how effective a household responsibility system was in increased productivity, that *baochan daohu* was legalized. By this time it had spread through much of rural China. In early 1984 the party-state encouraged household responsibility through the rest of rural China. Local governments leased land to farmers for periods that grew increasingly long term, now up to 30 years.[3]

Market capitalism enterprises also first re-emerged in rural China. State inefficiency in distributing goods led to shortages in towns and cities. An urban resident might have a coupon enabling him to buy food, but it might also require him (or more usually her) to stand in line for hours to gain access to a state store—and even then there might not be adequate food for every buyer. Once farmers had control of a substantial part of their product, they soon learned how to market it in the towns and cities. Since such activity was illegal, these new merchants faced police harassment, detention, and confiscation of their goods. They learned to either avoid or bribe the authorities. Eventually, farmers' markets were established in the towns and cities, and they grew so numerous that they were nearly impossible to control. Over time, food sales were supplemented by services long denied to rural and urban dwellers alike: repair operations, personal services, small shops, restaurants. Rural people did not have to execute complex enterprise plans; they merely had to respond to pent-up demand by furnishing a varied supply of goods and services. This was truly market capitalism from the bottom up, and it swept China once *baochan daohu* was established in the countryside.

While very small-scale individually owned businesses of under five employees were more or less tolerated after 1978, larger businesses were clearly illegal until the center legalized private enterprise in 1987. However, local collective enterprises were clearly allowed, and had been functioning since private enterprise had been made illegal in 1958. As *baochan daohu* worked its entrepreneurial magic in the countryside, farmers began to establish more substantial businesses. These were financed by family *hui* investors, and by overseas Chinese contacts in Hong Kong and Taiwan. In order to protect the business operations, these entrepreneurs "wore a red hat," which meant that they cut deals with local governments to recognize the businesses as TVE collectives, although in reality they were privately owned and operated. This arrangement protected what otherwise would have been illegal enterprises from government harassment, and later on from the excessive taxation imposed on private firms. Local officials received a percentage for the protection, and also benefited from the employment of newly excess labor in their neighborhoods.

In 1978, there were about 1.5 million TVEs, and no recognized individually owned small businesses. By 1984, there were about 1.9 million TVEs, and over four million individually owned businesses. TVE firm counts fell off to about 1.5

million by 1996 as private firms could by then identify as such (and some "red hat" operations transferred to urban areas under protection of officials), but individually owned small businesses exploded to over 20 million. These very small businesses continued to average three employees, but the remaining TVEs grew in employment count over the period. Township enterprises with an average of 39 employees increased employment to an average of 73 between 1978 and 1996; village enterprises also grew average employment from 13 to 26 over the period. Consumer goods manufacturing, construction, transport, and services were all in the mix, areas of pent-up demand. It is interesting to note that "industrial" firms accounted for 74 percent of value added in these small-scale enterprises, with an average per firm employment of ten people (Naughton 2007; Maddison 2007; Zhou 1996).[4] It should be noted that as private enterprise became increasingly tolerated many small-scale private enterprises developed into much bigger businesses, sometimes continuing to operate in their rural birthplace, and sometimes relocated to urban areas—particularly coastal areas with good access to materials, markets, and money, which came mostly from non-state informal access (Tsai 2005; Huang 2008).

Implementing reforms post-1978

As Chinese economic reform began to develop after 1978, market processes would move gradually from a position of illegality to limited toleration. SOEs would be challenged to operate more efficiently, and incentives to managers and workers would be based on SOE profits. Four coastal cities would be opened to worldwide commerce as special enterprise zones (SEZ), with the hope that business operations in an SEZ would discipline some of the SOEs and at the same time provide much-needed foreign investment and advanced technology. Private enterprise would continue to be greatly restricted, limited to the SEZ and very small-scale enterprises. Local government collectives would provide some competitive pressure to the center's SOEs. Key prices would continue to be controlled to prevent high inflation, particularly important as the center acknowledged the need to devalue the yuan as international trade increased. State enterprises would continue to be the key component of a socialist economy, and by managing modest economic liberalization the people of China would prosper even as the Party retained its monopoly on political power.

Had this been the full extent of economic liberalization, Chinese economic reform would probably have had the same results as in other communist societies. However, for a number of reasons, reform did not stop in the comfortable place originally envisioned by Deng and his group of reformers.

First, real markets emerged in China. Entrepreneurs seized opportunities to compete with the SOEs, at first under the protection of the "red hat" (pretending to be a TVE rather than a private enterprise by paying off a local official), but eventually out in the open (Zhou 1996, 2009; Huang 2008). Moreover, a number of entrepreneurs were successful at subcontracting to SOEs. So pressure was placed on the SOEs to rid themselves of redundant employees, and to cut back on the benefits to SOE workers, in order to meet the direct competition and to subcontract work to more efficient providers. Moreover, as China engaged in ever-greater international trade, her export-led economy required the ability to compete internationally (Zhou 1996, 2009). SOEs had always contributed monopoly profits as revenues to the party-state. In the new environment they required state subsidies to stay afloat, and it became a state interest to push the SOEs toward more efficient production.

Second, as SOE employees were terminated, the state needed healthier private enterprises to absorb the displaced workforce to higher uses. Grudgingly, the party-state accepted a much wider role for private firms than the marginal position envisioned in market socialism (White 1998). Post-legalization, private firms have been encumbered with special taxes, at times at almost confiscatory levels, with a variety of market barriers and regulations, and with lack of access to bank financing. Entrepreneurs have negotiated this adverse landscape through *guanxi*—payoffs to party-state officials. Everyone knows that to be internationally competitive Chinese firms, whether SOE or private, must operate efficiently, and that private enterprise drives efficiency throughout the economy.

Third, by the mid-1990s, it was clear to leaders that the two-tier pricing system they had constructed for many key goods (one price for state-supplied goods; a second, higher price for privately supplied goods) was causing more problems than it was solving. The SOEs were getting smaller revenues than the market price allowed, while also operating less efficiently than private firms. This required state subsidies from a government that was no longer acquiring forced savings from SOE monopoly revenues. At the same time, people were getting rich by arbitraging the price differentials. By the mid-1990s almost all prices had been freed from state control—with one important major exception related to banking (to be discussed later).

Fourth, not all SOEs are owned by the center. Most SOEs are owned by local or provincial governments, and while they are smaller than the "national champions," there is substantial competition among themselves and with center SOEs. The center produces Five-Year Plans for the economy, and tries to execute these plans through the SOEs. However, local SOEs do not always do what they are told, especially if it means cutting back on production and having to lay off workers. While this may not be an example of private-enterprise-style capitalism, it certainly reflects a certain level of market competition.

Fifth, the levels of FDI and exposure to the international trading system are substantial. When the four SEZs were opened, FDI flowed into China, much of it generated by Hong Kong and Taiwan businessmen who knew the ropes of doing business in China. According to the Chinese government statistics, FDI increased from $2 billion in 1985 to $108 billion in 2008. An estimate of $1,336 billion represents the cumulative FDI in the period 1979–2012 (Morrison 2013: table 3). This disciplined capital helped create enterprises that could compete on world markets. And this competitive ability stimulated ever-increasing imports of materials, and even greater amounts of exports of finished goods. China became the workbench of the world. China's export-led economy began to show a positive trade balance by 1990, and by 2008 peaked at nearly $300 billion (although the trade balance has fallen to about 60 percent of that level due to the global economic slowdown). In 2009, China launched the Chinese Investment Corporation for FDI outflows as an alternative to parking ever-increasing foreign reserves in low-yielding assets such as U.S. Government securities. In 2012, $84 billion was invested abroad (Morrison 2013: table 4, figure 12).

So, with increasingly developed markets, multiple competitors both public and private in most industries, prices set by the market in most instances, and market discipline enforced by huge exposure to international trade and capital, China's economic reform was far more substantial than that conducted by any other communist party. Party leadership since Deng Xiaoping has referred to the economic system in China as "socialism with Chinese characteristics." Especially considering the income inequality tolerated by the party-state ("Let some get rich first"), with significant regional, rural–urban, and individual disparities, the system looks much more like capitalism. The real question is: free market capitalism or state capitalism? The answer to that question may decide China's future growth prospects. So is China best characterized by state-directed planning for SOEs, or by market-directed independent capitalism? As we shall see, that is not an easy question to answer. As the Chinese entrepreneur was bringing market capitalism to China, the party-state was developing a system of "national champions" in strategic industries, and has been increasingly interventionist in the economy in recent years. China's "socialism with Chinese characteristics" is best understood as an authoritarian capitalism that modulates between a free market model from below and a state capitalism model from above.

The current economic structure in China

The exact percentages of production from state-owned/controlled firms vs. privately owned/controlled firms are very difficult to determine. There are good data on what China defines as an SOE: assets fully owned by center, province, or local governments and managed by the State-owned Assets Supervision and Administration Commission (SASAC) of the State Council, or by other government commissions. (There are local SASACs for province/local SOEs.) However, since 2002 qualified foreign institutional investors have been able to purchase renminbi-denominated shares of Chinese companies in the Shanghai or Shenzhen stock markets. The state holds either majority or controlling shares in these companies. These are structured as state-holding enterprises (SHEs), and do not enter government statistics as SOEs, although they essentially operate under state control. There continue to be small collective enterprises, which are considered public entities. There are also firms that are subsidiaries of SOEs and SHEs that are not clearly identified with the parent, and some foreign invested enterprises (FIEs) where both public and private Chinese money is "round-tripped" through Hong Kong and Macao for tax purposes. Szamosszegi and Kyle (2011: table III-5) reviewed data from China's National Bureau of Statistics, and published a table comparing the private sector (as best could be determined) with the observable state sector (state-controlled entities, or SCEs) on various industrial measures (see Table 11.1).[5]

Table 11.1 Private sector compared to state sector

	1998–2001		*2002–2004*		*2005–2009*	
	Priv	*SCE*	*Priv*	*SCE*	*Priv*	*SCE*
Gross Industr Output Value(RMB bil.)	483	3,804	2,921	6,314	11,491	12,729
Industrial Value Added(RMB bil.)	120	1,291	745	2,129	2,256	3,628
Total Employmt(urban+rural, mil.)	18	83	46	68	76	64
Industrial Taxes (RMB bil.)	17	326	103	506	427	1,002

Even with the limitations as indicated in the notes, it is clear that while both private industrial enterprise and state-controlled industrial enterprise have expanded over the period, private enterprise has been expanding faster. While SCEs tend to be concentrated in industries requiring heavy capitalization, the SOE employment figures are declining as international competition forces layoffs of surplus staff. If private enterprise was not available to soak up the otherwise unemployed in more labor-intensive businesses, the party-state would be facing an employment crisis. Comparisons of business shares in both contracting and services are even more difficult to determine. After reviewing those statistics that are available, Szamosszegi and Kyle (2011) estimate that SOEs and SHEs were responsible for 40 percent of China's GDP and 45 percent of China's non-agricultural GDP in 2007. Less observable state-controlled situations would probably bring state share of the economy into the 50 percent area, a much larger estimate than those found in studies that rely on Chinese SOE statistics and categorize everything else as "private" enterprise.

There is little doubt that the party-state is much more comfortable with the state-controlled sector of the economy. Various industries are categorized as "strategic" and "pillar" industries, including defense, aviation, shipbuilding, resources, communications, utilities, heavy manufacturing, metals, chemicals, and construction. These industries receive heavy public investment (via the banking system), subsidies, and other forms of state assistance. Multiple SCEs can be found in these sectors, and they tend to dominate. How well these industries would operate without state assistance is an open question. Naughton (2008) discovered that the state-formed assets management office (SASAC) in 2003 in attempt to separate ownership from management and to enforce shareholder interest without interfering in the operations of SOEs. But in reality, SASAC is ineffective on both accounts (Ye 2014). Given the fact that Chinese corporate leaders are promoted by a political leader, their real concern is not corporate profit (unlike chaebols in Korea); corporate efficiency is sacrificed.

China has kept its economy growing through a strategy of exports, high investment, and neglect of externalities. A review of World Bank data reflects these strategies (World Bank 2013).

In 2008, just prior to the worldwide financial crisis, Chinese exports were 35 percent of GDP and imports were 27 percent, yielding a net export number of

8 percent of GDP; a very attractive result. In 2009, exports fell to 27 percent and imports to 22 percent due to the crisis, especially in the United States and Europe, where China runs its large trade surpluses. After an uptick in exports in 2010 and 2011, but a further reduction in the margin over imports, China's exports in 2012 were 27 percent while imports were 25 percent, with only a 2 percent margin. While there are a number of modern nations heavily exposed to trade, most of these are part of the European Union where the economies are highly integrated. China is a continental nation like the United States, and should have extensive internal trading among provinces. In the United States, exports tend to run at about 13–14 percent of GDP, and imports are 16–18 percent of GDP.

Why is a huge continental nation like China so dependent on international trade? Consumption spending in China is an unusually small component of GDP. Total private plus government consumption spending was only 48 percent, and private alone was 35 percent, of GDP in 2012. This compares with the United States at 84 percent and 69 percent respectively. Most modern nations have total consumption expenditures above 75 percent of GDP, so the Chinese situation is a real outlier (World Bank 2013).

China's real GDP growth rate has run close to 10 percent for many years (although it ran in the 7–8 percent area during the financial crisis period). A reason for this is unusually high investment within China. Gross capital formation (GCF) was 44 percent in 2008 (compared to 18 percent in United States), but additional investment spending has occurred during the financial crisis with GCF rising to 48 percent in 2009 and remaining at that level in 2010 and 2011 (while GCF was falling in the United States to 15 percent), and even rising a bit higher in 2012 to 49 percent. This has been financed internally by a gross savings rate far above world norms at 51 percent of GDP in 2012, most of it from household savings (World Bank 2013). Chinese are champion savers, and minimal social insurance from the government has driven household savings way up since the mid-1990s (as personal consumption has fallen as a percentage of GDP).

The Chinese banking system is heavily controlled by the party-state, and lends primarily to SCEs, forcing most private firms to access informal credit arrangements (shadow banking). Admitted inflation (CPI) in China has ranged from –1 percent to +6 percent over the period 2008–2011 (undoubtedly lower than the actuality). The banks have been lending at 5.3 to 6.6 percent over this same period, and depositors have received 3 points less than the lending rates, below the admitted rate of inflation in three of the four years. This has been a common practice for many years, and the banks are the only practical savings vehicles for most people. So the government has benefited from paying savers below the rate of inflation, and this is unlikely to change any time soon, although we often hear that the Chinese banks are just on the verge of reforming to market-based rates for deposited and loaned funds.

China has ridden this export-driven, investment-juiced economy for two decades now. On a purchasing power parity basis, China's GDP was $12.3 trillion compared to the United States at $16.2 trillion in 2012, or 76 percent the

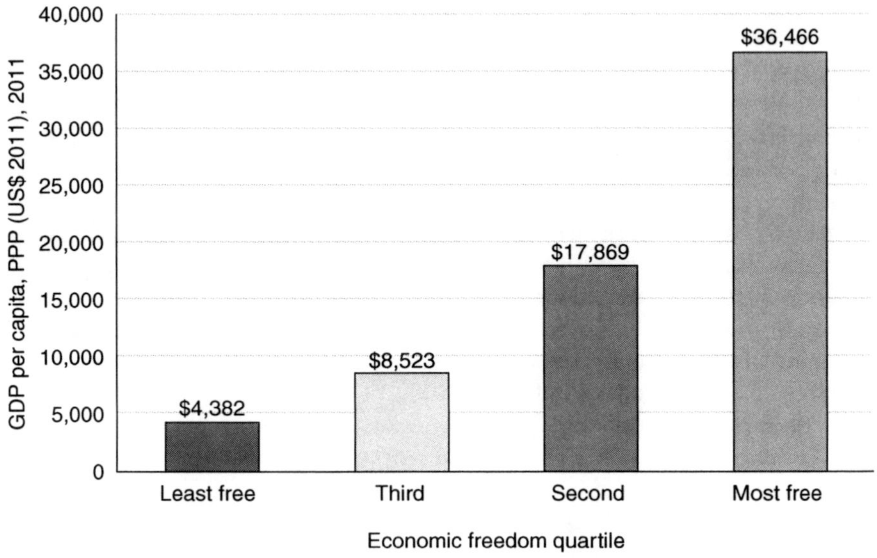

Figure 11.1 Economic freedom quartile/GDP per capita (source: Gwartney *et al.* 2013: 21).

size of the U.S. economy. However, on a per capita basis, the 2012 numbers were $9,083 in China vs. $51,749 in the United States.[6] So China has quite a way to go to become a truly wealthy nation. It is unlikely that its current development model is sustainable in out years. Potential problem sources include: (1) banking system problems; (2) export resistance in the United States and Europe; (3) product quality and environmental problems; (4) excessive corruption costs; and (5) inefficient investment spending. China admits to an unemployment rate of around 4 percent, but the real rate is undoubtedly higher than that. As growth slows and these potential problems are actualized, economic dislocations will threaten the stability of the party-state. A choice will have to be made whether to continue along an inefficient, unsustainable, and highly unbalanced state-controlled path, or a more dynamic market capitalism path. While authoritarian regimes have had some successes in the early stages of economic development, they have had to transition to higher degrees of economic freedom (and usually political freedom as well) to achieve higher levels of economic development, which require the liberation of productive forces.

Banking system vulnerability

On October 7, 2012, *The Economist* reported the findings of an independent Chinese study of the SOEs. The conclusion was that if all the government's grants and hidden subsidies were taken away, the SOEs would lose money. Moreover, they are vehicles for enriching SOE chiefs and political patrons, often children of Party leaders. SOEs have returned less than 3 percent on assets since 2008 (based on reported data), and their recent performance has been heavily driven by large increases in debt rather than improvements in underlying profitability (Batson 2013). As Chinese urbanization has increased, local governments at town, city, and province levels have raised funds to finance real estate development, infrastructure projects, and even normal operating expenditures. These local governments have created off-budget lending platforms (local government financing vehicles, or LGFVs), and this debt has surged since the worldwide financial crisis began. This spending has been a large contributor to continued economic growth. Local government debt via these platforms was estimated at $1.7 trillion in 2010, and has undoubtedly passed $2 trillion since then. This government audit of local debt, covering the larger local entities and perhaps a quarter to a third of outstanding debt, raised concerns about possible repayment and even service of these loans (McMahon 2013).

There is a two-tier banking system in China. Over 90 percent of commercial bank lending goes to SCEs and local governments. Non-performing loans (NPLs) have been a regular problem in Chinese banking. Loans are made on political considerations. Suspension of payments and even loan forgiveness to favored entities have been recurring features of Chinese banking. Private firms have been forced to the "shadow banking" sector (private trust companies, leasing firms, and wealth management products) at high rates of interest, and this poorly regulated market (conducting illegal lending operations) has created financial problems by financing bubbles (Huang 2008). Trust sector assets have expanded ten-fold since 2007 and are now estimated to be worth around $1 trillion. Local governments are beginning to look to shadow banking as the commercial banks become ever more skeptical of ability to service and repay (Hamlin 2013). Failure of shadow banks may have some spillover to regular commercial banking, since some shadow bank funding has come from loans to local businesses obtained from commercial banks (as seen in the Wenzhou underground banking crisis).

The legal commercial banking structure in China includes: (1) three wholly state-owned "policy" banks financing agricultural/rural development, infrastructure projects, and promotion of Chinese exporters (8 percent of banking system assets); (2) five "equitized" commercial banks where the state owns majority (or in one case controlling) shares (49 percent of banking system assets); (3) city commercial banks initially established by city governments in which the city owns controlling shares (8 percent of banking system assets); (4) rural cooperative banks, gradually being transformed into equitized banks with controlling public ownership (11 percent of banking system assets); (5) joint-stock and foreign-owned banks (16 percent and 2 percent respectively of banking system assets); and (6) other banks (6 percent of banking system assets) (M. Martin 2012). The interrelationships with central and local governments are clear, and the result is misallocation of capital and high levels of NPLs.

Bank leverage ratios are high in China. Capital to assets has hovered around 6 percent, as compared to 11 percent in the United States. Chinese banks are reluctant to write off bad debt, and have reported NPLs to total gross loans on a descending path from 1.6 percent to 0.9 percent between 2009 and 2012.[7] Nobody believes those figures. U.S. NPLs over the same period have ranged from 3.9 percent to 5.4 percent, and U.S. banking is not as politically driven as Chinese banking.

In 1999, China's banking system was essentially insolvent, awash in NPLs from SOEs and local governments that had defaulted on their loans under the assumption that the center would raise sufficient funds to bail out the banks. In 2000 and then again in 2004/2005, the State Council transferred a total of $566 billion of bank NPLs to four newly created asset management companies (AMCs). The AMCs were undercapitalized by the state, and NPL recoveries have been modest (well under the assumed 30 percent). Moreover, funding for the AMCs has been supplemented by bank "investments" in AMC bonds and equity, thus transferring the NPLs back to the banking system under a recategorized asset category. So the Chinese banking system faces pressure from legacy NPLs and from emerging NPLs (Martin 2013: 29–31). An honest audit of banking system assets might well result in an insolvent system. The IMF has warned China of its concerns over local government reliance on financed off-budget activity supported by land sales to service the debt, and there has been a flurry of regulatory activity to respond to the concerns (Evans-Pritchard 2013).

In Chinese banking, and in Chinese state capitalism more generally, politics trumps financial discipline. China needs to determine the real position of its banking system, use its stash of foreign currency reserves to recapitalize the public banks, gradually privatize the system, and as this is occurring establish audited policies that require all banks (including local banks!) to make loans based on capacity to repay. This must include ending the preferences for SCEs/local governments and begin making loans to more efficient private firms. This will probably also require a more stable funding source for local governments than land sales.

Export vulnerability

In 2012, the United States and European Union reported trade deficits with China of $315 billion and $187 billion respectively (Morrison 2013: 23). These were not unusual numbers, and trade with these partners has accounted for China's overall favorable trade balance. It is an open question how long the United States and European Union will permit this situation to continue.

China acceded to the WTO in late 2001. It promised to follow WTO trade norms, which are based on transparency, non-discrimination, efficient administration, and independent judicial review (rule of law). Its record has been a disappointment. Since about 2006, the trend toward state intervention in the Chinese economy has intensified. China pursues a mercantilist policy of managed trade, controlled through state capitalism practices. China has failed to enforce intellectual property rights, supports its "national champions" and other SCEs through excessive government support, mandates the use of unique national standards to deny market access, pursues restricted government procurement, imposes investment restrictions and arbitrary licensing provisions for services, and pressures foreign businesses to transfer technology in order to gain access to the market. Subsidies to SCEs are known to be excessive, although China has refused to disclose detailed information on their magnitude as required by the WTO (and provides no information at all on subsidies at the provincial level). As we have seen with the banking system, SCE loan payments are often suspended or forgiven, presenting another avenue of support to domestic businesses (Punke 2012). China's unwillingness to float the yuan (leaving it undervalued) is another irritant in international trade.

The World Bank ranks ease of doing business in 185 countries. The United States ranks 4, China 96. The European nations are generally in the top 20 percent of the rankings.[8] The idea behind WTO accession was that China would liberalize access to its markets (very limited success) and protect trade arrangements through rule of law (also very limited success), and that the resulting specializations in production would benefit wealth creation both for China and her trading partners. This has not occurred, and probably had no chance of occurring.

One problem no one considered was the situation in Chinese agriculture. Farmers are an important political constituency in most countries. Trade in agricultural commodities can be a very sensitive matter. China's farms tend to be quite small. Agricultural land in China is 56 percent of the land mass. In 2011, 35 percent of the workforce was engaged in farming that 56 percent of the land. In comparison, agricultural land in the United States is 45 percent of the land mass, and only 2 percent of the workforce farms the land. Agricultural value added per worker was $749 (2012) in China, $49,817 (2011) in the United States. Even though Chinese farming is more efficient than it had been under state control, it is still very inefficient compared to more highly developed countries.[9] At accession, both the United States and European Union expected to find markets for agricultural products. However, various strategies have been employed by China to retard the development of agricultural trade. Agricultural products did not make the list of major imports identified by Morrison (2013: 25).

In our current low-growth world we can expect the United States and European Union to begin erecting trade barriers until China fulfills the expectations promised at accession in 2001. This flies in the face of the Chinese export-led, high-investment economic system. If China wants to continue trading with the developed nations, there will need to be significant improvements in market access, transparency, and rule of law. This will require more efficient operations, disciplined by market forces rather than the artificial supports of state capitalism.

Product quality and environmental vulnerabilities

In 2005 and 2006 American building materials distributors came to China to buy drywall in order to meet increased demand from the home rebuilding that occurred in the aftermath of southeastern hurricanes. Major Chinese suppliers included a Chinese subsidiary of a German company, Knauf Plasterboard Tianjin, and a Chinese company, Taishan Gypsum. Impurities in the product caused sulfurous smells, corroded wiring, black coating of pipes, and health problems for the homeowners. The only way to remedy the situation is to tear out the defective drywall, and reinstall better drywall while also fixing any damage inside the walls. This is an expensive process. Up to 20,000 homes may have this problem, and there was recently a class action settlement in which parties (mainly Knauf) are to make $1 billion available for remediation. Taishan has not yet settled, claiming they were not responsible, but legal activity continues. Major homebuilders are trying to recover remediation expenses from Taishan (A. Martin 2012; Associated Press 2013).

U.S. consumers have heard about the poisoned milk, contaminated pet food, lead-based toys, and the like in the consumer goods area. However, some recent problems with building materials suggest that quality problems of Chinese goods are widespread over many markets. It is not that China is incapable of producing high-quality products. Manufacturing of Apple products has gone rather well. Paul Midler, a Chinese-speaking consultant to Western businesses who want to subcontract production to China, has identified the major issue of "quality fade." Initial negotiations go very well, and the Western company can't believe how good a product can be produced so cheaply. It can't. Over time, the Chinese factory begins cutting corners and replacing high-quality components with ever-lower-quality components. The Western company doesn't want to believe this is happening, because it means replacement of an important production process with a new supplier. As a result, quality edges down until it reaches sometimes dangerous levels (*The Economist* 2009).

State officials pushed Chinese solar panel companies to accept billions of dollars of debt to control the market. This was to be a Chinese "winner" in development of solar power. Poor planning led to overproduction of the panels and falling prices. The Chinese solar panel companies were then under extreme pressure to cut costs. The result has been defective panels that fail well before their 25-year lifespan. Some Chinese manufacturers have ignored specifications, swapping in cheap Chinese materials to save money. A Massachusetts company doing business with China audited 50 Chinese solar panel factories, and reported defects of 5.5 percent to 22 percent, well above a tolerable error rate. There has been so much pressure on the solar panel industry in China that the government allowed a Chinese bank to place Suntech, a darling of the solar power industry, into bankruptcy reorganization. The parent company, Suntech Power, is traded on the New York Stock Exchange. It had a market capitalization of $16 billion at its peak (five years ago), was then trading at $88.35 a share, and is now trading at 59 cents a share. Foreign lenders are in a subordinated position to the Chinese lenders in any recoveries. The shine is coming off investments in China Inc. (Bradsher 2013).

A problem for Western trading partners is that it is very difficult to recover damages on product liability cases from Chinese firms. There has been some exploration of how to remedy this situation, and it is likely that the United States and European Union will eventually require financial responsibility arrangements for Chinese products. Should that occur, there will be even more pressure on China to better oversee exporter business practices, and to refrain from destroying markets by poorly planned overproduction. Market discipline (as opposed to state preferences), combined with acceptance of financial responsibility, is really in China's long-term interest. China says it wants to move up the value chain, but its actions speak louder than its words.

China's pollution externalities have reached crisis levels. The 2012 Environmental Conditions Report, issued by the Ministry of Environmental Protection, found that nearly 60 percent of the groundwater in 198 cities was "bad" or "extremely bad." More than 30 percent of China's major rivers were either "polluted" or "seriously polluted." Air pollution reached record levels, not only in the cities, but also in industrialized areas of the countryside. Smog is everywhere. The center keeps promising action to promote clean energy, but local governments have been unwilling to sign on to requiring pollution control expenses that may retard industrial production at competitive prices (Duggan 2013). Pollution is a major concern of the Chinese people. Only if inefficient SCEs are replaced by more efficient market competitors is it likely that sufficient funds will become available for cleaning up industry discharges. And even then remediation is likely to take many years. It is unlikely that Western countries will continue to do business with a Chinese economy that is absolved of its responsibility to protect the air and water.

Excessive corruption vulnerability

There have been two patterns of corruption in China. The emergence of *baochan daohu* and market-driven firms in the countryside required bribes to Party cadres. In effect, the bribes were a cost of achieving freedom of action. We might consider this petit corruption. The grand corruption has emerged from top-down state capitalism. Important officials and their children have raked off billions of dollars from SCEs, and from multinationals allowed market access to China—for a price. This has been a detrimental kind of corruption in that it has promoted state capitalism inefficiency and has drained huge amounts of funds from victims of state enterprises. People are losing confidence in "capitalism" as they watch fortunes made on political contacts rather than customer desired advances in goods and services. The land sale revenue of local governments has caused ferment due to expropriation of farmers' lands, at modest or non-existent compensation levels. Rural dwellers watch local governments steal their land while the connected people attached to a project earn millions.

At the power transition from Hu Jintao to Xi Jinping in November 2012, Hu warned that the party monopoly on power could not be maintained unless corruption was addressed. Xi Jinping echoed these sentiments. There has been both skepticism and optimism regarding steps Xi has taken to deal with the problem. It seems to go beyond using anti-corruption as a way to purge opponents (although the Bo Xilai trial may be an example of that). Wang Qishan, the named anti-corruption czar, has launched a campaign to address cadre corruption, and displays of wealth are now thought to be inadvisable. Still, there are reasons to distrust the sincerity of the current campaign. It does not appear to be addressed to the "big fish" of high officials and princelings. There have been attacks on multinationals for corrupt practices, while domestic firms have been ignored for similar issues. This could be a convenient way to further limit competition in China's state capitalism.

The vested interests within state capitalism have become so powerful that they have squeezed out many private firms in profitable industries like real estate, services, extraction, and steel. As part of a publicized anti-corruption campaign launched by the Xi government, oil and gas magnate Zhou YongKang was arrested, as were several of his subordinates (Lim and Blanchard 2014; Areddy *et al.* 2014). Considering Zhou's close relations to the CCP power structure, this is one case that may test how real the anti-corruption campaign is. At the end of 2013, the new government under Xi Jinping and Li Keqiang launched three new AMCs to provide some reform of SOE operations. However, new strategies of industrial investment, investment holding, and capital operation does not touch the real problems of the SOEs—the problems of soft budget constraints, and of corrupt cronyism. It is likely that the main effect of Xi's anti-corruption program is to move control of the vested interest groups to Xi's faction, the new leadership group in the CCP.

China's economy is not sustainable if it is embedded in grand corruption. Political power leads to corruption, and only institutional reforms such as a more market-based economy and political competition (at least within the Party) is likely to reduce the adverse impacts of corruption. While there have been relatively optimistic reports of the new anti-corruption campaign (Moses 2013), Human Rights Watch has reported police harassment of activists for "illegal assembly," where demonstrators were urging a new law requiring disclosure of assets of government officials and their families. Public dissatisfaction with corruption may well put the position of the party-state at risk.

Infrastructure spending vulnerability

When the economy slowed due to the worldwide financial crisis, China faced the possibility of two different answers to deal with economic contraction. China could really focus on building household consumption, backing off on investment spending. This has been promised now in two successive Five-Year Plans. Or China could juice the economy in the old tried and true way: expand infrastructure spending. It was the latter course that was chosen. The center approved projects totaling $157 billion (Sweeney and Chiang 2007). Even more such spending occurred in subsequent years. *The Economist* (2014) reported that the Chinese government's own audit showed that China's local governments (and the investment vehicles they sponsor) occupied a third of China's GDP, a total of 17.9 trillion yuan.

Investment spending approaching 50 percent of GDP cannot be executed efficiently. It is an impossible task to manage such a project-intensive portfolio. Considering the level of corruption in China, projects are often built with substandard designs and materials in order to make budget after payoffs to officials. Infrastructure quality must suffer, and it does. Former Chinese Prime Minister Zhu Rongji, observing the level of poor planning and shoddy construction, often referred to the problem as "bean curd projects." China has built wasteful little-utilized projects that do not justify the money spent on them, such as airports built in remote locations to promote tourism that never materialized. Moreover, collapsing roads, bridges, dikes, buildings, and dams are a problem throughout China. An example is the steel and concrete Rainbow Bridge over the Qijang River near Chongqing. Forty people died in the bridge collapse, and later it was learned that the faulty welding was a consequence of the $12,000 in bribes given to officials to overlook problems. Money was siphoned off the project to build a karaoke bar (Hays 2011).

The investment program is unsustainable and unmanageable. It has been state capitalism's answer to preserving high levels of employment. It is really a waste of resources, and a transition to markets will never occur if excessive infrastructure spending continues to be the party-state's answer to all economic problems. International observers are beginning to take notice—and to worry. BBC Economics Editor Robert Peston (2014) has summarized the situation:

> It is a story of spending and investment on a scale never seen before in human history—30 new airports, 26,000 miles of motorways and a new skyscraper every five days have been built in China in the last five years. But in a situation eerily reminiscent of what has happened in the west, the vast majority of it has been built on credit. This has now left the Chinese economy with huge debts and questions over whether much of the money can ever be paid back.

When 50 percent of GDP is being "invested" year in and year out, private and (mostly) public debt are likely to be accumulating to unmanageable levels. The state capitalism from above thinks it is engaged in "bailing out" the system, but instead it is endangering the very stability it has been trying to protect.

A new "Chinese dream"?

China's new president, Xi Jinping, started his presidency in 2013 by promising to deliver a "Chinese dream" (*zhongguo meng*), consisting of economic prosperity and strength of the country (*guojia fuqiang*), rejuvenation of the nation (*minzu zhenxing*), and the happiness of the people (*renmin xingfu*). This is to mean a more balanced system with an expanded social safety net and a narrowing of the income distribution gap (which is among the widest in the world). Pollution is to be addressed. Rule of law will continue to be the socialist "rule of law," which is rule by law, or rule by CCP leadership, which will continue to hurt balanced Chinese economic development. The party-state will continue to deal with demands for political rights through increased spending on stability maintenance activities (Human Rights Watch 2013).

The productive part of the Chinese economy is that which is market driven. It serves the demand generated by the Chinese consumer, and, in some markets, by the foreign consumer. It is not an integral part of Xi's Chinese dream, not associated with any national champion. It is tolerated, not celebrated, and considered a potential pocket to be picked rather than a strategic path to the future.

The state capitalism of the SOE is part of the dream. The state can direct the economy so that all the resources remain employed, whether usefully or not. But China is coming to the end of an ability to invest 50 percent of its GDP year after year through a politicized banking system. Questions are being asked. The loans will have to be serviced. An unbalanced economy will have to be allowed to come into balance. It is impossible that such can happen without a reconsideration of what economic reform really requires. Dreams will have to encounter realities.

Conclusion

In the 1980s, Japan was considered a formidable competitor. Americans were told they needed to develop an industrial policy like that of Japan. Soon after, Japan reached the limits of possible growth from "directed" capitalism. The Japanese stock market and real estate market collapsed, the banks weakened, and Japan went into a slow growth period that lasted for decades.

The same thing is likely to happen in China. State capitalism is not an effective way of running a competitive economy. Pressure will grow on China's irresponsible trade practices, just as there was pressure on Japan's managed trade by trading partners. Limits to investment-led growth have been reached, and undoubtedly exceeded. The China situation is far more dangerous than was true of Japan. The party-state knows its position depends on continued economic super-growth. As China grows closer to the production possibility frontier, and as state capitalism retards rather than stimulates high growth, China will face an important decision. Will it try to retake a market path, as it started to do after WTO accession, or will it double down on state control of the economy? The choice will determine if China is to be an economic success story over the long run, or if China will become a danger to the worldwide economic system.

How China will manage this choice is not clear. In *How China Became Capitalist*, Ronald Coase and Ning Wang (2012) show how China's road to capitalism arose in part from enhancing incentives of SOEs, but mainly and more dynamically from first tolerating and later embracing grassroots movements and local initiatives to revive agriculture and establish rural industrialization. While Beijing still preached socialism, local authorities explored market-oriented approaches to revive local economies, and competed for economic development as laboratories of regional development. Beijing mainly kept out of the way, insisting on keeping key sectors under state monopoly, while exposing those sectors to greater levels of somewhat protected competition. This was "state-led capitalism," where the real driving force emerged from a growing private sector. Still, China's leaders have never given up on socialism. And China has reached the point where it has to address its lack of a marketplace of ideas if progress is to continue, if it is to move up the value chain. Its industrial revolution must become innovative, and that requires a society in which there is a free flow of ideas. Will the party state be willing to allow the liberalization and reform that will accompany a marketplace of ideas, the freedom of thought so essential to the creativity necessary to innovative capitalism? The answer to this question will determine the choice that China will make (Areddy *et al.* 2014).

Notes

1 China's economic statistics are often questioned, and pre-reform government statistics are particularly unreliable. Unless otherwise noted, all statistics concerning the pre-reform period or comparisons of the pre-reform period with post-reform years are those published by OECD based on Angus Maddison's comprehensive studies (2007). See Maddison (2007: table 3.13) for the data on agricultural share of employment and GDP.
2 For an excellent detailed discussion of this confused period, see Zhou (1995), Vogel (2011), Riskin (1987).
3 A full description of the freeing of Chinese agriculture through a spontaneous, unorganized, leaderless, non-ideological, apolitical movement (SULNAM) may be found in Zhou (1996).
4 These data on small-scale enterprises were developed by Maddison (2007) from official statistics. See Table 3.18.
5 Note that value added includes only 2006–2007, the most recent data available. Note also that the employment data does not include SHE employment. According to World Bank Data, the current Chinese economy on a value-added basis is 47 percent industrial, 43 percent services, and 10 percent agriculture. This compares with the world's predominant economy, the United States, which on a value-added basis is 20 percent industrial, 79 percent services, and 1 percent agriculture.
6 World Bank data (2013). Indicators "GDP, PPP (current international $)" and "GDP per capita, PPP (current international $)," in topic "Economic Policy & External Debt."
7 World Bank data (2013). Indicators "bank capital to assets ratio %" and "bank nonperforming loans %," in topic "Financial Sector."
8 World Bank data (2013). Indicator "ease of doing business index," in topic "Private Sector."
9 World Bank data (2013). Indicators "agricultural land (% land area)," "employment in agriculture (% total employment)," and "agricultural value added per worker," in topic "Agriculture & Rural Development."

References

Areddy, J., Spegele, B., and Grimaldi, J.V. (2014) "Chinese Dragnet Entangles Family of Former Security Chief, Zhou Yongkang," *Wall Street Journal*, March 31. Online: http://online.wsj.com/news/articles/SB10001424052702304020104579432881771992704 (requires subscription).

Associated Press (2013) "Chinese Drywall Settlements Approved in Five Class Action Cases," February 8.

Batson, A. (2013) "The SOE Irritant in U.S.–China Relations," *Wall Street Journal*, July 7.

Bradsher, K. (2013) "Chinese Solar Panel Giant Is Tainted by Bankruptcy," *New York Times*, March 20.

Chow, G.C. (2002) *China's Economic Transformation*, Malden, MA: Blackwell Publishers, pp. 24–45.

Coase, R., and Wang, N. (2012) *How China Became Capitalist by 2012*, Basingstoke and New York: Palgrave Macmillan.

Dikötter, F. (2010) *Mao's Great Famine: The History of China's Most Devastating Catastrophe, 1958–62*, New York: Bloomsbury.

Duggan, J. (2013) "China's Environmental Problems Are Grim Admits Ministry Report," *Guardian*, June 7.

Economist, The (2009) "Chinese Manufacturing: Poorly Made," May 14.

Economist, The (2012) "State-Owned Enterprises Are Dragging Down China," October 7.

Economist, The (2014) Counting Ghosts: China Opens the Books of Its Big-spending Local Governments," January 4. Online: www.economist.com/news/china/21592628-china-opens-books-its-big-spending-local-governments-counting-ghosts.

Evans-Pritchard, A. (2013) "China Orders 'Urgent' Audit of Debts after IMF Warnings," *The Telegraph*, July 29.

Gwartney, J., Lawson, R., and Hall, J. (2013) *Economic Freedom Dataset*, Canada: The Fraser Institute, p. 21.

Hamlin, K. (2013) "China Poised for 2013 Rebound as Debt Risks Rise for Xi," *Bloomberg News*, January 3.

Hays, J. (2011) "Chinese Labor Rights: Laws, Trade Unions and Lawsuits," *Facts And Details*. Online: http://factsanddetails.com/china/cat9/sub60/item363.html.

Huang, Y. (2008) *Capitalism with Chinese Characteristics*, New York: Cambridge University Press.

Human Rights Watch (2013) *World Report 2012: China*. Online: www.hrw.org/world-report-2012/world-report-2012-china.

Johnson, C.A. (1982) *MITI and the Japanese Miracle*, Stanford, CA: Stanford University Press, 412.

Kornai, J. (1993) "Market Socialism Revisited," in P. Bardhand and J. Roemer (eds.), *Market Socialism: The Current Debate*, New York: Oxford University Press.

Lim, B.K., and Blanchard, B. (2014) "China Seizes $14.5 Billion Assets from Family, Associates of Ex-Security Chief," Reuters, March 30. Online: www.reuters.com/article/2014/03/30/us-china-corruption-zhou-idUSBREA2T02S20140330.

McMahon, D. (2013) "Audit Office Shines Light on Local Government Debt," *Wall Street Journal*, June 11.

McNulty, M. and Lee, H.C. (2003) "East Asia's Dynamic Development Model and the Republic of Korea's Experiences," World Bank Policy Research Working Paper No. 2987.

Maddison, A. (2007) "Chinese Economic Performance in the Long Run," OECD Development Centre Studies, 72.

Martin, A. (2012) "Turning Point for Suits over Chinese Drywall," *New York Times*, October 12.

Martin, J. (2009) *When China Rules the World*, London: Penguin.

Martin, M. (2012) "China's Banking System," Issues for Congress.

Morrison, W. (2013) *China's Economic Rise: History, Trends, Challenges, and Implications for the United States*, Washington, D.C.: Library of Congress, Congressional Research Service.

Moses, R. (2013) "Why China's Current Anti-Corruption Campaign Is Different," *Wall Street Journal*, May 30.

Naughton, B. (2007) *Economic Transition and Development in China*, Cambridge, MA: MIT Press.

Naughton, B. (2008) "SASAC and Rising Corporate Power in China," China Leadership Monitor, No. 24.

Park, J.H. (2012) "The East Asian Model of Economic Development and Developing Countries," *Journal of Developing Societies*, 18(4): 330–353.

Peston, R. (2014) "How China Fooled the World," BBC documentary, first broadcast February 2014.

Punke, M. (2012) "Statement by Deputy U.S. Trade Representative at the World Trade Organization's Trade Policy Review of China," July 12, 2012, Geneva, Switzerland. Online: www.geneva.usmission.gov/tag/michael-punke/page/2.

Riskin, C. (1987) *China's Political Economy*, London: Oxford University Press.

Sweeney, P., and Chiang, L. (2007) "China Approves US $157 Billion Infrastructure Spending in Bid to Stem Slowdown," *Reuters*, September 7.

Szamosszegi, A., and Kyle, C. (2011) *An Analysis of State-owned Enterprises and State Capitalism in China*, Washington, D.C.: U.S.–China Economic and Security Review Commission.

Tsai, K. (2005) *Capitalism without Democracy*, Ithaca, NY: Cornell University Press.

Vogel, E.F. (2011) *Deng Xiaoping and the Transformation of China*, Boston: Belknap Press.

White, L., III. (1998) *Unstately Power: Local Causes of China's Economic Reforms*, New York: M.E. Sharpe.

World Bank (2013) *China Data*. Online: http://data.worldbank.org/country/china.

Xu, C. (2011) "The Fundamental Institutions of China's Reforms and Development," *Journal of Economic Literature*, 49(4): 1080.

Yang, J. (2010) *Tombstone: The Great Chinese Famine, 1958–1962*, New York: Farrar, Straus & Giroux.

Ye, M. (2014) "China Invests Overseas: Does the Strong State Help China's Outbound Investment?" In K. Xiao Zhou, S. Rigger, and L.T. White III (eds.), *Democratization in China, Korea and Southeast Asia? Local and National Perspectives*, New York: Routledge.

Zhou, K. (1996) *How the Farmers Changed China*, Boulder, CO: Westview Press.

Zhou, K. (2009) *China's Long March to Freedom: Grassroots Moderization*, New Brunswick, NJ: Transaction Publishers.

Zhou, Q.R. (1995) *Chinese Rural Reform and the Development of National Growth*, Oxford: Oxford University Press.

12 Rule by virtue, the mass line model, and cadre–mass relations

John Kennedy and Shi Yaojiang

Introduction

The East Asian Development Model is the alternative to the liberal market (Western) model of economic development and modernization. It is an amalgamation of government intervention into the economy and cultural traits of the East Asian region. The East Asian Model has enabled countries in the region to develop a different type of capitalism and path to modernization. According to Berger (1988: 6), the Western model of modernity is predicated on individualism, while East Asian modernization is grounded on communalism and "collective solidarity." Thus modernization and development can take on different cultural forms (Tu 1989: 93).

One of the key elements of the East Asian Model is Confucianism. While traditional North American and Western European theorists such as Max Weber and Karl Marx viewed Confucianism as a hindrance to capitalist (and socialist) development, the evidence suggests that Confucianism has been conducive to economic development in East Asian countries during the 1970s and 1980s. Over 25 years ago, Peter Berger (1988: 5) suggested that "Now, no one is likely to question that these social and cultural features are also, somehow, part of the 'East Asian Model.'" It is the Confucian values of benevolence and harmony that make the East Asian model distinct from the North American and Western European conceptions of modernity. Benevolent leaders both national and local rule by virtue and these authorities guide social and economic development. Harmony is the social goal that can be reached through responsive authorities and shared community and national development rather than strictly personal (individual) gains (Qin 2008: 70; Tu 1989: 92). While most of the focus was on Japan, South Korea, and Taiwan, there was a renewed focus in the 1990s and after 2000 on mainland China (Baek 2005; Bell 2008).

Yet, Confucian values alone cannot achieve social harmony and there needs to be institutional and social mechanisms to ensure responsive leadership or even authoritarian accountability. As Lenin applied the democratic centralism and the notion of the vanguard party to Karl Marx and *Das Kapital*, there needs to be political mechanisms that can enhance virtuous behavior and sustain social harmony. However, popular elections rarely produce virtuous leaders and a harmonious society. While popular elections in developed and developing countries are institutional measures to promote responsive government leaders, the election process alone does not make accountable leaders. In fact, authoritarian regimes also use elections to gain political legitimacy without direct accountability (Levitsky and Way 2002: 54). Thus, an East Asian governance model may be an alternative to popular election that is a different type of representation.

The East Asian model of governance focuses on the ideals of Confucianism connecting good governance with virtuous leaders rather than solely relying on political institutions and elections to shape the behavior of leaders. Indeed, Chinese national leaders, such as Jiang Zemin and Hu Jintao, as well as leading Chinese intellectuals, have promoted the notion of "rule by virtue" (德治) for local cadres in China. Virtuous cadres are committed to improving the well-being of citizens (or subjects depending on the historical period). These committed cadres must first understand the concerns and needs of the citizens, and then put the needs of the citizens above their own political and personal ambitions (Li 2012: 416; Tong 2011: 142). The general assumption of this model is that corruption and growing distance between cadres and citizens is due to the lack of virtuous local leaders. Indeed, central leadership tends to shift the blame for social problems, such as uneven policy implementation and corruption, on to local officials. Thus the East Asian Model that emphasizes rule by virtue is an important concept for the national leadership as well as local officials.

One of the most important mechanisms that the Chinese Communist Party (CCP) uses to connect cadres and citizens is the "mass line." The basic assumption is that local officials at the county and township level of government will accurately report conditions in villages and identify villager needs and concerns (Steiner 1951: 422). The mass line depends on the personal commitment of local cadres to improve local conditions and seek out citizen views and concerns. At base, this reflects the virtuous cadre. Thus, a close examination of the mass line can be a real test of the Confucian model and rule by virtue. While China scholars have debated the use of the Confucian model in contemporary China, few have actually attempted to measure and evaluate cadre commitment (or understanding) of citizen concerns. Although the mass line has a deep political history and implications for China especially during the Maoist era (1949–1976), the mass line assumptions and practice remain important tools for the CCP in shaping the behavior and values of local cadres. The practice of the mass line also includes a feedback loop where cadres communicate with villagers and learn about their situation then this knowledge of villagers' life will generate more empathy for them (Blecher 1979: 107). Greater cadre understanding of villagers may contribute to their commitment in helping local residents. In essence, cadres can learn to become virtuous. Thus, at the heart of the Confucian model and the connection with the mass line is that local cadres can be taught to become more responsive and accountable to citizens.

Rather than using competitive elections with an open nomination process or strict laws to shape cadre behavior and responsiveness, the CCP continues to rely on the mass line. For example, in 2011, several mass line campaigns were introduced to improve the relations between county officials and rural residents throughout China such as the "linking hearts" (连心工程) and "connecting with villages and villagers" (联村联户), where county officials were assigned a poor household to learn about their conditions and help out the family. The old-style campaign is intended to bring county cadres closer to villager constituents through face-to-face interaction and improve communication with villagers. In 2013, the central leadership launched a broader "Mass Line Education" campaign to increase the effectiveness of the mass line. These campaigns reiterate the importance of the "flesh and blood connections" (血肉联系) between the people and the CCP. In early 2013, there were a plethora of national news articles and media reports in the *People's Daily* and CCTV as well as the provincial and municipal news outlets on the mass line. The message is clear that local cadres need to become closer to the people (masses). The main political tool is the mass line where local cadres learn about the conditions and preferences of local residents so that the voice for the average citizen is included in the policy-making process. Local officials observe and report citizen attitudes and needs to higher officials providing information from the masses, then the CCP leaders take these reports into account during the policy-making process. The national policies are then implemented down to the masses. Hence the term used for the mass line: "from the masses to the masses." However, scholars have criticized and even dismissed the mass line as a systematic tool to improve local cadre–mass relations and shape the (moral) behavior of local cadres.

The mass line improved cadre–mass relations in the 1930s and 1940s when the CCP sought to gain mass support of the rural population for their policies, but maintaining the same practice after the CCP established a national government in 1949 was a challenge. The mass line was implemented in communist-controlled areas in Northern Shaanxi after the Long March, and it is tied to the revolutionary tradition of connecting the party to the population. The concept and practice worked well in the smaller rural districts because the CCP leadership was able to monitor local cadres in these revolutionary base areas (Hsu 1945: 47–51). There was a clear line of communication between the villagers, local cadres, and policy-makers. Moreover, local cadres had a uniform understanding of district villager preferences through cadre study sessions and shared information (Chen 1986: 5–6). However, when the CCP came to power in 1949, the leadership continued to adapt the same practice on a national scale. This weakened central monitoring of local cadres and vastly expanded the line of communication between the policy-makers and citizens. Indeed, lack of communication between lower-level cadres and higher authorities during the Maoist era (1949–1976) has had devastating results such as the Great Leap Forward (1958–1960). In the post-Maoist era during the 1990s, there was a dramatic increase in villager taxes and fees (villager burdens) and a further breakdown in cadre–mass relations. Villager concerns were not accurately reported to higher authorities or local cadres completely ignored villager concerns, so villagers took matters into their own hands by attempting to alert central leaders to the local cadre abuses through protests and petitions (O'Brien and Li 2006: 54–56).

Since the 1990s, citizen satisfaction with local officials has been declining while satisfaction with the national leadership remains relatively high (Saich 2007).

Despite the deteriorating relationship between local government officials and residents, the CCP continues to rely on the mass line as a mechanism for improving cadre–mass relations. There are two general criticisms of the mass line from the within the CCP and among Chinese and foreign scholars. First, much of the blame falls on the local cadres for not effectively understanding and communicating mass opinions and preferences (i.e., lack of virtue). The central leadership has focused on improving individual cadre contact with their constituents especially in the rural areas in order to "correct the mistaken viewpoints among cadres." The official problem is commandism and bureaucratism (Steiner 1951: 427). Commandism is where local officials blindly enforce policies. That is, local officials at the town and county levels strictly carry out administrative duties without educating the public and communicating with the masses. Bureaucratism refers to "paper pushers" at all levels and complacent cadres who use their position for personal advancement without regard for the masses. These condemnations of local cadres have occurred since the inception of the mass line in the 1930s and continue today. Indeed, much of the official language in the 1930s and 1950s is also used in contemporary accusations of bureaucratism (Guangming 2013). Foreign academics have also suggested that mass line practices when implemented at the local level were effective in incorporating mass preferences given the limited scope for mass participation through other available channels during the Maoist era (Blecher 1979; MacFarquhar 1974). Still, the burden was on the local cadre's "selfless service" to the people to ensure implementation. The official way to resolve the problem is to increase contact between cadres and local residents through study groups and field observations (考查). This includes requiring local officials to meet and interact with villagers such as the recent Linking Hearts campaign. Thus, officially the mass line is conceptually sound, but the problem is the implementation and practice.

Second is the conceptual (academic) criticism that the mass line is systematically flawed both theoretically and in practice. One scholar aptly suggests the mass line is conceptually inconsistent with democratic practices because it is "compatible with the traditional Chinese obsession with benevolent leadership, which is always for the people, but never by the people" (Shih 1997: 355). Indeed, Townsend (1977: 1007) suggests that the mass line in China "serves as an alternative to elections, competing political parties, and constitutional restraint." He also suggests that the mass line has been in decline as an effective institution for mass participation since the late 1950s. This notion of a waning mass line that is used only as a propaganda tool is echoed throughout the (English) literature (Whyte 1974; Burns 1988; Shi 1997). As Townsend stated (1977: 1013):

> In general, then, the post-Mao succession will bring a more cautious use of mass line institutions in which their primary role is to serve the goals of the central leadership. They will be more subject to central controls, more

> limited in their scope, and less open to spontaneous popular action. As long as they remain in place, however, the possibility remains that they might be reinvigorated, particularly in times of national crisis.

This is a profound observation and seemed to ring true for the following decades. Xi Jinping's current revival of the nationwide "Mass Line Education" may reflect the central leadership's response to the national crisis of deteriorating cadre–mass relations. Nevertheless, no matter how foreign scholars view the mass line, it seems clear that the central leadership takes the concept seriously and there are very real attempts to implement the mass line at the local level.

Despite the rich literature on the mass line both conceptually and in practice, there is little or no empirical data to examine the *vertical* relations among local officials and their understanding of mass attitudes. While many Chinese and foreign studies have criticized the mass line, few have empirically tested the assumptions and clearly identified the problems. The three key assumptions of the mass line are that (1) local officials learn from the masses (collect information/data); (2) they summarize (concentrate) mass attitudes for a uniform understanding of villager preferences; and (3) report the mass preferences to higher authorities. The CCP has recently attempted to resolve cadre–mass relations with nationwide programs to improve the cadre knowledge of villager conditions and fully carry out all three assumptions. Thus, has the recent mass line reforms improved cadre knowledge of villagers' preferences? How do local cadres collect and share information at town and county level? That is, do local officials at the county level have uniform information about villager conditions and attitudes? Is it possible to identify these problems with the mass line? These questions have significant implications for the mass line and Confucian model based on rule by virtue. If the mass line fails to influence the behavior of county officials, then this put into question the whole notion of learning to be virtuous and "rule by virtue" as well as the East Asian governance model.

This study will closely examine the first two assumptions using a unique *vertical survey* of villagers, village cadres, and township and county officials to assess cadre–mass relations and identify the strengths and weaknesses of the mass line. We find that the mass line has completely broken down due to lack of coordinated efforts to collect and evaluate information regarding villager preferences and opinions. Moreover, the recent efforts to revitalize the mass line suffer from the same systematic problems. While these results are not surprising, we offer a novel approach to identifying the key issues and problems. We also believe that the key problem with the mass line is not solely due to poor cadre behavior, but rather the methods (lack of methods) local cadres have at their disposal for collecting and evaluating mass preferences and attitudes. Although we find that local officials are not learning to be virtuous, we believe they can learn to be more responsive with better information and sanctions from high authorities.

This chapter is divided into three sections. The first part provides the basic assumptions of the mass line and measures for evaluating cadre performance and their shared understanding of villager preferences. This includes an introduction to the survey instrument and sampling methods. The second section is a descriptive analysis of the data and the testing of the assumptions of the mass line. The final section is the conclusion that narrows the critique of the mass line and closely examines some possible alternative "research methods" for local officials and implications for the Confucian model of governance and rule by virtue.

The mass line and basic assumptions

> In all the practical work of our Party, all correct leadership is necessarily "from the masses, to the masses." This means: take the ideas of the masses (scattered and unsystematic ideas) and concentrate them (through study turn them into concentrated and systematic ideas), then go to the masses and propagate and explain these ideas until the masses embrace them as their own, hold fast to them and translate them into action, and test the correctness of these ideas in such action.
>
> (Mao 1967: 118)

A number of scholars have quoted this famous line that provides the basic assumptions of the mass line. The notion of "take the ideas of the masses" is a key because individual opinions and attitudes are typically "scattered and unsystematic." Meeting with one or two villagers will not provide adequate information and even with dozens of interviews and observations it is difficult to assess and summarize attitudes. Therefore it is necessary to have a collection of opinions and attitudes from several sources (cadres) and then "concentrate them through study" and "turn them into concentrated and systematic ideas." Thus the basic assumption is that local cadres must create a uniform and relatively objective understanding of villager experiences, attitudes, and needs.

The mass line is meant to reduce individual subjective cadre views of villager experiences and concerns that lead to miscommunication and a breakdown of cadre–mass relations. Indeed, Mao states that, "Many comrades do not see the importance of, or are not good at, summing up the experience of mass struggles, but fancying themselves clever, are fond of voicing their subjectivist ideas, and so their ideas become empty and impractical" (1967: 119). One of the goals of the mass line is to unify local cadre understanding of villager experiences and needs especially at the village (brigade), township (commune), and county levels. The success of the mass line depends on the uniform understanding and knowledge of villagers among local officials. In more concrete terms, Mao warned that a collection of disparate views on villager attitudes among officials within the same level of government, such as the county agricultural bureau, is a serious problem for local cadres as well as the CCP.

While the CCP continues to call on cadres to follow the mass line, only recently has the CCP attempted to provide more "guidance" in the mass line practice. In 2011, counties in Shaanxi province experimented with several mass line methods to bring county cadres closer to villager experiences and eliminate commandism and bureaucratism at the county level. The "linking hearts project" was introduced as a means to connect county cadres with poorer residents so they can understand their experiences and needs (Xi 2013). The idea is to assign each county cadre a poor household and meet with the villagers to learn about their general needs as well as identify a problem they can address. Once the county cadre identifies an issue, such as limited funds for a child's high school education or minor repairs for the house of an elderly couple, the cadre will work with the family to resolve the problem. Since 2012, the experiment has become a campaign and spread throughout Shaanxi and other provinces using the same name or more local variations such as "linking village, linking household" (Gansu 2013). News articles and county government reports directly connect the "linking village, linking household" with rule by virtue (德治) and "virtuous education" (Jinchang 2013). The broader goal of this mass line campaign (practice) is to create a common source for county cadres to collect information about villager preferences and needs so they can "turn them into concentrated and systematic ideas" referring back to the basic assumption of uniform understanding of villager experiences. Thus, how well has the current mass line campaign helped to unify cadre understanding of villager preferences? Has the "linking hearts project" help bridge the gap between villagers' stated preferences and cadre perception of villager needs?

The data used to test the mass line assumptions is a unique survey conducted in 2012 and 2013 (third round in 2014). The 2012 random survey includes 541 village households from 36 villages in 6 counties as well as 328 county and town officials and village cadres. There are 217 county officials from the agricultural bureau (县农业部) and county cooperative medical offices (县合疗干部), and 111 township agricultural and health officials as well as village cadres (village leaders and party secretaries). We used seven separate questionnaires that asked about specific duties as well as similar (and same) questions for official and villager respondents. In addition, we conducted 60 opened-ended interviews of county and township officials as well as village cadres in 2013. This is a vertical survey of the county and subcounty party-government officials, and this data set allows us to examine the relations and knowledge between county, township, and village cadres.

In this study, we examine shared knowledge of farming practices and policies from the county agricultural bureau to test the assumptions of the mass line and provide an analysis of the mass line using empirical survey of cadre and villager attitudes and knowledge. The assumptions of the mass line generate several testable hypotheses. First is the mass line assumption of unified understanding. Thus *H1* is that the *majority of cadres have the same understanding of villager preferences*. This hypothesis does not assume that all (100 percent) of the county agricultural officials have the same knowledge, but at least the majority has a similar knowledge. The second hypothesis is the effectiveness of the new campaign for linking county officials and the villagers. The assumption underlining the campaign is that the officials who participate in the campaign will have a closer understanding of the villager preferences. Thus *H2* is that *county officials who participate in the "linking hearts" campaign and visited with villager households will have a better understanding of villager preferences.* That is, the participating "linking hearts" county officials estimate of the villager preferences will be aligned with the majority of the villager stated preferences.

Cadre "shared" knowledge of villager preferences

County officials from the agricultural bureau have a wide range of duties and they need to work with other officials within their bureau as well as lower-level cadres at the township and village levels. The services provided at the county level include seed and fertilizer inspection, pesticide control, mulching technology, agricultural marketing, agricultural technology training, and agricultural infrastructure. These duties make up the bulk of their activities. The inspection of seed and chemical fertilizer quality is an important duty. Many villagers acknowledge that poor-quality seeds or fertilizer can destroy a farmer's livelihood within a season. Mulching technology is also important in rural northwest China. This usually involves the use of plastic sheeting that covers the ground to conserve irrigation water and increase harvests. County agricultural officials will introduce technics used in the process and well as the type of plastic materials. Agricultural marketing involves increasing local and regional markets for agricultural products. For example, if the local product is apples, then county officials work with villagers to expand sales through advertisements and connecting with buyers within and outside the county. Agricultural infrastructure involves irrigation development and access to machinery. Agricultural technology training is also a crucial service that county officials provide. This includes greenhouse construction and maintenance for cash crops such as varieties of fruits and vegetables. Unlike inspection duties, technology training is where county officials work face-to-face with villagers. Thus, activities for officials from the agricultural bureau range from inspection to training, and they have a variety of ways to interact with villagers.

Yet, a typical county agricultural bureau may consist of 20 to 30 civil servants, and they all have different tasks that may or may not overlap with one another. In our survey, 152 agricultural bureau officials (from six counties) were interviewed and completed the questionnaires. We asked about their activities and work assignments. Only 23 percent of the officials conduct seed and fertilizer inspection, and only 25 percent are involved in agricultural marketing. However, 49 percent of the agricultural bureau officials are engaged in agricultural infrastructure duties, and over 45 percent are involved in pesticide control and mulching technology. The most common activity is agricultural technology training, where 67 percent of the officials provide this service. While some officials have specialized activities, there is an overlap in agricultural duties among county officials. Indeed, there are shared service responsibilities within the county agricultural bureau. This should facilitate a shared knowledge of villager preferences and agricultural needs.

In the survey, we ask the officials in the county agricultural bureau to estimate villagers' most important agricultural service need. The goal of this question is to determine whether or not the officials have a shared understanding of villager service needs. Figure 12.1 displays the distribution of the responses. There is a wide range of answers among the respondents. Although 67 percent of the county officials are involved in agricultural technology training, only 21 percent believe this is the most important villager service need. There is no uniform understanding of villager agricultural service among the 152 officials. Figure 12.1 is the combined total of all agricultural officials across six counties. However, the results might be more uniform within *each* county. Therefore, we examine the distribution of responses within the counties. Figure 12.2 displays the responses for County 1. While only 8 percent of the total respondents estimated agricultural marketing as the most important villager service need, 28 percent of the agricultural officials in County 1 estimate this as the most important service need. The distribution is similar for County 2 as well (see Figure 12.3). Indeed, data from the other four counties reveals the similar lack of uniformity among officials within the same county agricultural bureau.

Yet, at the county level, it is still possible that villagers' preferences are just as diverse and scattered as county officials' estimates. In the full household sample of 541 villagers, 68 percent stated that agricultural technology training is the most important farming service. At the county level, the percentage varies from 58 to 80 percent of the villager respondents. Thus the majority of villagers in all six counties believe agricultural technology training is a vital county service. In Figure 12.4, we compare county agricultural bureau officials' assessments of villagers' top service needs with villagers' own estimate of their most important service need. The gap between cadre and villager estimates is large,

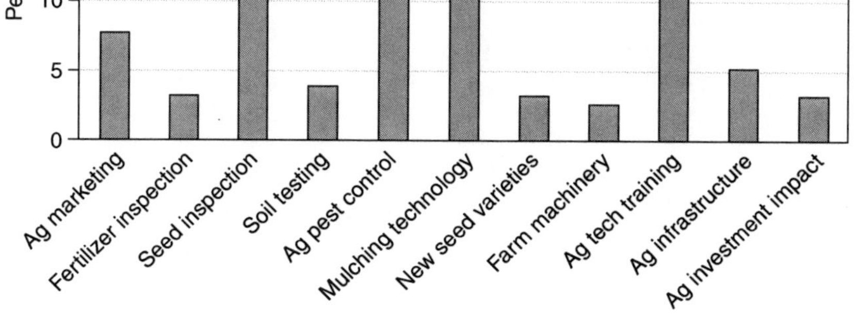

Figure 12.1 All county agricultural cadre estimate of villagers' greatest needs (source: author survey (N = 152)).

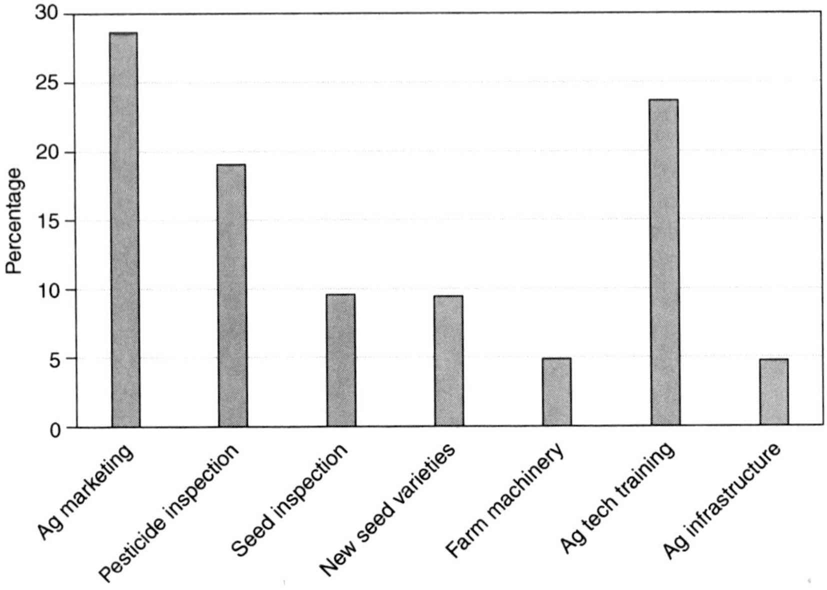

Figure 12.2 County 1 agricultural cadre estimate of villagers' greatest needs (source: author survey (N = 21)).

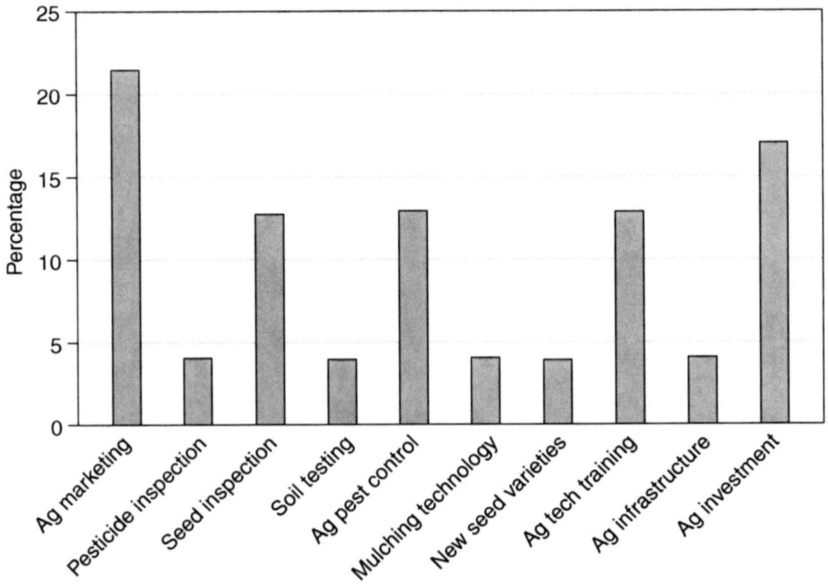

Figure 12.3 County 2 agricultural cadre estimate of villagers' greatest needs (source: author survey (N = 24)).

but it also varies among counties. It ranges from over 60 percent in County 2 to 23 percent in County 4. It is possible that county officials' individual backgrounds, such as age, level of education, and gender, may be a factor in the variation in estimates as well as the gap between county officials and villagers. However, when we control for these individual characteristics we still observe similar variation among counties. This suggests possible institutional or county-level influence.

One of the defining institutional features is the full implementation of the "linking hearts" program within each county. Within the sample, 23 percent of the county agricultural bureau officials had *not* visited a villager household at the time of the survey. In fact, the "linking hearts" program began in 2011, but there is still a variation in officials' participation, especially among counties. For example, in County 2, 25 percent of the county officials had not visited a poor household. This might explain the huge gap (68 percent difference) between cadre and villagers' estimates in Figure 12.4. However, the gap is lower in County 3 (28 percent difference) and over 30 percent of the county officials did *not* visit a villager household. While the evidence in Figure 12.4 is suggestive, it is still important to examine the variation in cadre estimates between those who fully participated in the "linking hearts" program (i.e., visited poor rural households) and cadres who did not within the same county. Figure 12.5 displays the variation in County 2 where only 10 percent of the participating county officials were aligned with villagers' agricultural service preference and none of the non-participating officials guessed correctly (agricultural technology training). This suggests that the new mass line program may be slightly effective. Yet, Figure 12.6 from County 3 shows a completely opposite

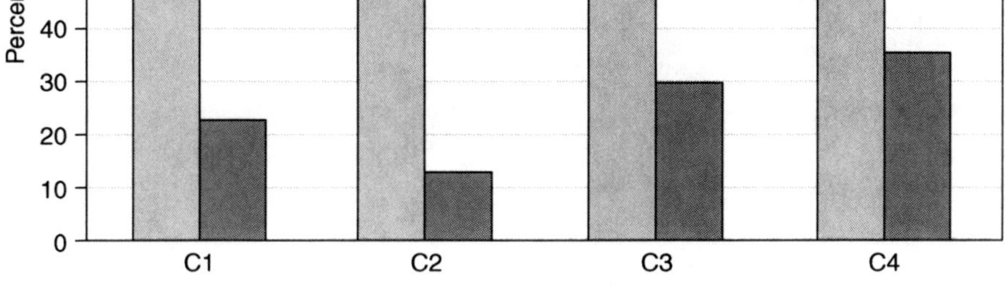

Figure 12.4 Percentage of villagers who believe agricultural training is most important need and percentage of county cadre's estimate that this is a most important villager agricultural need (source: author survey (N = 452)).

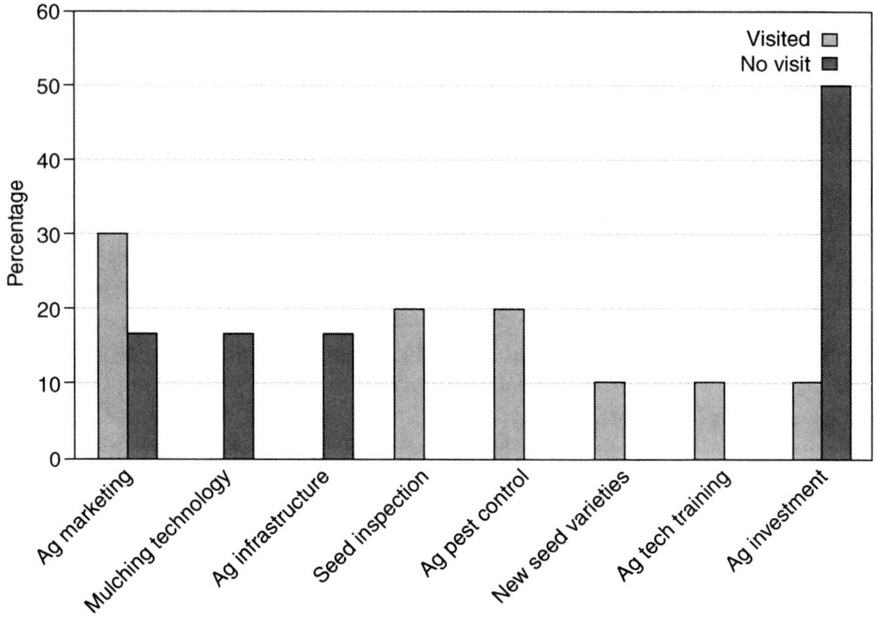

Figure 12.5 County 2 cadre's estimate of villagers' most important needs and whether or not the cadre visited villagers' homes (source: author survey (N = 114)).

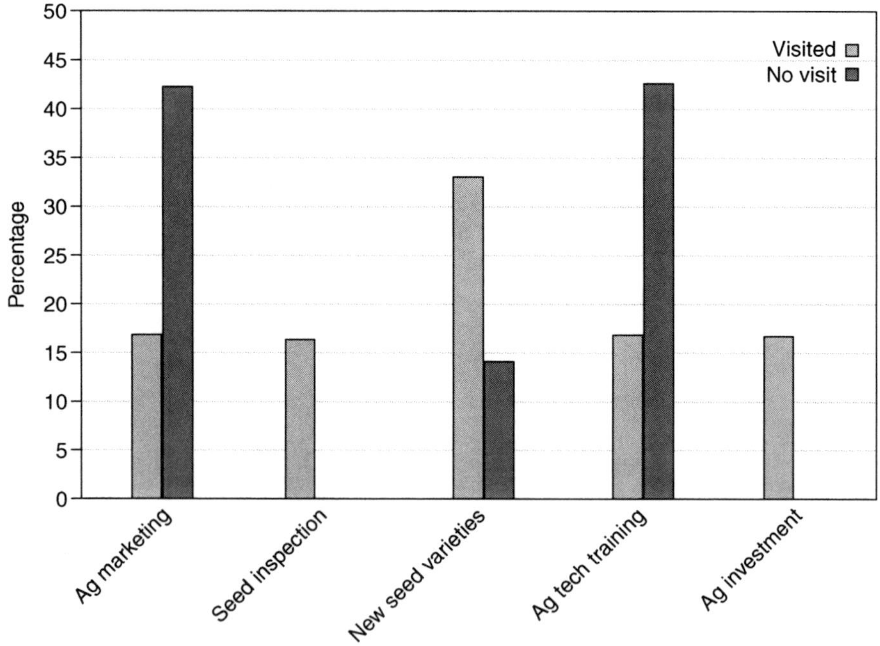

Figure 12.6 County 3 cadre's estimate of villager's most important needs and whether or not the cadre visited villagers' homes (source: author survey (N = 112)).

pattern where over 40 percent of the non-participating officials had estimates aligned with villagers' preference. This is 25 percent higher than officials who actually participated in the program. There are other factors that are influencing county cadre estimates of villager preferences. Indeed, visits to poor rural households do not seem to have a significant effect on cadre understanding of villager preferences.

Of course, individual cadre interactions with several villagers within a single household will not offer enough information to provide accurate estimates of county- or even township-wide villager preferences, but the mass line and the "linking hearts" program include study sessions and meetings to discuss the campaign. It is in these study groups where county agricultural bureau officials should be distilling their experiences and create a uniform understanding of villagers' needs. However, study sessions discuss policy directives rather than data. County officials in our sample are not systematically collecting and sharing the information they obtain through work experience and "linking" villager household visits. Moreover, government study sessions are designed to educate cadres about central and provincial mass campaigns and policies. This is related to the traditional (and contemporary) educational method of learning and absorbing party-government material rather than an open discussion. The basic mass line assumption of taking "scattered and unsystematic ideas" of the masses and then concentrating them into "systematic ideas" requires interaction and dialog among cadres. As Mao Zedong suggests, county officials need to reconcile the diversity of cadre opinions and estimates of villager preferences and service needs.

We believe the concept of the mass line is intact, but the mass line requires cadre training and a unified methodology. The data from the survey (Figures 12.1–12.6) provide a unique look at county officials. It also clearly identifies significant problems with the mass line. At first glance, the findings suggest that the fault with the mass line and "linking hearts" program falls on the county officials and their inability to move beyond their own subjective opinions regarding villager preferences. It seems that county cadres are *not* learning to be virtuous. Indeed, previous academic studies and the current "mass line education campaign" would also support this interpretation of the survey data. The central government solution is to create more opportunities for county officials to hear villager concerns and educate cadres on the mass line concepts. The CCP is still holding on to the mass line practice as a means to create virtuous local officials. If the current programs are not educating local officials, then there needs to be more intensive campaigns. However, as the survey data suggests, cadre interaction with villagers does not improve general understanding of villager conditions. The problem is not with the county officials' lack of mass line education or their lack of virtue. Instead, it is the lack of a unified mass line methodology and cadre training in data collection and analysis technics. The central leadership needs to shift the blame for the failure of the mass line away from local cadres and focus on the implementation process and training local cadres rather than "educating."

Conclusion

The East Asian Development Model is based on the notion of Confucian values and virtuous leaders. Of course, finding purely benevolent and virtuous leadership is a difficult task, especially among a large number of subnational authorities. Referring to Taiwan, South Korea, and Japan in the 1970s and 1980s, Tu (1989: 93) suggests that "governments in industrial East Asia are by no means 'benevolent,' but, to the extent they are seasoned Confucian culture, their sense of duty compels them to be publicly accountable." The East Asian nations at the time were also going through political reforms and institutional changes. Yet, there seems to be a combination of institutional mechanisms as well as "sense of duty" that compels them to be more accountable or at least knowledgeable about the public concerns. The empirical evidence in this chapter challenges the basic assumption of the East Asian model of governance and the ideals of Confucianism connecting good governance with virtuous leaders. We use the basic concepts of the mass line to test the notion that local cadres, given the opportunity, will be willing to learn about villager concerns and become more empathic and responsive toward villagers (i.e., learn to virtuous). The evidence suggests that even through central and local mass line campaigns, county officials are not learning about villagers concerns.

This also reflects the challenge in teaching local officials to become virtuous. However, the current mass line practices put the burden of learning about villagers concerns on the individual local official. Even a virtuous county official cannot estimate the needs of several thousand villagers within the county. Thus, training local officials to understand villager concerns and to be more responsive requires a change in the mass line approach. In fact, the root problem is not the lack of individual cadre virtue, but the lack of unified data collection and analysis among cadres at the county level; that is, the lack of methodology.

Mao Zedong set the tone for the mass line in 1943, but he also relied too heavily on the individual cadres and their individual commitment to selflessly serving the people. Mao did not address methodology for local cadres. According to Mao,

> Details concerning methods of leadership are not dealt with here; it is hoped that comrades in all localities will themselves do some hard thinking and give full play to their own creativeness on the basis of the principles here set forth.
>
> (Mao 1967)

Indeed, Mao Zedong, Jiang Zemin, and Hu Jintao did not directly address the need for a unified data-collection method. However, without uniform data and a common research language it is nearly impossible to summarize or "concentrate mass experiences" and attitudes.

While there are broader public opinion surveys such as citizen satisfaction surveys conducted by Chinese universities and collaborative opinion surveys with foreign academics as well as Chinese government institutions, these surveys and the methodology are limited to a few elite government institutions and universities (Thornton 2011; Saich 2012; Gao 2012). The real need for methodology is at the local level. The "flesh and blood" concern is local cadre–mass relations. The central leadership enjoys a significant level of support, but this is being eroded at the local level and central leadership needs to find ways to improve this local relationship. The revival of the mass line is the most recent attempt, but the mass line is missing a "mass methodology." A shared methodology including random survey samples, questionnaire design, systematic case studies, structure open ended interviews, as well as simple data-analysis technics are important tools for the cadres to summarize and concentrate mass attitudes at the local level. As Mao wrote in 1931, "without a survey, there is no voice; an incorrect survey similarly has no voice" ("没有调查, 没有发言权, 不做正确的调查同样没有发言权"). Mao used the word survey (调查) rather than investigation (考查). This is an important distinction and leaves open the possibly for a more unified mass line methodology.

Although broader more philosophical discussions on the East Asian Model and governance (rule by virtue) are important, a new direction for the Confucianism model may focus on a collective notion of understanding and information gathering rather than individual virtue. At base, the virtuous leader has empathy and learns about the people so he (or she) can address the concerns of the population. However, responsive leaders need representative information or data to make effective policy decisions that will meet the needs of the population and maintain social harmony.

References

Baek, Seung-Wook (2005), "Does China Follow the East Asian Development Model?" *Journal of Contemporary Asia*, vol. 35, no. 4, pp. 485–498.

Bell, Daniel (2008), *China's New Confucianism: Politics and Everyday Life in a Changing Society*, Princeton and Oxford: Princeton University Press.

Berger, Peter L. (1988), "An East Asian Development Model?" in Peter Berger and Hsin-Huang Michael Hsiao (eds.), *In Search of an East Asian Development Model* New Brunswick, NJ: Transaction, pp. 3–11.

Blecher, Marc (1979), "Consensual Politics in Rural Chinese communities: The Mass Line in Theory and Practice," *Modern China*, vol. 5, no. 1, pp. 105–122.

Burns, John (1988), *Political Participation in Rural China*, Berkeley: University of California Press.

Chen, Yung-fat (1986), *Making Revolutions: The Communist Movement in Eastern and Central China 1937–1945*, Berkeley: University of California Press.

Gao, Jie (2012), "How Does Chinese Local Government Respond to Citizen Satisfaction Surveys? A Case Study of Foshan City," *Australian Journal of Public Administration*, vol. 71, no. 2, pp. 136–147.

Gansu (2013), "Linking Villages and Linking Families" webpage (联村联户网). Online: www.gsny.gov.cn/lclhwmfm/meitbd/2013/03/20/1363743352016.html (accessed July 20, 2013).

Guangming (2013), "Practice the Mass Line Must Overcome Bureaucratism," (践行群众路线必 须克服官僚主义), 《光明日报》07月23日, p. 11.
Heilmann, Sebastian (2011), "Policy-Making through Experimentation: The Formation of a Distinctive Policy Process," in Sebastian Heilmann and Elizabeth Perry (ed.), *Mao's Invisible Hand: The Political Foundations of Adaptive Governance in China*, Cambridge, MA: Harvard University Press.
Hsu Yung-ying (1945), *A Survey of the Shensi–Kansu–Ninghsia Border Region*, New York: Institute of Pacific Relations, pp. 1–159.
Jinchang City Report (2013) "The Long Term View of 'Linking Villages, Linking Households' for Enriching the People," "立足实际联村联户着眼长远为民富民." Online: http://nmj.jc.gansu.gov.cn/art/2013/6/20/art_8203_ 82705.html (accessed January 5, 2014).
Levitsky, Steven, and Lucan Way (2002), "The rise of competitive authoritarianism," *Journal of Democracy*, vol. 13, no. 2, pp. 51–65.
Li, Fangchun (2012), "Mass Democracy, Class Struggle, and Remolding the Party and Government during the Land Reform Movement in North China," *Modern China*, vol. 38, no. 4, pp. 411–445.
MacFarquhar, Roderick (1974), *The Origins of the Cultural Revolution, Vol. 1: Contradictions among the People*, New York: Columbia University Press.
Mao Zedong (1967), "Some Questions Concerning Methods of Leadership," in *Selected Works of Mao Tse-tung*, Vol. 3, Beijing: Foreign Languages Press, pp. 117–122.
Meisner, Mitch (1978), "Dazhai: The Mass Line in Practice," *Modern China*, vol. 4, no. 1 (January), pp. 27–62.
O'Brien, Kevin and Li Lianjiang (1999), "Selective Policy Implementation in Rural China," *Comparative Politics*, vol. 31, no. 2, pp. 167–186.
O'Brien, Kevin and Li Lianjiang (2006), *Rightful Resistance in Rural China*, New York: Cambridge University Press.
Qin, Guoji (2008), "The Thinking Way of Confucianism and the Rule of Law," *Journal of Politics and Law*, vol. 1, no. 1, pp. 68–75.
Saich, Anthony (2007), "Citizens' Perception on Governance in Rural and Urban China," *Journal of Chinese Political Science*, vol. 12, no. 1 (Spring), pp. 1–28.
Saich, Anthony (2012), "The Quality of Governance in China: The Citizen's View," HKS Faculty Research Working Paper Series RWP12–051, John F. Kennedy School of Government, Harvard University.
Shi, Tianjian (1997), *Political Participation in Beijing*, Cambridge, MA: Harvard University Press.
Shih, Chih-Yu (1997), "The Mass Line Approach to Democracy in China," *Peace and Conflict*, vol. 3, no. 4, pp. 353–371.
Steiner, Arthur (1951), "Current 'Mass Line' Tactics in Communist China," *The American Political Science Review*, vol. 45, no. 2 (June), pp. 422–436.
Thornton, Patricia M. (2011), "Retrofitting the Steel Frame: From Mobilizing the Masses to Surveying the Public," in Elizabeth J. Perry and Sebastian Heilmann (eds.), *Mao's Invisible Hand: The Political Foundations of Adaptive Governance*, Cambridge, MA: Harvard University Press, pp. 237–268.
Tong, Yanqi (2011), "Morality, Benevolence, and Responsibility: Regime Legitimacy in China from Past to the Present," *Journal of Chinese Political Science*, vol. 16, no. 2, pp. 141–159.
Townsend, James R. (1977), "Chinese Populism and the Legacy of Mao Tse-Tung," *Asian Survey*, vol. 17, no. 11 (November), pp. 1003–1015.

Tu, Wei-ming (1989), "The Rise of Industrial East Asia: The Role of Confucian Values," *Copenhagen Journal of Asian Studies*, vol. 4, pp. 81–97.

Whyte, Martin K. (1974), *Small Groups and Political Rituals in China*, Berkeley: University of California Press.

Xi (2013) "Xi Jinping Promotes 'Mass Line Education'," ("习近平推进"群众路线教育"), *XinHua News Agency* (新华新闻), April 21, 2013. Online: http://news.xinhuanet.com/zgjx/2013-06/19/c_132466321.htm (Accessed July 20, 2013).

13 Beyond win–win

Rethinking China's international relationships in an era of economic uncertainty[1]

Brantly Womack

In July 2012 the International Monetary Fund (IMF) reduced its estimate of China's economic growth in 2012 to 8 percent and its estimate of 2013 growth to 8.3 percent (IMF 2012).[2] Robert Zoellick, president of the World Bank, cautioned China that it must shift its economic focus away from exports and toward increasing domestic consumption (Ding 2011). Lower expectations are not good news for China, but ironically they say more about the anticipation of continuing basic strength of the Chinese economy than about its vulnerabilities. The reason given for Zoellick's admonitions was that the world economy, and especially that of the developed world, is facing stagnation, and flat demand abroad for Chinese products dampens exports. The IMF sees the major downside risks of the world economy in Europe and the United States, and notes that the other members of the BRIC (Brazil, Russia, India) have also slowed. In this context China is still doing relatively well. China's anticipated 2013 GDP increment is equal to the combined estimated increments of the other top ten national economies, as well as the size of the entire Turkish economy in 2011, the world's seventeenth largest (IMF 2012; CIA 2012). In 2011 China's GDP in purchasing power parity was 75 percent of the United States; if the IMF's estimates are correct it will be 84 percent in 2013, making plausible the Economist Intelligence Unit's estimate of convergence with the United States by 2016.[3] Economic capacity is important in its own right and as a foundational dimension of military power and of political influence.

China's current global prominence is the result of successful domestic policies and of successful diplomacy. On the domestic side, Barry Naughton argues that economic growth has resulted not only from market forces but also from the positive interaction of state-owned enterprises, foreign-invested firms, and small-scale private enterprise guided by the government (Naughton 2010). Equally impressive has been China's emergence from diplomatic isolation during the reform era. While China's global relationships began to improve with admission to the United Nations in 1971 and the historic visits of Kissinger and Nixon, its relations within Asia generally lagged behind. Since 1990, however, China's attention to good neighbor relations has resulted in strong institutional and diplomatic ties that undergird remarkable expansion of trade and investment. "Win–win" is the latest in a series of slogans that articulate China's enthusiasm for deepening its regional and global ties.

Despite success, or rather because of it, China now faces a new context that requires the reorientation of both its domestic development and its diplomacy. Zoellick's recommendation of promoting consumption touches only the tip of the iceberg of domestic challenges. In order to move from a strategy of maximum economic growth to one of sustainable growth, inequalities must be addressed, welfare promoted, innovation and entrepreneurship encouraged, and an aging population cared for. These challenges are addressed in the Twelfth Five Year Plan (2011–2015) and will occupy China's leadership for the foreseeable future. On the political side, the rule of law needs strengthening, transparency and representativeness improved, and intra-party democracy expanded (Womack 2010b).

The need to adjust China's diplomacy is less obvious. After all, everyone wins with "win–win," so why change? In a nutshell, I argue that the current era of global economic uncertainty combined with the remarkable increase in China's relative capacities make China's credible reassurance to partners more important to them than mutual benefit. Economic uncertainty has made the fear of risk more vivid than the prospect of gain, and China's peaceful leap forward since 2008 greatly increases its partners' sense of exposure to China's actions. Diplomacy that prioritizes reassurance would limit China's options, but it is necessary in order to preserve the favorable international environment created by the earlier win–win policies.

Underlying this argument is a rejection of the realist assumption that disparities of capacity inevitably imply domination by the larger and stronger side. The actual effects of asymmetry are more complex. Cooperation is possible to the extent that the benefits of the relationship are credible to both sides. If the larger side imposes its unilateral preferences, the vividness of the smaller side's perception of threat is likely to produce determined resistance rather than submission. As Andrew Mack argued in his classic reflection of the American war in Vietnam, the larger side can be frustrated because the limited aims and commitments of its "small war" pose a mortal threat to its opponent (Mack 1975). Traditional Chinese diplomacy was sobered by many "small war" experiences (Zhou 2011). Although the frustration and unintended consequences of domination are most striking in military conflicts, there are more subtle analogues in economic interactions.

Changes in asymmetric relationships make more acute the challenges of diplomatic management, and China since 2008 has simultaneously increased its asymmetry with most partners while it approaches GDP parity with the global power. Other states have therefore become hypersensitive to China's actions and apparent ambitions. If China alienates them, it will isolate itself. If it maintains current win–win policies but is insensitive to their increased concerns they will become more cautious. If China adds credible reassurance to win–win, it will maximize its opportunities for cooperation.

I begin with a brief review of the course of development of China's diplomacy, and then discuss the effects of the contextual change in global politics since 2008. The controversy surrounding the South China Sea is presented as an example of new diplomatic challenges. The specifics of reassurance are then discussed in the framework of China's increasing asymmetry with smaller and developing countries and decreasing asymmetry with developed economies, especially the United States. Finally, the conclusion addresses the counterargument for greater Chinese assertiveness.

Roots of win–win

Despite the retrogression of the Cultural Revolution era, the roots of current win–win policies go back to the beginnings of PRC diplomacy (Womack 2010a: 183–212). China's critique of imperialism and its identification with Third World nations rising out of colonialism after World War II led to the formulation in 1954 of the Five Principles of Peaceful Coexistence:

1 Mutual respect for each other's territorial integrity and sovereignty;
2 Mutual non-aggression;
3 Mutual non-interference in each other's internal affairs;
4 Equality and mutual benefit; and
5 Peaceful co-existence.

China did not claim sole ownership of these principles. They were jointly announced with India and Burma, and they became core ideas of the 1954 Asia–Africa (Bandung) Conference and subsequently of the Non-Aligned Movement. They remain part of China's credo in any establishment of diplomatic relations. As Sophie Richardson points out, while they were not particularly relevant to U.S.–China relations, with developing nations they have defined China's core diplomatic priorities most of the time, and with most places (Richardson 2010).

From the late 1950s to 1970 the solidarity between China and Third World governments was increasingly vitiated by China's support for continuing revolution both at home and abroad. As decolonization succeeded and tension with the Soviet Union grew, China's condemnation of imperialism evolved into a critique of hegemonism. While anti-hegemonism did not target Third World states, most postcolonial states were aligned with one or another superpower, and few were attracted by the rigid isolationist stance of China and Albania. Even Vietnam, the largest recipient of Chinese aid, expanded its relations with the Soviet Union during the 1960s. Moreover, postcolonial states faced ongoing domestic insurgencies, and China's attitude toward popular disturbances was ambiguous. Actual assistance to insurgent groups was limited, but there was vocal encouragement in many cases and also the example of Chinese leftism.

In 1970 China's diplomacy shifted to revolutionary pragmatism, and while support for some insurgencies continued, the general picture of diplomatic relationships was transformed by admission to the United Nations in 1971 and the Shanghai Communiqué in 1972. The rhetoric of anti-hegemonism continued, but given China's new relationship with the United States anti-hegemonism came to mean anti-Soviet Union. The exchange of visits between Marshal Tito and Hua

Guofeng in 1977 and 1979 highlighted China's shift from critique of Soviet revisionism to opposing Soviet expansionism. The groundwork for a new era of international relationships was laid: formal relations with most states and no longer an outsider in global organizations.

Deng Xiaoping's "second revolution" in domestic policy was mirrored in external relations. In both, the most novel and important element was the new priority of maximum economic growth. Revolutionary pragmatism was replaced by economic pragmatism. January 1, 1979 marks the turning point, in part because of the completion of the process of normalization with the United States and in part because of the shift in Taiwan policy from "liberation" to "peaceful reunification." Even though war with Vietnam began less than two months later, China shed its reputation as a revolutionary troublemaker. Indeed, China's hostility with a fellow communist state that had occupied its neighbor Cambodia reassured other Southeast Asian states and provided an avenue of cooperation. In any case the primary emphasis of China's foreign relations was on trade and investment. Anti-hegemonism faded into a background drumbeat in diplomatic discourse, though it was used as late as 2003 to criticize American unilateralism (Xinhua 2003). It was replaced as a diplomatic organizing principle by multipolarity[4] and later by globalization (Yu 2009: 149–156). In its 1998 Defense White Paper China presented a "new security concept" stressing that "security should be based on mutual trust and common interests" (Information Office of the State Council 1998). "Win–win" (*shuang ying* 双赢) appeared in discussions of WTO negotiations in 1999 and quickly became a favorite term for bilateral relationships.

The events of June 4, 1989 led to a major setback in China's relations with the developed world, but they also led to a self-effacing diplomatic posture and a reorientation toward China's Asian neighbors (Womack 2003–2004). Normalization with Vietnam, Indonesia, Singapore, and South Korea in 1991–1992, as well as with the new post-Soviet states of Central Asia, completed China's diplomatic circle, and "good neighbor" policies encouraged the rapid growth of economic and other ties. China resolved most of its land border disputes, and tensions over maritime claims were secondary to a general improvement in economic and political relationships. The creation of the Shanghai Five in 1996 and holding the value of the RMB steady during the Asian Financial Crisis of 1997 were especially important for China's new Asian face. In Southeast Asia, China proved itself to be a reliable partner in contrast to the World Bank, the United States, and Japan. In Central Asia, the smaller states were relieved not to be the cockpit of Sino-Russian competition, while Russia and China shared concerns about American unilateralism.

Until 2008, China's win–win bilateral policies and its enthusiasm for regional cooperation (the Shanghai Five became the Shanghai Cooperation Organization in 2001, and the China–ASEAN Free Trade Area was launched in 2002) were in stark contrast to American unilateralism and its fixation on the "war on terror." Economic relations with neighbors grew exponentially. In 2000 China accounted for 4 percent of ASEAN's total trade; by 2009 China was ASEAN's largest external trade partner at 12 percent total trade, roughly equal to half of intra-ASEAN trade. Within a decade, trade with China had moved from being a welcome and growing sideshow to being a major part of every Southeast Asian state's economic outlook. And trade was only one aspect of thickening relationships including political exchanges, investment, and tourism. Win–win, confidence in mutual benefit, made possible China's peaceful rise.

Win–win since 2008: from panda to dragon?

Since the onset of global economic uncertainty in 2008 China has become vastly more important to its neighbors and to the global economy, and yet its same policies of win–win have met with considerably more anxiety and resistance. Similarly, in the remaining areas of disputed sovereignty China's claims have not changed, but tensions have escalated. China has not threatened, and yet its partners feel more threatened. Why?

There are two contextual changes in China's foreign policy environment that have affected the attitudes of its partners. The first is that the economic troubles of 2008 began at the core of the global system and have vastly increased the unpredictability of everyone's economic outlook. The second is that China's continued growth despite the global downturn has increased the disparity between itself and smaller states and at the same time has decreased the disparity with the United States and the European Union. Perhaps more importantly, the rapidity of the change in relative asymmetry causes China's partners to anticipate even greater changes in the future.

The financial crisis that has reshaped the global economy since mid-2008 is the first systemic crisis of the globalized world. Previous post-Cold War crises had been local (Russia, Mexico, Argentina) or regional (Asian Financial Crisis), but they did not challenge the stability of the global system. The current crisis began in the United States and has had severe repercussions on the European Union. Even the world depression of the 1930s is a poor comparison. Not only is the volume and intensity of global interrelationships much greater, but there are many more sovereign units, there now exist international and regional organizations that can provide venues for cooperation, and there is a dominant world paper currency rather than a gold or silver standard. Thus the global politics of the new era are as novel and uncertain as its economics. While everyone assumes that the crisis is part of a cycle, there is no prior experience that credibly predicts its depth or duration. Recurring doubts about each major segment of the global economy, including China, underscore the extent of global uncertainty.

For nations and for many of the world's families, a situation of multidimensional uncertainty has replaced an overly optimistic and complacent mentality of reliable progress. A profound shift in priorities has occurred. If progress can be relied on, then risk is downplayed and marginal benefit becomes the chief criterion for decisions. But if the future becomes uncertain, then caution and the protection of present assets becomes more important than risky marginal gain. This is not simply a psychological reaction. If, for example, a company is considering an international investment but the relevant currency exchange rates have varied +/– 10 percent, then profitability of less than 10 percent could be wiped out by currency fluctuation. And of course the outlook for investment might itself be affected by unforeseen global reverberations. At the national level, governments want to restore their previous levels of prosperity, but they too must face the risks that they once ignored. Caution becomes the global watchword.

No country, including China, has profited from the global downturn. The crisis has exacerbated China's domestic challenges of political and economic sustainability. However, China is the least damaged major economy, and in an era of caution and confusion its continued high growth rate is even more impressive. Moreover, as other economies wobbled, China's relative growth became more prominent. As a rock of stability in turbulent waters, it attracts more international investment that in turn contributes to more growth. With its surplus foreign exchange earnings and concerns about resource security, China's own foreign direct investment (FDI) has become one of the few growth areas of foreign investment. China's holdings in dollar-denominated assets has made it America's biggest foreign creditor and thus banker to the banks, a situation unimaginable a decade ago. With the continuing troubles of the developed economies, the arrogant exclusivism of the G-7 has given way to the expanded G-20. Given China's unique position among rising economies and the unique position of the United States in the current economic disorder, talk of a "G-2" is not unreasonable, though as a leading interaction rather than as an exclusive club.

Table 13.1 illustrates China's economic importance to its neighbors and to the world. With the exception of Afghanistan, China is one of the top five export destinations and top three import sources not only for its neighbor states but also for the United States and European Union. It is of course well known as the world's factory, so the high number of top ranks in imports is not surprising. Most are in the 15–25 percent range, with the high exceptions being neighbors particularly dependent on China. The high exporters to China fall into two groups, the suppliers of advanced intermediate goods (Japan, South Korea, Taiwan) and sources of energy and raw materials (Australia, Iran, Kazakhstan). In general, Southeast Asia is less involved in trade than Northeast Asia or Central Asia. But Chinese trade and investment are key growth areas for all its partners.

Clearly, China has become more than merely one good neighbor among many. Now its economic centrality matches its geographic centrality to Asia, and it is approaching parity with the United States as a global economic mass. While these developments make relations with China more important for its neighbors, it also makes them nervous. Has their neighborhood become China's backyard? Is China becoming strong enough as a regional actor to dictate the terms of relations, and also becoming strong enough on the global stage to control the interference of other global powers in Asia? Will China remain a good neighbor when it has the power to be otherwise, or will it yield to the

Table 13.1 China's trade rankings: 2011

Country	*Exports to China*		*Imports from China*	
	Rank	*%*	*Rank*	*%*
Japan	1	19.7	1	21.5
DPRK	1	67.2	1	61.6
ROK	1	24.4	1	16.5
Mongolia	1	85.7	1	43.4
Taiwan	1	28.1	2	14.2
Vietnam	2	11	1	22
Laos	2	23	2	11.1
Cambodia	1	28.3	9	2.3
Thailand	1	12	2	13.4
Malaysia	1	13.1	1	13.2
Singapore	4	10.4	3	10.4
Indonesia	2	11.3	1	14.8
Australia	1	27.4	1	18.5
Burma	2	18.8	1	38.8
India	3	6.2	1	11.9
Pakistan	4	9.2	2	15
Iran	1	21.4	2	17.4
Tajikistan	4	6.7	1	45.9
Kyrgyzstan	4	7.8	1	59.7
Kazakhstan	1	21.7	1	30.1
Russia	2	6.4	1	15.5
US	3	7	1	18.4
EU*	2	14.0	1	11.1

Source: CIA (2012); * Directorate General for Trade (2013).

temptations of hegemonism? These are Asia's new, unsettling questions, made more urgent by the general uncertainty of the post-2008 era. They arise from China's peaceful leap forward and the anticipation of its further growth rather than from changes in China's policy. However, these questions make China's neighbors acutely sensitive to any indication that China's intentions might be aggressive. How will China behave when its economy is twice its present size—nine years, at 8 percent average growth? As far as neighbors are concerned, the difference between an extremely large panda and a dragon is one of attitude, and they wonder if China's attitude will change.

There are similar concerns at the global level. In 2007 Juan Tokatlian, a leading Argentine expert on South American foreign relations, welcomed China's growing involvement in the region and suggested a strategy of "reliable engagement" (Tokatlian 2007). In 2011 he had a more cautious attitude (Tokatlian 2011). Not only does the proportional increase in China's presence require rethinking, but there are also various worrisome trends. China's investments in food and energy are tempting, but will they condemn the suppliers to permanent primary resource economies? What about the poor environmental reputation of China's mining operations? Will corruption reinforce local elites at the cost of the citizenry? These and similar concerns are felt throughout Latin America and Africa.

Among global powers the concerns about China are of a different order. They see the distance narrowing between themselves and China. Indeed, in GDP China has surpassed all but the United States, though it is still distant in GDP per capita and in technological sophistication. For Europe and Japan, deep concerns about their own continued growth make linkage to China more attractive. To hold their positions they must engage with China. Yet at the same time, as the Senkaku/Diaoyu island dispute shows for Japan and tensions over human rights for Europe, China's rise raises questions about their own stature. The American situation vis-à-vis China is even more ambivalent. As the world's only superpower, American diplomacy was increasingly unilateral in the post-Cold War era, and military burdens in the Middle East increased its financial burden at the same time that its domestic economy was undermined by imprudent policies. China's continued rise since 2008 presents economic opportunities for the United States, but it also faces the United States with the prospect of losing its unilateral status. Since the fall of the Soviet Union the United States has defined its security in terms of global invulnerability. China's military growth now challenges American invulnerability in the Western Pacific.

Meanwhile, public pressures on all governments are likely to make diplomacy more difficult. In China and Vietnam proliferating organized interests both inside and outside the state structure fragment and complicate decision-making and diplomatic management (Lampton 2001). More dramatically, the Internet and social media have cost the party-state its monopoly on information and communication, and netizen voices tend to be extreme, especially on current foreign affairs (Hao 2012). Since netizen voices and dissonant bureaucrats are heard outside China as well as within they amplify China's image as becoming more aggressive. Although the challenge of the connectivity revolution is most evident in political systems that exclude organized opposition, it also has a polarizing effect in democratic states. Public sentiment can be stirred more quickly and at less cost than earlier, and extremist opinion groups are less limited by location. Strangely enough, globalization does not mean that we share the same world, and governments must cope with domestic pressures as well as external realities.

We cannot leave the description of changes of attention toward China since 2008 without pointing out that they are based in part on a distorted projection of current rates of change. Dramatic relative change—especially in an atmosphere of increased caution and worry—encourages exaggerated focus on China and also unrealistic projections of current changes. As most economists inside and outside China agree, China's future growth will be slowed down by a sluggish global economy even as its relative strength helps others to recover. Domestic problems such as over-investment in real estate have yet to exert their full negative effect. It may turn out that the sub-phases of the era of global economic uncertainty will be the initial shock of China's peaceful leap forward, 2008–2012, followed by a few years of concern about a faltering China.

The longer term might not be so China-centric (Johansson *et al.* 2012; Ward 2011; World Bank *et al.* 2013). China is only the largest of a number of middle-income countries, including but not limited to India, that are likely to persist in high relative growth for the foreseeable future. The middle third of the world economy is moving closer to the upper third, and China is only the largest and fastest part of that cohort. Moreover, the multifaceted, accumulated economic advantages of the United States, the European Union, and Japan will preserve their status as per capita giants and innovation leaders. Lastly, China faces major challenges of domestic sustainability over the next few decades. Its proportion of working-age population will diminish, raising wages and increasing welfare costs. Environmental constraints on production will become more prominent. The political system will have to keep pace with an increasingly complex, diverse, and sophisticated society. None of these challenges portend a looming crisis that will stop China's growth, but all are likely to reduce China's absolute rate of growth and its growth relative to the rest of its middle-income cohort.

The Spratly Islands as material symbol of uncertainty

The situation and policies of any of China's neighbors over the past five years could be used to illustrate the effects of increased asymmetry.[5] But the area attracting the most attention has been the South China Sea (Womack 2011: 157–175). The basic cause of tension is the ambiguity of China's claims. In an era of heightened anxiety China's win–win policies are not enough to calm neighbors' fears.

Three features put the Spratlys at the center of regional tension. First is the complexity of conflicting sovereign claims. China (PRC and ROC) and Vietnam claim the entire cluster, while Malaysia and the Philippines claim part, and Brunei claims a reef and some waters (Parameswaran 2012). Sovereignty is necessarily an absolute and exclusive claim. However, the islands cannot sustain populations and were not accurately mapped until the nineteenth century, so none of the historical claims are convincing. The struggle to assert and defend claims involves acting as if one's own claims are not disputed and reacting officially and vocally when other claimants do the same. If a claimant does not protest another claimant's "encroachment," he is implicitly yielding his claim. The less dry land, apparently, the louder the dispute. For example, the Scarborough Shoal, the scene of a standoff between China and the Philippines from April to June 2012, consists of a lagoon with no more than five rocks protruding above the surface (Beckman 2012).

Second, the Spratlys are deep in the middle of Southeast Asia. China is both the most distant and the most powerful claimant, and not part of the region. Moreover a claim to the islands anchors vast and even more problematic claims to the waters of the South China Sea, conflicting not only with other Spratlys claims but with coastal and continental shelf claims. Thus the Spratlys are perfectly situated to symbolize conflicting interests between China and Southeast Asia.

Third, there are likely to be important oil and gas reserves in the South China Sea waters, and the Spratlys claims make exploration contestable and unilateral development dangerous (US Energy Information Agency 2013). Thus each state can imagine having its energy and budgetary problems eased by possessing the Spratlys, and Southeast Asian states can fear that China will grow so powerful that it will simply take over the South China Sea to slake its own thirst for energy.

Regional anxieties concerning the South China Sea came to a head in 2010. Besides the occasional small-scale confrontations, China reissued its claim to South China Sea waters—the so-called "nine-dash line," or "cow's tongue"—and also it was alleged that State Councilor Dai Bingguo had called the South China Sea a "core interest" of China during discussions with American diplomats. Although the evidence for the claim is weak and no ranking Chinese official has applied the term in public, neither has the claim been officially denied.[6] In a general atmosphere of increased caution and concern about China's leap forward the ambiguities of the nine-dash line and the "core interest" assertion were interpreted, regionally and globally, as signs of a new aggressive attitude.

Anxieties about the possibility of China becoming more assertive have heightened the tensions of small confrontations in the South China Sea. There are many possible examples, but perhaps the best is the alleged blocking by the Chinese navy of an Indian naval ship making routine port calls along the Vietnamese coast. According to the *Financial Times*, on September 1, 2011, "A Chinese warship confronted an Indian navy vessel shortly after it left Vietnamese waters in late July [2011]" (Bland and Shivakumar 2011). The report was immediately picked up by the regional and Indian press. The Indian navy clarified on September 2 that their ship had received an open-channel message that it was entering Chinese waters from an untraceable source identifying itself only as "the Chinese navy," and no naval vessel was in sight.[7] Despite the Indian statement, the regional and Indian media continued to see the non-event as a provocation.[8]

While the pushing and shoving among all claimants is a constant reminder of tensions, in fact the risk of major conflict is minimal and there is no foreseeable threshold of Chinese power that would make unilateral seizure of the Spratlys a practical policy. It is important to note that there have been no military casualties there since 1988, that the economic importance of China's relations with Southeast Asia outweigh the potential gain from seizure, and that in a hostile regional environment the platforms and logistics of energy in the South China Sea would be vulnerable. As China's power grows so will its economic ties, and many of those relationships—not only in Southeast Asia—would be damaged by a unilateral aggressive move on China's part. China would certainly lose its reputation as a good neighbor, and it would not acquire a friendly or submissive backyard.

Even if we grant that major conflict in the South China Sea is unlikely either now or at some tipping point in the future, its role as the focal point of regional anxieties about China is not unreasonable. It is the material symbol of the perceived ambiguities of China's future direction and of the region's increasing vulnerability. The nine-dash line has been claimed by China since 1947,[9] but only now does China have increasing naval capabilities to enforce the claim. In 1947 the Republic of China could not control the advance of the People's Liberation Army in China's civil war; it was hardly in a position to confront French and British imperialism and the American naval presence at Subic Bay in the Philippines. What once had the harmless softness of a KMT dream-bubble now has become the threatening ambiguity of the major regional power. And unofficial but uncorrected statements from China magnify the apparent threat. In the same article of the Chinese newspaper *Global Times* that dispels the story of the Sino-Indian naval confrontation, an expert with the Naval Research Institute of the PLAN is quoted as saying that "China has indisputable sovereignty over the South China Sea islands and adjacent waters, and any foreign warship sailing through the area is not in accordance with international law" (*Global Times* 2011). Since the U.N. Convention on the Law of the Sea (UNCLOS) to which China is a signatory allows innocent passage of foreign naval vessels through Exclusive Economic Zones (EEZs), this assertion is either untrue or it implies that the nine-dash line is claiming most of the South China Sea as territorial waters, usually 12-mile zones in which foreign militaries can travel only with permission. The latter would truly be a scary claim, and the ambiguity of China's position does not exclude it. Even more hawkish articles are published in China (Dao 2011),[10] and while they do not express official positions, the ambiguity of China's position makes them plausible as possible future intentions and they are not prohibited in the official press.

China's maritime claims touch on the common ground between regional and American interests, but the overlap can be misleading. The United States has always been neutral regarding conflicting claims in the South China Sea. However, it claims that UNCLOS (which it has not ratified) permits military intelligence activities in EEZs, an interpretation of "innocent passage" that China and some other states dispute. The EP-3 spy plane incident of 2001 and the confrontation with the sonar ship *Impeccable* in 2009 have highlighted the differences in interpretation, and China's naval and aerospace modernization threatens the invulnerability that American forces have in enjoyed in the Western Pacific since the defeat of Japan. Thus it is not surprising that Secretary of State Hillary Clinton claimed common cause with Southeast Asia in her July 2010 Hanoi speech, emphasizing freedom of navigation and peaceful resolution of conflicts. And given the ambiguity of China's maritime claim there is common ground. However, if Southeast Asia agreed with the American definition of "innocent passage" then it would countenance Chinese as well as American intelligence activities 12 nautical miles off their coasts.

Despite China's record of good neighbor policies and its emphasis on win–win, its neighbors are justifiably concerned about its claims in the South China Sea, especially in an era of caution and uncertainty. The claim that China's sovereignty is "indisputable" flies in the face of four disputants. The nine-dash line was and remains a unilateral and vague assertion that reaches almost to the shores of Vietnam, Philippines, and Malaysia. China's demand that a multilateral dispute be settled bilaterally can be interpreted as a delaying tactic. Meanwhile the submarine base on Hainan Island and the launching of China's first aircraft carrier are reminders of China's growing military reach. The frequent small confrontations are constant reminders of unsettled conflicts of interests. Even the increasing economic ties between China and Southeast Asia can create the impression of being sucked into a relationship of dependency.

China does have legitimate interests and claims in the South China Sea, and it would be foolish to expect it to yield simply to appease the neighbors. The challenge, therefore, is how to delimit and manage differences so that neighbors are not unduly alarmed. The China–ASEAN 2002 Declaration on Conduct of Parties in the South China Sea (DOC) (Association of Southeast Asian Nations 2002) was an excellent beginning, and the July 2011 announcement of Guidelines for the Implementation of the DOC marked some progress. But binding guidelines have not yet been achieved, and Southeast Asian states themselves have hindered useful steps such as a moratorium on construction in the Spratlys (Le Mière 2011). The 2012 ASEAN summit saw progress on formulating a code of conduct, but differences over confronting China led to ASEAN's failure to issue a concluding communique for the first time in 45 years (Emmerson 2012). Joint management and joint development are the only feasible paths to preserving fisheries and exploiting mineral resources, but the confidence-building necessary to such undertakings must be built with credible reassurances and rules of interaction.

Adjusting win–win

The largest question facing world politics for the next 20 years is how the United States and China will relate to one another as China reaches American levels of overall productivity. However, the largest question is not necessarily the most important one. How China will relate to its neighbors will determine, to a great extent, its vulnerability in its relationship with the United States. If China has a neighborhood that stands with it, then it cannot be contained. Moreover, the diplomacy necessary to maintain a friendly neighborhood will be a deeply positive influence on its global and great power relationships. But mutual benefit is not a high enough standard for China's diplomacy. China must think beyond win–win in order to maintain the good neighbor relations that it has created over the past 20 years.

These are strong claims, and they must be defended. How could relationships with smaller states, incapable of challenging China's security either individually or collectively, be more decisive in China's global security than its diplomacy with the United States? The United States is not only capable of threatening China militarily, its current spectrum of attitudes toward China ranges from engagement to hostility. Recently the Obama administration's new interest in Asia appears to exclude China, and its Air–Sea Battle concept is clearly aimed at China (International Institute for Strategic Studies 2012; Bumiller 2012). It is not unimaginable that America's fear of decline and the desire of its military for a high-technology opponent could confirm it in a Cold War mentality vis-à-vis China. How could this development be less important than the opinions of Russia, Japan, and India, much less Thailand, Indonesia, and Kazakhstan?

As General Rupert Smith argues in his bold updating of Clausewitz, "War no longer exists" (Smith 2007: 3). He goes on to explain that "war as a massive deciding event in a dispute in international affairs: such a war no longer exists." While the French Revolution introduced an era of massive armies and "industrial war," that era ended with the arrival of nuclear weapons. The Cold War was a face-off between the United States and the Soviet Union, and there was an arms race, but its conflicts were on the periphery and they had their local causes. The assurance of mutual destruction in total war led to the development of protocols and treaties to reduce its likelihood. The Soviet Union failed; it did not lose a war. It contained itself by isolating its economy and people, dominating Eastern Europe, scaring Western Europe, and acting in its narrow self-interest even in alliances. Consider the contrast between the American Marshall Plan in Western Europe and the Soviet pillaging of the industries of Eastern Europe. The full weight of the Soviet strategy was on military development and domination of neighbors. In the end, even the Russians themselves were not sad to see the Soviet Union go.

China has more neighbors than the Soviet Union did, and after three decades of reform and openness its economy is infinitely more enmeshed internationally than the Soviet command economy ever was. If interdependence is seen by China and its partners as a benefit, then China exists in a world in which a threat to China is an indirect threat to all. If China's neighbors do not consider China a threat, and on the contrary highly value their peaceful relationships, then China has an invaluable strategic asset. Not only do the mutual ties strengthen each economy and bring societies in greater contact, but they raise the cost and risk of losing the relationship. In short, if China does not contain itself by alienating its neighbors, it will be highly unlikely that any other state could persuade its neighbors to contain it.

Confidence in mutual benefit is a more fundamental bond than a formal alliance, but more subtle.[11] In a regional asymmetric relationship, the smaller parties can be reassured of mutual benefit only if the relationship is open-ended rather than exclusive. If the regional power requires a closed relationship then it is at the same time depriving the smaller parties of possibly beneficial relationships with others and restricting them to an unequal, monopolized relationship. In effect, the regional power is putting a fence around its backyard, and an exclusive regional structure serves its interests rather than those of its neighbors. This is domination, and it is unstable because it is only tolerated by others under duress or for lack of an alternative. Smaller states would rather buffer their disparity with a regional power by developing multilateral regimes, participating in global regimes, and developing extra-regional relationships. These actions are not against the interests of the regional power. In fact, if smaller states are confident that they are not alone they can deepen their relationship with the regional power. For example, after Vietnam joined ASEAN and normalized relations with the United States in 1995 it could be more confident in deepening its relation with China. Likewise, Vietnam's entry into the WTO in 2006 and expansion of trade with the United States allowed it to afford a larger trade deficit with China.

The problem with win–win as a regional strategy is that it is not sufficiently sensitive to the greater exposure and risk of smaller states in asymmetric relationships. The caution of smaller states is not a matter of resenting the gain of the larger—indeed, in proportional terms the smaller side benefits more. But risk is a more vivid concern than gain, especially since 2008. Greater asymmetry means greater exposure, and smaller states will be alert to the ambiguities of the intentions of the larger state as well as to their degree of isolation. Thus the key to a sustainable regional order beyond (but of course including) win–win is formal commitment of the regional power to acknowledgment of other regional interests, to forms of interaction that preclude domination, and to regional openness. Bilateral reassurance would be confirmed and enhanced by the evolution of multilateral and global regimes. But at the same time that diplomatic reassurance becomes more necessary, the rising voices of domestic opinions and interests will make it more difficult.

China's diplomatic challenge with the United States is of a different sort. China's relative growth is making it more equal to the United States rather than less equal, and its relative growth gives it a new capacity to be assertive. Given the economic shocks since 2008 American confidence in its future global role in shaken, and it projects China's growth and assertiveness into the future. While the United States does not oppose China's prosperity, it does not welcome its own loss of relative standing. The basic diffidence of American China policy is well described by Swaine (2011a). Inevitably China has become for the United States the symbol of a future in which its control is diminished. This leads some to proclaim a "China threat,"[12] and others to wonder how the United States can get along peacefully with a more equal China.

The quality of China's regional relationships is the strategic key to being prepared for either direction in U.S.–China relations. If the United States becomes cold and hostile, then the stability of China's external relations, both economic and political, will depend on the mutual commitment of other states, most importantly its neighbors. Alienation of neighbors, whether through domination or self-isolation, was the key strategic mistake of the Soviet Union. It made anti-Soviet containment possible. If the United States attempts to draw the line between its friends and China's friends, it is to China's interest that they would refuse to make the choice. Currently China's successful good neighbor policy has created a situation in which the worst nightmare of its neighbors is a new Cold War. But they also worry about a changing China. Maintaining a positive neighborhood and expanding it globally will require China's increasing attention to the anxieties of small states.

Even if the United States continues the path of peaceful engagement with China, it is likely to have a competitive mentality. However, if China continues to develop its friendly external relations, then the global competition might itself be win–win. A good example would be China's accession to the ASEAN Treaty of Amity as the first non-ASEAN party. China's action first caught the attention of India and then Japan, who also joined. Finally in 2009 the United States joined. Clearly the other states were trying to catch up with China, but their efforts have benefited Southeast Asia and they have not hurt China. Indeed, Southeast Asia can now feel more confident in its global status, and this makes it more confident in its relations with China.

Under President Obama the United States has emphasized peaceful and cooperative relations with most states outside of the Middle East. As former Deputy Secretary of State James Steinberg has said, "That's the single most important achievement of the Obama administration" (Kato 2011). The United States is quite confident of the strength of its soft power and it has always prided itself on its peaceful relations. To a certain extent its current interest in improving its relationships in Asia is related to a competitive mentality vis-à-vis China, but if the competition is one of peaceful emulation, then that is a strategic success for Chinese foreign policy.

Conclusion: should China care what the neighbors think?

China's present and projected relative growth puts China in a strategic situation of decreasing vulnerability vis-à-vis neighbors. This is the flip side of the increasing anxieties of smaller states and the concerns of global powers. Therefore there seems to be less need for the caution of Deng Xiaoping. China's peaceful rise has been accomplished. China has risen. If China is now Asia's pre-eminent regional power and can hold the United States to stalemate on its periphery, then why be concerned about the opinions of the neighbors, or of the world for that matter?

This is the basic idea of hegemonism, long condemned by China. For this reason it is unlikely ever to become China's official policy. However, hegemonistic thinking can enter through the back door. China can declare itself to be righteous, generous, and friendly, but if its diplomacy with its neighbors rests on its relative capacity advantages then it is acting hegemonically. To be sure, China has its own national interests and it should not sacrifice these to its neighbors. But ultimately the judgment of hegemony does not lie with the hegemon, but with those who are dominated.

Besides the moral problems of hegemonism there are practical strategic problems. If China enforces its interests on its neighbors or appears likely to, they will hedge their interests against China. Even in a confident asymmetric relationship smaller states will buffer their bilateral exposure, but if they are unsure about the intentions of their big partner then they will prepare for the possibility of hostility by hedging. If they become convinced that their identities will be threatened and their interests will suffer they will move from hedging to balancing against China. As other states fear an alienation of interests between themselves and China, they will move to protect their interests.

Likewise, if developed countries see China's rise as the emergence of a new and hostile hegemon they will behave defensively. If their perception of a "China threat" is mistaken and in fact China's external relations are positive, they will find little global support for a suspicious or hostile attitude. However, if other states are also worried about China's rise, then they could unite to protect the existing world order against a new, more threatening one. It would certainly be against China's strategic interests to behave in ways that increased global alienation and resistance.

China's win–win strategy has been successful because it has been sensitive to the needs of its neighbors and of its global partners. Before 2008 all faced a strong global system that had little respect for local interests or regional organizations, and China's different attitude was welcome. Win–win is still welcome, but now, in an era of global economic uncertainty in which China stands out as the successful power, reassurance concerning China's future path has become more important. Dai Bingguo's reassurance that China is not pursuing and will not pursue a "Monroe Doctrine" (Dai 2010) is important, but the ambiguities that drive anxieties need to be addressed. Neighbors need to be confident that China's continued growth will not be at their expense, and that China's increasing power will not be used against them. The controversies over the South China Sea illustrate the depth of concern and also the kinds of ambiguities regarding China's intentions that produce anxiety about the future. But this is not simply a problem for China's neighbors, or for the rest of the world. China's own future also depends on international relationships that are sustainable in uncertain times, and mutual confidence in mutual benefit is the fundamental prerequisite.

Notes

1 This chapter first appeared in *International Affairs* (London), vol. 89, no. 4, July 2013, and is reproduced with permission. For comments on earlier drafts I would like to thank Herman Schwartz and audiences at Academia Sinica, Guangxi Academy of Social Sciences, U.S. Pacific Command Headquarters, and Asia Pacific Center for Security Studies, as well as anonymous reviewers, though the views expressed are my own.
2 International Monetary Fund (2012: 2). There are more pessimistic analyses. See for an overview McDonald (2012).
3 Data as presented in Morrison (2012: figure 4, p. 10).
4 Beginning with Huan Xiang's 1986 analysis of Cold War stalemate. See Pillsbury (2000, especially ch. 1).
5 For example, Mongolia has been seeking to develop relationships with "third neighbors" in order to buffer its exposure to both Russia and China. See Wachman (2009).
6 Michael Swaine provides a very careful analysis; see Swaine (2011b).
7 Such a message can be sent ship-to-ship by anyone.
8 See, for instance, Karnad (2011).
9 Originally an 11-dash line, with two dashes in the Gulf of Tonkin. After the Gulf delineation agreement with Vietnam in 2000 and the implementation protocol of 2004 the top two dashes were removed.
10 See, for example, Long Tao (2011).
11 A contrary position is presented by Yan Xuetong (2011).
12 Most recently Friedberg (2011).

References

Association of Southeast Asian Nations (2002) *Declaration on the Conduct of Parties in the South China Sea*. Online. Available at: www.asean.org/asean/external-relations/china/item/declaration-on-the-conduct-of-parties-in-the-south-china-sea (accessed August 31, 2013).

Beckman, Robert (2012) "Scarborough Shoal: Flashpoint for Confrontation or Opportunity for Cooperation?" S. Rajaratnam School of International Studies (RSIS), RSIS No. 072/2012.

Bland, Ben, and Shivakumar, Girija (2011) "Beijing Flexes Muscles in South China Sea," *Financial Times*, September 1.

Bumiller, Elisabeth (2012) "Words and Deeds Show Focus of the American Military on Asia," *New York Times*, November 10. Online. Available at: www.nytimes.com/2012/11/11/world/asia/us-militarys-new-focus-on-asia-becomes-clearer.html?_r=0 (accessed August 31, 2013).

CIA (2012) *The World Factbook*. Online. Available at: www.cia.gov/library/publications/the-world-factbook (accessed July 16, 2012).

Dai Bingguo 戴秉国 (2010) "Jianchi zou heping fazhan daolu" 坚持走和平发展道路 [Remain on the Path of Peaceful Development], *Xinhua*, December 7. Online. Available at: http://news.china.com.cn/txt/2010-12/07/content_21495078.htm (accessed August 31, 2013).

Ding Qingfen (2011) "Structural Challenges Ahead," *China Daily*, September 5. Online. Available at: www.chinadaily.com.cn/business/2011-09/05/content_13620305.htm (accessed August 31, 2013).

Directorate General for Trade of the European Commission (2013) *EU Bilateral Trade and Trade with the World: China*. Online. Available at: http://trade.ec.europa.eu/doclib/docs/2006/september/tradoc_113366.pdf (accessed August 31, 2013).

Emmerson, Donald K. (2012) "ASEAN Stumbles in Phnom Penh," *Asia Times Online*, July 17. Online. Available at: www.atimes.com/atimes/Southeast_Asia/NG17Ae02.html (accessed August 31, 2013).

Friedberg, Aaron L. (2011) *China, America, and the Struggle for Mastery in Asia*, New York: Norton.

Global Times (2011) "China, India Deny Naval Confrontation," *Global Times*, September 2. Online. Available at: www.globaltimes.cn/NEWS/tabid/99/ID/673749/China-India-deny-naval-confrontation.aspx (accessed August 31, 2013).

Hao, Yufan (2012) "Domestic Chinese Influence on U.S.–China Relations," in D. Shambaugh (ed.), *Tangled Titans: The New Context of U.S.–China Relations*, Berkeley: University of California Press.

IMF (International Monetary Fund) (2012) *World Economic Outlook Update*. Online. Available at: www.imf.org/external/pubs/ft/weo/2012/update/02/index.htm (accessed July 16, 2012).

Information Office of the State Council of the People's Republic of China (1998) *White Paper on China's National Defense*, Information Office of the State Council, People's Republic of China. Online. Available at: http://csis.org/files/media/csis/programs/taiwan/timeline/sums/timeline_docs/CSI_19980727.pdf (accessed August 31, 2013).

International Institute for Strategic Studies (2012) "New US Military Concept Marks Pivot to Sea and Air," *International Institute of Strategic Studies*, 20. Online. Available at: www.iiss.org/publications/strategic-comments/past-issues/volume-18-2012/may/new-us-military-concept-marks-pivot-to-sea-and-air/?locale=en (accessed August 31, 2013).

Johansson, Åsa, Guillemette, Yvan, and Murtin, Fabrice (2012) *Looking to 2060: Long-Term Global Growth Prospects*. Online. Available at: www.oecd.org/eco/outlook/2060%20policy%20paper%20FINAL.pdf (accessed August 31, 2013).

Karnad, Bharat (2011) "No Buckling Down to China," *New Indian Express*, September 9. Online. Available at: http://newindianexpress.com/opinion/article359964.ece (accessed August 31, 2013).

Kato, Yoichi (2011) "James Steinberg: U.S. Leadership Restored in 10 Years after 9/11," *Asahi Shimbun*, September 23. Online. Available at: http://ajw.asahi.com/article/views/opinion/AJ2011092111598 (accessed August 31, 2013).

Lampton, David, ed. (2001) *The Making of Chinese Foreign and Security Policy in the Era of Reform*, Stanford, CA: Stanford University Press.

Le Mière, Christian (2011) "Can ASEAN Ease Tensions with China?" *IISS Defense News*, August 14. Online. Available at: www.iiss.org/whats-new/iiss-experts-commentary/can-asean-ease-tensions-with-china.

Long Tao 龙韬 (2011) "Nanhai dongwu shiji chengshu, suoding Fei-Yue yi zhan zhi zhan" 南海动武时机成熟 锁定菲越以战止战 [The Time Is Ripe to Use Force in the South China Sea; Lock on to the Philippines and Vietnam, Use War to Prevent War], *Huanqiu Shibao* 环球时报 [*Global Times*], September 27.

McDonald, Mark (2012) "China's Economy: Apocalypse Soon?" *International Herald Tribune*, July 9. Online. Available at: http://rendezvous.blogs.nytimes.com/2012/07/09/watching-the-china-stress-index-its-rising (accessed July 16, 2012).

Mack, Andrew (1975) "How Big Nations Lose Small Wars: The Politics of Asymmetric Conflict," *World Politics*, vol. 27, no. 2, pp. 175–200.

Morrison, Wayne (2012) *China's Economic Conditions*, Washington, DC: Congressional Research Service.

Naughton, Barry (2010) "China's Distinctive System: Can It Be a Model for Others?," *Journal of Contemporary China*, vol. 19, no. 65, pp. 437–460.

Parameswaran, Prashanth (2012) "China and Brunei: Ties that Bind?" *China Brief*, vol. 12, no. 21 (November 5, 2012). Online. Available at: www.jamestown.org/single/?no_cache=1&tx_ttnews[tt_news]=40069&tx_ttnews[backPid]=589#.Uh-0uT8phng (accessed August 31, 2013).

Pillsbury, Michael (2000) *China Debates the Future Security Environment*, Washington, D.C.: National Defense University Press.

Richardson, Sophie (2010) *China, Cambodia, and the Five Principles of Peaceful Coexistence*, New York: Columbia University Press.

Smith, Rupert (2007) *The Utility of Force: The Art of War in the Modern World*, New York: Knopf.

Swaine, Michael (2011a) *America's Challenge: Engaging a Rising China in the 21st Century*, Washington, D.C.: Carnegie Endowment for International Peace.

Swaine, Michael (2011b) "China's Assertive Behavior Part One: 'Core Interests'," *China Leadership Monitor*, 34, February 2011. Online. Available at: www.hoover.org/publications/china-leadership-monitor/article/67966 (accessed August 31, 2013).

Tokatlian, Juan (2007) "Latin America, China, and the United States: A Hopeful Triangle," *Open Democracy*, February 7. Online. Available at: www.opendemocracy.net/democracy-protest/hopeful_triangle_4336.jsp (accessed August 31, 2013).

Tokatlian, Juan (2011) "Una nueva estrategia hacia China" [A new strategy vis-à-vis China], *La Nacion*, August 29. Online. Available at: www.lanacion.com.ar/1401402-una-nueva-estrategia-hacia-china (accessed August 31, 2013).

United States Energy Information Agency (2013) *South China Sea*. Online. Available at: www.eia.gov/countries/regions-topics.cfm?fips=SCS (accessed August 31, 2013).

Wachman, Alan M. (2009) *Mongolia's Geopolitical Gambit: Preserving a Precarious Independence while Resisting "Soft Colonialism,"* East Asia Institute Fellows Program Working Paper no. 18, Seoul: EAI.

Ward, Karen (2011) *The World in 2050: Quantifying the Shift in the Global Economy*. Online. Available at: www.hsbc.ca/1/PA_ES_Content_Mgmt/content/canada4/pdfs/personal/120508-the-world-in-2050.pdf (accessed August 31, 2013).

Womack, Brantly (2003–2004) "China and Southeast Asia: Asymmetry, Leadership and Normalcy," *Pacific Affairs*, vol. 76, no. 3, pp. 529–548.

Womack, Brantly (2010a) *China among Unequals*, Singapore: World Scientific Press.

Womack, Brantly (2010b) "Political Reform and Sustainable Development in China," *Fudan Journal of the Humanities and Social Sciences*, vol. 3, no. 1, pp. 32–54.

Womack, Brantly (2011) "The Spratlys: From Dangerous Ground to Apple of Discord," *Contemporary South East Asia*, vol. 33, pp. 157–175.

World Bank, Development Research Center of the State Council, the People's Republic of China (2013) *China 2030: Building a Modern, Harmonious, and Creative High-Income Society*. Online. Available at: www.worldbank.org/content/dam/Worldbank/document/China-2030-complete.pdf (accessed August 31, 2013).

Xinhua News Service (2003) "Year-Ender: World Witnesses Drastic Changes in 2003," *Xinhua*, December 26.

Yan Xuetong 阎学通 (2011) "Zhongguo zhengduo daoyi zhigaodian xu jiejiao mengyou" 中国争夺道义制高点需结交盟友 [To Achieve the Moral High Ground China Must Find Allies], *Xinhua*, December 5. Online. Available at: http://news.xinhuanet.com/herald/2011-12/05/c_131284250.htm (accessed August 31, 2013).

Yu Keping (2009) *Democracy Is a Good Thing*, Washington, DC: Brookings.

Zhou, Fangyin (2011) "Equilibrium Analysis of the Tributary System," *Chinese Journal of International Politics*, vol. 2, pp. 147–178.

Index

Page numbers in *italics* denote tables, those in **bold** denote figures.